SEATTLE

ALSO BY NARD JONES

Pacific Northwest
(WITH STEWART HOLBROOK AND RODERIC HAIG-BROWN)

The Great Command

The Island

Evergreen Land

Still to the West

Scarlet Petticoat

Swift Flows the River

West, Young Man!
(WITH J. GORDON GOSE)

All Six Were Lovers

Wheat Women

The Petlands

Oregon Detour

NARD JONES

SEATTLE

DOUBLEDAY & COMPANY, INC., Garden City, New York
1972

Photographs courtesy of Seattle *Post-Intelligencer*

ISBN: 0-385-01875-4
Library of Congress Catalog Card Number 72–79397
Copyright © 1972 by Anne and Nard Jones
All Rights Reserved
Printed in the United States of America
First Edition

TO ALL THE OLD-TIMERS
AND ALL OUR WELCOME NEWCOMERS

ACKNOWLEDGMENTS

The present volume, linking Seattle's past with its present and future, has been on the author's mind for so many years that it is impossible now to recall the scores who have been of assistance. But it is fresh in my memory that I am particularly indebted to Dr. Dixy Lee Ray, Henry Broderick, Roberta Byrd Barr, James Faber, Hilda Bryant, Bruce Chapman; Dr. William Moore, Jr., Jay Rockey, Mr. and Mrs. William P. Woods, Harold Shefelman, John Reddin, Dan Coughlin, Giacomo Pirzio-Biroli, M.D., Don Page, Roy Edenholm, John Owen, Elizabeth Gustison, Miner Baker, Dewayne Kreager, Joseph Frisino and my daughter Deborah Anne Jones. Special thanks are due the library of the Washington State Historical Society, the Seattle Museum of History and Industry, the library of the University of Washington, the library staff of the Seattle *Post-Intelligencer*, the Seattle Public Library and the Bellevue Public Library.

Finally, I would like to express my deepest gratitude to Emmett Watson and his assistant, Ruth Howell, for some fine pinch hitting during a period when illness took me away from the typewriter.

CONTENTS

SEATTLE

1

From Mud to Sky

SEATTLEITES have their favorite vantage points from which to gaze upon the city they view with that combination of admiration and irritation which so often goes with long-standing love. My own favorite spot from which to look at its skyline—and I have a passion for skylines—is Duwamish Head.

Close up, a city's faults cannot be missed. But a skyline is the truer essence of a city. A sprawling city with few dramatic spires means little to me. A city which every now and then thrusts ever higher toward the sky is a city of spirit and one determined to grow, to stand tall among other cities of the world.

Seattle is such a city.

The long view from Duwamish Head is much like the one to be had from the forward decks of an incoming ferry. But our state-owned automobile ferries are fast-moving as well as sleek and beautiful, and therefore the perspective on the skyline is constantly changing. It is my opinion that to look properly at a skyline one must be motionless, with only an occasional walk to another point of view.

This pedestrian stillness gives one more time to look and to think about what he sees—to consider what the city is, how its people regard it, how it has changed since the last time he studied its outline against the sky, and, of course, to remember its past. So I will view Seattle in this introductory chapter, from Duwamish Head.

Seattle's past is a brief one, beginning in 1851. This means that the skyline you see today is a hundred and twenty-plus years old; young for a city. When you look at the skyline in the coming century, in the onrushing year 2000, the city by Elliott Bay will still be young as major cities reckon their decades. What indeed will be a hundred and fifty years to a city in the Age of Space, when more and more human beings will live a hundred years and "tourism" will become a word familiar to much of the universe?

The city with the curious name, hardly pronounceable in many parts of the world, rises on a strip of land between Elliott Bay, a part of Puget Sound, and the huge freshwater Lake Washington. Whirl your library globe, find the state of Washington in the upper left-hand corner of the United States, and you will discover Seattle marked there in comparatively prominent letters, because it is the seat of King County and the largest city in the Pacific Northwest.

We are a hundred and twenty-five nautical miles from the Pacific Ocean and our passageway to that greatest ocean in this world is the Strait of Juan de Fuca. By highway we are only a hundred and ten swift miles to the Canadian border on the north. To the south, just a hundred and forty-seven miles away are two rivers—the Willamette and the historic Columbia, and the Oregon metropolis of Portland. The Washington state capital, Olympia, is just sixty miles away.

In the beginning there was a moment in time when the founders of Seattle were planning to build a city on the sands and tideflats near Duwamish Head. But, for reasons we shall examine, it began its infancy on the other side of the bay, to the east. There it was expected that it would rise on seven hills, like Rome. Well, it did rise, from a sea of mud and not very fast. And those hills, some of them five hundred feet above the almost fathomless harbor, were covered with a forest which often looked black, but in sunlight proved green—evergreen, all year around, in various shades. That is why the region is still called the Evergreen Land by old-timers. The newcomers rarely if ever call it the Evergreen Land now, for much of that forest is gone, and so are some of the hills.

The city is nudged by other communities which, like Seattle, keep growing, showing skylines of their own. King County embraces some of these, and so does Snohomish County on the north. Fast becoming cities are Bellevue, Renton, Kirkland, Issaquah, Redmond, Auburn, and Kent in King County. In Snohomish County are other communities, some new, some older, and there is Everett, the historic lumber town whose citizens never dreamed it would be a neighbor of a Boeing unit that is the largest aircraft building in the world.

Some of these jostling neighbors are really great shopping centers, urban nuclei ringed with modern apartments and "country houses." Nobody in our part of the world is ever quite certain whether a shopping center is going to remain a mercantile operation or become a city with a mayor and council and a host of troubles, like Seattle.

The Seattleite, who would die rather than give up his car and the freeways (and sometimes does indeed depart this life as a sacrifice to his stubborn gods) considers it all part of Seattle and speeds and dodges from one to the other for a bargain or two. The suburban communities, however, do not consider themselves part of the big city and their official spokesmen frequently are heard to say so. Seattleites are welcome as customers, but the citizens of what is really no longer "suburbia" are reluctant to become a part of the great municipality insofar as government is concerned.

As I sit on the sand at Duwamish Head, or on a log whitened and smoothed by years of rolling with the tides, I look across one of the great harbors of the world, a fact which seems to escape most of today's Seattleites, so firmly bigamist are they in their wedding to sky and freeway.

Between the city and me are billions of silver crescents twinkling and disappearing and twinkling again, sparkling jewels of the bay on a clear day. On such a day from Duwamish Head there is a peculiar blend of atmospheric conditions which creates the illusion that one is looking at the city through a glass which sharpens and even magnifies. I have witnessed the same phenomenon across channels in smogless Alaska. Under such conditions the details of the buildings and wharves are amazingly clear.

That great deep harbor is five miles across from West Point on the north to Alki Point on the south. It almost encircles what we call the east, west and Duwamish waterways, which extend inland on the south side of the bay.

Of course I have chosen a clear day, one of those magnifying days, to have still another look at my beloved, but so fickle, skyline, and so can see Smith Cove on the north and realize that beyond my vision is Shilshole Bay with its hundreds of moored yachts, its marinas and the huge seaside restaurant called The Windjammer.

Shilshole is the western outlet of the Washington Ship Canal, not a great canal as canals of the world measure. It is six and one half miles long and has a depth of about thirty feet. But its looks fascinate tourists, and even Seattleites, particularly early and late on Sundays, when the attendants of the Hiram M. Chittenden Locks are letting hundreds of pleasure boats and an occasional tug pass through. The man for whom the locks are named was a distinguished pioneer engineer, but locally the folks usually refer simply to the "Ballard Locks" because they are in the neighborhood of that name. Ballard residents have a deep affection for the locks because many of them for years have been connected with commercial fishing. Few of the little ships which use the locks are unknown to them; they regard them affectionately as old friends.

Seattle is sometimes called "the boating capital of the world"— a term whose validity I shall try to prove later on—so the Hiram M. Chittenden Locks are indeed a busy sight to set before strangers and locals alike. Why such locks? Well, they adjust for the twenty-six feet of difference in water levels between the Sound, Lake Union and huge Lake Washington on the east of town.

Of course from where I sit on Duwamish Head I cannot see all this, except in my mind's eye. You scan a skyline as you do a sentence in a book, from left to right; you find yourself doing this naturally, from habit developed in childhood when you were learning to read. It is as if the skyline forms a sentence, which in essence it does; a brief story of a city. This is all the more true of Seattle, where the taller buildings are not in clusters as yet, as they are in many older cities.

So as I look at the harbor and the skyline many things in time and space cross my inner vision, just as they come between you and the pages of this book—I hope not too distractingly. Often when people say they love Seattle and would live nowhere else, they do not always mean the town itself, or alone, although they may not realize this fully. They are really thinking also of Seattle's awesome and varied natural setting.

They may be thinking of its broader outer frame, of northern Oregon and southern British Columbia, or the Rain Forest of the vast Olympic Peninsula in which are uncounted square miles where no human being has yet set foot.

Or, if lovers of flora, subconsciously they may be seeing broad prairies decorated with yellow lupine, or in thick bracken the pink or red rhododendron (our state flower), or they may be recalling the sight of wild azaleas, or salmon-pink salal, or snow-white dogwood as lovely as a gardenia. Or great spreads of Scotch broom, which bring a golden color into a land predominantly green.

Far behind me, far from Duwamish Head, are the those eternally snowcapped jagged peaks of the Olympic Range. Beyond them, and somehow rather frightening, are stygian rock monoliths not far from the rugged coastline. Once, surely, they were part of the coastline, and not even geologists are agreed as to how long ago that was.

Miles southward on my right is a sandspit twenty-eight miles long, and near it the cranberry bogs, and hidden in the sand the big razor clams of purplish hue, and that strange and ugly shellfish called the goeduck, in which foreigners refuse to believe until they see one. And oysters—oysters, many chefs have told me, with a flavor that surpasses that of any other oysters in the world.

As I sit in a tiny part of our water-oriented world, something on the skyline—perhaps a building that stood there in my youth and is somehow connected with that youth, and love, and wonder at the world—makes me recall for a moment the Blue Mountains that lie over in eastern Washington, miles upon miles from the Cascade Range, which is nature's own skyline beyond the one I see. Then suddenly, and for seconds only, the Blue Mountains remind me of one of Seattle's most beautiful sights, the Arboretum, bordering the boulevard which once was the town's invitable "Sunday drive" and the south shore of Union Bay. Was it an ancient trail in the Blue Mountains along which I walked with a girl whose name I cannot remember that connected those mountains with the Arboretum and its lovers' paths? Perhaps so; for the skyline of one's city has a way of bringing parts of one's life back.

Whatever the tricks of memory association, my modern man-

made skyline rather blocks out the view of the Cascades, which
separate eastern Washington from the Puget Sound country. The
two areas are as different as night from day. When I was a boy only
unpaved roads, parts of which were single-lane, connected eastern
and western Washington, and people would say that Washington
should have stretched along the coast to the California border, and
that from British Columbia to that border should be an *inland* state
called Oregon. It was not a good idea, we now realize. Oregonians
would never have let it happen even if it were.

The Olympic Peninsula memory makes me think in turn of the
wild coast storms from which our inland waters are protected. I
have seen those terrifying combinations of wind and waves which
seemingly are ready to roll up the continent like a carpet, taking
trees and plains and houses and whole cities and pushing on and on
with all the power of the greatest ocean in the world.

And thus I sit, looking at a skyline of a beloved city, but with
wayward thoughts bringing the whole state together, past and present. Wayward thoughts are impractical, however, and of no use to
anybody, so I must confess it is the superferries and the bridges
and the freeways that pull it all together for modern man, co-operat-
ing with him to destroy time and space and, all too often now,
beauty.

So I read the skyline of Seattle, left to right. On the left,
which is roughly north from my point of view on Duwamish Head, I
see almost cheek by jowl with Magnolia Bluff—a beautiful residential section with many harbor views of its own—the tips of the lacy
towers of the Pacific Science Center. Dr. Dixy Lee Ray, on leave
from the University of Washington, keeps the center lively and instructive the year around. Certainly those lacy towers bring Doctor
Ray to mind. Tacoma-born, she is one of the most vital and important forces in Seattle and the Puget Sound area. For a moment I see
her speeding along in her Jaguar equipped with a Paris taxi horn,
then paddling furiously in a rubber boat in a white-water stream.
I see her sunny smile, which comes most often when she describes
the interest of children and youth in the Science Center, and when
she tells of projects which help them understand science. Then there
is the pleasantly serious expression I had seen earlier in the week as
we talked across her big, cluttered desk.

She was talking with enthusiasm about Seattle's selection as

West Coast headquarters for the National Oceanographic and Atmospheric Administration, a powerful conglomerate of departments that are pertinent to the city's harbor, the skyline, the Puget Sound country and actually to the wide world. I choose to believe that Seattle would have been overlooked by the NOAA had it not been for Doctor Ray. For years this distinguished scientist has preached the importance of the sea, always emphasizing that Puget Sound is ideal for its study. But her interests are wide, and although she is keen about the probable future uses of "sea space" to mankind she has never allowed the Science Center to slight the promises of outer space as well. "In July of 1972 we celebrated the tenth anniversary of the Pacific Science Center Foundation," she said. "And to mark this occasion we'll open the newest, most sophisticated, most advanced planetarium in the world."

She accepted her position as director of the Science Center in 1963 because of two broad convictions. She arrived at them during three years with the National Science Foundation in Washington, D.C.

"One of my convictions was that our modern society is to a large extent built and powered by scientific knowledge, yet few government leaders, and even fewer members of the general public, understand the most basic concepts of science, either its powers or its limitations," Dixy Lee Ray said. "My second conviction was that the extraordinary rise of science and technology through support from the federal government was a temporary phenomenon, and that a reaction against science was certain to come and result in reduced financial support."

In addition to Doctor Ray's well-founded convictions, she believed as an educator that the public should have a better means of finding out what science is really all about, that science could be lifted out of its mystery for those who want to be informed.

"So at the Science Center we work hard for better public understanding of science. I admit that we are far from the goal, but perhaps someday there will be a better understanding of what constitutes 'a natural environment' and less fear and more rationality."

Dixy Ray's work and the Science Center have become well known in all parts of the civilized world. "But," she says, "the most wonderful thing to me has been the growth of real community pride in the Science Center. This is reflected in a membership of over five thousand, an annual use by school classes and teachers of more than seventy-five thousand a year, and a public attendance of more than three hundred and fifty thousand."

The most discouraging thing, I hear Dixy saying, was the lack of financial support. And there, I remembered thinking, she was putting a finger on one of the traditional problems in the history of Seattle.

Doctor Ray is not the kind of person who is easily discouraged. "As for the future," she said, "we'll continue and we'll grow. That growth will accelerate now that the Pacific Science Center has become the first (possibly the only) arm of the Smithsonian Institution. The fundamental nature and purpose of the Science Center will remain the same."

Naturally when you glance at our skyline as a whole you spot the taller buildings first. Near the Pacific Science Center is the famous Space Needle and we'll have a look from there in due time. After the World's Fair of 1962 it was the city's tallest structure. Then in 1969 there began to grow—toward the end of one of downtown's periodic building booms—the Seattle-First National Bank's fifty-story headquarters building, descended from the safe in Dexter Horton's general store before the Great Fire of 1889. It was Seattle's tallest skyscraper, topping the Space Needle by forty feet unless you want to count the Needle's slender spire, atop which its gas flame flares against the night sky.

Seattleites are definitely proud of the Sea-First building, yet a bit startled as well. In rain or overcast it may appear almost black from a distance. This is because of its dark metal facade, but certainly the facing is not black. It is pleasantly dark and coppery. The Sea-First cloud duster brought something new to the amenities of Seattle. The directors felt that the institution should reflect a civic cultural interest, and stated this explicitly. Even more explicit was the half million dollars budgeted for sculpture and paintings, and the commissioning of a cosmopolitan restaurant called the Mirabeau for the building's forty-sixth floor. The bankers anticipated by two years the first Urban Arts Conference to be held in this country. Convening in Seattle in February of 1971, the conference's thesis was that artist and architect must begin to co-operate in the creation of urban structures. It is interesting and relevant that the meeting was organized by local architect Fred Bassetti, who is strong on quality environment and influenced his profession markedly in that field.

One way or another we mix pioneering with our imitative characteristics.

From my view at Duwamish Head the heights of Seattle's "tall ones" are deceptive. That is because a great part of the business district is built on hills that were too expensive to sluice into the bay, and not high enough to impede progress. So the circular Washington Plaza Hotel, forty stories high and sometimes irreverently called "The Corn Cob," seems at a distance not much taller than the Northern Life Tower, a twenty-seven-story building raised toward the end of the Roaring Twenties.

The Washington Building is white, which has become a favorite color of many of our newer skyscrapers. It was erected in 1960, standing both tall and broad, like a handsome fullback. It began a decade of new skyscrapers.

The International Business Machines building, also a gleaming white, appears to rest its twenty-two stories lightly on corner arches. There is an architectural poetry about it that is at variance with the endless jibes at computerization and the alleged sober pragmatism of IBM personnel. South of the Sea-First giant, which dominates the central part of the skyline, is the Federal Office Building, of thirty-eight stories. And in the early seventies, when Seattle was plunged into gloom by the drastic cutbacks at Boeing, came an announcement that Peoples National Bank, one of Seattle's staid and older financial institutions, would build a new twenty-story building. That is not a skyscraper, really, but figuratively it is considered so—for two reasons. Peoples National is an influential statewide institution, and its board chairman is Joshua Green, who made the announcement at the age of one hundred and two and is himself an institution. The swiftly moving, shrewd-minded Josh Green came to Seattle as a boy and began his career in the small freight-passenger steamers which in his youth darted back and forth across the harbor. He is often heard to say that the maritime business was a lot more fun than banking.

There on Duwamish Head I remember that incorporated into the design of the new Peoples National building is the graceful Grecian facade so long admired as the entrance of the old building. It was beginning to look as if we were learning to control that wrecking ball which had been swinging so indiscriminately, destroying so many of the town's most beautiful landmarks.

Something else happened to raise the low spirits of Seattleites early in 1971. Across the bay I see the dazzling forty-story skyscraper of the Bank of California. Due to its location—adjacent, but one steep block higher—it seems almost to be taller than the Sea-First headquarters.

Over there toward the south end of the bay rises, on the scene of the earliest history of Seattle, the nineteen-story Norton Building. For that one we give thanks to Norton Clapp, board chairman of Weyerhaeuser. He did not name it for himself, but in memory of a timber baron relation. In 1959 it was the first office building to fully consider the quality of the downtown environment. The entrance on Second Avenue is a broad and airy plaza, and its First Avenue entry is a gardenlike portal which integrates the interior with the free outdoors.

I sit and admire and let my heart swell with pride at this still young skyline of the town where I was born and reared.

I have "read" most of the skyline now, knowing it will change—but over there at the southern tip of downtown is the daddy of all our skyscrapers. It is white, as some of the later ones are, and was christened the L. C. Smith Building because it was erected by the typewriter king. Now called the Smith Tower, it was slowly pushed upward in 1914. In that year it was something to gawk at indeed, "the tallest building west of Chicago." It was publicized as forty-two stories, but the assessor's office now calls it forty-one stories above ground level. Seattleites once would have set up a howl about that, but we don't mind now. We have other and taller skyscrapers and more to come.

On this clear day I see behind Smith Tower a skyscraper nature had ready when the founders arrived, although they didn't see it for some days because of the rain. To the old Indians it was a god, not to be approached too closely. One Indian legend calls it "the mountain that walked" because the story had been passed from generation to generation that in anger it had left its neighbors on the Olympic Range and strode east to its present location. In the legend was the belief that it would one day return to its old home, and perhaps we should not smile. Modern geologists say that slowly—very slowly, in the way of geologic time—it is moving west.

It may be this legend that gives me the feeling that Mount Rainier is faintly ominous as well as beautiful. I think perhaps it is just as well that we do not see it often. When "The Mountain" —as most Seattleites call it—decides to come out from behind a veil of rain and fog it is overpowering. It seems close enough to touch, and looks down upon us impassively. Since childhood I have never read approval there.

"The Mountain" can be dangerous as well as awesomely beautiful. By 1971 it had claimed more than a hundred and fifty lives in seventy-five years, and there may have been unknown deaths. It is a volcanic peak, although Seattleites don't worry about that. At some time in the past it was sixteen thousand feet in altitude, but blew two thousand feet off its top. They say that two million years ago it was part of the Pacific Circle of Fire that included Krakatau, Fuji, Popocatepetl and Erebus. Today, every so often, one reads in the newspapers that parts of its glaciers are melting when and where they should not, indicating a buildup of gas and heat.

Yet it fascinates us all, and every year will attract far more than a million and a half people, three fourths of whom are from the state. Of course, with occasional exceptions, they do not attempt to reach the peak. They come to admire, or to hike, or to ski. The mountain is part of that great framework I mentioned, one of the reasons people express their admiration for Seattle although they may not mean the city itself. I feel that we take less notice of the mountain now, because driving on a freeway is not a time to let your attention wander. Anyhow, nobody in Seattle gets to see The Mountain every day, and visitors may stay a week or more without visible proof of its existence. If you are host to such a luckless one, take him to the Mountain Room of—where else?— the Rainier Brewery, 3100 Airport Way South, where may be seen the most complete collection of photographs and paintings of the mountain. The great mountain was not named for the beer, of course; it was the other way around.

There is far more to Seattle than its skyline and The Mountain (which belongs to Tacoma and all the towns around us), so I get to my feet and and begin walking north on Duwamish Head, searching the harbor itself now. I glimpse the bright awning stripes of the plaza next to a popular restaurant called Ivar's Acres of Clams. Ivar Haglund is almost as well known as his restaurants, and I am particularly fond of him because—well, because he is Ivar, and tells a good story, and gently sings folk songs to the ac-

companiment of his guitar. He rose from dishwasher in a big
Seattle hotel to his present eminence as a leading citizen. A clue
to his delightful humor was revealed when his page advertisement
appeared in both Seattle newspapers. The essence of the "copy" was
that really he didn't need new customers, although they were always
welcome, but that as a dishwasher he had dreamed often of owning
a chain of restaurants of his own and inserting what advertising
salesmen redundantly call "a full page ad." So now, the message
went on, he had the restaurants and here was the full page ad.

I'm fond of Ivar, too, because he is not afraid to reflect
Puget Sound tradition in the decor of his restaurants, whereas others
of his profession seem intent upon making their patrons forget where
they are. One of Ivar's cafes is an almost exact replica of an old
Indian long house. His waterfront spot may not be an interior
decorator's dream, but it is pure Puget Sound. The walls are decorated
with fishnet, cork floats, gum boots, clam-guns and clam shovels.
"If I could," Ivar Haglund told me once, "I'd let a few sea gulls
romp around in here, but—well, you know it just wouldn't work
out in a restaurant."

As I walk along the sand with eyes on the waterfront I seem
to hear his quiet voice singing against the picking of his guitar:

> I've traveled all over this country
> Prospecting and digging for gold
> I've tunneled, hydraulicked and cradled
> And I have been frequently sold.
>
> So rolling my grub in a blanket
> I left all my tools on the ground
> And started one morning to shank it
> For a country called Puget Sound.

This folk song of the Old Settler tells how he arrived in one
of our little mists, flat broke, and chopped at the forest for two
years "but never got down to the soil." If he hadn't been broke
he might have moved on, but finally he became "an old settler"
and was stuck.

> And now that I'm used to the climate,
> I think that if man ever found
> A place to be peaceful and quiet
> That place is on Puget Sound.

No longer a slave of ambition,
I laugh at the world and its shams,
As I think of my happy condition
Surrounded by acres of clams.

I turn and look southward toward what we call Harbor Island and its waterways. These are a couple of miles from the hotel windows out of which our visitors believe they are looking at our port. Actually they are missing the most important part of it.

Harbor Island is the biggest man-made island in the world, dredged out of the tidelands. Comparatively few Seattleites themselves are more than vaguely aware of it, just as relatively few of the town's more than 650,000 population are really aware of the waterfront at all. It is odd, and to me an inexplicable paradox that hundreds of thousands of people have come to Seattle or were born here, and almost turn away from the great harbor that is partly natural and partly man-made.

Yet we *are* a port city, one of the great ones—a fact that often escapes the majority of our citizens. The exceptions, of course, are those whose businesses connect them with the waterfront, or those "waterfront buffs" who stroll along, perhaps yearning to climb aboard some ship destined for a far-off tropical island. Unfortunately, the waterfront is walled off, in a sense, by the elevated, two-level Alaskan Way Viaduct. But Seattle's central waterfront has grown in popularity, attracting tourists and natives alike.

Along with Ivar's is the wonderful Ye Olde Curiosity Shop, that venerable attraction beloved by generations of Seattleites. Joining these colorful fixtures are import shops called Trident and Pirate's Plunder, a proliferation of fish and chip stands, and farther north on Pier 70 a colorful complex of shops, stores and restaurants not unmindful of San Francisco's Ghirardelli Square. A free access "fishing pier," complete with benches, tables and sea gulls, is a further attraction that brings out hordes of gawkers, strollers and shoppers on warm and windless days. Even these almost never walk beyond the southern area, below the foot of Columbia Street, where the waterfront becomes somewhat grubby and noisy freight train sections block the way as they roll on the spur tracks of the wharves.

So they miss entirely the Harbor Island I am looking at from the beach of West Seattle. They do not see the capacious 700-foot moorages, or glimpse even the tops of the busy yellow cranes that in an hour can load into a ship thirty of those big truck trailers you have seen on the highways.

All too few Seattleites are familiar with the official "Port of Seattle," the organization to which the city's progress owes so much. This is a phenomenon in a seaport town and must be due to our often mentioned schizophrenia. Yet every Seattleite should know that the "Port of Seattle" officially began more than sixty years ago, and has grown into a $120-million municipal maritime corporation guided by five elected commissioners. Thus the city owns about twenty waterfront terminals, the $35-million Seattle-Tacoma International Airport, a multimillion-dollar small boat marina and a commercial fisherman's wharf. This latter facility is north by the Ballard Bridge, on the ship canal, and can accommodate more than six hundred vessels, some of which have brought their catches from a thousand miles out in the North Pacific.

So what I see from the West Seattle beach is by no means the boundary of the Port of Seattle. That boundary is the same as that of King County. All the while, perhaps as I stand there looking at Harbor Island, the port commissioners, in meeting assembled, are making plans for new facilities, new equipment, new sites and of course the continuing program for keeping the Sea-Tac airport up to date.

These alert and confident men (we have been most fortunate in our selection of port officials) do far more. They work steadily to attract additional water-oriented industries and bend their efforts toward the promotion of still more sea and air commerce.

My pedestrian route bends with the shoreline, and as I head toward Alki Point I am conscious that somewhere beneath me, obliterated now by tides and time, are the ways of the trails used by the Indians and the founders of my city. Those founders were almost wholly dependent on maritime trade, so they and those who soon followed them were indeed aware of the waterfront. In their time the waterfront was the city.

But as the years rolled by, the face of the city changed; its commerce became more diversified, the merchants took hold and have never let go, and thus the population of landlubbers increased day by day. There, I think, we really put a finger on the reason why too many Seattleites are only mildly, or not at all, interested in the waterfront.

Still the movement of cargo across our wharves, and the increase in air traffic over the years, contribute more and more to Seattle's economy. In the early 1970s the gross annual volume produced by water and airborne commerce was more than $600 million and growing fast. The annual payroll is about 35,000 jobs producing more than $200 million.

I follow the turn of the shoreline, thinking: so, despite what many people believe, there is more than Boeing here, although Seattleites see a bigger future for Boeing, too. Do you know what happened when the American SST got into trouble? Thousands of bumper strips appeared, reading:

SST—Seattle Stands Tall.

True enough, I thought, with that ever growing skyline in mind. Suddenly, forgetting that I had turned onto Alki Point, I almost stumbled into the tiny granite monument that commemorates the beginning of it all.

The skyline was supposed to begin about where I slogged through the sand and nearly collided with the modest landmark. For here is where the first settlers pictured a town and decided to call it New York—here by this modest spire hardly six feet tall, on whose stone are engraved the names of the twelve children and twelve adults.

They soon changed their minds about both the location and the name. But there will remain, as long as man, the wonder of what twelve adults and twelve children can begin, and what tremendous hazards they can overcome.

I'm not very high on effusions to attract tourists. But when I look across the water at the Seattle that came to be, I am more than ready to endorse a slogan coined by our tourist bureau: Seattle is a site to see with a Sound to match.

2

Overground and Underground

A MAP of Seattle doesn't help anybody much, except to show that it rather resembles Manhattan Island in shape—and part of it is indeed an island in its peculiar way.

Of course the map will be of some assistance in illustrating how our street system, if you can call it a system, is difficult for many natives and puzzling indeed to visitors. Some slight differences of opinion between two of our leading pioneers caused curious platting in the lower downtown area. And years later the highway engineers insisted upon slicing the city with a freeway plan which made streets hardly more than access and exit roads to freeways current or programmed, so our one-way streets have a way of adding to the confusion. Strangers have been known to inquire whether, in laying out the city, we followed cow paths or Indian trails. A map at least will prove that we did neither. We followed no pioneer paths, but simply made our own mistakes. Now we are attempting to correct some of them, and being careful not to make others.

As to the "island," it takes shape because the city is divided west to east by that Lake Washington Ship Canal which joins Shilshole Bay, a lively and decorative pleasure boat marina, with Lake Union and thereupon proceeds to freshwater Lake Washington. On the west is Elliott Bay, and on the south the waterways of Harbor Island.

Thus, you see, considerable of Seattle *is* a sort of island. The busiest part is south of the ship canal, but plenty goes on to the north as well. It is north of the canal that you find the huge University of Washington, second largest employer in the city as well as a splendid educational institution. North also is the important Museum of History and Industry, the lively "Avenue" bordering the University, picturesque Fisherman's Wharf and the area which forever—and properly enough—will insist upon being called Ballard, as if it were not a part of Seattle at all. I say this is proper because Ballard is indeed a community with its own characteristics, a sizable percentage of Scandinavians in its population, many of them commercial fishermen with a natural affinity for the sea.

Today when Seattleites want to show all of Seattle to visitors they inevitably and wisely take them to the Space Needle. There's an observation deck, but Seattleites like to treat their guests well, so the party more often than not settles down in the circular restaurant, which is known for its delectable Puget Sound food and the almost unbelievable view. The trip from ground level and the look all around the town is made in a gold-colored elevator which arrives at the top in forty seconds, meaning that it travels eight hundred feet per minute, not bad for a lift.

The whole restaurant moves, almost imperceptibly, a full 360 degrees an hour. This means that, no matter where your table is located, you see just about all the Seattle country there is to see. It is a lovely and awe-inspiring sight, day or night. Before you begin to examine the surface of the city and its surroundings, raise your eyes skyward if it's night. The stars are near, and usually because of a low overcast they may seem fewer and not as bright as the ones you see on the Plains or the East Coast.

This is not due to smog. We are beginning to have some of that, but not at all comparable with Los Angeles. Most Seattleites are unaware that we have less smog than we did in the past. Half a century ago in summers the overcast was as real as the ash which you brushed from your coat sleeves. Those were the wasteful days when lumber mills burned bark and chips. They were the days when forest fires raged and there was rarely such a thing as preventive measures against such blazes. Given the dry weather and carelessness on the part of loggers or campers, the "blowup" might come almost anywhere around the Sound. Such holocausts were fought by loggers and volunteers with shovels and wet sacks, and it was rain that usually came to the rescue. So if a Seattleite encounters a visitor who comments that we're getting smog like other big cities, tell him it's better than it used to be and watch his eyes bulge.

The view is breathtaking, but so far the Needle has been host to only one prominent character who discovered that he could not overcome his acrophobia. That was Phil Harris, the comedian of television fame, who was visiting the World's Fair. He gazed fearfully from his chair, and when the waitress said, "Your order, please," his swift reply was, "Two double martinis and get me on the ground again!"

As the restaurant revolves you can see to the west those Seattle waters which are salt: all of Elliott Bay, much of Puget Sound. On very clear days you also get a glimpse of the inland end of the Strait of Juan de Fuca, which connects us with the great ocean and, in fact, the whole Pacific Rim. You'll surely see sleek white auto ferries, which the state operates, and at least half a dozen vessels of other types, sometimes many more. Once upon a time, before the coming of the automobile ferries, the salt inland sea was streaked with the wakes of what old-timers called "the mosquito fleet." These were for both passengers and small freight. They served in a period when roads and cars were few indeed. Those little ships of Puget Sound were vital to the commerce and progress of the region.

Out there to the west, too, you'll see that beautiful snow-capped Olympic Range. You may not have heard that we *really* would have a reputation for rain were it not for the rugged Olympics. They protect us from about 140 inches of coastal rainfall annually. Some of that rainfall does slip around the south end of the range now and then. The Olympics also contribute to our mild summers, summers so pleasant that visitors are enchanted if they stay a while to see how it works. Snow? Yes, we have a little, usually in February and March, and newly arrived Easterners and Midwesterners push through it at top speed, splashing slush as they pass us more timid natives, who have never quite learned the trick of driving in snow. We don't get enough practice.

As you dine or lunch or brunch in the Needle you must keep your eyes above highball, fork or spoon, or you will miss something. Out there on the north is Lake Union, whose shoreline has become rather nondescript. But we have plans drawn up to make it more picturesque. Like Union Bay, on its east, it is the site of many houseboats in all sizes and degrees of obsolescence. But many are architecturally first class, and I happen to be a Seattleite who hopes that our houseboats do not disappear from the scene.

In this same quarter, as you and your table slowly revolve, you can see a part of the ship canal and Lake Washington. One of the purposes of the canal was to help "industrialize" that big and beautiful lake. Thanks be to God, it never happened. In very early days Peter Kirk planned an iron manufacturing plant on its northeast shore. But something was not quite right about the ore back in the Cascades. Nonetheless, Peter Kirk has important monuments dedicated to his memory: the lively, growing town of Kirkland, and a red masonry building of Victorian style. The latter has been declared a permanent historical marker by Kirkland's city fathers.

At one time the Navy had a notion that Lake Washington would be a fine site for a navy yard. Fortunately for our ecology and Kitsap County's economy the Puget Sound Naval Shipyard was built at Bremerton, founded over there to the west by a pioneer named George Bremer. Forsight was not involved, but the decision was fortunate indeed. Big wars were ahead. Imagine a modern warship trying to squeeze through our miniature ship canal, and a fleet bottled up in Lake Washington!

As you and your Space Needle dessert move around slowly you may be looking toward the south end of the downtown area. The newer skyscrapers block your line of vision a bit, but beyond them was once the center of the city Arthur Denny and his party founded. Actually it was just about the entire community. As we shall see, the founders who landed originally on Alki Point decided quickly that the point was not the right spot for a port city.

As early navigators remarked in salty language, Denny's choice was a hell of a place to start a town. Even when I was a boy, and Denny long gone, there were clay cliffs jutting up from the tideflats and some were more than two hundred feet high. If you and the Needle had been born a few decades ago, you could not see a thing in this direction—except a great mound of earth called Denny Hill. At one time, atop this little clay mountain, there stood fast an ornate hotel, some stubborn residents, a Catholic school and the historic Denny School. You reached these places by twisting, slippery paths, or very long wooden stairways. Finally, Seattle tired of it all and literally, in an amazing feat of engineering, pulled the hill down with sluicing-hoses, steam shovels and sheer manpower used on picks and shovels. Now and then, when a glacial rock of size was encountered, a few sticks of dynamite were employed.

You can't see Denny Hill now because it was transported by endless belts and horses and wagons to Elliott Bay. From shore it was floated on special barges out into deeper water, where it lies fathoms deep, doubtless still spreading uneasily with the countless tides that have ebbed and flowed since the "Denny Regrade Project" was Seattle's first and most steadily attended spectator sport.

Most of the hilltop citizens moved reluctantly—the view was superb—even though they were paid for their property. One resident proved so stubborn, with a lawyer adept at delaying tactics, that the city ordered the work to begin around him. They thought that once he saw the hill actually disappearing he would relent. But for a long time he did not, and Seattleites were treated to the sight of a house standing a couple of hundred feet high on a treacherous spire of clay. Still undaunted, the fearless Seattleite built a series of ladders on which to "commute" from and to the leveled ground. About the time that the municipal lawyers were ready to bring drastic condemnation orders into play, the stubborn citizen tired of hauling supplies up those ladders and surrendered. Meanwhile he had furnished the hundreds of "regrade watchers" many hours of entertainment.

For years most of the level ground created by the disappearance of Denny Hill was taken over by parking lots and almost all one could have seen from the Needle in that area were the uninteresting metal tops of cars. That was early in 1971, when Paul Thiry, nationally known architect and chief force behind the design of the Seattle Center, said, "Our ground area is not being properly utilized, and Seattle has become an automobile city." At this time, aside from a few small apartment houses rapidly reaching the obsolescent stage, the only notable buildings were the Grosvenor House tower apartments, and adjacent to it the *Post-Intelligencer*, which in 1970 added a third story and completely redesigned its interior.

So as you have brandy and coffee and begin a second revolution in the Needle you might keep in mind that the mayor's "In-City

Living Task Force"—a plan for the future—visualizes more than fifty thousand persons in high-rise apartments on the level ground where Denny Hill once stood. Obviously that stubborn early resident of Denny Hill had the right "high-rise" concept, but was too early.

Critics in the Space Needle who note mistakes will also see, if they look carefully, that we really are learning. The time is here when we will give a second thought to destroying such buildings as are represented by the classic Burke Building, which crumbled under the wrecking ball early in 1971 after eighty-one years. Crashing down with it came the old Tivoli Theater, scene of thousands of burlesque shows. There were many who regretted this, but hardly for environmental reasons. One local wit remarked resignedly, "The Tivoli was about to collapse anyhow, after all those years of bumping and grinding."

From the Needle you'll see the main Freeway here and there. Paul Thiry objected to the Alaskan Viaduct along the waterfront, but his feelings on that project hardly match in heat his attitude toward the routing of the Freeway, and plenty of Seattleites agree with him.

"It was with the Freeway, cutting through the very heart of the city, that Seattle began one of its wrong turns and started to lose its identity as a city," the famous architect contends. "I proposed a lid covering the Freeway from Columbia Street north to Olive Way." Others often talk about that now. Such a "lid" would have afforded an avenue of trees and parklike malls for resting, a refuge for contemplative Seattleites afoot. If the Freeway does get its covering, it will be far more difficult and expensive than it would have been during the initial construction.

But from the tall, wide perspective of the Space Needle even our major errors of planning appear to be overcome by the broad, varied and spectacular view.

There are, of course, many other towers with inspiring vistas of the city. There is also a breathtaking view when arriving by plane. I recall such an after-dark experience when our high-tailed Boeing 747 had word from the control tower to make another circle before landing. My seat companion had slept all the way from Chicago, and I had rather enjoyed his bourbon-scented snore. But now he was wide awake and assuming I was a newcomer.

"Look at that!" he exclaimed in the ecstatic tone which revealed him as a proud Seattleite, too. "Just look at it. Did you know that it is the most beautifully lighted city in the world?"

"I didn't realize that," I said. "But it's a sight to see, all right."

It thrilled me as always. I haven't looked down on all cities of the world, but from a slanting plane I have seen many. Patriotically, I am ready to believe my brother Seattleite that—at least perhaps—my city is indeed the most beautifully lighted in the world. Even Rome and New York and London and Paris have their dark patches at night—but somehow Seattle seems *all* lighted until a mountain range cuts it off at some faraway boundary.

Of course we are noted for our comparatively cheap electricity. But I choose to think that the main reason for the brilliance of our town at night is commercial, the traditional determination of our merchants to get every dollar they can. The smaller shops and many larger stores stay open late several nights of the week, or even all nights of the week. Their windows and signs blaze in many colors. The hundreds of restaurants, large and small, are open, their lights flashing enticing messages to the skies as well as to drivers on the highway.

The bridges—and heaven knows Seattle has them—wear necklaces of light which they reflect on the dark waters. Also that night, as the plane circled again, I saw the lights of buoys on the Sound and the flashing light of Alki Point, where it all began.

As I finally walked down the stairs that had been pushed against the landed plane I was proud, too, of the brightly lighted airport. Certainly it is one of the finest in the nation, and makes many of them look like deteriorating bus stations. That night there were signs of major expansion. But, as Don Shay, director of aviation for the Port of Seattle, says, "It's a well-known fact that you can't build something and have it at the same time." Seattle-Tacoma International Airport was in the midst of a $125-million expansion and modernization program. This phase of changes at Sea-Tac made the airport one of the finest in the country, but it was amazing how the construction planning was under way with a minimum of inconvenience to travelers.

Unfortunately, not all of Seattle's portals are attractive and surface traffic is slow. It's a common saying in Seattle that you can reach Portland by air in less time than it takes to move from the airport to the city. However, an introduction to Seattle from east of the mountains across one of Lake Washington's floating bridges is enchanting, and so are entrances by train from the east and north, as well as by ship into the fabulous harbor. Despite the short-comings of other routes, few if any other cities can offer such variety to the traveler.

Not all Seattle hosts take visitors only to the lofty places. Many thousands of tourists and natives each year discover The Forgotten City Which Lies beneath Seattle's Modern Streets. The Forgotten City really exists, just as does the rotting sailing vessel which lies beneath the Colman Building on First Avenue.

There were rumors of an old underground "city" for many years. John Reddin of the Seattle *Times* was one who partially penetrated the debris and he wrote an article about it which many readers considered a hoax. The valid discoverer of the whole eerie curiosity is William C. Speidel, publisher of the *Seattle Guide* and author of *Sons of the Profits* (sic), whose title reveals his good-natured cynicism about the ancestors of our present-day businessmen. Speidel is a determined protector of Seattle's classic buildings in the lower part of town, although he and his small army of preservationists don't always win. He was a leader in the refurbishing of many of the buildings in the Occidental Avenue area. He practiced what he preached by creating a beautiful office for himself in an old building restored by architect Ralph Anderson.

In the mid-sixties, Speidel was poking around below the street level and found a tunnel which led to what seemed to be an old arched stone footbridge over a stream. That the arched brickwork turned out to be protection for an old sewer box failed to dampen Speidel's conviction that he had made a discovery he was willing to compare (in some respects) with the ruins of Pompeii. He had, he was convinced, discovered the long forgotten "hidden city" of Seattle. He spent more than nine months proving his case, poking around buried alleys and dead-end tunnels and what had once been streets. Speidel by no means takes all the credit. He estimates that at least six hundred people volunteered part of their time establishing that there *is* a buried city, and showing how it came to be buried.

What, then, is Seattle's "hidden city," and how did it come to be? In the beginning, Seattle was a sea of mud punctuated by stumpage. The first buildings sat on wooden pilings. The mud was caused by the tides and by the hills alive with springs. The first water system was a crazily built affair of hollowed-out scrap logs which, by gravity, brought water from the springs in the forest high behind the town. These erratically routed log "pipes" on stilts gave the pioneer city an appearance that startled mariners making their first landing in Elliott Bay. Even today, close by the Olympic Hotel, there runs an underground river. Water has always been a problem in Seattle—too much of it from above, a lot of it below.

The tides and the low level of the pioneer street system created problems which the early citizens coped with as best they could. "In those days," Speidel contends, "kids were raised on the tide tables instead of Doctor Spock." Toilets were flooded and backed up at high tides. Some ingenious settlers solved the problem by raising the water closet to such a height that three or four steps were required to climb aboard. Small wonder then that Ezra Meeker, a Puyallup settler friendly to Seattle, was moved to remark: "You can smell Seattle a couple of miles before you can see it."

According to Speidel, the first water closet was installed in the White House in 1851, the very year of our city's founding. It was inevitable that some of the later settlers would bring the contraption along for their new homes. It was not long until Seattle merchants carried a stock of them, and it is reported that one enterprising store-keeper had a "demonstrator model" modestly enclosed, and the report contends that people lined up for a block to try it out. Not everybody approved. The irascible and penny-pinching Henry Yesler is alleged to have asked, "Who in hell would want a privy right next to his bedroom?"

Quite a number of these bedrooms were devoted to sin. There were no town assessments in those days (Yesler and other pioneers objected to such a preposterous idea), so there had to be other ways of raising money. Why not tax sin? This is the primary reason why Seattle did, indeed, import sin. It was licensed and taxed to the limit.

They found other means of municipal income besides taxing sin. One interesting method was to charge ships, arriving empty from San Francisco for lumber, the sum of five dollars for every load of stone ballast the vessels dumped at the foot of Washington Street. Speidel, in his historical digging, discovered that this was the original extension of land west of First Avenue. Although most of these smooth round stones were simply dropped in the bay, some later served on cobblestoned streets. Today there are still a few of these extending for a block or two here and there around town.

So the tides came, toilets were raised, sin flourished—such was Seattle's condition at water's edge before the Great Fire of 1889. At least 90 per cent of the "downtown" buildings were of wood, and all of the structures dedicated to sin were built with second-grade lumber from Henry Yesler's mill. The few sidewalks were of wood and the areas of "paved" streets (as few as the sidewalks) were of rough planking. If ever a town was ready for a big fire, that community was Seattle.

When the Great Fire struck in 1889, it leveled whole blocks of wooden buildings, many at the water's edge. The ultra-conservative Yesler, who had strong influence with the City Council, led a movement within the council to rebuild the damaged area on the old, tide-plagued level. That vote lasted about a week. The majority of Seattleites who had suffered wet backsides for years were so outraged that they frightened the political-minded council. The first vote was rescinded; it was decided not to build on the original level. The council passed a new law that would raise the streets and create a sewer system which would not give strangers a chilling surprise at high tides. The people voted the biggest bond issue in the city's history up to that time—$190,000 for a new sewer system. This was the origin of Seattle's hidden city.

New buildings, sidewalks and streets were raised above the old, damaged level, in some cases two stories above. For a time, storekeepers able to salvage things out of the Great Fire, found themselves doing business far below the streets—in fact, steps were created to get customers down to the stores. But so many people stumbled and fell under this weird arrangement that the city eventually paved over much of its one-time city. In time, the lower-level stores were abandoned and forgotten. It remains an incredible fact that some ten and a half acres—a sizable portion of downtown Seattle—is built above the old city.

Speidel's discovery of the "hidden city" brought a remarkably enthusiastic response. Of all the folks in Seattle who wanted tours of the underground portion of the city, the students of Cleveland High School were most active. In the spring of 1965, Cleveland students, with groups from other schools, spent many a weekend cleaning out debris in order to make tours of the "hidden city" safe for everyone.

Today, an underground tour of Seattle consists of five and a half blocks. Literally thousands of Seattleites and visitors have taken these remarkable journeys—and Seattle's underground is listed in the Automobile Club of America's roster of major national attractions. Those forgotten underground streets were tough enough for pedestrians and horse-drawn vehicles before the Great Fire of 1889. They are tricky even now, so everyone who joins a tour party must come equipped with a flashlight or battery-powered lantern. There is a guide, sometimes Speidel himself and sometimes a member of his staff. The stories they include in their historical lectures on Seattle's sin-prone "hidden city" are nearly as racy as some of the graffiti and drawings in the ruins. Because of the stubborn work of Speidel and his helpers, the City Council has made an official historical site of the invisible area once called Skid Road.

The modern, visible Seattle is still in the throes of creation, and doubtless always will be. After viewing Seattle from the tall towers, the air, and then beneath the ground, it is time to walk on its surface.

Impressions of Seattle on the part of both natives and visitors vary, which is to be expected. Even hometown folks cheerfully agree that we don't seem to have decided whether we want to be a great city or a more modest version of a metropolis. In the 1970s the streets reflect this well-known split in our collective personality. Before World War II the principal streets and avenues each had their own characteristics. But for the time being there is a sameness about them. Of course there are exceptions to this generalization, but in the overall view there is a similarity. Not long ago First Avenue was a honkytonk trail much admired by bluejackets from visiting warships. Now it is relatively tame, and bears a resemblance to Second Avenue, and the latter to Third Avenue and Fourth Avenue, and to Sixth and Seventh avenues.

Fifth Avenue now has nosed out Second Avenue as the quality street where you find most—but not all—of the high fashion shops. Its most stylish stretch lies between the circular Washington Plaza Hotel, built in 1970, and the remarkably attractive Public Library. Yet it would be stretching things a bit to compare our Fifth Avenue with the site of Manhattan's Easter Parade. But on it, and around about it, are high-class shops and department stores, office buildings and hotels.

Yet because of the general sameness of the streets, and the fact that our newer and taller buildings parade in a line from upper downtown to lower downtown, rather than stand in clusters, one does sometimes get the feeling of walking through a moderate-sized town decorated with towering monuments.

So far the "monuments" seem grafted onto a somewhat provincial city, and not yet rooted in that city. This, naturally, will change with time's passing, and the trend is visible already if you look sharply.

Steven V. Roberts of the New York *Times* encountered a transplanted Chicagoan who told him that "in some ways Seattle is really a provincial town. They still think something from New York or San Francisco has got to be good, and they keep apologizing for things like the rain. I tell them, 'Don't apologize, you don't have to shovel it.'"

The former Chicagoan's reference to "they" reveals that he had not yet been here long enough to think of himself as a Seattleite. When that happens, the criticism may remain but the tone will change. And the man from Chicago was a bit behind the times. True, Seattle was once markedly imitative, and there are still aspects of other cities which we covet. We preen our feathers when the New York *Times* pays attention to us, or we receive notice by some widely known national magazine. Yet much of our old imitativeness disappeared with the success of the World's Fair in 1962. That fair, although relatively small, was marvelously conceived and was an outstanding success. It gave us a faith and confidence which we had not had since the Alaska-Yukon-Pacific Exposition of 1909, and which we would need badly toward the end of 1969, when Boeing took a downturn.

Nonetheless we still take pride in the favorable notice of other and bigger cities. Naturally we were pleased and proud when Mr. Roberts of the New York *Times* noted that Seattle has nationally known restaurants, and stores chic enough to attract eastern fashion editors. He saw also that we had a flourishing anti-war movement, a drug problem and a seemingly continuous fight as to what constitutes urban renewal. These are not precisely signs of provincialism. But he seemed amused when he viewed a television commercial advertising a special sugar for canning and preserving fruit, and when he learned that it was "a big thing" to send a whole salmon to friends or relatives in the old hometown.

Because of its location in the farthest reach of the U.S.,

Seattle may never quite shed itself of this folksiness, and I hope it doesn't.

Naturally Mr. Roberts of the New York *Times* perceived at once that in normal times the economy was tied so heavily to Boeing that the aircraft company was employing about one in every five Seattle workers. Soon after his departure came a serious recession at Boeing and in the airline business, which affected Seattle and the surrounding area both economically and psychologically. This moved the city leaders and Boeing executives to thoughts and programs that will diversify the business of the area. Boeing chiefs were as anxious for this change as were the city leaders.

"We are examining all possibilities," a Boeing executive told me. "Even when our plants were going at top speed, it was never comfortable to feel that Boeing was responsible for so much of the area's progress and prosperity. It was not a healthy situation. Nevertheless, we still have confidence in the future of the commercial airlines and our part in that."

Seattle was suffering from the inevitable result of being almost a "company town," as it had been so many years before when so much depended on Henry Yesler's sawmill. It seems probable that this concentration on Boeing has affected the appearance and pragmatism of the downtown section. There one notices the almost total absence of places not wholly devoted to merchandising. Paul Thiry, the architect already mentioned as designer of the Seattle Center, and a member of the National Planning Commission by appointment from President John Kennedy, puts it this way, "What Chief Seattle said—'There is no place dedicated to solitude'—is actually true now in the city."

Thiry urged acquisition of property for parks around the periphery of the center. His suggestion was not followed, and possibly now it is too late. Thiry's comments had a direct bearing on the appearance of the downtown area at the beginning of the seventies.

"I think Seattle could be one of the great places in the world, and that it still has that possibility," Thiry contends. But he is pessimistic about our approach to change. He sees us as failing to isolate our problems, then relate them to the whole area.

The downtown blocks reflect the sporadic and disorganized efforts toward urban renewal, although there is coming to be a better understanding of what city renewal means. Small shops go into business, then hold closing-out sales with disheartening regularity. It is as if much of our activity is the result of persuasive sales talks by owners of so-called income property. Thiry lays considerable blame on city officials. He says, "The public leaders should exercise all their power to keep the community intact, and I think they have done just the opposite. They tax us for everything, and that ruins the city, drives people out of it. There is nowhere to be safe from encroachment. You are always in the way of some so-called urban renewal, of street widening, of land condemnation, of the grab for parks, or of viaducts."

So people move to the suburbs, and in those havens do not help support the city in which they earn their incomes. One is reminded of New York and other cities with a large daytime commuter population. Commercially, the battle between the downtown stores and suburbia is vigorous and Seattle shows the scars. Most large department stores have opened branches beyond the city boundaries, and the branch inventories have grown to the point where they almost match that of headquarters stores in the city.

The newcomer is certain to notice that Seattle has made itself "an automobile city." Almost 60 per cent of the town is covered with cement for freeways, streets and—increasingly—parking lots and buildings. It is this startling situation which gives an overall impression of dullness. The sight of thousands of motionless cars somehow contributes to the often heard charge that the city is smug, self-centered and provincial. But loyal Seattleites insist that such an impression is deceptive and out of date. The viewpoints of newcomers—until they settle in and adjust themselves—are often confused. For example, the wife of a utilities director who moved with her husband to Seattle some years ago comments:

"When we first moved here from New York State I discovered a lack of knowledge of the East, but I remembered that in the East there is more than an equal shortcoming regarding the West, particularly the Seattle area."

Perhaps the charge of provincialism was never valid. Certainly it wasn't in the pioneer days, when Seattle had connections with the whole West Coast and nations around the Pacific Rim, and when newcomers—as now—represented a great many regions of the nation and brought their thoughts and ways of living with them. Anyhow, if the city was rampantly provincial in 1960 it has changed now—

or I have. I'm sure that the World's Fair of 1962 had a great deal to do with setting us on a broader course.

"There are plenty of unusual aspects in the life of an alert Seattleite. I remember how amusing I thought it was to get to the football stadium by water as passengers in a friend's cruiser. But now I take it for granted, just as did my friends during my initiation."

She found the more or less constant apology for the weather a bit monotonous. "So many Seattleites talk about the weather to newcomers as if they may get around to changing it if they have the time. I catch myself doing this, so I suppose this makes me a bona fide Seattleite. At least we've developed a sense of humor about it. There's a local joke wherein the visitor asks a Seattleite what the folks do in summer, and the Seattleite answers, 'If it comes on Sunday we go on a picnic.'"

Her husband recalls years in the South and East when Washington State was considered overly liberal or even "sovietized" and he feels that in the past this deterred eastern financing for Seattle. But as a Seattleite he discovered that his early impressions, by long distance, were wrong. "Or perhaps I have simply learned to live with a strongly unionized state," he admits. "At any rate, I have plunged in and tried to be a good local citizen and make what contribution I can. I've found the response heartwarming. There is nothing smug or provincial about Seattle if the newcomer makes an effort of his own."

The Pike Place Market is another feature which any newcomer finds typical of Seattle's charms. For a time in the early seventies, the market seemed doomed. But the people saved it. In the process, the market became the center of one of the more dramatic battles involving urban renewal.

There is no question that the market was most unusual in a young and modern city. You entered its crazy-quilt but practical world through a short narrow opening that was the foot of Pike Street. But the foot of Pike Street did not reach the bay. Halted by a steep bluff, it turned abruptly north to become Pike Place Way, once ample for the maneuvering of moderate-sized horse-drawn vehicles.

The names of the "discoverers" on this haven are lost to history, which is a pity. They were truck gardeners from the small farms that had developed in the valleys south of town. They saw in it a trading mart to which they could bring their fresh vegetables before dawn, with time enough to stack them attractively and to fill the sprinkling cans which would bring hourly sparkle to their cabbages and berries and peas and all the other edibles that grow in the lush climate of the Puget Sound country. The prices were more than fair, and the market quickly became known to the bargain hunters and the poor. Some farmers placed hand-lettered prices on their wares, but as the hectic day wore on there was always a chance for dickering between buyer and seller. No matter what the daylight hour, the market was easily the busiest spot in town.

In November of 1907 a "formal" market was opened by John and Frank Goodwin, who had returned rich from the Alaska gold fields. This meant that the Pike Place Market had become a business, rather than a conglomerate friendly clash between customers and the farmers. Until then, farmers staked out stalls much as early settlers sat firmly on land of newly opened territories in days past. The Goodwin brothers laid out stall space and built shops, but they were careful to preserve the pioneer character of the market. Commission men and other "middle" entrepreneurs were firmly shouldered out.

The opening by the Goodwins was truly a gala occasion. Flags fluttered, banners waved and every single band in Seattle was on hand. It seemed as if all citizens except the halt and lame were present and accounted for. City officials made unnecessarily long speeches to which few listened; the audience was busy exploring. Some were making their first market purchases and thereby beginning a lifelong habit.

By 1927 more than four hundred people were selling direct to the consumer. When the Goodwin brothers tired of the enterprise and offered to sell the market to the city the council pleaded lack of funds. Thus the hurdy-gurdy collection of stalls and stores became in a sense co-owned by the men and women who rented space. Firm friendships developed between buyers and sellers, and even among competitors. Second and third generations came along to carry on the businesses. The market became by all odds one of the happiest places of commerce in Seattle. Family resemblances among the market people were often strong, and many an old-time customer was startled—after some years absence—to see a face he felt certain he had known when shopping in knee pants for his frugal mother.

It was in the sixties that the worshipers of Urban Renewal cast eyes on the crumbling, run-down Pike Place Market and some of the obsolescent buildings in its vicinity. The inevitable followed. Ambitious planners soon were at work, showing drawings of a "modernized" market surrounded by multi-family apartment towers and dotted with tiny malls with trees and benches and ponds.

At first the market people took no notice. To them the market always had been and always would be. And so busy was trade that they hardly took notice of the weakening underpinnings, the sagging ramps, and makeshift repairs. Indeed, the gradual decay became a part of the market's unusual charm. To the market people the place was not just a way of making a living. It was a way to live; they knew no other, and they liked it. To them it was a continual adventure, beginning each day with the coming of the farmers' trucks in the chilly hours before dawn, and the taking down of shutters on the wildly varied shops. When the young long-haired people discovered the market some of them opened shops of their own, selling trinkets and iconoclastic posters. Antique shops, galleries and restaurants opened and flourished. They were welcomed, when and if they were noticed at all, by the old-timers of the market.

But it grew apparent that the planners of Urban Renewal were serious. Mark Tobey, world-renowned Seattle artist living abroad, was alerted. The tall, distinguished white-haired painter had pleasant memories of the market. In 1964, from across the Atlantic, he was one of the first to issue a call to battle. His book *The World of the Market*, a collection of his market sketches, carried a warning:

"Our homes are in the paths of freeways; old landmarks, many of them of rare beauty, are sacrifices to the urge to get somewhere in a hurry; and when it is all over progress reigns, queen of the giants to whom the intimacy of living is of no importance."

The market people, both buyers and sellers, began to realize that the market was really a prime target. They heard the mayor saying, "We must get the machinery rolling!"

Victor Steinbrueck of the School of Architecture at the University of Washington, already had heard them—before almost anyone else. It was he who had alerted Mark Tobey and pleaded with the co-owners of the market to stage a counterattack. But they were not worldly people; and they knew little of the power of politics and organized commercial adventures.

So Steinbrueck began appealing beyond the market itself. He organized the Friends of the Market, pulling away from most of his other interests as one of the town's leading environmentalists. Literally, he began devoting his "moonlight" hours to an attempt to save the place where he had spent so many happy hours sketching or simply watching the very special people there.

With limited funds, mostly out of the pockets of individual Friends of the Market, they fought. Every Friday their battle plans were sharpened or completely redrawn. The logistics were planned at lunch around a plyboard table on trestles in front of The Copacabana. That was Ramon Pelez's little cafe, which featured two delectable entrées, and only two, and like all the tiny bistros scattered throughout the market it paid little attention to decor. Ramon Pelez knew something about loss of freedom and the power of the Establishment. In Brazil he had lost his newspaper because he published the truth about the government. So he fled north, as far north as he could get on the mainland of the United States, and opened The Copacabana. He was cook, waiter, cashier and dishwasher. His reputation grew and he had offers from backers who wanted to set him up in a larger establishment uptown. Ramon steadily refused; he was a free man, running his cafe as he pleased; and, when it pleased him, hanging a sign on the door: *Taking a vacation. Back some day soon.* But he tried not to miss a Friday, when he served the Friends of the Market as well as his regular customers.

For eight long years the struggle went on between the Friends of the Market and those whose banner bore the all too familiar device: *Progress!* The Friends succeeded in delaying those who waved that banner, and they developed a renewed and deeply sentimental interest in the market. The two newspapers had been understanding, and the place always had been a good source of stories and photographs. Then suddenly the papers withdrew their subtle, sentimental support. The essence of their new message was that the Friends of the Market should become "friends of the city, and let progress march on."

For the first time sellers in the market recognized that they would have to move or give up—or fight to preserve their place in the market. Most preferred the latter. Rallied by Victor Steinbrueck and Friends of the Market, petitions were circulated. In fact, petitions fanned out all over the city.

The battle was joined between what was known as the Pike Place Project and those Seattleites who wanted the market to remain as it is. The Pike Place Project, backed by downtown business interests and the newspapers, was a rather grandiose plan to build parking garages and high-rise apartments. Mayor Wes Uhlman joined the downtown forces, which felt that the Pike Place Project would stimulate in-city living and downtown business. The market people and their friends, however, felt that the project would stifle the market, change the character of the residents in that area and ultimately destroy the whole nature of this unique Seattle institution. Part of the Pike Place Project depended on ten million dollars in urban renewal funds.

The Pike Place Project plan envisioned leaving 1.7 acres of the market intact, and indeed its backers argued that they were really trying to "save" the market, which, they argued, was doomed without their help. But the petitions circulated by Friends of the Market and many volunteer groups as well, called for designating seven acres of the market area as an historical preservation site. Enough signatures were obtained to put the issue on the ballot—so the fate of the Pike Place Market rested with the voters of Seattle.

Known officially as the Pike Place Market Historical District measure, its presence on the ballot became the hottest issue in Seattle's spring of 1971. By election eve, it was clear that Seattle loved its market too much to endanger its future. The pro-market forces defeated the mayor, the downtown business interests and the Pike Place Project by a vote of 57,934 to 50,641 For the time being, at least, the market will remain as it was, and for one of the few times in its history, Seattle voted for preservation against "progress." In the fall of 1971, Seattle voters defeated two freeway proposals by resounding margins, a sign that some feel is all to the good—that Seattle is awakening to the reality that concrete is not always an unmixed blessing and that a beautiful city should be treated with care.

3

Mr. Denny and Doctor Maynard

It ALWAYS has been difficult to characterize the average Seattleite, and I am not too certain today that there is such an animal. Yet it is by following the lives of Arthur Armstrong Denny and Dr. David Swinton Maynard, two extremely large figures in the founding of Seattle, that we can come to a better understanding of the modern Seattleite—who is, like the city today, somewhat schizophrenic.

It is difficult to imagine two more opposite types—yet Mr. Denny and Doctor Maynard were archetypal of two kinds of leading Seattle pioneers. They added up to a perfect example of human polarization. Viewed from one angle, Maynard was a failure. Viewed from another he was, like Denny, a success. Both helped build the city. Without these two there might not be the kind of Seattle we now have.

Denny was pragmatic and somewhat close-fisted. He also was a teetotaler. Maynard often imbibed—indeed, to the despair of his friends and certainly to the chagrin of Mr. Denny. Denny was a

Whig and later a Republican, conservative and taciturn. Maynard, a Democrat, was outgoing, friendly and profligate. Yet in each there was streak of Populism, a strain now and then visible in our modern politics.

Except when Maynard was drunk, which was rather often, he and Denny got along. It behooved the founders and the trickling of newcomers to be companionable. They needed one another, not only in peace but in threatened warfare. Maynard and Denny seem to have come to direct loggerheads but once. This was over the platting of the town. The doctor insisted that the Organic Act, under which the village was formed, demanded that streets run north and south and east and west, all neat and—as his Indian friends would say—*copacete*. The doctor stuck to his belief when he laid out his land, which ended at Yesler Way.

Denny, on the other hand, had laid out his own streets northwest by southeast, mindful that in the interest of business it would be well to more or less follow the shoreline. Denny was not a man of ready humor, and the only light touch in his memoirs, published when he was sixty-six, refers to this platting argument. "The doctor," he wrote, "had taken enough to make him feel that he was not only monarch of all he surveyed, but monarch of what Boren and I had surveyed as well."

Later on, the city engineers did their best to twist the streets so that they joined at Yesler Way—more or less. As soon as the town grew big enough to stretch north of Denny Way the streets straightened out in accordance with the Organic Act. Today, given these origins, plus one-way streets and the imposition of the freeway, downtown Seattle is not easy for the tourist to navigate. In fact, it is almost impossible to explain to a stranger how to reach a certain destination or to extricate himself from some pocket into which he has wandered. I half suspect that it was in Seattle that there originated an old story. "How do I get to such and such a place?" the stranger asks. Whereupon the native city dweller furrows his brow, gives the matter long thought and at last confesses, "Fact is, you just can't get there at all from here." (It should be noted, however, that what we call "scenic routes" are well marked and carry the symbol of Neptune's trident.)

Arthur A. Denny had a good deal of moody Irish in him, being born of parents of Irish descent on June 20, 1822, in Salem,

Indiana, to which his father and mother had moved from Kentucky. He completed a common school education and soon thereafter married Mary Ann Boren. By 1850 he was surveyor for Knox County, Illinois, which might indicate that he was right, and Maynard wrong, in that argument about the laying out of the infant community. Sparse with words, he never explained fully his reasons for leaving home to travel toward the sunset shore. Actually, no full explanation is necessary, for those were the days when thousands of North Americans were under the spell of the *Zeitgeist*. For Denny, as for many others, the Donation Claim Act was an invitation to a man unafraid of hard work and the unknown. There was free and open land in the Pacific Northwest, as once there had been where Denny lived. He had had ample opportunity to see what could happen to the people who got to the free land first.

California did not excite his imagination, but the vast Oregon Country did. He was just twenty-nine in 1851, and doubtless felt that it was time to make something of himself if ever he was going to do so. His sparse memoirs do not make clear whether the men, women and children who would found Seattle traveled as a party. They do make clear that Seattle was founded by twelve adults and twelve children.

There is no evidence that the twenty-four founders of Seattle knew or cared about earlier explorations to Puget Sound.

Initially they seem not to have known that an aged Greek named Valerianos, who called himself Juan de Fuca, told seafarer Michael Lok that he had discovered the strait which leads from the Pacific into the great Sound.

The sparse journals and letters of the founders make no reference to the discovery of the Sound by Captain George Vancouver in his appropriately named *H.M.S. Discovery*. But they knew its name, if not the fact that Vancouver christened it after one of the least of his junior officers, Peter Puget. Although Vancouver appreciated its beauty and could see some of the awesome mountains which ringed it, he seems not to have been greatly impressed. But he may have been in irksome humor that day in May, probably having heard that he had missed in "the stinking fog" the wide mouth of the Columbia River to the south. In that year of 1792 he left the finding of the great River of the West to Captain Robert Gray, in his trading ship *Columbia*, out of Boston and sponsored by canny merchants. That discovery would be important to a young United States in later debates with Britain as to which nation had genuine claim to what was then known as "the Oregon country."

Nor do the early settlers mention the much later exploration of Lieutenant Charles Wilkes of the U. S. Navy, who had explored the Sound and sent a party far inland. Wilkes was not too long out of the naval academy, a naval officer through and through, with a good eye for prospective harbors.

Fortunately, Arthur Denny wrote a memoir of the earliest period called *Pioneer Days on Puget Sound*, which, unlike most pioneer accounts, is barely saved from dullness by its brevity and cogency.

"We left our Illinois home on April 10, 1851," he wrote, and does not say why. He makes little romance or adventure about the crossing of the Great Plains. Here is all of it:

"We crossed from Burlington in Iowa to Kanesville, a Mormon town [now Council Bluffs] on the Missouri River, traveling via New London, Mount Pleasant, Fairfield, Agency, Ottumwa, and Eddyville. We crossed the Missouri River on May 5th, and traveled up the north side of the Platte River, and passed Fort Laramie on Friday, June 6th. Estimated distance from Missouri River at 530 miles. On Saturday the 21st of June we crossed the summit of the South Pass. We reached Fort Hall on July 4th, distance estimated at 1,104 miles.

"From Fort Hall our line of travel was on the south side of the Snake River, and Saturday, the 5th, we camped a mile or two above American Falls."

It was at this point that they had their first encounter with unfriendly Indians, who confronted the party of four wagons and seven men (the rest were women and children), but the little wagon train simply drove through, refusing to stop. The Indians fired a few shots from the rear, but Denny kept going until he found "an advantageous position," where he halted and awaited an attack which did not materialize.

Despite Denny's phlegmatic account and the fact that the time preceded the Indian wars, it seems probable that his party did have a narrow squeak. A few weeks later a family by the name of Clark, traveling two or three miles ahead of the main train (a bad mistake) was ambushed and killed by the same band of renegade Indians near the site of Denny's adventure.

They reached Portland, and Denny's memoirs barely hide his dismay at finding a town of two thousand. He considered that too large for the quick opportunity he sought.

"On leaving home for what we called the Pacific Coast we had no other purpose or expectation than to settle in the Willamette Valley. But we met a man by the name of Brock who gave us information in regard to Puget Sound. . . . and I formed the purpose of looking in that direction."

Clearly Denny wanted a spot where he would be first on the mark, but just at this moment he, his wife and one of their children were stricken with ague, the pioneer's name for malarial fever, "most effectively defeating all my plans for examination of that country."

The man named Brock fired up Denny's desire to look at the Puget Sound country. Arthur was deeply disturbed, even embarrassed, by the illness which held him back. Yet Brock's first word picture to Denny was important; had it not been for this dimly glimpsed adventurer, Seattle might never have been founded—at least not as soon or on its present site. Denny had little patience with illness—particularly his own—and he continued to be considerably upset as the malarial chills held him in Portland until the early fall.

Meanwhile, in September, Denny's brother David, along with Low, drove the latter's cattle to the Chehalis River area for winter range, and Arthur commissioned them to examine the Puget Sound country about which Brock had been so enthusiastic. What Denny visualized was virgin land. He wanted to be "first"—no doubt of that—with all the advantages that gave to the early settlers. Apparently it had not occurred to him that there were still vast lands in the Pacific Northwest settled only by the Indians.

David Denny, Low and Terry, following Arthur's orders, explored that part of Puget Sound now known as Elliott Bay. As noted in Arthur's journal, they decided to settle on Alki Point. This historic location is on the west side of the bay and is encompassed today by the large area known as "West Seattle." It was on this spot chosen by the trio that later citizens erected a modest granite shaft on which are engraved the names of the twenty-four people who were Seattle's founders.

Terry and David Denny remained on the claim while Low returned to Portland to report to Arthur Denny and gather up the rest of the Low family. When Low arrived in Portland, it happened that a Captain Folger was fitting out his schooner *Exact* for a voyage to the Queen Charlotte Islands, where gold had been reported. It is characteristic of the Denny party that they ignored the dream of gold for the reality of salable timber, but Arthur—still shaking and pale with ague—determined to join the passengers of the *Exact*, since Captain Folger was willing to touch lower Puget Sound on the way north.

Says Denny in his journal: "The *Exact* sailed on the 5th of November, 1851, and cleared at Astoria, as shown by the custom house records, on the 7th. We crossed out [over the Columbia River bar] on the same day, and on Thursday, the 13th, our party, consisting of myself and family, John N. Low and family, C. D. Boren and family, William N. Bell and family, and Charles C. Terry landed at Alki Point, added to which were my brother David T. Denny, and Lee Terry, making in all twenty-four persons and twelve children—all living at the present time [November 13, 1887, when Denny published his memoirs] but six."

Scenic descriptions are almost entirely absent from Denny's account of the long journey westward to Portland; they are even absent when he finally arrived on the Puget Sound he came to love. "Our first work," he records in his direct, unemotional journal, "was to provide shelter for the winter, and we finished the house begun by my brother and Low. We all took shelter in it from the rain which was falling more or less every day, but we did not regard it with much concern and seldom lost any time on that account."

A passenger on the *Exact* described the scene as the schooner pulled away for the Queen Charlotte Islands. She said her last glimpse was of the women, weeping copiously, and with sunbonnets pasted to their cheeks by the rain, trying to stretch muslin over some berry bushes as temporary shelter from the downpour.

Sunbonnets seem strange head gear for the Puget Sound country, yet as a boy, a very small boy when Seattle was hardly sixty years old, I remember women wearing sunbonnets for summer gardening. And I remember the bracken of vacant lots dotted with wild roses and other flowers which had spread from seeds the founding women had brought across the plains in the pockets of their aprons. By then, say in 1910, the flowers were growing wild in every vacant lot and grass parking strip. At the time, of course, I had no idea how this came about. But then neither did most Seattleites.

The next big step was the building of a house for Arthur Denny and his family. "This," he later wrote, "increased our room very materially and made us all more comfortable." Today's Seattleites would find small comfort in a situation which divided twelve adults and a dozen children in two small log cabins. No sooner had the winter quarters for the party been completed than Captain Dan Howard in the brig *Leonosa* appeared. Noting white men on the beach he took to the ship's boats and came ashore to make a contract for a cargo of piles for booming San Francisco.

Inasmuch as there were no animals for hauling, Terry was dispatched to find a team of oxen. Some of the Denny men at once went to work cutting the timber nearest the shoreline. They chopped, sawed, trimmed and rolled logs to tidewater, where Captain Howard could float them to his ship. Arthur Denny was not losing time, rain or no rain, and by the time Terry returned with the ox team (he had driven them along the beach from grazing land the Indians called Puyallup) a sizable part of the cargo had been made up. Seattle was in business months before it became Seattle.

Low and Terry, by spring, already had laid out a town and the latter being a New Yorker decided on the name New York, which later became, less optimistically, New York Alki, meaning "New York bye and bye."

But Arthur Denny, Boren and David Denny were not quite satisfied with the Alki situation. They looked up the coast toward Puyallup and voted against a site there. In February they took soundings in the bay which Alki Point protected, using horseshoes spliced to clothesline as weights, and noted that the eastern shore of the bay offered extremely deep water and that the heavy forests reached to the tideflats. Also they discovered meadows which would provide feed for their stock.

On February 15, 1852, they located and marked three claims in one body. This was the Seattle that would grow to embrace Alki Point and spread eastward toward the huge body of water to be called Lake Washington.

The founding was not an easy one, or very adventurous as we now view adventure. But it was rugged labor, for men and women both. Denny saw nothing wrong with that, and he made a halfhearted apology for the advantages of the Donation Claim Law by which the government gave free land to original settlers:

"The object of all who came to Oregon Territory in early times was to avail themselves of a donation claim, and my opinion today is that every man and woman fully earned and merited all they got."

Clearly there had been criticism from latecomers, for he adds: "But we have a small class of *very small* [italics his] people who have no good word for the old settlers that so bravely met every danger and privation, and by hard toil acquired, and careful economy saved the means to make them comfortable during the decline of life."

For the first time in his memoirs Denny heats up: "These, however, are degenerate scrubs, too cowardly to face the same dangers that our pioneer men and women did, and too lazy to perform an honest day's work if it would procure them a homestead in Paradise. They would want the day reduced to eight hours and board thrown in."

On March 23, 1852, the *Exact* put into the bay on her return from the Queen Charlotte Islands, where passengers and crew had found the gold reports "a bust." Boren and David Denny then took return passage on the *Exact* as far as Olympia, on the way to pick up their stock. Arthur Denny and Bell remained behind in charge of the claims and families.

Unfortunately, the malarial chills again struck Denny; actually he had never quite recovered at the difficult time when piling was being cut and loaded for the *Leonosa* and when he, Bell and Boren were exploring Elliott Bay for a more advantageous town site. Before the return of the younger men with the stock, almost all of the remaining party were down again with the ague.

It was at this point that Doctor David Swinton Maynard arrived in company with the big Indian called Sealth. Practically exiled from Olympia by his brother-in-law and competing merchants, the physician brought abounding optimism to the drenched community. It is probable that he had immunized himself against disease. In any case he had had plenty of experience with both ague and the far more serious cholera on his way across the plains and mountains. He may have treated Denny and his family as his first patients on the Sound, but neither he nor the straightlaced Denny records any such thing in his journal.

Maynard's basic profession was not as interesting to Denny as was the doctor's plan to pack salmon when the "run" came in the following month. "After an examination of the point," Denny recalls, "Maynard and his Indian friends whom he intended to hire as fishermen decided on the southern point of our claims. At first he declined to take a claim, saying that he only wanted a temporary location on which to salt down fish. But on further consideration he decided to accept our suggestion that he make a permanent location."

Thus began the first of a series of rearrangements, approved in general by Arthur Denny and his associate founders, particularly if the individual seemed willing to work and had an idea for a new commercial enterprise. Accordingly the founders moved their boundary north to what later would be called Mill Street to allow Maynard to get on with his fish-packing plan. Unfortunately Maynard's first attempt at industrialism went wrong. Either the barrels were defective or there was not enough salt in the packing. The fish spoiled, and Maynard lost money. This was not unusual in his life and failed to dampen his enthusiasm for the location.

Soon Arthur Denny was moving again. The front of his claim was so rough and broken that it was difficult to gain access to the shoreline. He was in for another disappointment. Still shaking now and then with malarial fever, he dug a forty-foot well at the bottom of the gulch near the new cabin "and got mostly quicksand with only a limited amount of water."

It seems strange that Denny would have selected such an unhappy site or failed first to examine the possible water supply. But wholly undaunted, he built still another cabin. He made certain this time that he was in an area fed by several springs which bubbled to the surface in the forests above on the hill. Like most of the cabins, his boasted a brick chimney of impressive dimensions. There is evidence that the early settlers built several small kilns to make the bricks.

About this time another "industrialist"—much more practical than Maynard, and with a full knowledge of his business—appeared on the bay. This was Henry L. Yesler, who arrived from Portland with a view to establishing a steam sawmill. There had not yet been filed at Oregon City any official claims, and Yesler fancied a spot where Maynard and Boren joined. Yesler had his complete sawmill equipment stored in Portland and it did not take Boren and Maynard long to agree to give Yesler a part of their territory. So once again the plan of the town was rearranged and all went well until that hour when Maynard imbibed beyond his normal capacity. This was the situation which led Denny to observe that the doctor felt monarch of all he had surveyed, and all of what Denny and Boren had staked out as well.

Denny saw that it was time to beat the doctor to the draw. Early on the twenty-third of May, 1853, he and Boren filed the first plat of the town. "When in the evening of the same day the doctor's fever had subsided," remarks Denny, "he filed his own plat." Denny was in no mood to annoy a man like Yesler, who was ready to do business on the Sound.

The town was growing very slowly. Doctor Maynard's area grew fastest because always he was quick and generous to give away part of his land to any newcomer with a business in mind. Early in 1855 it welcomed another newcomer from Alki Point. This was J. N. Low, who sold his interest at Alki to Charles Terry, the former New Yorker. Inasmuch as Terry's brother had returned to the East, Charles became the sole owner at the point. Later he bought the front half of the Boren claim on the east side of the bay and became a new resident of Seattle. In time he would sell his Alki property to Doctor Maynard, who took up his residence there. But that was at the beginning of Maynard's hard luck period and was yet to come.

Settlers began trickling over the mountain passes of the Cascades, and this led Arthur Denny to become one of several pioneers who began exploring the various defiles with an idea of establishing a wagon road that would give Seattle a connection with the interior.

Not all centered in Seattle. Other parts of the Sound's shoreline were coming alive. As Denny admitted in his memoirs, Olympia already was "quite a city"—actually it was a village—at the time the founders of Seattle first chose Alki Point in 1851. Later there were settlers on Whidbey Island to the north. The Duwamish area was welcoming newcomers and in the same year there were families taking claims on the shoreline that Captain Vancouver had christened Port Townsend. Being nearer the Strait of Juan de Fuca and hence the open ocean, Townsend enjoyed a period when its population was outstripping that of Seattle. Muckleshoot Prairie was coming alive, and Tacoma on Commencement Bay had announced that new-comers would be wise to watch how it was growing.

But newcomers were attracted to the settlement on Elliott Bay, many making their choices because of the white plume of Yesler's steam engine. That feather in the sky looked like the signal of a coming city.

What many an optimistic and acquisitive modern Seattleite likes to call "Pugetopolis" was beginning to form in rough outline, stretching from Whidbey Island and the mainland opposite to the Duwamish Valley on the south and the shores of Lake Washington on the east. Olympia ignored all this, considering itself a center of culture and commerce, and Seattle an upstart settlement. Although it would not quite fulfill its maximum hopes, Olympia would become the capital of Washington Territory and finally of the state. New counties were forming and the one encompassing Seattle was named for William King, who had been elected Vice-President on the Franklin Pierce ticket but died before his inauguration could take place. Tacoma's county took the name of Pierce himself.

Despite Denny's optimistic stressing of accommodations rearranged for newcomers, all was not easy in the first years.

In the winter of 1852–53 but few vessels visited the Sound over a period of months, and as a consequence it was a time of great scarcity, amounting almost to distress. Our pork and butter came around the Horn and flour in barrels from Chile, and sugar mostly from China in straw mats. That fall I paid $90 for two barrels of pork, and $20 for a barrel of flour. I left one barrel of pork on the beach in front of my cabin, as I supposed at high tide, until it would be needed. Just about the time to roll it up and open it there came a high tide and heavy wind at night, and like the house that was built on sand it fell, or anyway it washed away and disappeared. It was the last barrel of pork in all of King County and the loss of it was felt by many as a very serious matter. There were various theories about it. Some said it would float and had gone out to sea. Others thought it had rolled into deep water.

The whole town turned out with fir pitch torches. "But the pork," wrote Denny, "has not yet been heard from."

After the loss of the pork the settlers ran out of flour and hard bread. Yet they considered themselves fortunate to have a good supply of sugar, syrup, tea and coffee. With fish and venison they got along well enough—until the supply of potatoes ended. That meant a canoe voyage to an Indian settlement on the Black River, where the natives had been taught to raise what the pioneers called "spuds." Recalled Denny:

> This was the hardest experience our people ever had, but it demonstrated that some substantial life-supporting food can always be obtained on Puget Sound, though it is hard for a civilized man to live without bread.

In any case, the citizens had happier things to think about and knew that flour would eventually appear in the cargo of some good ship from South America and points between. What was most exciting to Seattleites now was the noise and clatter of Henry Yesler's sawmill.

"We vacated our log cabins as quickly as possible," says Denny, "and began the building of frame houses."

Now things were beginning to look more like home. Denny seems never to have been impressed by the awe-inspiring scenery surrounding his own place. What chiefly interested him was a shelter in which to live and the growth of commerce. According to his memory, the mill cookhouse and mess hall was the last log structure in use.

For some years, however, that mill cookhouse was the center of the town's communal activities. The building also did duty as a place of entertainment when traveling "professors" came to town to lecture on such esoteric subjects as phrenology, or tell of adventures in faraway places across the oceans. The lectures were usually illustrated with large maps, and it may be doubted that all the "professors" had really experienced the adventures described or visited the countries where their picturesque tales allegedly transpired. Few charlatans were unmasked, however, and these gentlemen, decked out in tailcoats and stiff collars, were the forerunners of traveling companies in later days when Seattle had an "opera house" (but no opera) and the audiences were less innocent.

Just north of Yesler's noisy mill had appeared a two-story structure which prissy historians called "Mother Damnable's." It was a respectable boarding house known to many a sailor who probably called it "Mother God Damn's," which more accurately reflected the favorite expletive of the amply built proprietress.

The mill—soon flanked by a mountainous pile of sawdust—was the end of the skid road over which logs were dragged by oxen. (And the word is *road*, not row, as several modern dictionaries erroneously insist.) Civic leaders and professional loafers gathered often at the cookhouse to consider the latest news and gossip, and listen to the tales of ship captains. The building was for a time the housing for town meetings; thus the seed ground for Seattle's political life as well as entertainment.

It was not long before Yesler's mill had to relinquish its distinction as the only sawmill on that part of the Sound. Arthur Denny was proud to see others follow even though they were not within the boundaries of the town. J. J. Felt erected a mill at Port Madison on Bainbridge Island. A firm comprised of William Talbot and A. J. Pope built a mill at Port Gamble. This pair was soon joined by Charles Foster and J. P. Keller of East Machias, Maine. The dark forests of giant trees around the Sound were much like those of Maine, and many early settlers who engaged in the sawmill business near Seattle readily recognized the great future of the timber business in the Pacific Northwest. Soon there were mills at Utsaladdy, which later became the property of the Puget Mill Company. Still another sawmill was built at a site called Seabeck.

Arthur Denny often visited the various mill proprietors for both business and pleasure. The men of Maine were his kind, and his memoir has much good to say about them. Denny was heartened to see more and more tall-masted lumber ships berthed around the Sound. Despite the admiration of settlers such as Denny, there would come a time when the lumbermen would be maligned as "timber barons" who practiced hell and high water logging, giving hardly a thought to the future. Reseeding and practices to reduce the possibility of fire, genuine concern for the workers in the mills and woods—these were not to be factors in the lumber business for years to come.

Denny's mode of travel to and from his friends at the mills was by Indian canoe in the early days. It was a great event when a steamer service was established between the northern part of the Sound and Olympia, with stops between. The initial rate to Olympia was ten dollars, later reduced to six dollars, which Denny thought a very reasonable rate.

The steamer brought Seattle's mail, but on August 15, 1853, this rating came to an end with a shipment of twenty-two letters and fourteen newspapers. On that day there was established a post office at Seattle. Denny was appointed postmaster and arranged a mail service in a corner of his second log cabin. It was a matter of pride to him to become the first postmaster, but the pride was not long lasting.

> I was not permitted to enjoy the distinguished honors and 'immense immoluments' for any length of time. Doctor Maynard and two or three kindred spirits represented to the Department that I was not only a Whig but 'an offensive partisan' and they got me relieved by a drunken little doctor who was a newcomer.

But Denny had friends too. When the Maynard petition had gone forward one of them, even though a Democrat, forwarded a protest, and on May 4, 1854 Denny was recommissioned by the First Assistant Postmaster General. "I declined the reappointment," Denny recorded haughtily, "and about this time the drunken little doctor left the country, forgetting to pay his bills before starting, or settling up with the Department. Charles Plummer then took the position."

Subsequent events do not indicate that Denny held the matter against Doctor Maynard; apparently all was fair in politics, then as now in the city of Seattle. Or perhaps he forgave Maynard because he believed that the doctor was under the influence of spirits, periods when Maynard's actions were not always predictable.

There are other evidences that Denny—except when laziness was involved—was fair-minded and had a forgiving heart. He did not approve of the settlement's method of punishing Indians for crimes, real or alleged. There were frequent murders of both white and red men in those early times, and Denny felt that the Indians always got the worst treatment. The natives rarely failed to take revenge when one of their race was the victim. They did not care whether the white men chosen to pay the price had anything to do with the original killing. What they wanted was vengeance and for this purpose they preferred a high-placed white leader. Any white of distinction would do, and Denny himself once narrowly escaped by disguising himself in a blanket and paddling swiftly out into the bay. The experience did not change his mind for equal law for Indian and white.

> Two Indians were hanged for a murder without legal trial, and near the same time another Indian was hanged, without trial, for the murder of his squaw. It is true that three white men were indicted for these offenses. One was tried and acquitted and the other two were discharged without trial at all. I have ever been opposed to mob law. It is a most dangerous method of punishing crime and settling grievances and where savages are concerned it is no better. . . . If they commit crimes against the whites and are dealt with and convicted under due process of law, I am very sure that the effect is likely to be salutary, and the penalty imposed accepted as a final settlement by the friends of the offenders.

Denny's character shines from his memoir—which refers far more often to others than to himself. His forgiveness of Maynard for slights, and even insults, and his attitude toward the Indians say much for him. As the elder of the city's founders his life was exemplary. His recollections say little or nothing of his political activities, which extended beyond the little settlement. One wonders how he found the time to help form the early laws of the area and state, but he was not a man to shirk his civic duties. He was a commissioner of King County, and served in the House of Representatives during its maiden session in 1854. During the next decade he was either a member of the House or Council. Staunch Whig, later Republican, he was elected as a delegate to Congress from the territory. This was the highest honor possible to an early Seattleite, yet one finds no mention of it in his recollections.

He abandoned politics at last when he was defeated for mayor by a mere forty-four votes. It was not defeat that discouraged him so much as the fact that his opponent, William Shoudy, was a member of the People's Party, whose platform was the opposite of every one of Denny's political beliefs.

A taciturn man, he makes in his memoirs only indirect references to his wife and children, although it is clear that he was an excellent family man and proud of "the issue" of all the founders of the city. He was loyal to his friends and, in times of general stress, even to his enemies.

In his lifetime he saw Seattle grow from twenty-four people to 42,000—yet nowhere does he assume the slightest credit for growth and progress. He died on January 9, 1889, a wealthy man for his times, and the nearest he came to a defense of riches was in his diatribes against the indolent latecomers who criticized the successful. Pragmatic he was indeed, and a booster, which makes him a Seattleite for all times. In his way he is the symbol of the best of Seattle, which is the city's good fortune today.

Doctor David Swinton Maynard was also typical of Seattleites, most of whom retain a bit of the frontier in speech, action, and thought. But in general his ways were not those of Arthur Denny.

Doctor Maynard remained somewhat undiscovered until this mid-century insofar as local historians are concerned, and of course he was not nationally known. There were regional rumors about him, and most of them were true. But writers did not dare to pounce upon him until the passing of his loyal widow, Catherine. She was Maynard's second wife and, for a time, one of two. Chiefly it was this tidbit of gossip that brought Maynard to life in the annals of Seattle. It was discovered at last that we had a pioneer who was a bigamist, a periodic drinker and a failure by habit, but who also had a way of occasionally bringing off a success, usually for others or the town as a whole.

It was in 1850, about a year before the founding of Seattle, that Maynard found himself in Lorain County, Ohio, with an unhappy marriage and a burden of debt. Much of the debt was due to Maynard's reluctance to collect bills due him, and he was known even to co-sign the promissory notes of patients. Too, through the years to come, considerable of his financial difficulties stemmed from his efforts to help others. As his wife Lydia could have told Lorain County, with her husband charity did not begin at home. He had tried to run a medical school but it went broke during the panic of 1837 and he had never been out of trouble since. When he decided to make a break for the Far West he was forty-two and concluded that it was high time for a change of scene and an attempt at a change of luck.

Certainly many a pioneer headed westward to escape an unfortunate marriage, although the majority of early journals were written by men (and women) who brought the whole family and as many of their household goods as space in the covered wagons permitted.

Maynard was among those who departed as "a loner" and—like so many who ended up on Puget Sound—he first had California in mind. He planned to recoup quickly, helping another former Ohioan in the gold fields. Fortune insisted that love intervene and that he stay on that part of the big trail that terminated in the Oregon country.

He left home broke, naturally, hoping to make his way as a doctor and promising himself that payment for every service would be cash on the barrelhead. His motive power was a decrepit mule. His possessions, aside from the clothes on his back, were a buffalo robe, a doctor's bag of instruments, plenty of various colored pills and a book or two.

At St. Joseph he encountered a wagon train not all of whose segments were headed for California. Maynard didn't worry much on that score. The long caravan offered business, and protection for a loner and his mule. Unlike Arthur Denny, he kept count of the graves beside the Oregon Trail. They indicated that business might be good.

It was. Cholera was the great common scourge of the plains and it was not long until the disease broke out among the caravan. Maynard himself was touched with it, but he treated his own case as Arthur Denny treated his ague: with contempt. Maynard did not inform others of his illness, correctly suspecting that folks would not trust a physician unable to keep himself healthy. He did confide his trouble to his diary, and four sentences in that entry are a bit puzzling:

> Go eighteen miles. Pass four graves in one place. Two more of the same train are ready to die. Got a pint and a half of brandy. Earn $2.20.

Was the brandy a fee, or part of the possessions of a deceased? There were no whiskey stores or forts in the vicinity. It would be interesting although irrelevant to know how much of the brandy went to Maynard's own malaise and how much was preserved for patients.

It was on June 7 that Doctor Maynard turned his way from California and headed toward the Puget Sound country, although he was not fully aware of it at the time. About eighty miles west of

Fort Kearney he heard of a cholera outbreak in a wagon far ahead. He wheeled his mount in that direction—and what a picture he must have made, dressed in the fashion of a country doctor and astride a mule as exhausted as its owner, riding up and down the long caravan which had split into sections, according to the practice of wagon trains in those years. In dry weather the foremost wagon had the favored position because it missed the dust that swept up from the huge wagon wheels. Next day the lead wagon would take its place at the tail end and gradually work up to the front again. Thus in the dusty weather the occupants of each wagon got their fair share of clear air—and of alkali dust.

By the time Maynard reached the wagon which had passed down the line the dread word *cholera*, one occupant was dead. Before morning three more passed away before the hopeless watch of Doctor Maynard. This left alone a new widow: Catherine Broshears, who, Maynard reported, was "ill in body and mind." Professionally he omitted the fact that she was attractive even in grief. She had no strength with which to cope with the yoke of oxen and a couple of cows. There were other wagons to call on, but the doctor promised to return to lend a hand. Every other male in the caravan either had his own duties or was down with cholera. It looked as if the doctor was elected as protector of the widow Broshears, although never in his life had he laid a whip to such stolid animals as oxen and cows. But glibly he entered in his diary that after the burial of her husband he had "transferred his duds to the widow's wagon" and tied his mule to the tailgate.

The widow was not headed for California, but for the southern tip of Puget Sound, where her brother, Michael T. Simmons, had settled five years before. This made Simmons and his party the first to settle on Puget Sound, and as the energetic leader he had established himself as a pioneer of considerable regional fame and influence.

After he transferred his effects to the widow's wagon, there is a noticeable hiatus in Maynard's journal—from June 8 to the Fourth of July. As doctor, ox driver and cowpoke, and what with keeping up the spirits of the widow, he must have been exhausted. Only the celebration of Independence Day revived him.

It was by now obvious that something more was happening. Maynard was ill, but this time it wasn't cholera. Maynard, at a susceptible age, was sick with love for the comely and charming widow. Moreover, there were signs that she was ready to forget the recent husband now miles behind them and under ground.

When Maynard had delivered Catherine safely to her brother, he also fell in love with the Puget Sound country. Mike Simmons, her brother, did not share all this love and contentment. When Maynard showed no sign of turning south for the California gold fields, Simmons changed his attitude from one of welcome to something akin to enmity. It had come out, of course, that Maynard had left a wife in Ohio. There was one ticklish moment when Simmons argued with Maynard from the butt end of a shotgun.

It took more than lack of brotherly love to discourage Maynard. He settled a few miles north of Tumwater. The spot was called Smithter and sometimes Smithfield after a divinity student named Levi Smith whose settlement there preceded a fatal attack of epilepsy. The memorial did not last long, for soon the area was encompassed by Olympia.

Although on the rugged westward trail Maynard made money, it did not last long, and the people around and about Olympia were disgustingly healthy. Unafraid of work—perhaps this is why Arthur Denny forgave him much—the doctor began cutting wood, and by the fall of 1851, about the time the founders of Seattle arrived downsound, he had four hundred cords piled neatly near the shoreline.

When Captain Leonard Felker arrived in his brig *Franklin Adams* the doctor signed an I.O.U. payable when the wood was sold, and took passage with his hard-won cargo to the Golden Gate. He realized two thousand dollars profit on the cordwood. It was more money in one chunk than Maynard had ever had. Under different circumstances the doctor might have drunk it up with merry companions in the exciting city of San Francisco. But a man of forty-two does not suffer from mere puppy love and Maynard kept the widow on his mind. With the two thousand dollars he bought up enough odds and ends to establish a store in Olympia.

The doctor's career as a merchant in Olympia was short-lived. Trouble with Mike Simmons and competing merchants exiled Maynard to Elliott Bay. He arrived at New York Alki in March of 1852, about five months after its founding, and at a time when earlier settlers were trying to decide whether to stick tight to Alki Point or find another area on the bay which would be more favorable to business.

With the salmon-packing scheme in mind, Maynard chose the east side of the bay and opened a one-room store near the waterfront and lived in the cramped attic quarters above. Thanks to a borrowed ax and the inspiration of the widow Broshears, the doctor was one of the settlement's immediate successes; perhaps for a time the wealthiest of all the settlers, even though the salmon-packing business did not work out. It was only later, when Maynard began trying to help others, that he got into trouble and made a few enemies. Too, some of his past life in Ohio would pursue him. It was not that his judgment was bad; the difficulties that now and then beset him were almost always due to a generous nature and, sometimes, overindulgence.

But whatever he could do to help Seattle the physician did. He cleared land and sold it cheap when he didn't actually give it away. Out of his exuberant love for the growing settlement he sold a lot to his friend Captain Felker for twenty dollars and the captain's promise to build a sizable residence on it. He established a blacksmith shop, found that he was not adept at shoeing the town's half a dozen horses, and sold the layout to a young newcomer—who had worked as a smithy—for ten dollars. He gave away two choice lots to Methodist missionaries in return for their assurance that they would start clearing and building immediately. Anything that looked good for Seattle he tried to help along. Atop all these activities he made frequent trips to Olympia to see Mrs. Broshears.

One of these visits was doubly important. He had been appointed a delegate to the Monticello Convention, which was a gathering of citizens from north of the Columbia who wanted a territory split off from Oregon and would eventually accomplish their purpose.

The other part of his business on this trip was to persuade the territorial legislature to grant him a divorce from his wife Lydia in Ohio. Maynard was equal to his unusual request. The legislature, largely Democratic, saw no reason not to accommodate this likable fellow. One cannot resist imagining a smoke-filled room and a bottle passing back and forth. Anyhow, only one member objected, and he was a Whig. He pointed out that Lydia would not even know she was divorced. This was unlikely; although mail was slow, Lydia would not remain in the dark indefinitely.

While the legislators were feeling warm toward Maynard they reorganized the counties north of the Columbia and designated his store as a county seat. To top the cake they made him justice of the peace and notary public. Maynard hurried back to Seattle to straighten up his meager living quarters, then returned to Olympia to marry the widow. The ceremony was a quiet one at a farm outside the settlement. Brother Simmons and shotgun were not present. Eight days later, as justice of the peace, the doctor performed Seattle's first wedding, joining young David Denny and Louisa Boren.

Soon thereafter he took "the bench" in Yesler's cookhouse to try the mate of a sailing ship. The mate was alleged to have appropriated some of the ship's money. The verdict was guilty, but the town had no jail and Maynard suspended the sentence with a warning that thereafter the mate keep his accounts in better order. The lecture must have provoked smiles and some elbow nudging from spectators who knew that in the keeping of accounts the justice was no master.

Maynard often has been recorded as "the friend of the Indians" and most certainly he was. While Arthur Denny believed in their right to trial and thought of them as human beings, his relation with the Indians was neither as close nor as warm as Maynard's. It was Doctor Maynard who saw most clearly, and with deep sympathy, the Indians' forced decline as unworthy of the land he loved. His foresight here went awry, of course, but his heart was with them. Of all his duties it was clearly his appointment as special Indian agent which most pleased him. He treated the illnesses of the Indians, and worked among them as friend and adviser with the zeal of a Jesuit, and his new wife Catherine was his devoted accomplice. Neither could predict what tragic problems this would bring into their lives.

When warfare broke out among the tribes, and some of the inland natives showed serious enmity toward the white man, the territory refused even a penny toward the expense of moving the friendly Indians to a place of safety. Mike Simmons, now adjusted to his sister's choice of Maynard, was special Indian agent in his own area and strongly he advised the doctor to move his charges.

This was much more easily said than done. Seattleites had rushed to build two blockhouses with a stockade between. This attempt at a fortress appealed greatly to the thousand or so natives in and around Seattle. Nor did they want to abandon their midwinter homes. "This is no time to move household goods and food by canoe," they told Maynard. Maynard argued persuasively, and made several promises he would not be able to keep.

.   Late in November he managed to borrow a schooner to carry Indian property and what food he could beg or borrow. By then there was open warfare in the interior. Report had it that the regular troops were not doing well. Volunteers at a blockhouse on the Duwamish were ready to be mustered out and showed no inclination to re-enlist. The rumor that Seattle would be attacked grew stronger, but the citizens felt somewhat easier when the navy warship *Decatur* anchored in the bay.

Within a few days nearly all the dwellings in King County, except those on Elliott Bay, had been wiped out. Seattleites of inadequate courage took ships for San Francisco. The merchants lost their Indian customers because Maynard had got them across the bay to Port Madison. It was a bad time in the town's history.

Maynard and Catherine did the best they could to keep the native exiles happy at Port Madison, but were not completely successful. The Indians were sullen at being separated from their winter homes, and mysteriously a few cases of whiskey showed up in the cargo of Maynard's borrowed schooner. Considerable of Catherine's time was spent in breaking up hair-pulling and face-scratching melees among inebriated squaws. Their men could handle liquor better, and Maynard confiscated what alcohol he could discover.

Through the rain and gray mist the Maynards were forced to worry through the attack on Seattle by ear. When the wind was right they heard the firing of musketry and now and then the booming of the *Decatur*'s guns. But they could not see the battle and had no idea of how matters stood in what came to be known as the Battle of Seattle.

It was at this confused time that Maynard's life in Seattle took a turn for the worse. Those settlers who had accepted the peaceful Indians now turned against all natives and half-breeds. And when Maynard and Catherine returned from Port Madison they noted a marked difference in the attitude of most citizens toward them. It was a most unhappy time for the doctor, although he explained as best he could that as Indian agent it was his duty to mix with the "redskins." He still had a few strong friends, but to the majority he was biased in favor of potential enemies. In another region and in a time soon to come he would have been called a Copperhead, and now there were Seattleites who called him worse.

And once again heavy debt rose to plague him. Most of the

money he had supplied to protect friendly natives was never repaid. There is no record that any of the settlers he had helped now came forward to help the man who had established their position. The growing schism in the United States between the North and the South, although far away as a practical matter, added to his unpopularity. Paradoxically, although a friend of the Indian, he was set against the Abolitionists. To make matters still worse, the political tide had turned on Puget Sound. Maynard was a Democrat and the town's top leaders were Republicans. When the drink was on him, and that condition was increasing, he would argue for Secession. The Dennys, Borens, Yeslers and other influential men found the doctor increasingly hard to take.

At last, with breaking heart, he decided that he must leave Seattle. He could not bear to get too far away, but he must—and Catherine, whose life must have become as unbearable as that of her husband, was willing.

Perhaps, he thought, the solitude of a farm was the answer. Accordingly, in 1857, he transferred 260 acres of his land to C. C. Terry in exchange for a farm of 319 acres on Alki Point. There, in one of the finest houses in the region, he and Catherine were hard put to find enough to eat, for Maynard was no farmer and the long-suffering Catherine also was not accustomed to the agricultural life. Furthermore, there was little doctoring to be done on that side of the bay.

Time after time Dr. Maynard walked southward around the point and there his wife would find him sitting on a log, staring across the bay toward the town he had helped to build.

Regularly, perhaps too regularly, he paddled across the bay to haunt the places he knew so well and seek out those he could still call friends. He also had some official duties. Despite the rise of Republicanism, the Democrats controlled the territorial administration by a narrow margin. So Maynard was reappointed justice of the peace for the Seattle area and court commissioner for King County. This meant considerable travel and Catherine considered it wise to accompany him on most trips.

After one such journey they returned to find their fine house burned to the ground.

It was doubtless just as well, although the probability of arson was a sad and shocking experience. Outwardly undaunted, Maynard returned to Seattle to open a hospital. It was encompassed in a couple of rooms in a two-story frame house, rented by the doctor. Catherine was not a nurse but she learned fast.

The hospital did not prosper. These were times when a citizen expected that the most serious illness should be treated at home, and operations were performed on kitchen tables. But the Maynards' hospital was boycotted by some because he treated both Indians and white patients there.

Now Maynard decided to try some lawyering, having been admitted to the bar in 1856 by his friendly legislators. Clients were few, Maynard was aging fast, and at last alcohol got the upper hand.

Yet now and again the old merriment came to the fore, and at unlikely times. When Maynard received word that his first wife, Lydia, was on her way via Olympia, he stopped at his barber's and asked for the works.

"What's going on, Doc?" the barber wanted to know, for Maynard had long since ceased to be a regular customer.

Maynard roared with the old laughter. "I'm going to give this town a sight to see," he answered. "I'm going to show the folks a man walking up from the waterfront with a wife on each arm!"

That is exactly what happened, and for a time the three lived together with no arguments the town's alert gossips could overhear. There was no emotion involved in Lydia's visit. She did not want her husband back. She had come to gain title to property that she had heard should belong to her. In the extended litigation Catherine stood aside. But Lydia failed in her mission because she had never lived on the land in question.

Maynard contained his delight as best he could, concluding that now Catherine would receive the property. But the final ruling was that the land the ladies wanted must be returned to the government because Catherine, too, had not settled on the property in time to create a valid claim. A number of citizens breathed easier at the decision, because a finding in favor of either of the women could have brought at least a dozen claims into question at law.

Catherine did not care too much. By now she was accustomed to ill fortune. Lydia took her leave in disappointment, but certainly not in envy of her rival. Maynard saw her off in gentlemanly fashion but not in sobriety. He was drinking more and more in these last days. As he pursued his path to a confirmed alcoholism, some of his old popularity returned, for he created a diversion almost every week.

Beneath his fading, ragtag exterior he had changed little. One of his last acts was to give a piece of property to Seattle's first Masonic lodge. They wanted to establish a graveyard. The doctor, perhaps in self-diagnosis, thought this an excellent idea. A few months later Dr. David Swinton Maynard died.

As so often happens at the ending, his enemies joined his few remaining friends, making the funeral the largest held in the town up until that year of 1873. His body lay in state in Yesler's Pavilion, the sizable new structure at First and Cherry, and it was not quite large enough to hold all the mourners who turned out. An unidentified citizen, whether friend or enemy is not known, stood up to say, "Without Doctor Maynard the town of Seattle will not be the same. Without him Seattle would never have reached its present size. Perhaps, had it not been for Doctor Maynard, Seattle might not be here now."

Arthur Armstrong Denny was there and it will never be known what thoughts passed through his mind as he heard these words.

The burial was as unorthodox as the life of the deceased. The long procession led from the pavilion up the steep, primitive streets, past trim white houses—some on land given away by Maynard—and around fir and cedar stumps which made the route difficult.

The destination was not the cemetery, because that had not yet been properly dedicated. The wooden coffin was unloaded from a wagon draped in black crepe and awkwardly the pallbearers headed for a tool house where Maynard had to rest until the Masonic ground could be consecrated. The bearers slipped and slid on the wet clay mud at one point and nearly dropped their burden. Maynard's last journey was a rough one, but no rougher than much of his life had been. The living regretted the need to store the remains in a tool shed temporarily, but surely old Doc Maynard would have felt content and amused.

Like his opposite, Arthur Denny, the doctor had dreamed of a city and helped to make the dream come true. Even at the last his vision had been clear; he had donated land for a cemetery and, appropriately, was the first to be buried there.

4

The Battle of Seattle

Much of what has happened—and happens—in our town has a comic operetta quality. I have never been able to fathom the reason for this. Yet the libretto for some of our events, seemingly quite serious at the moment of happening, appears in retrospect to have been written by Gilbert and Sullivan.

So it was with the so-called "Battle of Seattle," during which the youthful community was attacked by Indians and, naturally enough, the citizens were frightened out of their wits.

The battle took place soon after the Organic Act was approved by newly elected President Franklin Pierce on March 2, 1853. This separated Washington from Oregon, which was a happy event for those living north of the Columbia River. Nonetheless the four thousand white people of Washington Territory, the majority of whom lived beyond the limits of Seattle in isolation, had something else on their minds. The natives, watching the steady immigration and usurpation of their lands, were becoming restless.

Almost immediately after approving the Organic Act the President appointed Major Isaac I. Stevens as governor of the new territory. He did not hurry getting to his post, and it would have taken long enough in any case. Governor Stevens was an engineer and surveyed possible railroad routes on the way. Doubtless this was the most important part of his career, although the results would be a long time in coming.

Reports on the ability of Isaac Stevens differ widely. An early and official historian tags him as "one of the great men of his day" and adds that subsequent events would prove his wisdom. As yet, subsequent events have proved nothing of the kind. He was a pompous little man, unduly conscious of his position, and while making his surveying trip across the country seems to have been utterly unaware and incurious about what situations might confront him when he reached his appointed job. On the surface he was a man of action and quick decision, but some of his actions turned out badly, and the most eminent of these was his effort to make peace treaties with the Indians. He seems to have been in too much of a hurry and decades passed before realization that his treaty making was neither understood by nor acceptable to most of the natives.

His egotism popped out immediately upon his arrival. He sent word ahead of the date of his possible coming and so the folks in Olympia, the capital of the territory, made haste to prepare a banquet and suitable welcome signs. Stevens chose to appear alone as a ragged stranger, wanting to hear incognito what the people were saying about their as yet unknown governor, commander-in-chief of militia and superintendent of Indian affairs. By the time he made his identity known the food was cold, the women were worn out, and the men too filled with anxiety to appreciate what Stevens seemed to think was a joke. They were only partially revived by his maiden speech.

But they lost no time in trying to make him see the dangers of the Indian attitude. What he did thereafter was sensible enough, but time was fleeting. He embarked on a sailboat down the Sound, visited settlements, listened to complaints of both red and white men, took a census of Indians, and in February of the next year, 1854, he cautioned the legislature that the Indians did indeed own their lands. Then he recommended that Congress be memorialized to "extinguish" such ownership.

A frightened legislature agreed. But the memorial took a long time to reach Congress, and that somewhat unconcerned body also took its time in acting on it. The Senate and House empowered Governor Stevens to make treaties with the natives and to form a military system to protect the whites.

When the creaky machinery had been set to work the governor began a four-year task of treaty making. It must be borne in mind that the only means of communication were canoes and rugged Indian trails. In later years he regarded his treaty effort as the high point of his career, and perhaps it was. But there would lurk in the minds of most of the Indians, and gradually in the minds of their descendants, that Stevens was simply stealing their lands, yanking up their roots and depriving them of age-old fishing and hunting rights. In truth he was "extinguishing" their title to a domain larger than New England.

Due to their numbers and the fact that they were passing through, the earlier wagon trains encountered little or no trouble with the Indians. This began to change as the natives recognized the meaning of the seemingly endless stream from the East. There were massacres of white men, women and children—then retaliations on the part of the military.

Little Seattle lived in a nervous peace. The Indians around Elliott Bay were deteriorated in spirit before the arrival of the settlers and may never have been warlike; possibly in some earlier time they were subdued by the Haidas to the north.

But Seattleites knew that there were more spirited red men around Lake Washington and through the dense forest on the east, with ominous communication with really warlike tribes still further east across the Cascade Range.

There were other factors which made the Seattle Indians friendly. Henry Yesler employed numbers of them in his sawmill and thus exerted great influence. They adored the reckless Doctor Maynard and respected the more forbidding Arthur Denny. Moreover, their most visible leader, Sealth, for whom the town had been named, was friendly to the white man.

But there was trouble outside the town, and the citizens were cautious enough to build a blockhouse. In 1853 a man named James McCormick was killed and buried on the shore of Lake Union. The crime might have gone unnoticed except for a report by friendly Indians. The murdered man was a stranger, and it is somewhat of a mystery how his name was known. The investigation resulted in the arrest of four Indians, who were tried in the Felker home before a justice court.

An inevitable verdict of guilty resulted in the hanging of two Indians from a tall stump near the site of what would be the New England Hotel. C. D. Boren was sheriff and kept one of the younger Indians locked in his house. The temporary location of the fourth convicted Indian is hazy, but during Boren's absence some white men broke into his house and were on the point of stringing his prisoner up to a nearby tree when Boren returned and prevented it. After all, the murdered stranger was not a member of the Establishment which already had been taking shape in the town by Elliott Bay.

Even before this incident an Indian had been killed, without trial, for murdering his squaw, and in retaliation friends of the impetuous husband killed two white men. There is no record of the aftermath, but it was becoming evident that nobody was certain of safety even in Seattle.

So much was going on that Governor Stevens pompously prepared a much too voluminous paper setting forth the "duties" of both Indians and white men. The Indians could not read it, and not all the white men took it seriously.

The traditional policy of the federal government had been simply to move the Indians westward as the old colonial land and parts of the Midwest became more populous with whites. But Washington Territory was as far west as one could get, and in fairness to Governor Stevens it must be said that finding reservations where regional tribes would be happy was not a simple task.

By 1854 small fires of rebellion were being ignited all around Seattle. There were troubles at Bellingham Bay to the north. There was a massacre on the upper waters of the Green and White rivers near the present town of Kent. Nearly all those whites who had abandoned their farms during a previous scare and then returned were murdered. A few survivors fled to Seattle.

The following year it became known that Indians east of the Cascades were making overtures to the Sound Indians. The general war plan was that all tribes would strike settlements all over the territory simultaneously, wiping out the whites entirely or at least frightening them into abandoning the country. Thus the natives would regain the land they regarded as their birthright.

It was a grand plan but had no hope of success. The white

militia was growing; the army regulars, despite tardiness and occasional defeat, were learning how to cope with Indian strategy. Delays of the Army in Washington Territory were partially due to the reluctance of General Wool, western commander in San Francisco, to bail Governor Stevens out of hot water. On a visit to the Golden Gate the peripatetic governor had managed to insult Wool, and the latter had an ego at least as large as that of Governor Stevens.

Most fortunate of all for Seattle, the legislature had memorialized Congress to send a naval vessel into Puget Sound. This was done, but her "rescue" value was initially in doubt, for the *Decatur* had duties aside from Seattle. She doled out small arms at Olympia and made a voyage to Port Madison to protect the settlers from northern Indians. Then she struck an uncharted rock near Bainbridge Island on Puget Sound and had to be hauled up at high tide for repairs. Had the accident happened a few days later the story of the "Battle of Seattle" might have been much more tragic than it was.

Military and naval authorities wanted to put all the Seattle Indians in irons, but Denny and Doctor Maynard had other ideas. The doctor got busy transporting them in canoes to West Seattle across Elliott Bay. If the enemy succeeded in occupying Seattle the friendly Indians would be murdered outright or taken as slaves. It was probably unnecessary to explain that to the marines of the *Decatur* one Indian would look like any other.

News of the contemplated attack on January 26, 1856, allegedly came by a native called Indian Jim and his squaw. It was received by a settler who passed the word to Henry Yesler, who quickly transferred the intelligence to Captain Gansevoort in command of the *Decatur*.

There was a rumor that some hostiles had congregated in a certain hut on the waterfront, so the captain sent marines ashore with a howitzer to destroy the shack. The marines had excellent aim and blew the hut to smithereens but it is not clear from the records whether any Indians were inside.

Nonetheless the boom of the howitzer signaled the beginning of the battle. It is curious that despite all the excitements and premonitions most Seattleites were in bed asleep when the attack began. Perhaps they were simply worn out with preparations and tension.

In any case the sound of the howitzer was followed by a volley of Indian muskets from the dark forest behind the town. The smoke from the guns indicated that the front line of the enemy encompassed nearly the whole town.

The doors of houses burst open instantly and a stampede of men, women and children dashed for the blockhouse. Doubtless they escaped death because the Indians were reloading their muskets. The whites were half dressed or in underwear. One excitable settler had drawn on his wife's petticoat instead of his pants. If a child fell down his parents lost no time in dragging him like a sack toward the blockhouse. Most of the settlers had forgotten their guns.

The Indians continued their firing; some houses were pierced by as many as fifty bullets, and two white latecomers were killed. Survivors insist that hundreds of Indians were killed by the guns of the *Decatur* but nobody seems to have made a body count after the battle. Certainly the guns of the naval vessel were playing hob with the site of Seattle. The ground beyond Third Street was literally plowed up by exploding shells. Some homes were damaged by grape and canister. Huge logs and trees were splintered, and some say that above the noise of the battle could be heard the yelling of Indian women urging their warriors to further effort.

The jammed blockhouse became a madhouse, but there were no casualties there, except that a spark from a flint set a woman's hair afire. This unusual blaze was extinguished by covering her head with a blanket, effectively putting an end to her screams and the blaze.

Along about noon the Indians pulled back to feast on beef stolen from the settlers. The meat had been roasted to a turn by the squaws and surely their warriors discussed the balls from the howitzers which knocked over trees and later exploded or, as the Indian put it later, "mox-poohed." It was their first encounter with such a weapon.

During the lull in the battle most of the women and children in the blockhouse were taken aboard the *Decatur* and the bark *Brontes*, which happened to be lying in port. And while the Indians were feasting some of the settlers returned to their homes for guns and other valuables.

In the afternoon and evening the Indians kept up a useless firing, but by ten that night the "Battle of Seattle" was over. The enemy had melted back into the forests toward Lake Washington, pillaging and burning the few isolated cabins on the way. There were not many, and none was occupied.

The "Battle of Seattle" was over. Except for an occasional isolated incident there would be no more trouble with Indians until the seventies of this century, when descendants of the participants in that early war decided that rebellion was the only way to right the old wrongs. Except for the presence of the *Decatur* the battle would have turned out differently, and perhaps the grand strategy of the territory's Indians would have been successful. In any case it was certainly on January 26, 1856, that the long-lived love story between Seattle and the Navy began.

The report of Governor Stevens, written to his superiors a few days later, was dramatic but on the whole accurate as battle reports go:

> The people of the whole Sound region are living in block-houses or in their immediate vicinity. A band of hostiles, numbering according to estimates from two hundred to five hundred, are on the White and Green rivers, determined to prosecute the war. They attacked Seattle on the 26th, keeping up the attack all day, killing two people and driving families on shipboard. The town was defended by a vessel of war and over one hundred citizens. They have devastated the whole of King County, driving the whole population within the line of defenses of the Town of Seattle.

Seattle has always been lucky, and this was one of its lucky days. But for a long, long time Indians and white men would not live shoulder to shoulder there. On a reservation on the west side of the bay Doctor Maynard and his helpers built seven or eight shelters, and it was there that friendly Indians would live for a time—excepting, of course, those needed to help operate Henry Yesler's sawmill.

5

Noah Sealth

W HAT kind of man is commemorated in the name of the city of Seattle? The early settlers saw an aging Indian who was unusual and who sought the white man's friendship with a deep and somehow lonely longing. A man who broke through an intense pride to seek this friendship. A man clearly scarred by life and saddened by his recognition that the days of the Indian seemed finished. Only toward the end of his time did he perceive that perhaps he had been wrong, bringing forth the courage to challenge and question the white men's easy assumption that the land was theirs by right of discovery and occupation, and the white man's feeling that the Indians were somewhat less than human. "We may be brothers, after all," he told Governor Isaac Stevens at treaty-making time. "We shall see."

His name, as accurately as the settlers could understand it, was Sealth. At one time his likeness was seen in scores of places around the town, well into this century. Now that likeness is nearly forgotten, and newcomers show little interest in how, and for whom, the city got its name. But when I was a small boy the face of Sealth was visible all around the town. There were scores of horse-watering troughs of standard design cast in iron, and surmounting each was a bust of the man who came to be called Chief Seattle.

The only full-sized statue of Sealth is at Fifth Avenue and Cedar Street. Prior to the Century 21 Exposition a fountain base and pool were designed for it. The statue is by James Wehn, founder of the School of Sculpture at the University. The likeness is said to be the result of considerable research on Wehn's part, for he knew many of the old-timers who had seen Sealth. His statue shows the Indian wearing his blanket like a Roman toga, a bare arm outstretched toward Elliott Bay. His back is toward the monorail built to carry passengers to and from the exposition and Westlake Mall, where Seattle's shopping and business district begins. The statue gives the effect that Chief Seattle is pointedly ignoring the modern city and pointing toward Alki Point, where the first settlers landed and his meeting with them took place.

There is no question that Sealth was fascinated by the white man. This feeling may have been deep-seated from the period of his childhood. Often he told of an unforgettable experience when he was six or seven years old. He remembered the arrival of the *Discovery* in 1792. His Majesty's ship was commanded by Captain George Vancouver, who, fortunately for the United States, completely missed the Columbia River, which in the same year would be found by Captain Robert Gray of Boston. The outpouring of the great River of the West is difficult to miss when sailing as close to the coastline as Vancouver was. Perhaps the Englishman had encountered what Sir Francis Drake, who may have got as far north as the Rogue River, called "the everlasting stinking fog." Certainly Vancouver's miss, and Gray's good fortune, would soon negate a statement made by King George during the celebration of his birthday: "On this auspicious day I had long since designed to take formal possession of all the countries we had lately been employed in exploring, in the name of, and for, His Britannic Majesty, his heirs and successors." Whereupon he did that very thing, and had it not been for Gray's encounter with the Columbia, among other factors, King George might have made it stick.

But while Gray was sending small boats up the Columbia the master of the *Discovery* was blithely scattering over the Northwest landscape names such as Vashon, Rainier, Bainbridge, and those of other high-placed officers in the Admiralty. The youngish Vancouver was a politician as well as an explorer. The Indians had for unknown time called Mount Rainier "the mountain that is god" and referred to it as Takhoma. Naturally the settlers around Commencement Bay felt the Indian name should remain on maps and the lips of men, so Vancouver unwittingly had planted the seed for a feud between Tacoma and Seattle that would go on for years. "Rainier" was a sore point for Tacomans long after the federal Board of Geographic Names made Vancouver's choice official.

Vancouver was loyal to his own men as well as to powers in the Admiralty. After he died as a retired admiral, Puget would collaborate with his old commander's brother to finish the story of a four-and-a-half-year voyage that in many ways was more remarkable than that of Columbus. Sealth, like his tribesmen, ignored the name of Puget. Indians all around the Sound continued to call the Sound Whulge, as did Theodore Winthrop in his classic *The Canoe and the Saddle,* published just before the Civil War, in which the New England author was killed.

The arrival of the *Discovery,* all sails set in a light wind, greatly excited the natives. There was an ancient legend that one day gods would appear, so why not in a giant canoe with white wings? Many natives fled into the woods, but some overcame fear with curiosity and surrounded the ship in their canoes. Vancouver invited several aboard. Sealth and his father were among these. The latter was a leader of the Suquamish tribe, but in speech Sealth preferred the tongue of his mother's tribe, called the Duwamish.

Sealth thought he saw signs that Vancouver recognized the father as a great tyee, or leader, and his son as heir to that leadership. Actually there is no certain indication of a dynasty. Nothing is known of Sealth's grandparents, no title was passed to his sons. The title of princess was given Sealth's daughter, Angeline, by Seattleites, not by the tribe.

In Sealth's memory, which became more embroidered with the years, Vancouver had a special smile for the boy. Sealth claimed that the English captain removed uniform jacket and shirt to demonstrate that he was all white, not a red man with a painted face.

In the ship's log Captain Vancouver wrote that he had sent the natives away happy with a few gifts of no particular value. Because Vancouver was not traveling for furs to trade in China, and because these were the first white men the Sound natives had seen, they were easily satisfied. But they would have been crestfallen had they been able to read that log, for Vancouver added: "Encountered a party of natives this day. There were probably five hundred, dwarfed and in a low state . . . hardly better than animals."

Historians writing in the first and second decade of this century agree neither on the physical stature of Sealth nor on his temperament. One writer calls him "runted," probably because nearly all the Sound Indians were "canoe natives," small and bow-legged. Lacking the necessity to hunt, and without horses to ride, they often were either fishing or traveling from one shore to another in their cedar canoes. They did not need to go far on the trail for deer or bear. Those on the shorelands seemed satisfied with a diet of clams and other shellfish, which were more than plentiful and could be varied with smoked salmon. Hence their legs were not well developed.

Glass-plate photographs taken in front of Yesler's mill show groups of men, all wearing "Boston clothes," as the Indians called trousers and jackets. The Indians are easily distinguishable even though the quality of the photographs was not the best. The white men stand head and shoulders above the natives, and the legs of the latter are thin and bowed. Vancouver was correct in his view that the Sound Indians, like those along the lower Columbia, were a poorly constructed band.

The condition of these tribes had begun to deteriorate long before the coming of the traders with their trade whiskey and venereal disease. Some archaeologists and anthropologists cautiously venture that the physique of the tribes and their comparatively primitive culture were due to their distance from the seacoast, creating "a relative lag" in their development. But more recent discoveries indicate that at one time the culture of the natives trapped in the pit between the rough Olympic Peninsula and the Cascades was of a high order. The whole story is yet to be learned and recorded.

At any rate, Sealth must have stood out sharply against the majority of natives around the Sound. Dr. Henry A. Smith, a contemporary, insisted in later years that Sealth was the tallest native he had ever seen, "standing six feet in his moccasins."

Another feature which made him noticeable was his voice. There is a legend that in his youth he filled his mouth with small pebbles and, like Demosthenes, orated against the wind and storm waves. This may be true, for one diarist of Sealth's time wrote that when he was angry, his powerful voice brought lazy squaws to attention at a distance of half a mile. All who wrote about the man agree that he had a strong and persuasive voice.

As in many other tribes across the continent, there came a time in Sealth's younger life when he went off alone, fasting for days, praying for a sign that would tell him what species of wildlife would be his guardian. It was the custom to disappear into the forest for this tribal rite. But Sealth claimed in his old age that he found a lonely point of shore and turned to the sea for his sign. Fasting faithfully, he said, for hours on end he plunged into the inland sea, diving as deep as he could, holding his breath until his lungs seemed ready to burst. And at the end of many days of ordeal he recognized his guardian for this life and the next.

It was the sea gull.

Voice and stature were not Sealth's only reasons for his claim to leadership. He made a canoe and portage trip from Bainbridge Island to the mainland, through Lake Union and southward on Lake Washington to the Duwamish River, which he ascended for several miles. Sealth said that his purpose was to create a unity among the various tribes and plan defense against the warlike Haidas, who now and then swept out of the northern fog, setting fire to villages, killing men, women and children, and returning north with as many slaves as their great war canoes would accommodate.

This would have been a difficult and notable journey, although the main points touched are today within twenty-five miles of downtown Seattle. Although Sealth claimed success for his efforts, there are unanswered questions. The so-called unity of the tribes is not provable at this late date and there is some evidence that occasional warfare continued to break out among the Duwamish, the Muckleshoots, the Suquamish and other tribes.

Another unanswerable aspect of the journey lies in the fact that Sealth refused to speak other than Duwamish, and harbored a deep dislike for the Chinook trade jargon, not a word of which he would allow to pass his lips. Thus if Sealth's journey was successful we must accept that he carried a number of interpreters. Or that every village had an interpreter at least somewhat conversant with the Duwamish tongue. This latter seems unlikely, for although the Sound natives were of the Salish strain they used different languages. Tribes living within only a few miles of one another conversed through the Chinook trade jargon—and a hodgepodge jargon it was, made up of English words, occasional Indian words, sounds of nature and bastard French. For example, the word "Siwash," which the settlers used, in partial contempt, to cover all natives, came from the French *sauvage*, or "savage." The word "Siwash" was used well into this century and still is heard from whites who have yet to develop respect for the rights and dignity of the Indian from whom the land was, in effect, stolen.

Despite Sealth's dislike of the trade jargon and his loyalty to the Duwamish language, he must have picked up sufficient English for at least a basic communication. His close friendship with Doctor Maynard suggests this.

As to dress, Sealth remained adamant until his dying day. The founders discovered him in a breechcloth, which was standard attire for male Indians of the Sound. In excessively bad weather they added a conical cap woven from dried reeds, or a rough short jacket of animal skin. Later, probably in deference to the white women, Sealth adopted a blanket, regally draped as depicted in his statue. No matter what the occasion, he refused to adopt "Boston clothes" of trousers, shirt and jacket as did many of the younger Indians.

Sealth appears to have taken credit for the idea of bringing Doctor David Maynard to the settlement on Elliott Bay. It is far more likely that Sealth and his Duwamish paddlers happened to be in Olympia at a time when that settlement had become determined that the doctor must move elsewhere. At any rate, Sealth appeared at an opportune time. The good and generous doctor had been around Elliott Bay and up the Duwamish Valley, liked what he saw, and was more than willing to remove himself from Simmons' wrath.

He loaded his scant remaining stock in Sealth's canoe, and onto a makeshift barge. It was a rough three days' journey, but they arrived without serious mishaps and Maynard was made welcome on Elliott Bay. In later years Sealth seems to have contended that he was dissatisfied with native medicine men and, hearing of "a real doctor" in Olympia, went to fetch him.

Maynard and the aging Sealth became fast friends. At the time of the meeting of Maynard and Sealth the latter had been converted to the Roman Catholic faith by the itinerant missionary Father Demers. Sealth was overjoyed to find that Demers knew a little of the Duwamish, avoided trade jargon and prayed in Latin, which Sealth found pleasant to his ears. Sealth confessed his sins, and thereafter devoted himself to the white man's God.

Sealth apparently had been deeply attached to his first wife, who was a delicately beautiful young woman. He seems to have spoken of her often in later years, mourning her death, which was long in the past. He had little to say about his second wife, who bore him several children.

He was delivered another bitter blow when his first child, grown up as Angeline, eloped with a northern Indian. For a period of at least ten years he was in the dark as to her whereabouts and the conditions under which she might be living—if, indeed, she lived at all.

He may well have become embittered. His experiences with the Hudson's Bay factors at Nisqually turned him against the white man for a time, but later he concluded that "the King George men" were different than the Americans, or "Boston men." It is certain that Dr. W. F. Tolmie, chief factor for Hudson's Bay at Nisqually, had no use for the big Indian he called "See-at" and sometimes, in anger, "La Gros." Almost every time Sealth appeared at the post there was a quarrel with one of Tolmie's men. Tolmie at length decided that Sealth was truly dangerous and barred him from the stockade.

Sealth is often described as "ugly" by contemporary diarists, and perhaps at the last he was. His long white hair was always tangled and he took poor care of his blanket. Yet the only known photograph of him, taken in 1860, six years before his death, shows a strong-featured and clear-eyed Indian with plenty of character. He is staring at the photographer's magic box and there is a trace of concern in his dark eyes. Older Indians were superstitious about having their picture taken. It is easy to suspect that Doctor Maynard persuaded Sealth to go through the ordeal.

Many have scoffed at the stories growing from the recollections of Sealth in his old age, but some of them are verifiable. Perhaps the most important concerns the building of what was called the Old Man House, and it reveals something of the character of Sealth's father. The elder of the Suquamish decided to make neighboring tribes envious by building the largest "long house" ever known. The natives of the Salish tribes were hardly nomadic and did not live in tepees as did the nations east of the Cascades on the Great Plains. They constructed "long houses" of cedar, large enough for more than one family. Heat was provided by a small fire kept alive with fish oil or wood. Directly above was an opening in the roof to allow the smoke to escape, and the efficiency of this arrangement was much dependent on the weather. There was no furniture but only woven reed mats and ledges for sleeping, ranged around the walls. Sometimes families were separated by animal skins hung from the ceiling.

Old Man House, built under the direction of Sealth's father, was located on a low sand spit in Agate Pass on the mainland across from Bainbridge Island. The huge multi-family dwelling was missed by most of the earlier explorers. Lieutenant Wilkes, who investigated Agate Pass in 1841, apparently did not land on the spit and is vague as to what he saw there. He thought that it must be a Catholic mission house because he saw what looked to him like a cross. More probably this was a totem pole with a large bird replica near the top of the pole, the wings outstretched. However, in modern times archaeologists from the University of Washington and the State Parks and Recreation Commission have established that it was indeed a long house, but of far larger size than any yet discovered. Oddly enough, Sealth's father chose an unfortunate site, one in which the structure was eventually undermined by wind and tide. Not long ago a sizable part of the front of Old Man House was found, fallen flat beneath the newer sands of the spit. This section was remarkably preserved, even as to the colors used on the carved frontal posts.

The christening of Seattle seems to have been done on the spur of the moment. Doctor Maynard had applied to the territory for appointment as justice of the peace. Territorial officials approved, and accompanying his appointment was a copy of the plat of the infant community. It is said that someone in charge of such affairs had written "Duwamps" across the face of the drawing. This may have been meant to indicate the approximate location of the Duwamish tribe, or it may have been a bit of frontier humor. In any case, so the story goes, Maynard took it to mean that the territorial officials had chosen Duwamps as the name of the upstart village. He nearly hit the gray skies above him, and his neighbors were as upset as the doctor. A settlement that, a short time before, had been ready to call itself New York was not in a mood to have Duwamps thrust upon it.

The town had to find a name of its own, and Maynard suggested that it be called after Sealth, who, after all, was the central figure—certainly the tallest and most garrulous—of the predecessors on the bay. Others thought that the name Sealth, when pronounced Indian fashion, was too guttural. And that when the pronunciation was Anglicized it was "too flat."

"All right," retorted Maynard. "We'll call it Seattle." While this version of the christening may be apocryphal it seems to be borne out by Tolmie's reference to the big Indian as "See-at" in his journals. There were no serious objections, which certainly indicates the esteem in which Sealth was held by the leading citizens.

So Seattle it was, and is. For a long time Sealth was not happy about it; there was a superstition that whenever a dead man's name was mentioned he would be troubled in his grave. But before the end of his days he became proud of the honor, or at least accepted it because it was a decision made by his great friend Doc Maynard.

Not irrelevantly, that town plat was to undergo considerable change. The earliest settlers all moved their property lines a bit to accommodate Doctor Maynard, and they rearranged survey lines to accommodate Henry Yesler when he appeared with machinery to construct a complete sawmill. From the very first days, Seattleites were favorable toward new people—providing they showed signs of respectability and particularly if they brought a new skill or business. In far later times the city would gerrymander its southern city limits to spare a Boeing plant the pain of certain taxes and give it room to grow in.

It was in December 1854 that Governor Isaac Ingalls Stevens landed on the shores of Elliott Bay to forge a treaty and probably at least a thousand members of the local tribes assembled to hear what he had to say. His approach was nearly identical at every treaty-making assembly. He offered sums ranging from a hundred thousand dollars to twice that for the lands of a tribe. He promised schools and mills on reservations and the Great White Father in the East would provide teachers for the schools. When he thought it advisable he suggested there might be a little side money for chiefs who signed the treaty—say an annuity of five hundred a year for twenty years. A chief across the mountains suggested that it would have been well for Stevens to have brought the money with him so that they could take a look at it and make judgment. As yet the natives were in no position to understand the value of United States currency. Blankets, muskets, pieces of copper, metal containers and tools—these they could understand. Of course their main concern was the proposition that they move from their familiar lands to some strange environment chosen by the white man.

It was not the governor's fault that many of his promises never came to pass. There is no reason to believe that the promises were insincere, but the mills of the Great White Father ground slowly indeed. Today in the Pacific Northwest, as elsewhere, such treaties are the subject of litigation and rebellion.

In comparison with other tribes, the Puget Sound natives were amiable indeed, and this added much to Stevens' feeling that his work was well done.

First to speak at the gathering on Elliott Bay was, of course, Stevens himself. He was followed immediately by a tall native with straggling gray hair and a powerful voice. This was, of course, Sealth. The white officials were given to understand that he spoke on behalf of the Suquamish, the tribe to which his father belonged, and the Duwamish, from which his mother had come. Sealth had not talked long before Stevens received the impression that this towering Indian was speaking for all the tribes of the area.

There are many once famous Indian speeches, and this writer has regarded them with suspicion. They have seemed, at least to me, to carry ideas and expressions which would not be likely—perhaps not be possible—in the tribal language. First of all, there had to be a literal translation and then, I have considered, a revision by either a minister or some sentimental and highly literate white man. Also, there is often more than one version of the addresses of waning or condemned Indian leaders, each new one an improvement as the years go by.

The first time I read the valedictory of Sealth I had this same doubt, and even dismissed it as entirely apocryphal. But I have read it many times since over the years and somehow each time it has become more credible, possibly because, over those years, I was learning more about Sealth. Considering the man, his admirable points, his disappointments and grief, his changing temperament, his conversion to the word of the white man's God, I have come to believe that in essence this is his speech.

We know with certainty that he did make an address for Stevens and his aides, but what is most interesting is the subtle change from amiability to irony and finally outright challenge. Such subtle transition could hardly be that of a white man under the circumstances of its first publication. It may be that I have come to accept it because I am a native of Seattle and feel that it is part of our traditions. Certainly I have concluded that no book with the city as its subject would be complete without it. The version here was discovered, and admittedly translated, by Dr. H. A. Smith, who knew Sealth but was not a professional writer, and was resurrected in a limited publication, adorned with considerable comment by John M. Rich. It seems to this writer that in addition to its inherent value, it furnishes another key to the character of Sealth. And it is not without relevancy to our own time:

> Yonder sky that has wept tears of compassion upon our fathers for centuries untold, and which to us looks eternal, may change. Today it is fair, tomorrow it may be overcast with clouds.

> My words are like the stars that never set. What Sealth says the Great Chief at Washington can rely upon with as much certainty as our paleface brothers can rely upon the turn of the seasons.

> The son of the White Chief says his father sends us greetings of friendship and good will. This is kind of him, for we know he has little need of our friendship in return, because his people are many. They are like the grass that covers the vast prairies, while my people are few; they resemble the scattering trees of a storm-swept plain.

> The Great—and I presume—good White Chief sends us word that he wants to buy our lands but is willing to allow us to reserve enough to live on comfortably. This indeed appears generous, for the Red Man no longer has rights that he need respect, and the offer may be wise also, for we are no longer in need of a vast country.

> There was a time when our people covered the whole land as the waves of a wind-ruffled sea covers its shell-paved floor, but that time has long since passed away with the

greatness of tribes now almost forgotten. I will not dwell on nor mourn over our untimely decay, nor reproach my pale-face brothers with hastening it. We too may have been somewhat to blame.

Youth is impulsive. When our young men grow angry at some real or imaginary wrong, and disfigure their faces with black paint, their hearts are also disfigured and turn black, and then they are often cruel and relentless and know no bounds, and our old men are unable to restrain them.

Thus it has ever been. Thus it was when the white man first began to push our forefathers westward. But let us hope that the hostilities between the Red Man and his paleface brothers may never return. We would have all to lose and nothing to gain.

It is true that revenge by young braves is considered gain, even at the cost of their own lives, but old men who stay at home in times of war, and mothers who have sons to lose, know better.

Our good father at Washington—for I presume he is now our father as well as yours, since King George has moved his boundaries farther north—our great and good father, I say, sends us word that if we do as he desires he will protect us.

His brave warriors will be to us a bristling wall of strength and his great ships of war will fill our harbors so that our ancient enemies far to the northward—the Sinsians, Hydas and Tsimpsians—will no longer frighten our women and old men. Then will he be our father and we his children.

But can that ever be? Your God is not our God. Your God loves his people and hates mine. He folds his strong arms lovingly around the white man and leads him as a father leads his infant son—but He has forsaken His red children, if they are really His. Our God, the Great Spirit, seems also to have forsaken us. Your God makes your people wax strong every day—soon they will fill the land.

My people are ebbing away like a fast-receding tide that will not flow again. The white man's God cannot love

His red children or He would protect them. We seem to be orphans who can look nowhere for help.

How then can we become brothers? How can your God become our God and renew our prosperity and awaken in us dreams of returning greatness? Your God seems to us to be partial. He came to the white man. We never saw Him, never heard His voice. He gave the white man laws, but had no word for His red children whose teeming millions once filled this vast continent as the stars fill the skies.

No. We are two distinct races, and must ever remain so, with separate origins and separate destinies. There is little in common between us.

To us the ashes of our ancestors are sacred and their final resting place is hallowed ground, while you wander far from the graves of your ancestors and, seemingly, without regret. Your religion was written on tablets of stone by the iron finger of an angry God, lest you might forget it. The Red Man could never comprehend nor remember it. Our religion is the traditions of our ancestors—the dreams of our old men, given them in the solemn hours of night by the Great Spirit, and the visions of our Sachems, and is written in the hearts of our people.

Your dead cease to love you and the land of their nativity as soon as they pass the portals of the tomb—they wander far away beyond the stars, are soon forgotten and never return.

Our dead never forget this beautiful world that gave them being. They still love its winding rivers, its great mountains and its sequestered vales, and they ever yearn in tenderest affection over the lonely-hearted living, and often return to visit, guide and comfort them.

Day and night cannot dwell together. The Red Man has ever fled the approach of the white man, as the changing mist on the mountainside flees before the blazing sun.

However, your proposition seems a just one, and I will think that my people will accept it and will retire to the reservation you offer them. Then we will dwell apart in peace, for the words of the Great White Chief seem to be the voice of Nature speaking to my people out of thick darkness that is fast gathering around them like a dense fog floating inward from a midnight sea.

There in the circle of Stevens and his associates Sealth went on, and it is this part of his speech which, in years past, was most quoted.

It matters little where we pass the remnants of our days. They are not many. The Indian's night promises to be dark. No bright star hovers above his horizon. Sad-voiced winds moan in the distance. Some grim Fate of our race is on the Red Man's trail, and wherever he goes he will still hear the sure approaching footsteps of his fell destroyer and prepare stolidly to meet his doom, as does the wounded doe that hears the approaching footsteps of the hunter.

A few more moons, a few more winters—and not one of all the mighty hosts that once filled this broad land and that now roam in fragmentary bands through these vast solitudes or lived in happy homes, protected by the Great Spirit, will remain to weep over the graves of a people once as powerful and as hopeful as your own.

But why should I repine? Why should I murmur at the fate of my people? Tribes are made up of individuals and are no better than they. Men come and go like the waves of the sea. A tear, a tamanamus, a dirge and they are gone from our longing eyes forever. It is the order of Nature. Even the white man, whose God walked and talked with him as friend to friend, is not exempt from the common destiny. We may be brothers, after all. We shall see.

We will ponder your proposition, and when we decide we will tell you. But should we accept it, I here and now make this the first condition—that we will not be denied the privilege, without molestation, of visiting the graves of our ancestors, friends and children.

Every part of this country is sacred to my people. Every hillside, every plain and grove has been hallowed by some fond memory or some sad experience of my tribe. Even the rocks, which seem to lie dumb as they swelter in the sun or darken in the rain along the silent seashore in solemn grandeur, thrill with the memories of past events connected with the lives of my people.

The very dust under your feet responds more lovingly to our footsteps than to yours, because it is the ashes of our ancestors, and our bare feet are conscious of the sympathetic touch, for the soil is rich with the life of our kindred.

The noble braves, fond mothers, glad happy-hearted children and maidens, who lived and rejoiced here for a brief season, whose very names are now forgotten, still love these somber solitudes and their deep fastnesses which, at eventide, grow shadowy with the presence of dusky spirits.

And when the last Red Man shall have perished from the earth and his memory among the white men shall have become a myth, these shores will swarm with the invisible dead of my tribes; and when your children's children shall think themselves alone in the fields, the store, the shop upon the highway, or in the silence of the pathless woods, they will not be alone. In all the earth there is no place dedicated to your solitude.

At night, when the streets of your cities and villages will be silent and you think them deserted, they will throng with returning hosts that once filled and still love this beautiful land.

The white man will never be alone. Let him be just and deal kindly with my people, for the dead are not powerless.

Dead—did I say?

There is no death.

Only a change of worlds!

Sealth was probably around sixty-eight when he delivered that prophetic challenge. He had some twelve years more to live, but was already beginning to fail. He seemed old to Stevens and his men, to the settlers, who were comparatively young, and even to his tribesmen, who, except in rare instances, did not live nearly as long as is popularly supposed.

When he knew the end was close he asked that his white friends pass his coffin and grip his hand in farewell. This last request was honored, with his good friend Doctor Maynard leading the long single file past the open cedar casket. The grave was marked by a rude wooden cross. It was not until a quarter of a century later that Hillory Butler and Arthur Denny, dean of the founders, who mentioned Sealth only once in his unemotional and succinct memoirs, erected a granite tombstone. On its face is chiseled

SEATTLE
Chief of the Suquampsh and Allied Tribes
Died June 7, 1866
The Firm Friend of the Whites
For Him Seattle Was Named by its Founders

On the reverse side, and doubtless at the suggestion of Father Demers or some other Catholic priest into whose sect the Indian had been converted, are the words

Baptismal Name, Noah Sealth
Age Probably 80 Years

Honoring him today are this tombstone, a statue with the waters of the mountains pouring into a simple circular pool, and Noah Sealth's profile on the official seal of the city called Seattle.

6

The Mercer Girls

I n the brief history of the youngest major city in the nation Asa Mercer inevitably appears as a hero. But to many a woman-hungry bachelor of Seattle in the sixties of the last century he must have seemed a confidence man of astonishing stature. This suspicion is buttressed by the fact that soon after his return from the East with a second shipload of unmarried women, forever to be known as the "Mercer Girls," he departed from the town on Elliott Bay and took up residence in the western shadows of the Rocky Mountains. That was about as far away as a man could get without the protection of a wagon train or a ship. This despite the fact that he had been president of the university he helped to build, and one would expect that his future would rest most promisingly in the town which once had revered him.

My great good friend Stewart Holbrook, one of the finest writers ever produced by the Northwest, once threatened to shoot the very next writer who recorded the story of the Mercer Girls. He was sick and tired of them. I fear that the appearance of a novel called

Cargo of Brides may have hastened his passing. But by our loss he was spared the appearance of a color television series, shakily based on the story, called "Here Come the Brides." I am at a loss to know where the script writer found his research for this serial, in which early Seattle showed up as a kind of sanitized Peyton Place.

Yet the Mercer Girls are an inextricable part of any book about Seattle. The curious thing is that one never hears a Seattleite claim to be a descendant of a Mercer Girl, whereas New England and adjacent areas are jam-packed with descendants of passengers of the *Mayflower*. The reason for this may stem from a long period during which Seattle seemed somewhat ashamed of its history. Probably this was because Easterners considered the town, when they considered it at all, as chiefly populated by Indians, which was all too true.

In any case, the importance of the Mercer Girls to Seattle progress is evidenced in a public advertisement which appeared in the *Puget Sound Herald* on February 24, 1860—a little less than a decade after the founding of Seattle. The author was editor and publisher Charles Prosch:

> Attention, Bachelors: Believing that our only chance of a realization of the benefits and early attainments of matrimonial alliances depends upon the arrival in our midst of a number of the fair sex from the Atlantic States, and that, to bring about such an arrival a united effort and action are called for on our part, we respectfully request a full attendance of all eligible and sincerely desirous bachelors in this community to assemble on Tuesday evening next in Delin and Shorey's building to devise ways and means to secure this much needed and desirable emigration to our shores.

Certainly the great majority of the population of the town consisted of eligible bachelors, and there was no question about the sincerity of their desire. Many had coupled with Indian girls, briefly or permanently, in legal marriage or a simpler arrangement with their parents. This was frowned upon by the moral element of the town, and sometimes had its dangers because white sailors long ago had infected the tribes with venereal disease.

Also, the anxiety of the bachelors had been proved by one John Pennell, a former operator on San Francisco's Barbary Coast. He had heard of the problem in Seattle and so traveled north to build a long structure of cedar logs on a part of the sawdust pile near Yesler's mill. Inside he nailed down a dance floor. On one side he improvised a bar of planed boards riding sawhorses, and on the other side a series of small rooms with opaque curtains.

He then negotiated for the most promising Indian girls he could discover, and personally saw to their scrubbing down in a large wooden tub. They were not in the habit of bathing often (but then neither were most of the eligible bachelors) and Pennell discouraged them from the age-old practice of washing their hair in urine. As a final elegant touch he decked them out in calico.

From San Francisco he hired his combo: accordionist, fiddler and drummer. Customers could dance with a girl by the simple business of buying a couple of drinks, the female's drink being dark cold tea paid for as whiskey. A customer also had the privilege of taking his dancing partner into one of the rooms and drawing the curtain. Records do not disclose the price for this ultimate service, but we can estimate from the fact that as late as the twenties the price on Skid Road was two or three dollars.

Business was excellent, and Seattle became a center of entertainment. As one irreverent historian put it (and irreverent historians were scarce on Puget Sound) Pennell had "built the best mouse-trap on the Sound" and hobnailed boots beat a path to his door. Thus encouraged, Pennell enlisted from the Barbary Coast several out-of-work white prostitutes. A fancy lady unoccupied on the Barbary Coast could not have been either young or handsome, but under the circumstances on Elliott Bay they sufficed. The proportion of males to females west of the Cascades was about nine to one.

But Charles Prosch did not consider Pennell's The Illahee (later known locally as The Mad House) even a partial solution. He continued to editorialize for marriageable women. He sent clippings of his editorials to eastern newspapers in the rather forlorn hope that they would be reprinted. Few eastern editors bit, and if they did they usually added a warning or took umbrage at what they felt to be an outrageous suggestion. On his part, Prosch felt that he might be reaching an appreciative audience. The Civil War had cut off the cotton supply from the South and many of the New England textile mills were shut down. Thus women textile workers were unemployed. Also, the war had begun to produce its inevitable by-product of widows and orphans.

Prosch did not offer marriage alone. Knowing the female mind, he suggested independence as well. He pointed out that Seattle and neighboring communities had need of dressmakers, laundresses, cooks and helpers and—above all—schoolteachers.

Thus, over a period, the publisher suggested the problem and the solution. But the means to the solution were another matter. To travel across the Rockies to the Atlantic, find a willing female, and return with her would cost a bachelor a thousand dollars. Accomplishing such a miracle by ship passage would cost only a little less. A thousand dollars was a lot of money on Puget Sound in 1860. If a man had a donation claim, a flannel shirt, hickory breeches, logging boots and fifty loose dollars he was well off. If he had three hundred dollars he was considered wealthy.

Then into the breach suddenly stepped Asa Mercer. He arrived, fresh and volatile, from college about a year after the bachelors' meeting called by Prosch. As the younger brother of solid Judge Thomas Mercer, who had arrived in 1852, his credentials were good. Nor was his reputation harmed because he had ready-made friends in Dexter Horton and Daniel Bagley, who had known the Mercer family back in Illinois. Judge Tom Mercer had brought with him the town's first team of horses and become the first teamster. (I once asked Dave Beck if he knew the name of Seattle's first teamster and when he hesitated told him the story of Judge Mercer. The then chief of the International Brotherhood of Teamsters roared with laughter, and said, "By God, and all this time I thought it was me!")

The judge's young brother Asa quickly proved up in his own right by pitching in with his hands. He worked waist-deep in black wet bog, chopping at roots of great fir and cedar stumps to help clear ground for the first building of the Territorial University, which was to stand just east of where the Olympic Hotel and the IBM Building now prosper. He rested with smarting eyes in the silver-blue smoke while the stumps burned out. Doubtless he was there on the famous day when Dexter Horton came by, parted his long coattails, and backed up to a smouldering stump for warmth. At which moment there burst an unexploded cannonball from the U.S.S. *Decatur*. The incident was a reminder of the Battle of Seattle and propelled Mr. Horton several yards, considerably shaken but uninjured. Seattle's first banker was lucky as well as shrewd.

When the land was cleared Asa helped erect the university building. That done, he stepped in by acclaim as the first president and the entire faculty.

This was not enough to use up all his energies and enthusiasm. He became interested—perhaps as a civic leader and maybe as one of those sincerely desirous young men—in Prosch's project. Clothed in the dignity of the university presidency he discussed a plan with Territorial Governor Pickering and with members of the legislature. He insisted that the way to get suitable white women onto the shores of Elliott Bay was to go East and bring them back in groups of a hundred, two hundred, five hundred. But no politician dared support the idea actively, and anyhow the territorial treasury was empty.

Asa Mercer then decided that the sensible thing to do was to go East for the women and also for the money with which to return them to Puget Sound. His own finances were those of a pioneer schoolteacher, so he went from cabin to cabin, from merchant to merchant, to raise money for his passage East. He managed an undisclosed amount, at least enough to get him around the Horn to Boston.

His first trip was not the success he had hoped it would be. He could persuade not more than eleven young women, ranging in age from fifteen to twenty-five, to accompany him back to Seattle. Just how he raised the money for the return voyage is somewhat of a mystery, but he got them to San Francisco. They were wan from seasickness and already frightened of the rugged West Coast. Mercer thought it best not to wait for the monthly steamer from Puget Sound. He put some of his charges on the lumber brig *Tanner* and the rest on the lumber bark *Trent*. Thus they reached Port Gamble, which had become a booming mill town, and from there they reached Seattle in the sloop *Kidder*.

They arrived at midnight on May 16, 1864, and presently nobody was asleep in Seattle town. Everybody turned out, hair-slicked bachelors among them. There were only three pianos in the village, but immediately all were in use.

We can easily be certain that their welcome was merry because leading the parade to the wharf to meet the *Kidder* was Doctor David Swinton Maynard, the antithesis of all the earliest settlers, who were a sober and serious lot.

The ladies had come, too, to welcome the Mercer girls with open arms, and the bachelors—who would have liked to do the same—hung bashfully about, hoping the results of their grooming would make them shine out.

There was a reception in the common hall, and the pianos and singing lasted until dawn. (Two or three of the second shipment of young women brought their own pianos.) When at last everybody was exhausted, particularly the newcomers, the Mercer ladies were taken into various homes until permanent residences could be built, or until they found jobs or husbands with dwellings attached. When they awakened late next day they must have been awed by the primitive yet beautiful land around them.

For the time being the young ladies were put to use as schoolteachers around the Sound, and one was made assistant lighthouse keeper at Admiralty Head.

Asa Mercer was disappointed at having brought eleven women, but in the excitement his neighbors seemed to think he had done well enough and elected him to the legislature. Dazed, Mr. Mercer said, "They did it without my spending a nickel. I never bought a cigar or a glass of whiskey for anybody."

If his constituency was satisfied, Mercer was not. A year or two later he was off on another expedition. This time he was encouraged by the thought that Abraham Lincoln was President and as a boy he had sat on Abe's knee and listened to his stories.

Mercer's method of raising money for the second expedition is interesting. He zeroed in on bachelors who wanted to wive, and for a definite sum promised to bring them back a mate. Some records say the sum is not known, others suggest that the price was three hundred dollars. Nor is it known whether Asa himself chipped in three hundred or whatever for Annie Stephens of Baltimore, whom he eventually took unto himself in marriage.

In any case, Asa Mercer was never to forget the morning he came down into the lobby of a New York hotel, on the way to catch the train for Washington. Porters were hanging crepe and no one spoke. Outside, on the way to the station, he learned what had happened the night before at Ford's Theater.

Lincoln's death took much of the wind from Mercer's sails, but he saw Governor Andrew of Massachusetts, who turned him over to Edward Everett Hale. Not much seems to have come from either interview. He spent weeks in Washington, seeing everybody from President Johnson on down. All seemed to think that Mercer's idea was brilliant, a genuine contribution to the national welfare. But the politicians of Washington, D.C., had even less courage than those of Washington Territory. They were somehow frightened of the plan.

Then Mercer encountered General Grant. Emerging from the

scraggly hair was a particularly sympathetic ear. Grant had been stationed, as a young officer, in Oregon Territory, and had hated its climate. His memoirs do not report that on occasion he was carried dead drunk to his quarters by an Indian squaw. But then memoirs are notable for such omissions.

"I'm to appear at a Cabinet meeting this morning," Grant told Mercer. "You wait here and I'l try to bring the whole matter to a head, one way or another." He was back within an hour and had written out for Mercer an order on the United States Army for a vessel completely fitted out and manned for Puget Sound.

Mercer literally ran with it from the hotel to the office of the Quartermaster General. There he ran into a snag. "This is absolutely illegal and Grant knows it," said Quartermaster General Meigs. "I cannot honor this order. You'll get no vessel from the Army."

Mercer did not give up. He poured his story into the ears of strangers in hotels. Probably on advice from Grant, and at a discreet distance, he kept in touch with the Quartermaster General. Finally the officer relented to the extent of agreeing to allow Mercer a vessel upon payment of eighty thousand dollars to the federal government.

Word gets around fast in Washington and soon Mercer was confronted by a man named Ben Holladay, who would leave his mark on Oregon history. "Let me have the vessel," he told Mercer, "and we will enter into a contract. I'll furnish the money Meigs wants, buy the ship, and take your women to San Francisco at the going rate."

Mercer jumped at the offer. Rashly he indicated that as many as five hundred women had agreed to make the trip. Later he was to report home that anti-Mercer stories in eastern newspapers were seriously damaging his recruiting.

Mercer's figure of five hundred dwindled to two hundred. When Holladay learned of this he said that Mercer had not fulfilled the contract and that the passage rate must be boosted. Mercer could do nothing but agree. Meanwhile at home the citizens were finding that building quarters for even two hundred women was a problem, but not everybody was ready to criticize him. He was doing the best he could. But some of those bachelors who were out three hundred dollars, or whatever the sum may have been, were beginning to wonder if they had been taken.

A New York *Times* reporter joined the vessel and faithfully reported the rough journey via the Strait of Magellan, Rio de

Janeiro, Lota and the Galápagos. There were homesickness, seasickness and considerable bickering, some of which reached the hair-pulling stage.

At San Francisco, which was as far as Holladay's skipper would go, Mercer had just about enough money to telegraph Governor Pickering for passage money to Elliott Bay. The return message came collect and Mercer couldn't pay for it. Mercer offered to gamble with the Western Union man. "I think it's a money order from the Governor of the Territory of Washington. If it is, I can pay you. If it isn't, you need not read the message to me."

The telegrapher looked at the message and burst into a guffaw. Pickering had sent several hundred words of congratulations—collect—and no money.

Then Mercer played his last card. In New York he had bought a few farm wagons—where had he got the money for these?—and had them shipped as far as the Golden Gate, hoping one day to bail them out and sell them on Puget Sound, where the settlers were already making sporadic—and rather unsuccessful—efforts to build wagon roads inland, with the ultimate ambition of linking the settlement with the eastern part of the territory across the Cascades.

The financial source of Mercer's wagon business remains one of the several dim mysteries in the story of the Mercer Girls. One cannot help but wonder if the money was a no longer necessary part of his collections from Seattle bachelors, accrued due to his failure to persuade the "several hundred" he had hoped to bring home. If this is true, Mercer is absolved by his willingness to sacrifice his side business to the completion of the main part of his mission.

In any case he sold the wagons and began shipping his "cargo of brides" on several craft which had room for passengers and were heading north.

An interesting sidelight that helps to make the Mercer Girls real, despite the apparent lack of visible and audible descendants, comes from Mrs. Betty (Engle) Engstrom of Greenbank, Washington. Says she:

> Though the true character of the Mercer Girls has been distorted, I, as a granddaughter of one, am justly proud of my heritage. My grandmother, Flora Pearson Engle, was a mere child of fifteen when she came West on the second Mercer expedition, accompanying her mother and young

brother. Her father and two older sisters were passengers on the first voyage, as Mr. Mercer brought families as well as single girls West."

Mr. Pearson settled on Whidbey Island and was the lighthouse keeper at the Fort Casey site, and when Flora arrived she became assistant lighthouse keeper. The Pearsons, like some others, brought their piano around the Horn with them. Flora taught music to some of the children on the island and played her Chickering grand piano so many years that the center keys became concave. This I remember well from childhood. I now own that beautiful piano and a dainty floor what-not shelf and her lovely yellow taffeta formal dress complete with hoop-skirts.

After marrying William B. Engle, Flora and her husband lived at the lighthouse, where my father was born. This event was noted in the lighthouse log along with notice of an inspection by Admiral Dewey.

As for descendants, there are sixteen living on the island and nine others located in other areas, among them my son and daughter in Seattle. This all adds up to twenty-five, not bad for one Mercer girl who had just three children.

Recently I persuaded Susan Paynter of the Seattle *Post-Intelligencer* to see what she could find out about descendants of the Mercer Girls. Although a stubborn and thorough researcher, she was only able to trace somewhat more than a dozen, these not living in Seattle. It must be remembered that, although Seattle was slowly growing, there were many who drifted away, unable to adjust to the climate perhaps, or fearful of the mounting enmity of the Indians, or just possibly discouraged by the monopolies already beginning to form in the infant Establishment comprised of the very first settlers, such as Arthur Denny, Dexter Horton, the Borens and Terrys, Doctor Maynard and the like.

Nor did Miss Paynter's subsequent article in the newspaper's Sunday magazine bring forth more than two or three other admitted descendants. However, she did find three or four descendants in Seattle, one of whom was the great-granddaughter of Ida Barlow, who came as a very young girl just out of a preparatory school. She brought with her a "card of honor" from her school, printed in

fashionable French, attesting to her character and behavior. She left
her brownstone-front home in Manhattan with the dubious blessings
of her parents, and made the long voyage purely in a spirit of
adventure.

Ida Barlow's descendant, together with the testimony of Mrs.
Engstrom of Whidbey Island, seems to undermine the general myth
that the Mercer Girls were all widows and orphans of the Civil War,
desperate for marriage. Ida Barlow appears to have come to Puget
Sound with much the same attitude we find today in youth who join
the Peace Corps, or who feel that their easy home life is restricting
their outlook on the world.

In any case, her great-granddaughter denies that the Mercer
Girls were mainly husband-seekers. Their attitude, she feels, was
wholly different from that of the bachelors who awaited their
arrival. Ida's descendant feels also that the quietness of the Mercer
Girl lineage has been due to two other factors. "First of all,"
she said, "we haven't thought much about it. Perhaps I should take
more interest and form a club of some kind. Then, of course, some
years ago there was a feeling on the part of the first settlers and
their descendants that the Mercer Girls were upstarts and not true
pioneers."

Undoubtedly she was referring to what was then "high society"
in Seattle. These families are now somewhat fragmented, but prior
to the Great Depression they lived in winter on "First Hill" just
above the central business district, and in summer repaired to a
security-guarded subdivision called The Highlands. This hideout of
the wealthy still flourishes, but now the well-built homes are used
all year around and it is no longer "out in the country." If there
are still blue bloods in Seattle, a possibility which the majority is
willing to debate, you find them almost anywhere except in the so-
called Central Area, now largely populated by blacks. The prosperous still cling to The Highlands, and to a newer protected development called Broadmoor. But also they may be almost anywhere: in
the new skyscraper apartments with balconies viewing the Sound or
Lake Washington or the downtown area; on Queen Anne Hill or
Capitol Hill; in the more graceful suburbs springing up north of the
city or east of Lake Washington, and even in pretentious houseboats
on Lake Union.

And surely, here and there among them, is a quiet descendant
of a Mercer Girl with every reason to stand tall in the community.

I can't bring myself to agree with an early local historian who wrote: "Never in history was an equal number of women thrown together who had a higher average of intelligence, modesty and virtue." This unprovable statement seems to me overblown. But they were a courageous lot, and tremendously important to Seattle's progress in a very crucial period.

Nonetheless, upon their arrival at least three hundred rough, toughened bachelors who had contributed to the project were without a good woman. Certainly they were if Asa Mercer promised five hundred women before departing on his second expedition. And Asa did not come up short for himself, for he married one of them. I am sure that feelings ran high in some quarters, but I believe that he deserved his prize. He had the right idea and he put it into action under difficult circumstances.

It may or may not be significant that he no longer yearned to be a university president or a member of the Washington territorial legislature. Soon with his bride he was heading for the western foothills of the Rocky Mountains to become a rancher.

Meanwhile the Mercer Girls and their descendants carried on, modestly and quietly.

7

Seattle's Lost Language

On my grandfather's watch chain was a gold nugget which seems to me now to have been as big as a walnut. In one of my grandmother's trunks was a slim, long chamois sack long emptied of gold dust. In Alaskanese the chamois was a *poke*, the prospector's purse.

For my grandparents had been in the Klondike during the Gold Rush. My grandfather was a veteran of the Chilkoot Trail that wound from Skagway to Lake Bennett. Traces of that cruel, tortuous path can still be seen from the little narrow-gauge railroad that in summer is a favorite of tourists to the North Country.

Thus my family was a member of the fraternity of ex-Alaskans, no small distinction in Seattle when I was a boy. The city then was a community of hardly more than two hundred thousand, and all these former Alaska "rushers" seemed to know one another. Some had come back "outside" as broke as when they went north, some had struck it rich, and others had learned things in the Klondike that made them successes in Seattle.

The status of the former Klondikers and Alaskans was of no consequence in the brotherhood. They didn't care, for example, that Alexander Pantages had been a singing waiter in Nome. In Seattle the energetic Greek formed a vaudeville chain, built the Pantages Theater (with the clear blinking stars of the Northland in its ceiling) and was a wealthy man. The dubious background of certain women in the Gold Rush days made no difference to their membership in the club of the North. They were all one now; there were thousands of them in Seattle, and no questions were asked about the past.

The idiom of Alaska and the Yukon Territory was a part of their speech. I can remember being told to "mush on" instead of dawdling behind when I was out walking with my grandfather; it was a dog-sled expression. And regularly he would implore me to be "lead dog" as he tried to sharpen my initiative and activity.

Gradually, of course, as the "Gold Rushers" died the idiom began to disappear. But there was another language, a broader one, that hung on until World War II. This was called Chinook, but actually was a trade jargon—not the genuine Chinook language— chiefly derived from French and English and the language of several tribes. Naturally it was influenced by the ability or inability of the Indians to pronounce certain vowels and letters.

I remember sitting in the office of a former "Gold Rusher" as he answered the telephone. "Kloshe," he said. "Arctic Club, twelve o'clock. Alki, tillikum."

He replaced the receiver and turned to me as if he had not been speaking in code. In the Chinook jargon *kloshe* meant good or fine. *Alki* was soon or in the future or, as the Indians thought of it, bye and bye.

Tillikum was perhaps the most used word in the jargon after the jargon was no longer necessary. It meant friend, and it meant a particularly good friend. It is rather sad to see it disappear from Seattle's language. The late Miller Freeman, Seattle capitalist, attending a Whitman College commencement to receive an honorary degree, sat up half a night writing a Chinook speech, which of course began, "My tillikums." He had not pursued his education beyond the fifth grade. With typical frontier humor he said that in that grade he discovered compound interest, and that his immediate reaction was "How long has this been going on? Let me out of here!"

The Seattle overseers and trustees who accompanied him to Whitman to receive his honors knew of his lack of formal education.

Straight-faced they told him that the president of the college would present the diploma with a little speech in Latin and that Freeman would be expected to make a speech of thanks in the same language. He received the news unblinkingly and prepared himself as best he could with a speech in the Chinook jargon. I have always been sorry that he was not required to deliver the talk; it would have been a delightful addition to the legends of frontier humor, which, alas, is also disappearing.

Particularly in the Arctic Club of old you heard dialogue in the jargon. *Nika kumtux* meant "I understand." A very important combination was *chuck chako*: the tide is rising. If you were *chako Boston* you were becoming American or, God help you, civilized.

Skookum chuck was a rapid stream or coastal eddy. *Cultus* was "worn out, worthless." A pioneer often used it to describe the state of his health when asked *Klahowya?*

A *dolla* was a dollar, hard, round, heavy and worth one hundred cents. Every storekeeper knew that *tatoosh glease* was butter. *Hyak* was swift or quick, and *hiyu* meant much or plenty.

Illahee was the land or country where you lived and in which you found comfort, as Mr. Pennell knew when he founded Seattle's first house of ill fame and so named it. *Kalakala* was a bird or waterfowl and this word prolonged itself into the thirties, when the ferry company (the ferries were not then state-owned) applied the name to the rebuilt *Peralta*, a San Francisco ferry which had burned to its gunwales. The Seattle firm bought it, encased it in a huge, shining, streamlined metal frame, and christened it *Kalakala*. It became nationally famous for its dramatic appearance and a speed it could not attain without shaking itself to pieces.

If a friend asked about your *klootchman* you knew he was asking after the health of your wife. *Konoway* was the sum or the whole of anything. Your *lacaset* was your trunk, and *lum* was rum or whiskey or any drink with a respectable content of alcohol.

The derivation of some jargon words was apparent. Syrup was *melass*, deriving from molasses, a pioneer staple. *Moos-moos* of course meant oxen or cattle, and *muck-a-muck* meant to eat same. *Siwash* meant Indian, or savage, and later was to become unpopular with the Indians, although it hung on in white men's talk almost as long as *tillikum*.

Klahanie was the great outdoors around us, and if you think it is great now you should have seen it fifty years ago, when people spoke the Chinook jargon. In those days it was *skookum* or powerful and not so much dwarfed by Mount Rainier and Mounts Baker and Shuksan and the rugged Olympic Range far to the west of the Sound.

Tyee meant chief and in that earlier time the tyees of Seattle had a great respect for the word *potlatch*, a festival of giving, a word that had been strong medicine in the highly cultured tribes of Vancouver Island just north of the town. Indeed, that word hung on almost as long as did *tillikum* because, prior to World War I there was an annual week-long celebration called The Potlatch sponsored by three "tribes" of leading citizens.

But after the First World War the celebration did not return. Somehow Seattle had become a bit embarrassed about its early rough history. A celebration based upon Indian tradition might be all right for cities where the rough frontier days were a hundred or more years past. But Seattle's beginning at that time was uncomfortably close; in fact, not quite seventy years had elapsed.

Seattle had decided that perhaps it should take more care about being a civilized city. Several variations of annual celebrations were tried, and at last we settled on a borrowing from a Midwest winter carnival and called it Seafair. The name was proper enough, inasmuch as Seattle is one of the boating capitals of the world and a great seaport. But the story theme of Seafair involved King Neptune, a beautiful young queen, Davy Jones and pirates from his locker beneath the deep. It has about as much to do with Seattle as does the story of Little Red Riding Hood and is not half as interesting.

By then the Chinook jargon had almost disappeared, as now it has entirely. Only a few can speak it fully, men ninety or a hundred years old, like Henry Broderick, the realtor, and Joshua Green, the banker. We have a number of this hardy breed still active in Seattle. But they are hard put to find another person with whom to carry on Chinook dialogue.

When Seattle was young there were tens of thousands west of the Rockies who could speak Chinook fluently, with the gestures to help it along. Between Puget Sound and the Missouri River probably a hundred thousand persons—Indians and whites and mixed bloods—conversed in it. All the settlers, including merchants, loggers, seamen, traders, even housewives, used it, for it was a necessary part of living then.

Its decline began after we had fenced off the Indians on

reservations under conditions against which their descendants are now in rebellion. Yet for decades afterward you heard the language everywhere, even in the halls of exclusive clubs.

The offspring of the pioneers did not perpetuate it; there was no practical reason to do so. Seattle was the last major city to use the hybrid tongue and so the last to abandon it. Now this lost language exists only in the memories of a few ancients and in sparse, well-thumbed dictionaries almost impossible to find.

This shedding of the jargon was a signal that Seattle was entering a new era. We have entered a good many eras, and sometimes shied back at the shock, for that is a characteristic of the town. But this one was real; we had quietly and unwittingly taken a step from which there could be no return. We had abandoned the Chinook jargon, without which the Midwest and Far West could never have prospered.

8

About That Rain

Seattleites of light heart and momentarily at leisure have a way of picking up a few dollars on a bet involving the weather. Generally the routine works in this way:

The Seattleite climbs onto a stool in a bar in the hope that the next seat will soon be taken by a man who may or may not be from out of town. If he is from out of town, so much the better. If he is seeking shelter from a pouring rain, the conditions are even more propitious.

Being a friendly sort, as are most Seattleites, our citizen tentatively starts a conversation. If the stranger seems willing to talk, the Seattleite casually brings forth the subject of the weather. The other fellow, having shown sense enough to come in out of the rain, usually is ready and willing.

"Yes," says the Seattleite, "we do get considerable rain here. But —you know—New York City gets more rain than we do."

Even if the stranger has never been in Manhattan, which in these days of air travel is unlikely, he will almost certainly reply to the effect that this is hard to believe. If he has been in town several days, or months, even several years, he will work himself into a state of mind which makes the Seattleite's claim preposterous.

At this point, depending of course on the climate of the conversation, the Seattleite proceeds: "I know it's hard to believe. But it's a fact. If you care to make a small wager we'll call the weather bureau."

If the trap has sprung (and it will have if there has been more than one martini), a bet will be made and the pair will go to the bar's public telephone. The wily Seattleite (we are not all like this) looks up the telephone number of the weather bureau—a number he knows perfectly well, having pulled the dodge innumerable times. When the weather bureau answers he hands the receiver to his new companion and says, "Go ahead, ask him."

The weatherman, who encounters this question at least two or three times a week and can hear the juke box in the background, sighs, "The average rainfall in Seattle is 34.10 inches. The rainfall in New York City is 42.37 inches."

Whereupon the stranger says something to the effect that he will be damned, perhaps with the queasy feeling that the bureau is in league with the Chamber of Commerce or perhaps with all Seattle.

Back at the bar the subject is pursued and the wager settled. The Seattleite buys the next round and gently explains, "People get the wrong idea about Seattle's climate because the rain is fairly steady when it comes. It may go on for two or three days a week, with not much of a letup. In other cities they get a brief rainfall but while it lasts it can be a dilly, and over a year the precipitation adds up to a lot of inches. I could name you a dozen cities in the country—no, a hundred or more—where there is more rainfall than here."

If the stranger is sensible he'll reply, "Never mind."

Yet there's no question about Seattle's downpours. Maybe they do fall as a gentle rain from heaven, but they are persistent about it. Any honest Seattleite will tell you that it is fairly certain to rain on the Fourth of July and other summer holidays, or on a weekend when you've planned an outing, or a very important golf game. Of course Seattle golfers rarely let the rain stop them.

Some of our people believe we should stop being so sensitive about the rain, and get on the offensive about it. One such citizen is Walter Rue, retired newspaperman, who has studied weather for thirty years as a hobby. It is difficult for the Seattle Weather Bureau to accurately predict our weather because that weather comes in from the big Pacific or down the Aleutian chain. Also there is no way to predict whether our surrounding mountains will protect us, as often they do, or whether the wind may take a sudden change of direction and sweep around the ends of the Cascades or the Olympics. There's a long-standing jest in town that after the weather bureau has fiddled with its complex equipment and made its calculations the local chief telephones Walter Rue and asks, "Walt, what do you figure? We're a little puzzled down here." Surely the story is apocryphal—Rue denies it emphatically—but it's true that he is our most noted lay expert, and that newspaper subscribers give the weather report a dubious glance.

We can get some very rainy or overcast summers, but these may be leveled out by fall and winter weeks so warm that no raincoat or topcoat is needed. What is known as an overcoat in most cities finds no sale in Seattle. Until recent years a male Seattleite would not be caught dead with an umbrella; he simply set his hard derby foursquare and marched through the rain. But today's young men frequently carry a neatly rolled umbrella in winter, and when it rains they unlimber it. This may be partly due to the smartness of a rolled umbrella and partly due to the fact that few of Seattle's young men wear hats, a fashion that brings tears to the eyes of our haberdashers.

I have known Christmas days when one could sit on the patio in a light sweater—but when that happens a Seattleite watches out for a marked snowfall in March or even early April. "Our weather tends to balance up over the year," is how Walter Rue puts it. Yet snow is so rare that even a brief blizzard will be memorialized in school books for years afterward. Many winters pass without the sign of a single white flake—although one shivering exception was the winter of 1972.

Genuine hurricanes are almost unknown in Seattle. But in March 1875, a hurricane swept the Puget Sound region, the first within the memory of white men there. An eyewitness said, "It blew down thousands of trees, swept up several homes, barns and sheds. The storm was fearful, with trees crashing every instant. Both our lakes were lashed to a foam. A tree fell across an Indian camp and somehow it caught fire. The whole camp was ablaze and the

Indians had to run to the lake and stand in the lashing water up to their waists to save their lives."

Since that memorable year there have been on the Olympic Peninsula what are known as "williwaw hurricanes." These sweep downward, move horizontally for a mile or two, then disappear upward again. Evidences of such phenomena have been found by rangers and hikers in the interior of the peninsula. "They happen more regularly than people realize," says one old-timer. He claims that early in this century, on a stormy day when the sky was jet black over the peninsula, he heard the evidence of a williwaw hurricane. "I was sitting on a wharf on the bay, watching the white-caps and I hung to a big cleat to keep from getting blown into the water because the wind was pretty strong even there. Every once in a while I would hear a series of funny noises, as if maybe a hundred or so men were breaking matchsticks somewhere near me. It took me a while to realize what the sound was. That's a hundred miles out there to where hell was breaking loose, and what I was hearing was great trees breaking off just like—well, just like matchsticks."

There may be more evidences of such Olympic hurricanes than we know, for there are parts of that vast rain forest whereon not even rangers have set foot. It is this peninsula, as well as its great Olympic Range, which protects Seattle from the frequent rages of the Pacific. For the city is a hundred and twenty-five miles from the ocean coast, a fact missed by many a tourist from the Midwest who takes a look at Elliott Bay and believes he has seen the Pacific.

Those very early gentlemen, Lewis and Clark, who passed through a part of what is now Washington State, encountered rain and plenty of it. The spelling in their journals may not have been modern, but they knew when they were wet, and between the lines of their record one detects a certain annoyance with the elements of the continent's western edge: "It raned during the whole night and about daylight a tremendous gale of wind rose from SSE and continued through the day . . . The rane continued through the next day . . . It raned almost incessantly for three following days and sickness began to prevail among the men . . . Towards evening it began to rane . . . The morning was cloudy with some rane . . . It continued raneing the whole day."

Those passages, which are taken at random, and there are many more in the same vein, extend over more than a month. Although they were writing during parts of November and December, it is pertinent to note that they did not have to shovel any snow.

It may or may not be due to climate that Seattle has one of the highest suicide rates in the nation. This is a fact not issued by the Chamber of Commerce, and it could be because we have a large number of lofty bridges and it is from these that a great percentage of suicides jump. But whether their mood is shaped by rain and long periods of overcast skies the doctors, psychologists and psychiatrists cannot yet say. Some of these medical men have been working on the problem for years—and as yet have come to no satisfactory conclusion.

Seattle patriots like Walter Rue will have no part of the notion that our suicides are driven to the brink by our weather, and they refuse comment on the subject of our above-national-average liquor consumption and the number of proven alcoholics. "Seattle and her near neighbors lie in one of the healthiest climatic belts," says Rue stubbornly, "and you must realize that the moist air of fall, winter and spring has a soothing effect on the mucuous membranes. It has a beneficial effect on the general tone of the skin, and I have the word of reputable beauticians for this."

This writer, a native of long experience in girl-watching, will so testify on oath.

When Dr. James E. Stroh was head of the Department of Allergy at the University of Washington Medical School he advocated in all seriousness that the Chamber of Commerce should stress the total absence of ragweed in the Seattle area. "Ragweed is a principal cause of hay fever in other regions," Doctor Stroh said, "and we just don't realize how many people come here to avoid the misery caused by ragweed pollen."

Some Seattle physicians contend that our curious (almost seasonless) climate works to the advantage of our metabolism and circulatory systems. Cool nights for uninterrupted sleep are also given as a reason for the general good health of Seattleites. Statistics indicate that the life expectancy of a Northwesterner is more than a year longer than the national average, and that actually we seem to be healthier both mentally and physically. Paradoxically, perhaps, we have a high per capita number of doctors to keep us that way. This may be partly due to the fact that many young doctors are fond of the outdoor life, of hunting and fishing and boating. They may be attracted to the area for the same non-professional reasons as are so many Boeing engineers, university and college professors, and those engaged in timber and oceanography research. A truth obvious to us natives is that our newcomers—the emigration to the Northwest has never ceased—are more enthusiastic about the climate than old-timers. Not even the rain disturbs them unduly, for most are happy to have escaped sizzling hot summers and frigid winters.

Boosterism for the Northwest climate goes back a long way. The traders and mountain men were filled with tales of the health-giving qualities of what then was known as "the Oregon country." Kenneth Lynn in his fine study called *The Comic Tradition in America* tells the story of the mountain man who encountered a Britisher traveling in a steamboat down the Mississippi, secure in the belief that he was about as far west as he could go in the colonies. The Britisher confessed that he was traveling for his health as well as his education.

At this confession the mountain man hooted. "Hell, sir, you ain't even *begun* to see the West, and you can take that as gospel from this squirrel-eating alligator who has *really* been West. If it's your health you want to improve go out to the Oregon country. The Injuns out there almost never die, and white men there almost never kick out except from lead poisoning in the back or an arrow in the neck. I tell you, sir, that Oregon country is so damn healthy that they don't dare bury a body in the ground. That Oregon soil is so life-giving that they're afeared to bury a man because he's liable to come to, breathing again and fight his way out of the grave. You can see, sir, that this spoils the obsequies and causes all kinds of complications. So they embalm the body, wrap it in canvas and tie it tight high up in the boughs of one of those firs or cedars that are as big around as the pilot house on this steamboat."

Such mountain man tales, wild as they were, had effect not only on visiting Britishers; they impressed Europeans who had crossed the Atlantic and settled in the Midwest. There was always a small nugget of truth in such yarns as that "alligator" spun in the saloon of the paddlewheeler. Several tribes of Northwest Indians put their deceased high above ground.

The climate in Seattle is markedly less severe than it is in nearly all places across the nation in our latitude of 47° 36′ 32″. We are warmer, too, than many places farther south, thanks to the moderating effect of the Japanese current plus the protection of our mountains, which normally shield us from icy blasts from the north. Seattle's average annual temperature is 53.2 degrees Fahrenheit. The averages for our warmest and coldest months—July and January— are 65.6 and 41.2. Of course we have had some record breakers: 100 degrees on July 16, 1941, and June 9, 1955. The all-time low was three above on January 31, 1893. It frightened a good many Seattleites nearly to death; they thought the end of the world was on its way and not in accordance with the Bible.

Again as to that much publicized rainfall, here are some comparisons. Cities with more than Seattle's 34.10 inches, some with as much as 50 inches, include Indianapolis, Key West, Portland (Oregon), Pittsburgh, St. Louis, Atlantic City, Miami and New Orleans.

Because this is an age of air travel, we should see where we stand abroad on rainfall. Moscow has Seattle hands down on precipitation with only 21 inches, but then you know what the rest of Moscow's climate is like. It's about a standoff between London and Seattle, and generally our climate resembles that of England. The British Isles do have less rain but there is a great deal of what we here call "Oregon mist." Summers in Paris and Seattle are much alike, and the boulevardiers get only 22.6 inches of precipitation, so the late Maurice Chevalier, an occasional visitor to Seattle, had much to sing about.

All of us are becoming less innocent about climate and geography across the nation, but now and then something happens which irks us right down to our overshoes. A Boston paper announced that Seattle had suffered a fifteen-foot snowfall and published a photograph to prove it. Unfortunately for some Boston picture editor or caption writer the picture was taken at a high mountain junction called Hyak, whose small frame station stood at the eastern portal of the Snoqualmie Tunnel in the Cascades.

This was just too much for my old friend Douglass Welch, who popped off next day in his newspaper column:

> You gay, giddy people of Seattle don't realize it, but we had a fifteen-foot snowfall in Seattle recently and it all but covered one of our railroad stations.
>
> Fifteen feet—that's three squaws deep.
>
> The Associated Press's best guess is that Boston editors assumed that the word "Hyak" (plainly to be seen in the

photograph) is the Indian word for "Welcome" or "Gents Toilet." It is well known in Boston, where I was born, by the way, that all Seattleites speak nothing but Chinook and subsist on salmon-heads, dried.

I think it only proper to tell you readers where Boston is. It is situated between Hyak and Ellensburg on the Milwaukee Railroad. It is inhabited by Pilgrims and Puritans and the present Mayor is the Hon. Paul Revere. It is only a three-minute subway ride between Boston and New York City, the latter being situated on the Hudson, which empties into the Columbia near the town of Pasco near the Hanford Atomic Works. Incidentally, there was so much snow in Boston last week that both its north and south stations could not be found for a period of nearly a day and a half.

It is unknown whether clippings of Mr. Welch's column found their way to Boston or, if so, whether any Bostonians found it even mildly amusing. But of course it is this kind of broad frontier humor which delights Seattleites, even former Bostonians like the converted Mr. Welch.

So there you are. In essence, Seattle has a goodly share of rainfall throughout the year. Often it has gray skies, but—as the old vaudeville song puts it—who cares about gray skies?

In general Seattle has an oddball and unpredictable climate which both medical men and laymen insist is not only salubrious, but the finest in the world.

True or not, most of us love it.

9

The Shining Rails

WHEN Seattle overcomes its more or less regular periods of apathy it does so with an explosion that sometimes can be heard as far away as New York City. This happened in the last century when the little community on Elliott Bay approached a battle for rail connections with the "outside."

The struggle was a David and Goliath affair because the town was three thousand miles from the source of capital, and the chief enemies were successive presidents of the Northern Pacific Railroad.

Of course Seattle was not the only town on the Sound to suffer wounds and disappointments. But it was the only one which fought back, with a kind of guerrilla warfare of its own, and that was unheard of by the Manhattan tycoons.

Just about every populated spot around Puget Sound considered itself a candidate for the terminus. In truth, they all had points in their favor. It seems improbable now, but such settlements as Whatcom, Fairhaven, Port Townsend, Anacortes, Steilacoom, Holmes

Harbor on Fidalgo Island and Penn Cove on Whidbey Island aspired to be the end of those shining rails.

Naturally, the larger mainland communities figured that they were the front-runners. But population alone was not too important, for railroads made cities where they chose. So even Tacoma had hopes, although it was a while before Seattle took those hopes seriously. Seattleites were more fearful of Olympia. It was the largest and most solidly established town. Moreover, it was the seat of government for the territory. Tacoma was a loose-jointed community of not much more than two hundred people.

Actually most Tacomans did not hold high hopes, but a few indomitable souls were optimistic and from friends in Portland heard that the prize need not necessarily go to the big and strong. Seattle continued in confidence; it had population, vast forest lands, one of the great deep harbors of the world, and a certainty that its future was practically unlimited. Seattleites were all set to plan a celebration when in 1864 the powerful Northern Pacific received a charter to build a line from Lake Superior "to a point on Puget Sound."

A committee from the railroad got around to visiting the Sound in 1872, but already it had damaged Seattle's confidence by turning down Snoqualmie Pass as a route through the Cascades. Seattle felt that the selection of its favorite pass would have meant certain victory.

But Seattle was ready with other prizes, and when the Northern Pacific scratched Snoqualmie the whole Northwest went into a seizure of excitement. This accelerated when Congress amended the original act and granted the railroad permission to run a main line down the Columbia River, allowing only a spur to Puget Sound. Since Seattle had a broad, deep harbor looking toward the Pacific Rim, this action seemed idiotic to its citizens.

But the big eastern railroad had the choice and the chips, and Seattle did not. It began to shine up those prizes: 7,500 town lots, 3,000 acres of land, $200,000 in bonds and $50,000 in cash, together with as much waterfront as the road felt it would need for tracks and depot.

The railroad committee cruised around the Sound for about a week, and when the Manhattan financiers departed for home, about the only definite word they left behind was that Olympia had been eliminated. At least this encouraged Seattle and Tacoma and every remaining contestant on the Sound, no matter where or what size.

A year went by with no further word from the East, and apparently this let Seattle slip into lethargy. But the town was awakened with a rude shock on July 14, 1873, when Arthur Armstrong Denny received a telegram almost insulting in its brevity and omission of regret:

A. A. DENNY, SEATTLE

WE HAVE LOCATED THE TERMINUS ON COMMENCEMENT BAY.

R. D. RICE

J. C. AINSWORTH

The telegram was not from New York, but from the village of Kalama, the point at which the proposed spur line would take off. Ainsworth was a Columbia River steamboat magnate from Portland, Oregon, and hand in glove with the Northern Pacific. Commencement Bay, of course, meant Tacoma—and the ferocity of Seattle's feelings easily may be imagined.

Within minutes after the telegram arrived there was a gathering around Yesler's mill. A good many businessmen, thrown into panic, announced their intention to move to Tacoma as soon as arrangements could be made. But the majority of Seattleites were of sterner stuff, although for several days most citizens were in a state of shock. When this had subsided the town leaders made the only move left open. If Northern Pacific would not come to Seattle then the town would build a road of its own, through the Cascades to the east.

To outsiders this seemed a quixotic notion. But if it could be brought off there were some points in its favor. Selucius Garfielde, twice elected territorial delegate to Congress, pointed out that a route through Snoqualmie Pass to the fertile Walla Walla country in the southeastern part of what would become Washington State, could bring produce from the Inland Empire (as Spokane would later call it) and bring it cheaper than transportation by the roundabout route chosen by the Northern Pacific.

The town acted on Garfielde's premise. As Northern Pacific got the word and understood that Seattle was serious, it was the tycoons' turn to go into a rage. It was now open warfare, and one president of Northern Pacific announced, "If I had it in my power, a locomotive would never turn a wheel into Seattle." Without Seattle's spirit that could have happened, but fortunately for Arthur Denny and his followers the Northern Pacific was not the only railroad on the map.

Yet for sixteen years after Seattle did have a railroad connection with the eastern seaboard, it was impossible for an Easterner to buy a ticket to the town on Elliott Bay. The name Seattle did not appear in the timetables; the magnates of the NP eliminated it from their main plans and hoped to wipe it off the map literally. Of course this was not mere vindictiveness at the audacious attitude of the scraggly-haired frontiersmen. It was business. The railroad wanted all Seattleites to give up and move to Tacoma, where, on Commencement Bay, the magnates expected to build the one great city on Puget Sound. From their viewpoint this hope was a sensible one. It was in and around Tacoma that the railroad owned the land. And probably it was beyond their imagination that Seattle could fight them and win.

To a degree, the New Yorkers were wrong. Nothing like this had ever been attempted, but Seattle decided to try it anyhow. A company was formed called the Seattle and Walla Walla Railroad and Transportation Company and the stock was subscribed, for men like Denny had a temper, too, although they did not have much money to go with it in comparison with the powers in New York City.

The trustees (many of whom have active descendants in Seattle today) included Denny, John Collins, Franklin Mathias, Angus Mackintosh, Henry Yesler of the mill, James McNaught, J. J. McGilvra, J. M. Colman and Dexter Horton.

These new trustees traveled across the mountains on the wagon road and were warmly welcomed in Walla Walla. The farming town boasted considerable wealth from the broad wheat ranches. It resembled a New England town both in appearance and in the characteristics of the population. It was the site of Whitman College, oldest institution of higher learning in the territory.

It developed, however, that friendliness and enthusiasm were about the full extent of Walla Walla's support for the railroad. After all, "the town they loved so well they named it twice"—as Al Jolson said during a one-night stand—had avenues to Portland by land, and the great Columbia itself. At the time the Seattle and Walla Walla Railroad and Transportation Company was a far more important program to Seattle than to the cautious little ranching community. Walla Walla was mildly interested, and flattered by the visit of the Seattle men, but it was also content, whereas Seattle was desperate.

It had been estimated that it would take $4,179,910 to build the road by the lower Yakima River Valley, and $3,677,962 if the rails were laid by way of Priest Rapids near the big bend of the Columbia toward the sea. Leading Walla Wallans took a close look at the figures, and soon thereafter the problem was back where it began. In Seattle.

So the town on Elliott Bay would have to proceed on its own and refuse to let the cooling of the Walla Wallans discourage the bold plan to start its own road. There was only one way to overcome the lack of capital: the way of the founders. Inasmuch as there was a lack of money, the citizens would have to do the work themselves.

It came about that May 1, 1874, was to be a date written in bold-faced letters in the annals of Seattle. On that day few were missing from the gathering at Steele's Landing on the Duwamish River. There were no ceremonies or speeches. The male population had brought picks and shovels and everybody simply went to work.

The only gaiety came at noon, when the sweating, hungry, muscle-sore men were served a picnic-style feast by the women of the town. By nightfall a surprising amount of grading had been accomplished. The workers trudged home that night fairly well satisfied, and it was resolved that the work would proceed by voluntary labor. Every able-bodied man in Seattle would contribute a day's work each week. Nobody was exempt. Men like Denny or Yesler were expected to do their share along with those currently familiar with pick and shovel.

The beginning of the road was of course played up in the newspapers of the Sound and the news sped south and east on the wires. Considerable favorable publicity was spread across the country. It was not a good year for the nation's economy and Seattle enjoyed a new influx of population. Hundreds of young men in other parts of the U.S. decided that a town with this kind of spirit was a place of opportunity.

As might have been expected, the program of voluntary labor did not continue at the pace of the first few days. It was hoped that fifteen miles of road would be nearly ready for operation by the onset of winter. But by October there were only twelve miles of grading completed. That was not so bad, and Seattleites had no reason to relinquish their dream of shining rails topping the Cascades and sloping into the great agricultural area beyond the mountains.

Money was in short supply everywhere that year, but the trustees of the proposed road with the rather grandiose name never for a moment gave up their plans. Every little bit helped, and arrangements were made with the firm of Renton and Talbot to obtain their assistance in building a section of five miles from the coal mines at Renton to Steele's Landing.

This helped some, but there was a long way to go. Congress had turned a deaf ear to appeals for help. Even had there been a few friendly Congressmen they would have been helpless, for these were the days when the big railroads exerted power in both House and Senate.

Seattle was making the discovery that it needed a lot of things it did not yet have. It needed money, first of all. It needed friends in the national capital and New York, and it needed somebody who could lead the fight. It found such a leader in J. M. Colman, who had been sitting on its railroad board from the first.

Colman had come to Seattle in 1861 to engage in the lumber business. Four years later he was in control of Yesler's mill and a number of other enterprises. His fellow trustees could not have chosen a busier man, but they realized that the busy man is just the kind needed in times of stress and strife. He was asked to take complete charge of the Seattle and Walla Walla Railroad and instantly replied that he would accept the post, not as a compliment and honor, but as a civic duty.

After that, things began to move a bit faster. Back in Maine the new leader had been a born mechanic. But in his adopted town he had shown that he was also an organizer, financier, and possessed managerial capabilities, which the original Seattleites did not have to any marked degree.

His first action was to offer $10,000 cash on the line if five others would advance a similar amount. In connection with that proposal, he suggested that other Seattleites loan the company $30,-000, taking $60,000 in stock as security for their loan. Somehow that proposal did not strike pay dirt, so Colman—showing his own faith and earnestness—agreed to advance $20,000 if others would add $40,000. That was a lot of hard cash in those times and, wisely spent, could accomplish much. The few Seattleites who could afford it accepted his second plan.

Colman lost no time now. Immediately he consulted with Chin Gee Hee, a popular Chinese who later built a railroad system of his own in China. Hee had great influence over Chinese labor in Seattle and it was at this vital point that the Chinese assumed a prominent historical part in the building of the railroads and the Pacific Northwest. Chin Gee Hee knew where he could obtain cheap labor, a factor foremost in Colman's mind when he appointed the Chinese leader as a principal contractor in the construction of the Seattle and Walla Walla. With the line to Renton a reality, Colman's next step was to extend the rails to the little coal mining town of Newcastle. He hoped that profits from the coal routes, plus some passenger service, would impress eastern investors, perhaps to such an extent that the problem of the remainder of the line, into Walla Walla, would be solved.

With national conditions as they were, this was not to be. Even the Northern Pacific was having trouble with its financing. But this did not defer its efforts to make difficulties for Seattle. For example, any passenger wanting to reach Portland had to stay overnight in Tacoma and the same inconvenience was imposed on his return trip. The Northern Pacific was aided in this vendetta by its control of small steamboats running between Seattle and Tacoma.

During the sixteen-year battle there was an upheaval in the Northern Pacific which put Henry Villard in the president's chair. Seattle and Colman himself viewed the change with mixed feelings. Villard was looked upon as one of the great financiers of his day. When it came to railroads he knew two vital things: how to push track across the prairies and through the mountains—and how to raise money to do it.

In 1883 Villard visited Seattle and experienced a frontier welcome which demonstrated that, insofar as Northern Pacific was concerned, the town was willing to let bygones be bygones. Streets and buildings were strung with banners of welcome, cheering the name of Henry Villard. Also, Seattle was ready now with some money. It offered $150,000 to help build a standard-gauge railroad up the Cedar River Valley to connect with the Cascade division of Northern Pacific. Villard was wary of any direct comment on this proposal, but he did transact some business which made many Seattleites feel that perhaps at last they had a friend in Northern Pacific. He bought the Seattle and Walla Walla Railroad through his Oregon Improvement Company, which was an outgrowth of Portland banker J. C. Ainsworth's steamboat and portage combination on the Columbia.

From a profit standpoint the deal was favorable, and it looked as if it might be bad news for Tacoma. But all was not perfect. Seattle's connection with the rest of the nation would be by means of an extension of the Puget Sound Shore Line of the Seattle-founded company to Stuck Junction. There it connected with a spur line seven miles long and laid down by Northern Pacific to its old favorite, Tacoma. This wasn't much of a victory, and Seattle had to take comfort that its self-made Seattle and Walla Walla Railroad brought $250,000 and that $750,000 more was paid for the coal mines, landholdings and a fleet of coal ships. Financially Colman's early spadework had turned out well. But Seattle did not yet have what it wanted, and had to take temporary comfort in what seemed friendliness on Villard's part.

The bad news came the very next year after his visit. Seattle's initial uncertainty about him had been well taken, for Villard turned out to fall short of his reputation. He was forced from the presidency of the Northern Pacific and Seattle's old enemies were back in the seats of power. They refused to operate on the branch to Stuck Junction. The junction had been named long before to honor a pioneer, but now the wry joke in Seattle was that it was well named indeed.

Soon the town and the farmers along the rusting rails had enough. Once again they decided to take on the Northern Pacific. A mass meeting was held in Kent, a tiny farming community. Judge Cornelius Hanford of Seattle took charge of the program and outlined the complaints. Land for the road had been taken over by the Northern Pacific for active use, and inasmuch as that company had not performed it was time for the people concerned to take condemnation proceedings and operate the road themselves.

When the Northern Pacific officials received word of the meeting and its decision they came around—or rather, part way around. They began to "operate" the line, but on their own terms. The service was unpredictable and sometimes absent altogether. Moreover, the company decreed that Seattle merchants could receive goods only in carload lots, and extra charges were made on the slightest pretext or no pretext at all.

But new names were appearing on the Seattle scene now; a second wave of pioneers sprang up with the same indomitable spirit as the first. Judge Hanford was one, and in 1883 there arrived from the East, to stay, Daniel Hunt Gilman. He had influential friends on the Atlantic Coast, and he fell in love with Seattle and its determined citizens. He entered the railroad battle with zest.

Thomas Burke, a roly-poly little lawyer, was also beginning to be heard from. He and Gilman got together and a new plan was developed. It apparently was Gilman's suggestion that an attempt be made to secure money for the building of a line around Lake Washington to the settlement of Sumas, where a connection could be made with the Canadian Pacific Railway. The Canadians were more than willing, for they saw considerable new business as a possibility in the Gilman-Burke program.

It was Burke who circulated a petition to raise money. Circulating petitions for money was to become a regular procedure for Burke, and doubtless he recalled his first, and successful, attempt. When he had been in Seattle only a couple of years, he decided that there should be a two-plank sidewalk along First Avenue from Pike Street to Belltown near Lake Union. His own name headed the petition; he was down for a dollar and that was the amount he asked of others to whom he submitted the petition. The sidewalk, a real improvement for those days, was built. Years later Burke said, "In the East when they ask me what I do in Seattle I tell them that I'm a professional beggar. Over the years it seems to me that this is all I really *have* done—go begging for money." But Burke picked his targets with care, and was almost always successful.

He circulated his latest petition among a small group of citizens and raised money enough to send Gilman East to see what could be done with the friends he had there. Gilman returned with the welcome news that the money market there had improved.

Seattle learned a great deal in its sorties with the Northern Pacific. The earliest pioneers had been willing but somewhat innocent. Most had come from small towns, with little knowledge of money matters, and of how big business wags in the world. But now Seattle realized that a railroad took more than spirit and brawn. The later pioneers were more experienced; many had come from large centers like New York, Chicago, Pittsburgh, Boston and the like—a far different world from the little towns of the Midwest.

So new names appeared in the group that incorporated the Seattle, Lake Shore and Eastern Railroad Company. Like the first wave of fighters, they produced descendants widely known in Seattle today, and many streets and buildings perpetuate their names.

Among the incorporators of the proposed new road were Burke and Gilman, David T. Denny, younger brother of Arthur and the town's first bridegroom; J. R. McDonald, F. H. Osgood, Thomas Minor, John Leary, George Kinnear, whose great-grandson namesake would become prominent in state affairs; G. M. Haller, Griffith Davies, William Cochrane and J. W. Currie.

The trustees were Burke, Denny, Osgood, Minor and Currie. McDonald was elected president; Minor, vice-president; Burke, secretary and auditor; Osgood, treasurer; Gilman, manager; F. H. Whitworth, engineer; and Currie, superintendent of construction. Burke, who by now had fulfilled duties on a territorial bench, was of course the attorney. This appointment was the real start of his soon to be widespread reputation in the strange, rough world of railroading.

Then Burke and Gilman went East together and accomplished more than the latter had been able to do alone on his initial exploratory trip. One of the bankers interested was much impressed by Burke's liveliness and enthusiasm for Puget Sound. But he either wanted to test his faith or play a joke on the little lawyer from the big woods.

"We're ready to organize a building company and subscribe half a million," the banker told Burke. "But only if you will put in ten thousand dollars of your own."

Burke was startled. "My God, man," he spluttered, "I haven't got ten thousand dollars of my own and never did have." He paused a moment. "But I think I know where I can get it."

"I hope your hunch is good," the banker replied. "My feeling is that if you people out there can't raise at least ten per cent of the money I can't bring my associates along on the proposition. After all, from what you tell me and what I hear elsewhere, Seattle is prosperous and growing. No reason, it seems to me, why your well-to-do citizens should sit on their dollars and expect to bleed us Easterners." The banker laughed—but it was just that, a banker's laugh. He was serious and Burke knew it.

Back in Seattle, the judge made a beeline for the office of Angus Mackintosh. "Angus," he said, "we can get the money in New York, but a banker named Cotting insists that I personally put in ten thousand dollars. I don't have it, and I'm asking you to lend it to me."

"It's as good as done," said Mackintosh.

Meanwhile Gilman went ahead with his main task, the organization of the Puget Sound Construction Company. This was made up of practically the same men who had put together the railroad.

It was now one of the good times in Seattle and the country generally. The Canadians showed new interest. They saw no need to put up any money; they had a going concern in their transcontinental road. The Canadian Pacific had pushed across the Rockies—it is still the most beautiful route to the Northwest—and terminated at Vancouver, British Columbia.

The first division of the road out of Seattle was built onward to Issaquah, where new coal discoveries had been made. Today, over one of Lake Washington's floating bridges, the community is only a few minutes' drive by car. In Burke's time it was hidden in deep forests and coal seemed its only future.

The half million dollars from the Manhattan bankers was to take care of linking up Issaquah to the Sound. Future plans were to build rails to Spokane in the northeast of what would be Washington State. There it would meet any railroad that hit Spokane first, and already that city seemed a certainty as a railroad center east of the Cascades.

As the first division of the road neared completion, the initial money from New York was made available. The agreement was that every ten miles of road would bring partial payment from the East.

But near the end of that first ten miles Seattleites struck a snag. A bridge across the Snohomish River to the town of Snohomish touched the end of the first ten miles of the Seattle company's rail line. Eugene Canfield of Fairhaven, now a part of Bellingham, had his own notions about connecting Bellingham Bay with Seattle. From Congress he had received permission to build bridges across all the rivers that lay between his starting point and Seattle. He opposed the bridge plans of the Seattle company and behind this opposition suspicious Seattleites smelled Northern Pacific. Canfield obtained a writ to prevent the completion of the Snohomish bridge begun by the Puget Sound Construction Company. That put him in a position to halt the new line and interrupt the flow of money from Manhattan.

At this point Judge Burke entered the fray and what happened then would be repeated in various versions as the railroad struggle went on. Burke made haste to the depot where a group of passengers waited to make the maiden trip to Snohomish and way points. As a lawyer, Burke quickly spotted the man with the writ.

The judge realized this was no time for the slow grinding of the mills of the law. Recruiting lawyer John Leary, he climbed into the locomotive cab. Using his authority as an officer of the new road he ordered the engineer to uncouple the engine and speed him and Leary northward. The engineer entered a mild protest, but agreed to this unusual procedure if Burke would take full responsibility.

"I'll do that," Burke is reported to have promised. "Do as I say and I'll see that you don't get into trouble. All I want you to do is let her out full speed. Don't stop at Ballard. Run right on through to the Snohomish bridge."

Leaving irate passengers standing on the platform the engineer blew the whistle and followed Burke's orders. During this wild ride (the like of which would be repeated many times in the first silent movies) the judge lost his top hat, a part of the uniform of all successful Seattle lawyers.

At Snohomish the hatless and wild-eyed judge found Sheriff William Whitfield, a friend in need, and asked him how many deputies he had. The answer was two.

Asked the judge, "Don't you think there must be some desperadoes around the edges of Snohomish County and that you and your deputies ought to be trailing them for a couple of days?"

Sheriff Whitfield allowed that there were always desperadoes around the edges of Snohomish County and wanted to know what was in the air. The lawyer's reply was direct and honest. "Canfield and his crowd are trying to give us trouble in getting our bridge completed to this side of the river. There's a fellow with a writ on his way up here and we don't want it served. If you and your men keep after those desperadoes, you'll be showing enthusiasm for your job, which is stamping out lawlessness."

Burke's influence was demonstrated by the immediate departure of the sheriff and his deputies. "I'll send for you when the coast is clear," said the judge.

With all possible speed Burke and Leary put every willing man they could find to work on the bridge. It was simple trestle construction and almost finished. The volunteers made quick work of the completion. Then the engine returned to Seattle for such passengers as had been patient enough to wait. On the return journey the judge glimpsed his shining top hat in the higher branches of a cedar. The engineer offered to stop, but the trio were not adept at tree climbing and Burke decided his headgear would make a fancy abode for birds.

When the man with the writ reached his destination he found the river had been crossed and nobody appeared to know the whereabouts of the sheriff or his deputies.

It was such stories as this that soon would interest President James Hill of the Great Northern. By then, however, Burke was well off financially and the subject of an attack of respectability. His improved methods did not mar ingenuity and courage, however; he was even more effective in later years.

The first station of the Seattle, Lake Shore and Eastern was a tiny wooden structure near the foot of Columbia Street. Meanwhile the Northern Pacific built a stub line from Puyallup, near Tacoma, to the Black River and reached an agreement with the Seattleites to operate over the Seattle-built roadbed into the community on Elliott Bay. But at this stage of the game the big road was not ready to relinquish its enmity. The service was almost as bad as had been the Stuck Junction operation, and Northern Pacific's dislike for Seattle came into the open again.

Judges Cornelius Hanford and Thomas Burke persuaded the City Council to create Railroad Avenue, which is known now as Alaskan Way. It then was a broad planked thoroughfare on piling and shorelands, a hundred and twenty feet wide, set against the waterfront and its growing number of wharves. This was valuable property indeed, and Seattle offered the Northern Pacific gratis thirty feet for the new rails heading for Sumas. The NP officials never took advantage of the offer; they were angry because Gilman had moved quickly to take first choice for the Seattle, Lake Shore and Eastern.

The need for more money seemed endless, and to continue work on the Sumas route still another company was formed: the Seattle and Eastern Construction Company. The city leaders involved were those who had first shown spirit, faith and silver dollars. When they went into action again the New York bankers followed, and thus was completed a fund of a million dollars.

It was now beginning to dawn upon Northern Pacific that Seattle was in the railroad business to stay and intended to become a terminus of importance. So after nearly seventeen years of warfare the men who had tried to push Seattle into the bay made another purchase. They took control of the Seattle, Lake Shore and Eastern from stockholders in the East.

This at first alarmed the general public of Seattle. But men like Leary, Gilman and Burke recognized that the battle with the Northern Pacific was practically over and that Seattle was winning. The big wheels in Manhattan conceded, one by one, and with reluctance, almost every point that had been at issue over the years.

In the final analysis, Northern Pacific had not harmed Seattle. On the contrary, it had taught the community some valuable lessons in how a city is built. In the early nineties the town on Elliott Bay was basically prosperous. It boasted a population of more than 40,000 people, most of whom took pride in its modern buildings, its progress as a rail and maritime center and its beginnings of a street-car system.

Many years later when the town was fighting for more airlines to land at the Seattle-Tacoma International Airport (about halfway between Tacoma and Seattle and operated by the Seattle Port Authority), it set no limit as to the number of lines it would consider adequate and for which it could arrange accommodations.

A federal aviation official asked a city leader named Edward P. Carlson, "Just how many airlines do you people want out there, anyhow?"

"We'll fight for all the traffic will bear," Carlson answered. "Our skies are big, and the city has never stopped growing." Carlson had risen from a hotel garage attendant to board chairman of Western International Hotels, a worldwide chain with headquarters in Seattle. He didn't suppress a grin when he added, "If you'll look at that desk globe of yours standing up, instead of sitting down, you'll see that Seattle is, in a way, the geophysical center of the whole world!"

In 1970 the Western International Hotels merged with United Airlines and the holdings of the two created a complex called UAL, Incorporated, with headquarters in Chicago. A short time later Carlson became president of UAL and moved his office to the big midwestern city. Perhaps "moved" is not the word, for Ed Carlson is a true Seattleite. "I'm not really leaving town," he told a friend. "You're looking at a man who is going to be the busiest commuter in the country!"

It was Carlson, years after the railroad fight, who created the motto "All the traffic will bear." That was the feeling of earlier Seattleites when the subject was railroads.

There was another big railroad in Seattle's dreams of the future, after the Northern Pacific had been brought around to what Seattleites called plain horse sense.

That railroad was the Great Northern, headed by James J. Hill, the railroader who had heard of Thomas Burke and remembered his name. Hill was the kind of man that Seattle and other Pacific Northwest communities could understand.

The story that endeared Jim Hill to Seattleites involved an oral engagement he had with Jay Gould when Hill was relatively young and new in the world of high finance and politics. He was born in Canada and at eighteen turned up in a town called Pig's Eye and, on second thought, St. Paul.

Certainly Jay Gould, when his moment came, had never seen anybody quite like Hill. The transplanted Canadian was stocky, huge in chest and shoulders, with arms and legs which seemed just a bit short for the rest of him. Over one eyeless socket was a black patch hiding a childhood injury. The black patch, the grizzled hair, the beginning of a mustache and beard, the sharp clear eye which could change in an instant from an expression of thoughtfulness to ferocity—these all combined to create a human being exuding character and force.

The young wandering Canadian stopped in St. Paul because he was attracted by a job. This changed his original plan, which was to find a ride on a Red River cart, a two-wheeled vehicle that would carry him to some trappers' brigade headed for the Rockies and beyond. He had done a lot of homework and his amazing ambition on the way to St. Paul was to reach India and put Mississippi-type steamboats on the Hooghly and Brahmaputra rivers, and he knew exactly what sections of those rivers would be likely to furnish the most passengers and cargo. The boy—a man, really, by then—very probably would have accomplished his plan, and Seattle would have lost forever a favorite "son." But there were no Red River carts in sight when he arrived in the town that had been Pig's Eye.

There was, however, a job, and Jim Hill never wasted time. He had been in town twelve hours, in that year of 1856, when he heard of a job as clerk with J. W. Bass and Company. It was in that job that Hill became fascinated with the transportation possibilities in his adopted United States. When the Red River carts appeared he ignored them. He stayed with the Bass Company, and when it was sold he went with the deal as one of its finest assets. He was always working; he was always asking questions about transportation, and getting or finding the answers.

Jay Gould, the fancy New York financier, never forgot the brief visit of Hill years later and described him as "a veritable gorilla of a man . . . His beard burst asunder, the thick lips snarled back, and from between the huge teeth there came a series of hoarse, growling barks."

Gould was to find that Hill's bite was equal to his bark; they were combined and equal. The essence of what Jim Hill had to say to the most powerful millionaire in North America was this:

"I've got a railroad now and I intend to fetch it up on the shores of Puget Sound. I had Congress persuaded to allow me to build across Indian reservations, but now I find that your paid henchmen in our government are trying to block me. I say to you and to them that you have played hog in this matter as long as you're going to be permitted. Unless you call off your bushwhackers, I'll tear down the whole railroad business. I'm going ahead with my plan if I have to go to Washington and camp there until I nail every one of your crooks to the doors of the Capitol by their ears!"

It developed that no such heroic measure was needed, because lawmakers and lobbyists had found that Hill's threats were never mere words. One-eyed Jim got what he wanted. By 1877, with three partners, he had bought the sick St. Paul and Pacific Railroad, and out of that action grew the Great Northern Railway system. Eventually the line would be known as the "Empire Builder" and in Seattle the title meant the man as well as the road.

Almost every literate Seattleite could quote Hill's challenge to Jay Gould, and they knew that actually he did build empires. He caused great expanses of land to prosper, and in a genuine sense he formed the base for the Pacific Northwest lumber industry, a base upon which it built the complex and diversified wood-using business it is today.

Although others had made the claim, nobody in reality could push a rail line faster and cheaper than Hill. This allowed him advantages which literally staggered his competition. He was full of ideas; they were ideas he put into motion and they worked. Immigrants were pouring into New York by the shipload and Hill offered them a rate of ten dollars if they'd settle along the Great Northern tracks. For a few dollars more an immigrant family could use an entire freight car to carry household goods and even farm animals. Hill knew what would happen in a very few years; the hard-working foreigners along his route would prosper and furnish freight.

Hill was no absentee rail official as so many others had been. He was likely to appear anywhere, any time, where work was in progress. He was known to climb out of his special car and help shovel snow off the route. Wherever he was, that one sharp eye took note of the soil and water, and he gathered statistics on climate, too.

For a long time he had that eye on what would become Washington State and its fabulous resources. Years later at the Alaska-Yukon Exposition he recalled, "I called a group of lumbermen together and they said they could ship their lumber East if we made them a rate of sixty-five cents a hundred. I told them they were wrong, that they couldn't move any large amount if they paid more than fifty cents. Then and there I offered them a rate of forty cents on Douglas fir and fifty cents on cedar. I told them the rates would be effective immediately."

It is easy to imagine the hard jaws of those timber barons dropping. They had never heard talk like this from a railroad official. It was not long until a large lumber trade was in the making, some of the footage going clear to the Atlantic Coast. For the time being, however, the great bulk was distributed throughout the interior West, north of St. Louis and the Ohio River. Jim Hill wasn't just running a railroad. He was helping to build the United States.

Sometimes one of Hill's solutions created another problem. When that happened he rarely rescinded his first decision but went to work on the new problem. He found that he was carrying too many empty cars East. So he set to work creating new markets for Oregon and Washington lumber in the Midwest and East.

There were many facets to the genius of Jim Hill and an important one was his ability to pick men. He knew that this was vital, and it was in his character that he would hear of Judge Thomas Burke in Seattle and that he and the little lawyer would get together.

Hill visited Seattle and there was little in or about the town that he missed, but—and in this at least he followed the pattern of other railroad moguls—he left without leaving any clue as to what he thought or what his plan for Seattle might be. Undoubtedly that was because he hadn't yet thought the matter through, for he wasn't a man to hold back good or bad news if he had made up his mind. Spokane had found out that much about him.

However, he left Fairhaven in doubt also, although the town on Bellingham Bay had offered a free right-of-way, and more than that if he wanted it. This was unsettling to Seattle because Hill's proposed routing through Skagit Pass seemed to give Fairhaven a definite edge, and it was considerably closer to that avenue to the Pacific, the Strait of Juan de Fuca.

Better news was on the way, but it came quietly in the shape of Col. W. P. Clough, one of Hill's attorneys. He arrived incognito and not even the newspapers around the Sound got wind of this important stranger. For some time only Judge Burke knew of his arrival and the reason for it. The lawyer could hardly keep himself in his chair when Colonel Clough told him that One-eyed Jim had decided on Seattle as his western terminal point.

Clough stipulated, "We want a right-of-way and plenty of room for terminal facilities. I'm telling you because Mr. Hill wants you to represent him here. Within reason, he'll give you a free hand and full authority. In other words, you can do whatever is necessary—providing, of course, that it is reasonable from our point of view—to see that this city lives up to a promise of an unobstructed entrance and no trouble from the council or the legislature. Mr. Hill has reasons to believe you can manage that. Will you take it on?"

Burke said that he would be delighted, and honored as well.

Of course the news had to leak out due to the activities of Burke. The town had experienced plenty of disappointments, and no celebration took place or was planned. By now Seattle wouldn't believe anything about a railroad until it saw a chugging locomotive and a string of cars.

Hill was certain that he had chosen the right man in Seattle, but it was not long until he had definite proof. Burke began picking up lots and with every offer he made the promise that the Great Northern would not pay a higher price to anybody else with property of equal value.

However, there was a bit of a slip. One property owner was a resident of St. Paul and an acquaintance of Hill's. He held out for more money than Burke was paying, and in the rush of business Hill agreed to the price on the premise that not much difference in money was involved and the difference wasn't worth fussing about.

When Burke got the news—and he got it straight and casually

from Hill himself—he staged a miniature version of one of his boss's rages. At once he fired off a telegram to St. Paul:

IF YOU PAY YOUR FRIENDS MORE THAN YOU PAY MY NEIGH-
BORS PLEASE CONSIDER MY RESIGNATION IN YOUR HANDS.

Hill knew that he was in error, and realized also that out in Seattle he had a man who wasn't afraid of him and would risk a fat retainer rather than break a promise. As sheepishly as Hill could resemble a sheep he showed Burke's ultimatum to his friend. "It looks as if we're in a corner. The matter is in Burke's hands and you'll have to deal with him." The St. Paul man had a key piece of property; had he held firm he could have ruined the works, but also he could imagine what this would do to his relationship with Hill. At once he communicated with Burke to accept the judge's offer.

Obtaining the land for Great Northern was a long and arduous task for Burke, and the Northern Pacific tried to block every other move he made. But Burke had encountered the enemy before. He worked with speed and finesse that left the NP officials perpetually confused. Moreover, the judge was staging the battle on home grounds and he had plenty of influence in the City Council and the legislature.

Piece by piece Burke got the land together. But in a deal of this kind there is always at least one recalcitrant tougher than Hill's friend in St. Paul. Others had made sacrifices for what they felt was the good of the Empire Builder and the town. But this citizen— properly nameless in the records of Seattle—held out for $10,000 and refused to shave his price by a single penny.

Now it was Burke, not the boss, who was in a corner. His telegram to Hill months before had stated a position that now the judge was going to have to trim. Probably he didn't admit even to himself that he was faced with a situation which demanded a little bending of his character. Even more probably he excused it because it was for the good of Seattle. In any case, he didn't want Hill to know that he had managed to meet the price, and the railroad magnate never found out.

Burke's method was the usual one, with as much secrecy as possible involved. His argument to the sophisticated—who knew what was going on—was simply that Seattle had made promises to Hill and must not fail to fulfill them. If that happened, Burke warned, they would all be face to face with Northern Pacific again, and the fiery Hill would transfer his affections to Fairhaven.

Inevitably the point came when Burke was preparing another petition. He had salved his conscience for keeping from Hill the deal with the stubborn citizen. What he got for $10,000 was terminal room almost a mile long and two blocks wide. One-eyed Jim was pleased indeed.

So in his broad hand Burke put himself at the head of the petition for a thousand dollars. Practically on tiptoe and conversing almost in whispers, Burke circulated the petition among nine others: Jacob Furth, John Collins, John Leary, Angus Mackintosh, Henry Yesler, Arthur Denny, Dexter Horton, Amos Brown and J. M. Colman. Thus he raised the $10,000 for the greedy villain who lacked the Seattle spirit.

The Northern Pacific, which had wanted to ignore Seattle completely, now found itself in a complicated struggle as to who could get what in the stubborn city on Elliott Bay. Naturally Judge Burke was in the center of the fight, and the City Council was the body from which action must come. The Great Northern, whose admiration for Seattle had come tardily, had to see to its own arrangements and forget to hate Jim Hill. It did not get far with the council. Burke was pleased to be able to send to Hill a telegram reading:

CITY COUNCIL STOOD BY YOU TWELVE TO ONE AND THE ONE CAME IN TO MAKE IT UNANIMOUS.

One-eyed Jim was delighted. The message made him feel really a part of the town which already had adopted him. But actually it was Burke, as much as Hill, to whom the council gave its support. Some years later Charles Mellen, who had become president of the Northern Pacific, told E. H. Harriman: "I hear you plan to enter the city of Seattle. If that is true the first thing you had better do is get permission from Judge Thomas Burke out there. He was Hill's attorney and when it comes to railroading he's got everything in the bag."

Seattle now had railroads, but its depots were a disgrace to citizens who were beginning to feel they lived in a modern city. The Seattle stations were not much different from the hundreds of small wooden stations that still dot the continent from the Atlantic to the Pacific and from the Great Lakes to Deep South.

But everything cannot be accomplished at once, and Burke felt in need of a rest. He decided that he and his wife should take an extended trip through Europe. Of course on his way to New York he paid a call on Jim Hill.

The railroad magnate said he had some maps and drawings he wanted Burke to look at. He unrolled the plans and architect's sketches and Burke gasped. They showed a tunnel straight under Seattle, running north and south, a plan which previously had been suggested by City Engineer R. H. Thomson. "This plan," Hill said, "will give the people of Seattle a depot they can be proud of, and we won't have to be cluttering up your lovely city with surface equipment. A major depot for a major city, and trains hidden underground. What do you think of it all?"

The judge sighed, but there was a familiar lively look in his eyes and suddenly he seemed no longer tired. "I think it's magnificent, Mr. Hill, and I'm going to postpone my trip to Europe. I don't need to tell you that it's a big project and lot of preliminary work will be involved."

"I'm sorry to spoil your trip and please give Mrs. Burke my apologies."

"She'll understand," Burke promised. "Those places abroad have been there awhile, and they'll be there for a long time to come. And if I go back to Seattle with plans like these my neighbors will decide that they aren't getting tired of seeing me and my petitions, after all."

The modern station was a reality by 1905 and—wonder of wonders—the Northern Pacific and the Great Northern were running through the tunnel side by side, and sharing the depot.

Ed Carlson's motto "all the traffic will bear" was prevalent in Seattle in the latter days of the railroad battles, long before jet liners were dreamed about. Seattle was still hankering for more shining rails in and out of the city, and there was still disappointment because none of the big roads had chosen the city's proposed route, the Snoqualmie Pass through the Cascades.

Then, rather suddenly and without fanfare, the Chicago, Milwaukee and St. Paul decided to use the Snoqualmie Pass as its portal to Puget Sound. The road drove its first spike for the line in 1905 and by late 1906 the bright yellow cars were running clear through to Elliott Bay. It was a tremendous feat of speed in railroad construction, but what pleased Seattle old-timers most was that the Chicago, Milwaukee and St. Paul used the grading that the pioneers had begun with their own hands years before.

Seattle was by no means finished with railroads. In 1910 Harriman realized he had better get into the Puget Sound picture. This was no surprise, for the company had begun three years before to buy up tideflat lands south of town. J. D. Farrell, president of the Oregon-Washington Railroad, was determined that there should be a full-fledged link with the Union Pacific. An astonishing feature of his strategy was that he asked nothing from Seattle. Perhaps he realized that now the town was in the driver's seat and it was long past the day when citizens would bargain. Farrell was pleased when his interest in the tideflats created an exciting land boom in the lower end of town. For some years the tideflats had been considered a problem, and there was a difference of opinion as to whether they would ever be useful. Indian shacks bordered their inshore line, and high planked roads required an intricate system of piling. But the stirring of the Union Pacific created the kind of action that in its periods of euphoria Seattle has always admired. The land speculators went into action and fortunes accrued overnight. Too, fortunes were lost overnight, and that was part of the game.

The Union Pacific ran its first train into Seattle on New Year's Day of 1910, its destination a small temporary depot. But already it had broken ground for what then seemed a gigantic and beautiful station—the finest, Seattleites claimed, between the Far West and Chicago. This opened on May 1, 1911, and was used also by the Milwaukee, which ran its first train under the sheds on May 25 of that year.

In 1916 Clarence Bagley, one of the most definitive of early Seattle historians, summed up the situation by saying that Seattle's place on the railroad map was fixed "but there will be more rails to come." The forepart of his prediction was true enough, but as to the future Bagley naturally did not foresee what would happen in air travel, nor could he know that in another year a man named William Boeing would build his first airplane. Bagley did have a glimmer, no more than that in the year before our entry into the First World War, that the automobile would become important. In 1916 a car trip over the Snoqualmie Pass was an adventure.

In this mid-century most observers of the railroad situation—for example, Stewart Holbrook, author of *The Story of American Railroads*—felt that Seattle had become "over-railroaded." Four major lines: the Great Northern, the Northern Pacific, the Milwaukee, and the Union Pacific were chugging in and out of two great stations through a vast tunnel, or up and down planked Railroad Avenue, which subsequently became smoothly paved Alaskan Way, with a concrete overhead freeway for motor traffic. The four roads became three in 1970 with the merger of the Great Northern and Northern Pacific into the Burlington Northern.

Yet Bagley was partly right. There were more rail cars in Seattle's future. In effect, Seattle got a "new" road when, in 1972, the Milwaukee was awarded rights to serve Portland, Oregon. This action by the Interstate Commerce Commission meant that the Milwaukee could operate a direct freight service from British Columbia to Oregon. Fred Tolan, probably Seattle's most widely informed freight consultant, said, "This is really an exciting development. It stems from the Burlington merger and adds up to a widespread and new competitive action in the region's transportation industry. I should think it will mean another round of industrial development in rail-owned lands in the Green River Valley just south of Seattle." In other words, friendly as the skies may be, additional freight service by mail is still an incentive for expansion and a key determinant for plant location.

As to the passenger situation, Seattle is now the western terminal of Amtrack's northern route to Chicago. And for people who prefer a more leisurely pace and a closer look at our natural beauties, Amtrak provides one train a day to eastern points.

So really Seattle has not written *finis* to the battle for rails. Those early Seattleites had started it all when they gathered in shirt sleeves, with picks and shovels, in that May of 1874. Often the town is slow on the starting line, but once it has made a beginning it rarely stops and anything and everything seems probable.

The long and sometimes bitter fight for railroads left a deep impression on Seattle, and somehow that impression has passed from one generation to another. There is a legend that if in the pre-dawn you go into the dome car of one of our transcontinental trains—just as the pink is showing from the east behind the jagged white peaks of the Rockies—you may see a strange sight indeed:

the shades of Hill, Harriman, Mellen, Villard, and other railroad moguls of the past, all quarrels forgotten, marching arm in arm through the passes of the Great Stony Mountains. I used to know three or four old-timers who swore they had seen this through the misting windows of a dome car. As a native Seattleite, I believed them.

But I think had they looked more closely they would have noticed another figure, a stocky lawyer called Judge Burke, born 1849 in Chateaugay, New York, of Irish immigrant parents. It was somehow sad and fitting that when he died in St. Paul in 1926, he was brought back to his beloved city in a special Great Northern car—brought back to the town that was two years younger than he when he arrived at the age of twenty-five.

10

The Big Fire

Two decades before, Mrs. O'Leary's cow had kicked over a lantern in barn straw and set off a famous holocaust in Chicago, news of which went around the world.

On June 6, a Thursday in 1889, Seattle had a careless assistant in James McGough's paint and cabinet shop in the basement of a wooden building on Front Street facing Elliott Bay. The assistant remains nameless, which is a pity, for he was the man who really began a new city and created the "Seattle Spirit" about which much was said in years to come.

There had been no rain for more than a week. By days a gray ash from forest fires filtered down on a thriving town of more than 25,000 people—not, of course, counting Indians, whom census takers still pointedly ignored. At night the distant skies shone pink from such fires, which in those days were usually allowed to burn themselves out, or blow into fiery extinction by a self-created explosion called a "blowup," or be taken care of by an inevitable rain.

Most towns then in midwestern and western North America were built largely of wood, even down to the sidewalks and streets. Fires were common. In Washington Territory there were two others that year, one in Ellensburg and one in Spokane, across the Cascade Range. But Seattle was particularly vulnerable because much of its business district was built on piling, and when its fire began there was a ready-made draft beneath the lower streets, creating an impossible situation for firemen, both regulars and volunteers.

It was around two-thirty in the afternoon when the cabinet-maker's assistant allowed a glue pot to boil over on the stove. The flaming glue ran down onto shavings, which said little for the housekeeping of James McGough. And the flustered assistant, instead of looking around for a blanket or getting very busy with a broom, poured water on the fiery floor. This only spread the flames and Seattle's Great Fire was under way. The possibility had been in the mind of every thinking citizen. Indeed, Dexter Horton had built his bank—formerly operated from a safe in his grocery store —of stone. His foresight was thwarted because the heat was so terrific that in a few hours the walls were gutted—but not Horton's dream; its survival is seen today in the tall skyscraper called the Seattle-First National Bank Building.

Within a few minutes after the blaze in the cabinet shop, bells began to ring, steam whistles of docked ships sounded off, and the dread cry of "Fire!" moved throughout the town.

It was already too late. North of Columbia Street and on the west side of First Avenue was a waiting row of wood frame structures, mostly two stories in height, with a sawmill, lumberyards and many wooden sheds between them and the wharves. Streets and buildings were mostly on creosoted piles, so that the fire began traveling both above and below the downtown district.

The fire department was hopelessly inadequate, and its appearance on the streets brought cries of derision rather than encouragement. Water pressures were low or inadequate. Unfortunately, the fire chief was in San Francisco attending a meeting designed to help prevent what was going on in his town two thousand miles to the north. On the shore of the Golden Gate he listened attentively to lectures, having left matters in charge of an acting chief who was thoroughly inexperienced. The latter's duties were taken over almost at once by squared-jawed Mayor Robert Moran. The first equipment to arrive on the scene was a hose cart pulled by men and boys. Within a few minutes "No. 2 Hose" had got up steam at Second Avenue South at the corner of Main, and soon was directing a stream at the black mask of smoke pouring from retail stores. Already the owners of these establishments, with help from bystanders, had begun to carry their goods outside. As the fire spread, their inventories were moved farther and farther toward the hill on the east as flames and heat threatened them. And already there was a brisk business in tents.

It has been mentioned before that somehow great events in Seattle develop into a comic operetta, and the Great Fire—inasmuch as there were no tragedies and few casualties—was no exception. Soon a steamer pump came into view and made for a low wharf at the foot of Columbia Street. The idea was to pump from the bay, and it would have been excellent strategy had the tide not been out. The crisis was not far off; as each new hose was brought into play the strength of other streams was weakened. It did not take long to reach the capacity of the water main. Within an hour the most effective means of fighting the fire were the old-fashioned bucket brigades.

Already the telegraph office had clacked out messages for help to Tacoma, Portland and all the sizable towns between. Tacoma and Seattle were arch enemies, but this was no time for feuds. Even before its message arrived citizens of Tacoma had seen the black smoke rising over Seattle and were loading hose and men on a flatcar of the Northern Pacific. Unfortunately the town on Commencement Bay had no fire engine, but considering the state of the Seattle water pressure such equipment could have done little good. Yet the Tacoma firemen, having made the "run" from their hometown in sixty-three minutes, formed additional bucket brigades and helped in preventing the fire from spreading into the residential area on the forested hills.

Aid from abroad produced little more than good will at the height of the fire, but in a few days the women of neighboring towns, chiefly Tacoma, would be invaluable in helping with the distribution of food as Seattle struggled out of the ashes. Second in line with a Silsby engine was Olympia, which brought the equipment in less than four hours on the steamer *Fleetwood*. A little later a train from Portland arrived with a Silsby and a crew of men who were considerably delayed by the impossibility of finding a place to unload on the waterfront, which was now a shambles of goods, abandoned wagons and terrific heat blown in by the usual summer northwester.

Even as the first local hose crew arrived, the entire row of two-story buildings between Marion and Madison streets was masked with smoke so thick that merchants had difficulty in moving out their goods. Flames were not visible until planks were pried up from the sidewalk at the northern end. When that happened the fiery furnace erupted. To the realistic it was plain that the business area was doomed.

Yet fire fighters with their piddling hoses, their useless ladders and their sweating bucket brigades worked on through the day.

At such a time only the contemporary view is wholly dependable. Next morning, operating from a flatbed press under a tent, the *Post-Intelligencer* spread this story on its single page, twelve hours after its wooden plant had been burned to the ground:

A SEA OF FIRE

———

The Business Part of
Seattle in Ruins.

———

Sixty-four Acres of
Ground Swept

———

Thirty-Two Blocks
Of Smoking Debris

———

The Loss Will Exceed
Ten Millions

———

A little Blaze at Madison
Street Becomes a Giant of
Destruction Ravaging All
The Lowlands to the South
—Fire-proof Brick and

Frail Wood Alike Food For
the Forked Tongue—
The Phoenix.

The business portion of Seattle is in ruins. Between the hours of two and three o'clock yesterday a wall of flame sprung up at Madison and Front Streets, traveled southward to the waterfront in a column whose left swept long Second and Third streets and whose right licked up the docks, wharves and warehouses of the waterfront.

In this area, a spread of over twenty blocks, only blackened walls and ruins mark the spot where yesterday stood the city's commercial center. At this time the true loss is incalculable.

The fire was caused by the overturning of a glue pot in Jim McGough's paint shop, under Smith's boot and shoe store, at the corner of Front and Madison streets in what was known as the Denny Block.

In an instant the whole paint shop was in flames and the fire burst through the floor above before a single thing could be carried out of the room.

The Denny Block was a frame structure, extending along Front Street from Madison to Columbia, running back to the alley. The basement and hallways seemed to serve as flues to draw the flames, for black clouds of smoke poured from every window, door and crevice in the structure from one end to the other, within five minutes after the first alarm was given.

The flames, however, had only burst from the north end of the building and the fire department set to work to check the fire which at this juncture seemed easy to control. Engine No. 1 attached to a hydrant at the corner of Front and Columbia streets, and Engine No. 2 took its turn at the rear of the building and commenced pumping salt water.

A cheer rose from the crowd as the beat of Engine No. 1 was heard and two streams of water were turned on to the fire, but the cheer of hope died into a wail of despair when after a few minutes pumping the streams became so weak that they did not reach the top of the building, showing that there was no water with which to fight the fiend of fire, which by this time had reached the center of the building.

Almost given up was any hope from the fire-fighting equipment. Stores were broken into, not for looting, but for the purpose of carrying goods into the streets, where they were flung down in heaps. About twenty minutes were allowed for this. By then the whole block was in flames from one end to the other. There followed a Herculean effort to save the row of buildings on the east side of Front Street, just opposite the Denny Building. No thought was then given to the Opera House, despite the tiny puffs of smoke from some of its windows. Its solid walls looked impervious. But then someone cried, "The Opera House is on fire!" and, surely enough, an arrow of flame shot up from the mansard roof. By this time the Denny Block was a sea of flame, and it was out of the question for firemen to stand in front of that wall of fire to work on the Opera House.

The wooden buildings north of the Opera House were meeting the general fate of the theater and the rest of downtown Seattle. Men were driven back with scorched faces and smoking garments. The hoses even began to melt; the firemen dragged them back, detached them, and tried to meet the enemy from Second Avenue. Mayor Moran and Councilman Durie—ignoring the acting fire chief—attempted to bring some order out of the confusion. Parties were organized to bring merchandise and furniture out of the buildings and Police Chief Butterfield swore in a hundred deputies, instructing them to arrest—or shoot, if they had a weapon —every man found looting. It was probably fortunate that few were armed, for it was not always easy to distinguish a looter from some distracted clerk or store owner. But at least the mob took on a semblance of organization moved by intelligent leadership. Small boys were thrilled to see the big Preston hook-and-ladder truck tearing up Front Street, now First Avenue, and into Columbia to reach the rear end of the Opera House. But the building was already a skeleton. Canvas scenery and wooden-framed "flies" and "wings" had helped to fuel the flames.

"At four o'clock," wrote the publisher-editor of the *Post-Intelligencer*, "the flames leaped across Marion Street and the Colman Block on the West and the Renig Building on the east side of

Front Street became the center of the fiery sea." Busy with his pencil and notebook the newspaperman was the only able-bodied man not ordered into action—except for more than two hundred prisoners in the city jail. That is an interesting number of jailbirds in a town of hardly 30,000. Soon the busy mayor had them shackled together and marched to the relative safety of the Armory. The staggering line was made up mostly of drunks who shook their fists and wished the flames all success. One report says that the felons broke into song.

A traditional method of fighting the fire was brought into play at about this time. Large charges of dynamite and other explosives were shoved under the center of the Colman Block, but this effort proved abortive as the large building burned from one end to the other. The explosions shattered the windows of the the big brick blocks south of Columbia and several people were injured by falling glass. At five minutes past four the brick Kenny Block on the corner of Front and Columbia caught fire at the top. This forced Engine No. 1 to pull up and attach at the corner of Cherry Street. Before a stream could be started again every building north of Columbia Street was afire.

The San Francisco Block seemed to be the next possible barrier to the flames. Every window was covered with soaked wet blankets and once again a charge of explosives was tried. And once again the method was ineffective, only shattering the structures, and sending burning brands aflying. Retired General J. B. Metcalfe led a party of brave men to the roof of the White Building and a hose was pulled up by a rope. But when the valve was opened only a trickle of water showed itself and the daring party scrambled down again to the street.

"The breeze from the northwest freshened again," reported the morning paper, and this was a bad omen. "At twenty minutes past five the fire had reached the Seattle Hardware Building, adjacent to which twenty tons of cartridges were stored."

The fire fighters had already escaped a fusillade from the Gordon Hardware Building, and had learned what to do now. Run as far as possible until the ammunition was exhausted. The excitement of even an organized mob can be suggested by the fact that nobody, not even Mayor Moran, had thought to have the shells moved to some safe place on First Hill. But the fire was moving too fast now for considered thought. At almost exactly six o'clock

the fire jumped Cherry Street and only twenty minutes later reached
the southern end of the block. In half an hour the flames had
consumed the establishment of sign-painters Harris and Greenus,
Mrs. Story's music studio and Pieser's "culture studio" adjoining.

One by one of the basic businesses of the city were going.
The *Post-Intelligencer* resumed the toll:

> The Haller Block, a one-story frame structure, was
> reached in an incredible short time, and soon razed to the
> ground. This was occupied by J. A. Ames, printer; Mrs.
> Lynch, dressmaker; A. Fisken, stationery; McLaughlin and
> Bridges, hardware. These firms lost all except the small
> moveable items. Boy's photograph gallery, on the opposite
> corner, was next enveloped. The buildings in this block—
> the Northern Pacific Land office, the St. Charles Hotel, and
> the Congress Saloon, were swept away.

But all was not lost. The Boston Block was saved, and it was
one of the finest structures in the town. Two bucket brigades were
formed, one extending up the front stairs to the fourth floor
and another reaching across Columbia Street and into another entrance as high as the second story. This freed the fire department
equipment to concentrate on the Front Street brick establishments.
Despite the lack of water the Colonial Block was saved, but in
the next half-hour the buildings between James and Cherry, on
Second Avenue, were destroyed. This left the way clear for the
Occidental Hotel, reached by the flames at about six o'clock.

The flames had by now swept down Front Street nearly to
Marion before crossing to the north side of Madison. The Commercial Mills disappeared, and once again the flames found footing
beneath the piling, attacking the blacksmith shop, and then the
afternoon newspaper, the Seattle *Times*. Efforts on the latter
proved useless and, like its competitor, it would soon be operating
from a tent on the hill.

Now the warehouses and the wharving on the north side of
Madison ignited, and some of the bucket brigades were resorting
to the use of garden hose rescued from the destroyed hardware
stores. But warehouse after warehouse fell with resounding crashes,
sending up great showers of sparks. For a few moments an excavation for a proposed Holyoke Building checked the progress of the
flames and did save the next block and the residents of Second

and Third beyond Spring Street. But the west side to the bay's edge was one great fiery caldron.

The Starr brick block was in flames by 5:30. The fire was confined to this building for a time, but swept on back through the mills and warehouses and again reached Front Street through the burning of the Oregon House and the electric light works.

The fire at the north end was finally checked at University Street. A few doors south, on Front, stood a story-and-a-half frame house owned by Jacob Levy. Here another bucket brigade was formed with the aid of water from the Denny house. Levy's friends were enthusiastic, rallied to his support, and within a short time from sixty to seventy men were in the brigade. A pessimist in the crowd offered to bet a dollar against a hundred that the place would not be saved. The press reported:

> The bucket brigades were proving their mettle else-where. One outfit of perhaps two hundred men extended from the waterfront to the corner of University and Front Street, and by hard work prevented the fire from spreading by way of the wooden sidewalks on the south side of Front. It took several hours of labor to stem the tide at the north end. But by 8:30 p.m. all danger of a spread in that direction seemed at an end. The residents of the North End began to breathe easier and to thank God that they would not be burned out of house and home. The firemen performed miracles in this area when it is considered that not a drop of water was at their command.

It looked as if the fire was determined to concentrate its efforts on the merchants rather than the homes which sprawled here and there on the nearby hills. The flames were still at work along the waterfront. The docked ships, having loaded aboard much of the rescued goods, moved out into the bay to keep away from the hellish temperature. Everything was razed to the south, and Yesler's wharf, scene of so much of Seattle's commerce, was gone within the space of five minutes.

The morning paper reported this phase:

> The flames were increased by the violence of the evening wind. A squad of several hundred men, com-manded by Mayor Moran and H. W. McNeil of the Oregon

Improvement Company, commenced tearing down the wooden buildings on the north side of Yesler Avenue from *The Post Intelligencer* to the foot of the street. They were almost entirely successful, but to no avail, for the flames crept along the scattered ruins and then leaped across the street, taking everything in their path.

At this point began a new and destructive blaze. The tempest of flame was roaring down Front Street. Curiously, the Yesler-Leary Building resisted the onslaught for some time. But at last the flames entered by a rear entrance and the end was not long in coming for this Seattle landmark. The walls of the Poncin Block and the Merchants Bank had hardly fallen when the lofty peak of the Yesler-Leary structure burst aflame. The flames were walking with a steady beat along the wooden row toward Yesler wharf. By twenty minutes past six o'clock the fire had destroyed every building up to the Butler Block.

Now and then, above the roar of flames and the shouts of fire fighters, the frightened sound of the prisoners in the Armory could be heard. Obviously they felt that they were likely to be roasted like bricks in an oven. But martial law had been declared, and United States Marshal Hunt and the sworn-in deputies were brooking no nonsense. The offenders were never in danger, from within or without the Armory, but nonetheless Sheriff McGraw had encircled the building with an armed posse. Seattle had lost much that long frightful day but justice would be served.

The editor-publisher of the morning paper was furiously taking notes, which he had yet to transcribe into cold type on a printer's stick, then set on stone beneath a hastily erected tent beyond the ruins. But he never faltered. This was Seattle's biggest story since the founding in 1851 and he was well aware of it.

Straight to the south with even front moved the terrible wall of flame. Main street was reached by seven o'clock. The Squire Brick checked the flame only a few moments, then succumbed, adding to the intensity of the scene. The roadways from the buildings all had burned, making escape to the hills difficult.

In the district south of Yesler Avenue there were more than a hundred and fifty hotels and lodging houses. The inmates of these places were escaping with their lives and what they wore, and considering themselves fortunate. The Seattle Transfer Company saved its teams and most of its vehicles. South of Yesler Avenue the walls of Schawbacher Brothers, Harrington and Company's brick and stone buildings, and parts of their contents, are now, with the Dexter Horton Bank walls, the only standing monuments to this once busy mart.

The Arlington Hotel, once one of Seattle's finest, was gone. It was only there that death hovered near, when guests tarried too long in an attempt to save valuables and keepsakes.

It had been thought that the courthouse would be saved, but by nightfall its appearance was what the *Post-Intelligencer* could only call "magnificently terrible."

The setting sun showed blood red through a vast haze of smoke. The air was so charged with heat that breathing was difficult. The firemen, realizing now the futility of it all, had withdrawn to the comparative safety of the foothills and sprawled in exhaustion.

The little blaze that began in McGough's cabinet shop had become a giant and had its way. Seattle's downtown district was no more.

But it was the beginning of a new Seattle and an attitude that was to be known, proudly, as the "Seattle Spirit." While the embers still burned red, a meeting of Mayor Moran and leading citizens was held. The first decision was to send to sufferers of the Johnstown flood the sum of nearly seven hundred dollars which had been collected before disaster struck the city by Elliott Bay. That was a sizable sum for the time and could have been used at home, but charitable pride as well as spirit were at work that morning.

The records of the fire are told from the viewpoint of the Establishment and nothing is said about the hundreds thrown out of work by its devastation. Emphasis is put upon the fact that the residential section remained intact.

Promise of new employment was implicit, however, in the plans made at the post-disaster meeting. Representatives of banks promised loans for new construction, and it was determined that the new city would be of masonry and brick, designed against fire. The water system would be made adequate as soon as time would allow.

Said an editorial in the *Post-Intelligencer*: "From the ruins will spring a new Seattle, just as from the ruins of Chicago there sprang a new and mightier Chicago."

That is exactly what happened; and it happened, to use the frontier phrase, in jig time.

11

Gold—Yellow and Black

THE whole country was in one of its frequent doldrums. But citizens of Tacoma and Seattle felt themselves particularly marked by the evil fates as sites of what in the eighties were called "panics." The Tacoma unemployed were actionists. In 1897 they seized a hotel, stole all the food in the kitchen and storerooms, then began hauling out furniture with the hope of selling it for passage money to Washington, D.C. The governor stepped in with troops and the rebellion came to nothing.

Seattle's unemployed were more easily controlled. They were trapped by the police in the Skid Road area, like Indians on a reservation. That was their natural habitat anyhow, but they lacked the price of a "flop." They camped in the streets around small fires, subsisting on squirrels and rabbits, which could be found in the forests back of town. All they lacked was cheap wine, and this deprivation made them easier to control.

But Seattle in general, farthest community on the continent, literally sunk in hills of clay, overshadowed by great trees which looked black in the summer rain, was as badly off as Tacoma. As the natives put it, the town was "in the dumps for sure."

Isolated despite the railroads, which were of little comfort without passengers or cargo, and unable to diversify beyond its main industries of timber and fish, Seattle was what today would be called a disaster area. But it knew better than to appeal to Congress and the President. Any Seattleite could tell you that it had never had much help from the East Coast and the politicians.

Its merchants, slipping and sliding in the clay mud from their hilltop homes to their places of business near the waterfront, wore faces as long as their beards. True, they had built a "modern" city on the ashes of the Great Fire eight years before. But what good was that without commerce, with the sawmills dawdling or shut down completely because the San Francisco timber market had almost vanished, and fish were bringing lower prices than the skinned wild rabbits hanging in front of butcher shops?

Yet there was hope for the future—always there is hope for the future in Seattle, no matter how bad the situation. Let Tacoma call itself the "City of Destiny"; Seattleites knew that theirs alone was the city of destiny on the Sound. If Tacoma was afraid to define its "destiny" Seattle was not. Its destiny, proven throughout its brief past, was a lucky one, and Seattleites made it so. Refusing defeat from the powerful Northern Pacific Railroad, hadn't the city begun its own railroad twenty-three years before?

Now there was a new report that could mean a change for the better. A ship had landed at San Francisco with gold from the Yukon Territory up North. With the berthing of that ship came a report of a gold strike—a big one. If this new rumor panned out, the little fish and lumber town, ready with its practically new stone and brick downtown district, stood right in the path of a prosperity such as it had never known.

The proof came on Saturday, July 17, 1897. There really was gold in the Yukon Territory, apparently by the ton, by the millions of dollars' worth. On that Saturday in July the steamer *Portland* arrived, and its cargo and passengers brought Seattleites to attention, cheering their lungs out.

The *Portland* had made it through the Strait of Juan de Fuca and sent a wireless as she rounded Cape Flattery. Geographic conditions blocked the message for Elliott Bay, but the press wire services in San Francisco obligingly relayed the golden message.

Within minutes virtually all of Seattle crowded the waterfront. The planks and piling of the wharf assigned to the *Portland* began to creak, and the police had to push part of the mob back onto the railroad tracks stretching north and south behind the piers. They also had to fish from the bay several inebriated gentlemen who had begun their celebration early and with enthusiasm. Residential areas were emptied of men, women and children. Merchants locked their doors so that they and their employees, if any, could witness the great event. Already they knew it was a great event, because an enterprising newspaper had sent a reporter down the Sound to intercept the vessel. Via tugboat and Jacob's ladder he was able to board the *Portland* as she stood off Port Townsend for customs clearance, and the newspaper had an extra on the street a good five hours before the ship resumed her way toward Elliott Bay.

The *Portland* entered Elliott Bay as a heroine with whistle pluming and a cargo that would change the history of Seattle—as well as the great Northland—for all time.

That morning's edition of what was one of the biggest newspaper scoops on the Sound sold out in a quarter of an hour. Later in the day there were other extras, complete with editorials oozing optimism and predictions which, despite their fanciful language, turned out to be accurate.

The headlines served to fan the excitement. One five-bank banner read:

GOLD! GOLD! GOLD! GOLD!

Sixty-eight Rich Men On
the Steamer Portland

STACKS OF YELLOW METAL!

Some Have $5,000, Many Have More
A Few Bring Out $100,000 Each

THE STEAMER CARRIES $700,000

One Puget Sound paper carried a banner line which said simply: A TON OF GOLD ARRIVES! It was not quite accurate, but it was near enough for Seattleites who had awakened in gloom and now were almost incoherent with happiness.

Whatever the exact amount, the gold brought by the lucky passengers was the real thing. The stories of what was yet to come promised even more excitement. Nobody was concerned with the geological fact that many nuggets encase granite or compressed gravel. Seattle as yet had no assay facilities, but the citizens and banks soon would take care of that.

In Captain Kingston's cabin were three chests and a safe filled with bags of nuggets and gold dust. The estimates made on the southward trip did place the value at $700,000, which in 1897 was near enough to a genuine million to rock Seattle to its foundations. Also it is probable that some untrusting passengers in the *Portland* wore beneath their woolen shirts money belts crammed with gold dust and smaller nuggets.

All of the gold had been taken out of the ground the previous winter. The nuggets shown the reporter in the captain's cabin ranged in size from "that of a good-sized pea to the size of a guinea hen's egg." Of the sixty-eight miners aboard only one or two men had less than $70,000 worth of gold, and at least three reported that they owned $100,000 in the yellow metal. Captain Kingston, as protector of the precious cargo, endorsed the statements made by the miners and he was the man who had signed the receipts for what went into his safe and checked the contents of the chests which were stored in his cabin.

What's more, the miners all had stories of others who had made similar strikes and were awaiting ships in the North. Most of the miners had taken the treacherous overland trail from Dyea north and back, a route that meant mile upon mile afoot and considerable distances on homemade rafts or rude vessels built on the shores of wind- and snow-swept lakes and streams.

The first strikes were made in the Yukon in Canadian territory but Alaska herself would soon be heard from and thus would be forged a lasting marriage between Seattle and what is now the forty-ninth state. It would not be a marriage in which Alaska would find continuous happiness, but always Seattle has been overjoyed at any good fortune which comes the way of Alaskans. The reason is all too obvious: Seattle shares in the bounty and, over the years and particularly in earlier periods, has taken more than what might be called fair advantage of her geographic position in relation to the Northland.

A peculiar feature about the first strikes in the Yukon was that the tenderfoots—"cheechakos" became the word for them well into the present century—had fared better than grizzled, experienced miners who for years had been fighting, cursing, praying and hoping for a smile from Lady Luck. Literally thousands of these, over the years since gold was first reported in the North, had suffered unbelievable hardships with only a few hundred dollars—or nothing—to show for their efforts. But a few hundred in dust, or a stray nugget, or a report from over the mountain, kept them at it. On the narrow-gauge railway which now runs from Skagway to Lake Bennett there are still to be seen vestiges of the steep and ragged trail left by the boots of miners nearly three quarters of a century ago. It was plain hell to get to the "gold fields" and just as hellish to get back, and more so if the return trip was made without some gold in the pack.

As the first reporter to "cover" the Yukon strike put it: "Fortune seemed to favor the inexperienced men who went into the district only late last year. The stories they tell seemed beyond belief. Instances are noted where single individuals have taken out in two and a half months gold to the value of $150,000 or more."

Some of the miners had made their second try, however. Clarence Berry of Fresno, California, had gone North in 1890, prospecting for seven years without the luck a miner needs. He returned home, married, and went North a second time. The bride, who must have been the soul of optimism as well as deeply in love, brought him the good fortune he had missed as a bachelor. Mr. and Mrs. Berry were aboard the *Portland* with $135,000.

The Fresno man modestly reported that "with a miner it is all luck in the final analysis." Why the reporter failed to elicit comment from the wife will never be known. "I was real fortunate because last winter I took out $130,000 in thirty box-lengths. A box is twelve by fifteen feet. In one length I found $10,000 worth of nuggets and dust washed down. Also I got the second biggest Yukon nugget that's been heard about so far. It weighs thirteen ounces and is worth at least $300. I know men who have taken out a thousand dollars a day over several days in a drift claim. Of course you understand that gold is found in pockets, not in solid veins like some metals, and I tell you those pockets are not easy to find."

Berry was one of the few experienced miners who struck it rich. More typical among the *Portland's* passengers was Frank Phiscator of Baroda, Maine, who had gone to the Yukon as a tenderfoot and was returning with over $96,000. He had worked two claims with nine men for three months, and still owned the claims. Phiscator was one of the original discoverers of what came to be known as the new El Dorado district.

Knowing that the arrival of the ship would trigger a rush to rival that of the emigration to California years before, Phiscator too had sober advice for Seattleites, many of whom had already booked return passage in the *Portland*.

He told eager citizens who flocked around him that the Northland was not a poor man's country, that nobody should go there without at least a ton of grub (which had to be backpacked on the trails), a full outfitting of warm clothing, at least a year's supply of both—and, above all, a resignation to suffer great hardships. Other miners advised that a cheechako should carry enough money to hire help.

On the latter score already there had been labor troubles up North. The going wage was fifteen dollars a day, and some miners had tried to lower the rate to ten dollars. They had no success at all. That was understandable when one considers that many of the hired men fed themselves and that flour was sixty dollars a sack and other provisions proportionately high. My grandfather went to Alaska relatively late and found that a hen's egg might sell for a dollar. "And it would be a cold storage egg, at that," he told me. There were no vegetables, and no milk except the condensed kind in cans; my grandfather became so used to it that for years later, although living outside, he preferred it to fresh milk.

Only a few of the sixty-eight passengers from the *Portland* were from the Puget Sound area. Many came from California, where a great gold rush was a tradition of the state and the entrance to the harbor had been christened the Golden Gate forever. Most of the miners were from tiny unheard of towns in the East and Midwest, farmers and handymen, and loggers—men with callouses already on their palms, from climates not by any means beneficent.

Among the few Puget Sounders in the *Portland* was Richard Blake of Dungeness, a village on the Strait of Juan de Fuca. Bearded almost to the waist, his visible features red and blistered from his northern winter, he stepped off the gangplank and announced to one and all that he was taking his sack of nuggets to Dungeness and would stay there. "That's where I was born and that's where I intend to die, and I'm taking no more chances to get richer."

William Stanley was the only passenger who gave residence as Seattle. He had gone to the Yukon the year before and was coming home with $90,000 in gold; he had left two husky sons to guard a pair of claims in his absence. Obviously he intended to get richer.

T. J. Kelly and his son were from Tacoma and had made $10,000 the previous winter. He, like Stanley, was going to return. "I tried to get passage on this tub we came down on, but she was all booked up for the return trip."

There was another Tacoman, Jack Horne, known as a pugilist around the Sound. He had gone to the Yukon the winter before to work an interest in a claim, and was back with $6,000 in his poke. He admitted that was far more than he could have made in the ring, and added modestly, "I wasn't headed for the championship anyhow. I think I'll go back up there, but I want to get this stuff assayed and get the money in the bank."

Harry Anderson was from Sweden but well known in Seattle. He had sold half his claim on El Dorado Creek and was the only arrival with spot cash, $45,000 of it. "I'm going back," he said, "as soon as I can get a new outfit together."

None of the miners from the *Portland* expressed publicly a longing for a wild fling with part of the hard-won gold. But certainly in ships following the *Portland* would come many a got-rich-quick prospector who would run through his gains in record time, forgetting how hard the trail had been, how long the discouraging months, how backbreaking the toil. Seattle would be ready for such as these, too, and in record time. Not long after the news of the *Portland's* cargo had flashed around the world, business on the railroads picked up amazingly. Much of it was hastily ordered freight that would find its way into the stocks of the mercantile establishments. But prominently visible among the passengers were barkeepers, gamblers and fancy women.

In a 9 A.M. edition of the *Post-Intelligencer*, on the same day of the ship's arrival, two interesting advertisements appeared on page one.

The firm of Cooper and Levy warned: "Don't get excited and rush away half prepared. You are going into a country where grub can be more valuable than gold, and frequently can't be had at any price. We can fit you out quicker and better than any firm in town. We have had lots of experience and know how to pack and what to furnish."

Inasmuch as Messrs. Cooper and Levy had not been North their experience might have been questioned. But one must admire the swiftness with which they adapted their advertising copy to the new era. The rest of Seattle's merchants would be quick to follow.

On the same page was a message from Joseph Mayer and Brothers, who until then had been leading fairly quiet business lives as wholesale and manufacturing jewelers. Hastily they had changed their banner line to read "GOLD DUST" and inserted this copy: "We pay highest prices for gold dust and bullion. We keep a full supply of all sizes of gold scales."

Doubtless figuring that many a cheechako would be nearsighted, they reminded readers that in their store was Miss F. Wilzlaski, graduate optician. It would not be long before Miss Wilzlaski was advertising on her own, suggesting that departing miners buy several pairs of spectacles in the event of loss or accident, "both of which can be prevalent in the rugged North Country."

The man most responsible for tying Alaska and Seattle together inextricably was Erastus Brainerd, who, nonetheless, fares badly or not at all in the earliest histories of the town. A Connecticut Yankee who certainly could have sold sawdust for nutmeg, Brainerd, alone and unaided, sold the idea that Seattle was the Gateway to Alaska and the *only* such portal. No publicist or group of boosters in other towns could touch him; he was too energetic and too filled with ideas.

He had been an editorial writer on the New York *World*, then associate editor of the Philadelphia *Press* and the famous Atlanta *Constitution*. Handsome, urbane and highly cultured (he had written a book on art and was curator of a Boston museum), he was not the happiest choice for editor of the Seattle *Press*, which a Philadelphia friend had bought and sent Brainerd West to run. In 1890 Seattleites yawned at his scholarly editorials and his essays on foreign lands. But when gold was discovered in the North Brainerd found in himself an unsuspected talent. He was a public relations expert far ahead of his time. To a sizable advertising campaign in magazines and eastern and midwestern newspapers (Seattle merchants pooled together to foot the bill), he added ingenious devices of his own which cost not a cent. He brought Seattle plus Alaska to the attention of the nation and parts of Europe. He planted in the mind of the average non-Seattleite the notion that Alaska and the town on Elliott Bay were practically one and the same.

Brainerd himself did not cash in on the Gold Rush. When the

first excitement was over and his task as publicity man was finished, he experienced a brief period in Alaska as a "mining consultant," a role for which he was unfitted. Later he became editor of the *Post-Intelligencer,* and although he had learned much about frontier tastes he was no match for Col. Alden J. Blethen, who had come from Minneapolis to found the Seattle *Times.* Blethen's elegance in dress and manner disguised a rough, tough interior, and he ran Brainerd into the ground. Finally the former Yankee moved to Tacoma, where he died in obscurity in 1922.

While that Gold Rush was in progress the change in Seattle was phenomenal. This was due, of course, not just to the value of the gold itself. The population soared. There was a tremendous upsurge of commerce and of highly profitable sin. Genuine mansions (extremely ornate with every combination that a carpenter with a scroll saw could create) sprang up on First Hill with far more speed than a fir seedling. Front Street and Second Avenue came alive with new honky-tonk joints and houses of joy. One New York visitor came away convinced that there was a saloon for every fifty citizens and he expressed his convictions in a letter to the New York *Times.* Seattle was getting a reputation that rivaled that of the Barbary Coast in San Francisco, but in reality it was never quite that bad. True, now and then a bloated anonymous body washed up on the tideflats and bumped against the wharf pilings. The public servants were inclined to let sinful matters ride along. Not every murderer was apprehended or, if he was, got before a judge. When that happened his chances of freedom were good, because already the town had a fair share of criminal lawyers with friends in the right places.

Three of the whorehouses were so elaborate that not even the later film industry would be able to exaggerate their plush red velvet interiors hung with oil paintings of provocative nudes. Some of the gambling houses rivaled the joy palaces in furnishings and art. Certainly their owners were the best-dressed men in town. It would be a long time yet before other Seattle males would pay much attention to dress. We were still a frontier town. Businessmen, for the most part, looked as if they belonged in their surroundings.

Bankers, if unaccompanied by wives, tipped their derbies to the like of Diamond-tooth Lil, a leading madame who had decided that a large diamond imbedded in a front tooth would add something to her smile. It certainly did, and well might the bankers lift their hats to Lil. The accounts of the houses of prostitution were not to be overlooked, and neither were the girls Diamond-tooth Lil took under her protection. Whenever she received a shipment of new ones she attired them in a fashion so ladylike that the genuine ladies of First Hill were infuriated. It was Lil's habit to parade her flock up and down Second Avenue with the finest teams and open carriages available for rental. This was the most effective kind of publicity, and Lil had ceased to be concerned about the refusal of newspapers to carry her advertising. A petition to the mayor, signed by more than a hundred women who considered themselves respectable, pleaded that this blatant public appearance of prostitutes be confined to the vicinity of Yesler's mill and similar areas. But somehow the petition was mislaid among the mayor's official papers.

Alaska is still an unknown land to the great majority of Seattleites and the Alaskans properly resent this, too. Actually the Alaska "panhandle," which dips down through Canada and holds the town of Ketchikan precariously on a mountainside, is only a few hundred miles from Seattle. But the gold discoveries were much farther north, and when at last the excitement of the rush expired a renewed apathy of Seattle toward Alaska was noticeable.

Even today only a tiny percentage of Seattleites have visited the neighbor that has done so much for them. Not long ago I made my fifth sailing along the beautiful inside passage as far north as Skagway. In the passenger list of a hundred and thirty-five my family and I were the only ones from Seattle. The majority were from California, and many were from the Midwest. Today, of course, much of the travel is by air, and this communication is for business reasons mainly.

Regularly the Seattle Chamber of Commerce sends to Alaska a missionary committee of members particularly interested in the state. The trip is a bit rushed, usually led by the mayor of Seattle and other civic leaders. The Alaskans are hospitable, as always. But I think some of the chamber members would be a little downcast if they knew the true feelings of many Alaskans about these junkets. Recently I followed in the wake of one and in a bar or two posed as a man from Missouri, learning considerably by the shameless ruse.

One Alaskan commented: "Those characters don't come to really see the country and find out some of our problems. Of course, there are a lot of fine speeches about the historical relationship between

Seattle and Alaska. We reply in kind. What the hell, we're civilized. But damned near every one of those chamber pots has an order book in his hip pocket, and you can bet he'll flash it every chance he gets."

Alaskans have a tremendous pride in their land, and don't enjoy being regarded simply as a market that is backed into a corner without much chance to do a little dickering. The days of the Gold Rush are not forgotten; the stories have been passed on to the new generation. They know how Seattle merchants sold at the highest possible prices, and how they sent tenderfeet North with Rube Goldberg contraptions which were utterly useless.

The value of gold and commerce in the nineties is not a matter of accurate record. Curiously, insofar as Alaska is concerned, this situation has changed only a little. The Port of Seattle alone keeps open books on shipping to and from the Northland. As an example, the figures for 1969 (which dipped somewhat in the following year of recession) showed more than a million tons of cargo, valued at $800,000,000, producing a payroll of more than $30,000,000. In an average month forty vessels of various types depart Elliott Bay for Alaska, and this number is definitely due for a rise.

Added to this is air cargo, much on the increase with the building of larger planes. In one month it is not remarkable for 1,800 tons of freight to clear the Seattle-Tacoma International Airport and sail into the gray skies yonder. Nor is it unusual for 60,000 air passengers to depart for, or arrive from, the young state to the north. Yet there is still no central depository of facts which would indicate just how vital Alaska's commerce is to Seattle. We know it is important, but we don't know *how* important. As Dan Coughlin, business editor of the *Post-Intelligencer*, puts it, "It's an odd and pitiful state of affairs. The ups and downs of Boeing business should have taught us that full knowledge as to the value of Alaska to our economy is a necessity. There should be machinery for checking as to the value of commerce between other Puget Sound ports and Alaska. We ought to know exactly where we stand."

This curious lack of commercial data involving Seattle and Alaska is a reflection of something more than apathy or tardiness among the business community. Erastus Brainerd taught Seattleites, as well as others, to take for granted the liaison between Seattle and Alaska. We are hypnotized into a condition that makes us believe that we really *are* the main Gateway to the North. However, there are some Seattleites who fear that we may be in for a rude awakening unless we mind the store with a little more care.

These cynics point out that Vancouver, British Columbia, has grown into a metropolis which, some say, may outstrip Seattle and Portland together in the Pacific Northwest. There is a lot yet to happen in the provinces west of Ottowa, and Vancouver is the funnel through which must pass much of the commercial results of the dominion's agriculture, its tremendously strong wood-using industries, and its growing number of multi-industry complexes.

The same Cassandra types in Seattle see a greater future for Everett, once a straight sawmill town, jarred into the twentieth century by the huge expansion of Boeing in Snohomish County. And Bellingham, which has plenty of room to grow in, almost touches the U.S.–Canadian Boundary and is closer to Alaska than any Northwest city except Vancouver.

But when you invite the average Seattleite's attention to these conditions he is more than likely to say, "All right. So much the better for everybody on the Sound." Meanwhile insurance companies, machinery firms, general supply houses and food distributors are not anxious to throw into a public information pool the amount of business they are doing in Alaska.

Eagle-eyed old-timers of Seattle took notice that when, on January 3, 1959, Alaska became a state, there was an undercurrent of uneasiness in the city by Elliott Bay. True, the newspapers dutifully editorialized in favor of statehood for the rugged territory, and many papers on the Sound issued special editions when at last it happened. That was of course the neighborly thing to do. And for a week or two after the celebrations grammar school children repeated dutifully, "Alaska is the forty-ninth star in our flag. Her flower is the forget-me-not. Her official tree is the Sitka spruce. Her bird is the wild ptarmigan, and her motto is 'North to the Future.'"

But when the speeches were over, the editorials forgotten and the last firecrackers had exploded in Juneau and near Seattle's Totem Pole, there was speculation as to precisely what would happen now that Alaska was a part of the Union with true representation in Congress instead of merely a more or less powerless delegate. With the psychological surge which statehood brings would there be changes in the relationships between Seattle and Alaska? Actually a real concern pervaded some of the businesses which had counted the territory as an important customer. As the old history teachers used to ask, "Was this a good thing, or a bad thing?"

Thus far it looks as if it is a good thing, both for Seattle and Alaska.

In fact, a very good thing had happened already—and caught most Seattleites napping. The event was far more important to Seattle than the arrival of the *Portland* in 1897, and would have more lasting effects.

Again it was a discovery of gold, but this was Black Gold, as they call hot oil.

Seattleites had paid scant attention to the finding of oil in the Navy's Petroleum Reserve No. 4 in 1944. Although the Japanese had been chased out of the Aleutians, the North Country and the Pacific Northwest were still on a war footing. Furthermore, the Navy had played down its holdings of an oil reserve in the North. A few Seattleites noted that "Pet 4" was a 47,000-square-mile area just below Point Barrow, and some old-timers recalled that there was where Will Rogers and Wiley Post had met their deaths in a plane crash after a visit to Seattle. Those aware of "Pet 4" noted that the government had not opened the area to drilling and there was no sign that it intended to do so.

Nor did Seattle excite itself about some commercial drilling on the Kenai Peninsula and off Cook Inlet, southwest of Anchorage, which would become Alaska's liveliest city.

Then came the Big One—the discovery of Black Gold on Prudhoe Bay's north slope in 1968. This meant that Alaska, only 300,000 people in 586,412 square miles (making it the biggest state in the Union, nosing out Texas) had struck it rich again—and, by the shade of Erastus Brainerd, so had Seattle.

But curiously, when the name Prudhoe Bay popped up in the news, most Seattleites didn't even bother to find out exactly where it was. Some, however, had a vague idea that it was just about the northernmost edge of the western part of the continent, lying just south of the polar ice cap and the Beaufort Sea, which is an ocean of ice.

Of interest to the big oil companies was its location at the western end of the fabled Northwest Passage. That brought up the question as to whether icebreakers and barges could move oil eastward. Humble Oil Company built two ice-breaking vessels at a cost of fifty million dollars and made two voyages with them before deciding that this route was impossible. This heart-breaking and hull-crushing experience was more good news for Puget Sound—but Puget Sounders looked at photographs of the icebreakers, yawned, and turned to the sports pages or the comics. Yet a transPacific pipeline winding south to the ice-free port of Valdez on the Gulf of Alaska was now more important than ever; it was the only way to go. From Valdez gigantic tankers would move the oil down through Dixon Entrance at the Canadian boundary, then farther south to—where else?—Seattle and neighboring ports.

There was as yet no official signal from the federal government, but the oil companies were not wasting any time. Already they had shipped 600 miles of four-foot-diameter pipe and piled up the sections to await assembly. There would have to be 200 more miles of pipeline to come. The oil companies were getting ready, but was the federal government?

For a time the federal government was stalled by outcries from ecologists and conservationists. They warned that the hot oil in the pipeline, particularly where it ran above the surface, would melt the permafrost around and under the line. This, they said, would create a bog into which whole sections of the pipeline would collapse. Conservationists also feared that the line would interfere with the migration of caribou that numbered 600,000, twice the human population of the young state. The oil companies' rebuttal was that the line would create a warm belt against the sometimes sixty-five-below temperature in the central wilderness of Alaska.

Then the Eskimos, accompanied by lawyers, joined the conservationists. They were encouraged by rebellions of Indians "outside" over broken fisheries treaties. Were Eskimos citizens of the new state or weren't they? That would be a difficult question to answer in the negative, and lawsuits loomed on the horizon of the Northland. There would have to be a fight, or considerable negotiations, even though the Secretary of the Interior was Walter J. Hickel, who had been the second governor of the forty-ninth state. The oil companies were banking on the fact that Hickel was a tough Alaskan who knew first-hand the state's need for income, the kind of income that oil brings. But also Hickel had expressed concern over the quality of the North's environment, the necessity of preserving wild-life and wilderness areas. As governor he had shown concern for the Eskimos, an attitude at sharp odds with the attitudes of most "outside" governors toward the plight of the Indians.

Many others "down below"—including residents of Puget Sound and Seattle—expressed concern about such a huge movement of hot oil through the center of North America's last frontier. They were also wary of the big tankers because on both coasts and the Great Lakes there had been spillages which created havoc with wild-life and shorelines generally.

There would be a struggle, and concessions, but nobody—ab-solutely nobody—stops oil worth billions of dollars. Nobody stops oil, which is almost the central product in a modern nation's in-dustrial economy, and affects the mobility of the average citizen wherever he lives.

Doubtless it was on these premises that the oil companies kept moving. The former Trans-Alaska Pipeline System was reorganized into the Alyeska Oil Pipeline Service Company and set up head-quarters in Seattle. The chief executive was Edward L. Patton, a Standard Oil of New Jersey executive who knows a thing or two about oil, about refineries and about the politics that an oil discovery in-evitably arouses.

Alyeska is a consortium of eight companies, and the fact that its name is the Aleut word for "Great Land of White to the East" did not appease the Eskimos. The more astute of their leaders knew from the first that they would be fortunate to come away with a settlement, but with the ecologists and the conservationists they succeeded in stalling the project for nearly four years. Seattle had almost forgotten it.

The city stayed calm when Alyeska took up headquarters there, even though this had to mean that the consortium was moving from the planning and talking stage into preparations for actual construction. There was no such excitement as there had been with the discovery of gold in the Yukon. Seattle was basking in one of Boeing's periods of prosperity, and still recalling smugly that it had brought off a genuine, official world's fair. Prudhoe Bay, wherever it was, could lie frigid and white and quiet.

It took a recession, and severe cutbacks by Boeing, to make a lot of Seattleites start yelling for Alyeska oil and to hell with the risk of spillages. At last it had dawned on the city what Prudhoe Bay could mean.

It meant a million-and-a-half-dollar pipeline 800 miles long and thousands of new jobs. It meant ultimately two million barrels of oil a day rushing through that pipeline to Valdez. It meant that Alaska was already a billion dollars richer from north slope oil leases, and due to become a lot richer.

It meant the upsurge of attendant industries, some unknown. For not even the best geologists are certain about the total wealth that lies beneath a state largely unexplored. Oil revenue meant, first and foremost, that new roads can be built in the state, and these roads can lead to hard-rock mineral deposits which have been locked away for aeons of time since some cosmic upheaval created Alaska and the chain of islands that curve like a scimitar toward Kamchatka.

It could even mean, eventually, the realization of a dream of Senator Warren A. Magnuson of Washington State. He envisioned a railroad, with bridges and ferries, along the Aleutian chain, linking the United States with Kamchatka and Russia. That would take a lot of ferries and a lot of bridges and one gigantic bridge—but the senior senator comes from a state which has thousands of bridges of various kinds and operates the largest ferry system in the nation. When the friends of "Maggie" scoffed, he said, "All right. Then what about a combination rigid and floating bridge from a point just north of Nome? That's only fifty-five miles. Or an auto or rail ferry system?" Well, it is a well-known fact that Washington State's bridge engineers consider no span impossible. People kept telling them that they couldn't build a floating bridge across Lake Washington. So they went ahead and built one; then a second eight-lane crossing, which is the longest floating bridge in the world.

Whatever his dreams, the Senator knows for certain that Alaska oil means that some day, probably soon, Alaska can get at the eighty billion tons of coal on the north slope of the Brooks Range just to the west of Prudhoe Bay. On the south side of that range are huge copper deposits, and on the east commercial amounts of phosphate rock. Everybody who knows anything at all about Alaska knows that it is heavily mineralized, and there may be additional gold, far more than was found in the original discoveries.

Alaska needs highways and railroads. Oil is just the magic that can create them. Already there is talk of extending the Alaska Railroad from its Fairbanks terminal to Prudhoe Bay. Such an expansion would supply the oil region with equipment and might even assist in hauling oil to refineries and Alaska ports. Uncle Sam owns the railroad now, but would let it go for a hundred million dollars. That will look like chicken feed to Alaskans when the oil starts running south. The pipeline alone will begin with half a million barrels a day before reaching the probable maximum of two million barrels.

Then the word came from the Secretary of the Interior that the stringent requirements demanded by the government would be met by the Alyeska group. The latter had agreed to rigid inspection measures costing two and a half million dollars and posted a five million dollar bond to cover any damage to the Alaska ecology. Alyeska also had agreed to protective measures on the huge tankers that would be coming to Elliott Bay and neighboring ports. It had even agreed to a federal inspector aboard each tanker.

None of these protective measures completely satisfied the Eskimos, the ecologists or the conservationists—but the secretary had given the green light and hardy men would soon be working in sub-zero temperatures at nearly the top of the world. Valdez would be waiting, and Seattle would be waiting.

The day that new Secretary Morton gave the signal, I enountered Henry Broderick, pioneer Seattle realtor, returning to his office from the exclusive Harbor Club, which looks down on that part of Seattle where the city began. At eighty-two he had even more of a spring than usual in his step.

Grinning broadly, he looked up and down Second Avenue. "Where in hell *is* everybody? There ought to be dancing in the streets. That news from Prudhoe Bay should make the Alaska Gold Rush excitement look like a nickelodeon on a Sunday afternoon."

"Would you advise young men to rush North?" I asked the man all Seattleites know as "H.B."

The grin grew broader. "No. I'd give them the same advice I gave in 1901, the year I came from Minneapolis and went into real estate. Invest in land in and around Seattle. I haven't been wrong on that yet."

He knew that once again Seattle had turned toward a lucky streak. He knew that it could have a bad run of cards, but that it wouldn't lose the game.

12

The Seattle Revolution

A BRIEF period in Seattle's history which it chooses to
forget was a five-day general strike in February of 1919. It was the
first general strike in the nation. It frightened the United States
at many levels, but the scare was sharpest in the Pacific Northwest.

The region was already disturbed by the presence of representatives of the Industrial Workers of the World, unpopularly
known as the IWWs or "Wobblies" and believed by conservatives
to be as dangerous as German imperialism or Russian bolshevism.
Indeed, many thought that the IWWs were puppets of the bolshe-
viks, but the movement was wholly a reaction to the confrontation
of American labor and capital. It was, in brief, one result of the
quality of American life in the years between 1877 and the First
World War.

The strike had its origins not too far from the shores of Elliott
Bay in the fierce labor-management battles of the mining states of
the Rockies. It was a rebellion against the poverty of tens of
thousands of workers. It urged class warfare and believed in non-

violent direct action and promised revolution. Actually the "Wobblies" could claim little credit for the Seattle Revolution, but it
was easy for regional industry and capitalism to blame them. The
decline and fall of the Industrial Workers of the World was due
not so much to failure as to success. It did much to frighten the
contemporary Establishment into decent working conditions, particularly in the mining and logging areas, and was a spearhead
for today's respectable unionism.

Its marching song struck terror in the hearts of the majority
of Seattleites:

> Arise, ye prisoners of starvation!
> Arise, ye wretched of the earth!
> For Justice thunders condemnation.
> A better world's in birth.
>
> No more tradition's chains shall bind us;
> Arise, ye slaves! No more in thrall!
> The earth shall stand on new foundations;
> We have been *naught*—We shall be *All!*

Already blood had flowed in clashes with the American Legion
and the police, some of the latter in the pay of the timber interests.
There were tragic fatalities on both sides. The confrontations had
taken place in Everett, to the north of Seattle, and Centralia on
the south. This was close enough to alarm Seattle, and to shake
the beliefs of Mayor Ole Hanson, who had been friendly to labor
and was called radical by a town to which the big World War
had brought prosperity.

There was another individual—it did not take more than one
or two—to make lumbermen, cannery owners, bankers and shipyard
executives shake in their boots. This one was a woman: Anna
Louise Strong, whose path was certainly leading toward Moscow
although she seems not to have known this in the beginning of
Seattle's first serious labor uprising. For some years the lumber leaders particularly had been ignoring the grumbling of the workers,
and the fish cannery owners (most of whose plants were in Alaska)
had been buying cheap labor from Chinese entrepreneurs. The
cost for the season might be no more than several hundred dollars
and enough sacks of rice to keep the Chinese laborers going through
the salmon run. It was indeed a profitable picture, and the fish

canners were among the most valuable depositors in the city's banks. A mayor who had shown signs of radicalism and a determined woman turned labor leader were disturbing signs on what had been a happy horizon.

Anna Louise Strong was the daughter of a pacifist minister of Seattle and although she had been elected to the school board with the support of conservatives it was now remembered that she had issued pamphlets against war, strongly implying that young men should not volunteer. Naturally she did not long remain on the school board. A petition was issued for her recall and enough signatures obtained to put the issue before the voters. Anna Louise Strong lost, and the defeat crystallized her conviction that her country was on the wrong track. She took a job as a reporter on a left-wing newspaper named *The Call*, which quickly began to go under due to lack of funds and a boycott by advertisers. The *coup de grace* was delivered when a mob (probably composed of Legionnaires, many of whom were sons of the wealthy) broke into the plant at night and smashed the ancient flatbed press.

The Call was replaced by the *Union Record*. This was a labor paper with union funds behind it, and guards to protect its property during the night hours. Miss Strong became one of its editors. This was the move that convinced conservatives that bolshevism was really afoot on the shores of Elliott Bay.

Miss Strong was in Chicago attending a rally for Tom Mooney when she learned by telegram that a general strike was imminent in Seattle. It was not her invention, but its implied militancy appealed to her. She boarded the first train heading for Elliott Bay, resolved that the *Union Record* would support, and possibly guide, the only general strike in the nation's history.

Her first move was to write an editorial that would be remembered for several years. Although it supported a general strike it also revealed that the editor of the *Union Record* was none too certain as to where such a move would find the workers—and her beloved city—at its ending. She was too honest to pretend otherwise, although the businessmen and industrialists would read into her words meanings that were not there.

The handsome woman in her thirties was a graduate of Bryn Mawr, postgraduate from Oberlin, and possessed of a Ph.D. from the University of Chicago. But her editorial was uncomplicated in prose and uncertain in its conclusion. Nonetheless, a part of it would form the pattern of the "Seattle Revolution," revealing that Miss Strong had a following and considerable influence in the Central Labor Council:

> Thursday, February 6, 1919, at 10 a.m. there will be many cheering and there will be some who fear. Both these emotions are useful, but not too much of either. We are undertaking the most tremendous move ever made by Labor in this country, a move which will lead NO ONE KNOWS WHERE.
>
> Labor will feed the people. Twelve great kitchens have been offered, and from them food will be distributed by the provision trades at low cost to all. Labor will care for the babies and the sick. The milk wagon drivers and the laundry drivers are arranging plans for supplying milk to the babies, invalids and hospitals.
>
> Labor will preserve order. The strike committee is arranging for guards and it is expected that the stopping of the [street] cars will keep people at home.
>
> A few hot-headed enthusiasts have complained that only strikers should be fed, and the general public left to endure severe discomfort. Aside from the inhumanitarian character of such suggestions, let them get this straight: NOT THE WITHDRAWAL OF LABOR POWER, BUT THE POWER OF THE WORKERS TO MANAGE WILL WIN THIS STRIKE.
>
> The closing down of Seattle's industries as *a mere shutdown* will not affect the Eastern combinations of capitalists much. They could let the whole Northwest go to pieces as far as money alone is concerned.
>
> *But* the closing down of the capitalistically controlled industries of Seattle *while the workers organize* to feed the people, to care for the sick, the babies, and to preserve order —*this* will move them, for this looks too much like the taking over of *power* by the workers.
>
> Labor will not only *shut down* the industries, but Labor will *reopen*, under the management of the appropriate trades, such activities as are needed to preserve public health and public peace. If the strike continues, Labor may feel led to avoid public suffering by reopening more and more activities UNDER ITS OWN MANAGEMENT.

And this is why we say we are starting on a road that leads NO ONE KNOWS WHERE.

Businessmen, reading the editorial, thought they saw exactly where the road led. And while the fuse of the editorial was much delayed in Seattle history it is possible that it was precisely at this point that the city took a path that would lead to its being the strongest union community on the West Coast. For the moment, however, businessmen suffered the vision of naked Socialism although Miss Strong had not mentioned the dread word. What was most unnerving was that her editorial ignored the entire city government, including the mayor and the chief of police, and showed no fear of the power of business and industry.

The mayor read the editorial and felt his sympathy for labor slipping. Already he had been visited by a group of business leaders demanding knowledge of his intentions. Did he have a plan by which to break up the take-over of the city? Actually, at that moment, Mayor Hanson did not; Anna Louise Strong had caught him by surprise. But he promised an immediate conference with the chief of police, the calling of the militia, and if necessary troops of the regular Army from Camp Lewis near Tacoma.

Some of the more volatile business leaders had ideas of their own. They saw no reason why machine guns should not be mounted on the roofs of downtown buildings, and the bringing of strikebreakers and Burns detectives from California and the mining districts of Montana. Some suggested that Burns men, armed to the teeth, should see to it that the streetcars ran, and guard business houses where non-union employees would continue to work. So far as the records show, none of these drastic suggestions was translated into reality.

Miss Strong was in error when she wrote that eastern capitalists would not be alarmed at conditions in the Pacific Northwest. A general strike anywhere in the United States was to them a danger signal not to be ignored. Press wires were hot with stories datelined Seattle—most Easterners pronounced it *Seetle*—a city not heard from since the Yukon Gold Rush over thirty years before. The smell of bolshevism was in the air of every major industrial city, and soon Mayor Ole Hanson would be fanning that odor with interviews and by-lined articles in *Harper's* and the *Atlantic*. He now regarded the strike as a revolution and if he could put down the rebellion it entered his mind that for him even the Presidency was not an impossibility.

The shipyard workers were spoiled by the war. They were the highest paid among Seattle labor, and anti-union Seattleites called them "that silk shirt gang" because for Sundays and holidays they favored expensive striped silk shirts, a gaudy luxury that not even Seattle millionaires—there had come to be quite a number—allowed themselves. In the "silk shirt gang" was a tough and coming pugilist named Jack Dempsey, who had come over the Cascades from his Cle Elum training camp when the United States entered the war. He signed into a shipyard and thus escaped the draft, although nobody could be certain that this was his reason. After the war, as Dempsey began his sure climb toward the heavyweight championship, there was no more grumbling among the patriots.

The shipyard strike was triggered when a national contract was signed, making no allowance for higher living costs in the Far West. These were the days when almost every national advertisement carried the legend "Prices Slightly Higher in the West."

The yard workers had taken on rugged adversaries; even after the Armistice the yards were operated by a three-pronged group, the U. S. Shipping Board, the Navy and the owners. They refused to make a special allowance for the western workers.

It was in sympathy with this situation that the general strike was called, although Anna Louise Strong, the Wobblies and the Central Labor Council hoped that such a move would strengthen all labor in the Northwest.

Although at the beginning of trouble businessmen found Mayor Hanson of uncertain mind, he soon was making his position clear. He issued a proclamation:

> By virtue of the authority vested in me as Mayor, I hereby guarantee to all the people of Seattle absolute and complete protection. They should go about their daily work in perfect security. We have fifteen hundred policemen, fifteen hundred regular soldiers coming from Camp Lewis and will secure, if necessary, every soldier in the Northwest to protect life, business and property.
>
> *The time has come* for every person in Seattle to show his Americanism. Go about your daily duties without

fear. We will see to it that you have food, transportation, water, light, gas and all necessities. The anarchists in this community shall not rule its affairs. All persons violating the laws will be dealt with summarily.

OLE HANSON, Mayor

Thus the mayor answered Anna Louise Strong, although tardily. Inasmuch as the conservative newspapers were shut down, the proclamation did not enjoy a general circulation locally, although Hanson saw to it that it got onto the press wires. He did not go to the Labor Temple to deliver the message, sending his secretary instead. He later declared that as the audience heard the words "the strongest anarchists and strike leaders turned pale, realizing that the Mayor and his supporters were ready to go the limit in defeating their nefarious and un-American aims."

Old-time laborites who were at the Labor Temple that night do not remember any changes of color in the faces of the audience; they do remember a good deal of booing and catcalling, and recall that the mayor's secretary got through his reading with difficulty.

The proclamation was ignored. The general strike called for by the *Union Record* began as scheduled at ten o'clock on Thursday morning. It was signaled by whistles from the sawmills and from ships at the wharves.

At once an entire city of 250,000 people fell as silent as some ancient ruin. What most old-timers recall vividly is that silence on the first day after the whistles blew. It was somehow more unnerving than movement or even violence would have been. There was hardly a sound except those people had ignored or forgotten—the chirping sparrows in the eaves of buildings, the faint mourning of doves in the forests on the hills to the east, the angry cawing of sea gulls swinging in from the bay. Joshua Green, the hundred-year-old Seattle banker who is only semi-retired, recalls the sea gulls alighting in the streets. He was a ship master then and says, "The gulls rarely left the waterfront, and I'd never seen one light in the streets. It looked to me as if they had puzzled expressions, as if asking what was going on anyhow."

There was no whine of saws in the Georgetown district south of town or in Ballard on the north. Hotel beds were unmade and there were no bellhops at the ready to serve travelers. In fact, no travelers stepped from the trains on Front Street. Seattle had not yet become a target for tourists, and these would not have ventured the trip in any case. But there were no traveling men, or "drummers" as they were generally called in 1919. They had read the newspapers in California and the East and concluded that no orders were to be had in Seattle.

Elevator boys had locked the lifts in every building which boasted such equipment. Clerks and janitors stayed home, even the non-union ones fearing trouble. A few owners of stores and small shops ventured downtown to see what might be happening to their property. Now and then there was the sound of a horse's hooves, for some store owners chose equine transportation; large sections of the town's residential sections had not yet been zoned against animals and some of the larger lots harbored horses, even cows and chickens. The streetcars were not running, true to Miss Strong's promise. The growing numbers of citizens who owned automobiles chose not to risk such valuable property. Besides, they suspected that any unseemly show of wealth might incite trouble.

But there was no trouble, or even the slightest sign of it. Wisely, the mayor had asked that the troops from Camp Lewis be stationed out of sight in the new brick Armory near the waterfront, an imposing edifice (with gun slits instead of windows) that would be a Seattle landmark for decades to come. Ole Hanson's "fifteen hundred policemen"—surely many must have been temporary deputies —appeared warily, separating themselves into small non-belligerent groups, their revolvers invisible under the knee-length jackets which were part of the police uniform of the time. As always, they carelessly swung short mahogany clubs, a weapon used chiefly, if at all, on unmanageable drunks of the Skid Road.

True to the promise of Miss Strong's editorial, labor kept its head and preserved order—if indeed order was ever in jeopardy. If a crowd formed, the mayor's police let the labor guards take care of the situation. Any sizable group of curious loiterers was invited to break it up and move along. One of the laborites committed to preserve the peace jocosely suggested that it was a fine day to be home weeding the garden, although a cold February rain was slanting out of the southwest and the smell of the tideflats was heavy in the air. The man's jest became current and must have helped relieve some of the tension.

So passed the first day and with it some of the fear, although of course the conservatives were not happy and merchants moaned that they were being ruined. Before the strike began it had been planned that delegates from each union would "run" the city. It was realized quickly that this would be an unwieldy and confusing plan. Thus was formed a Committee of Fifteen, a term that frightened conservative Seattleites who had read of the French Revolution and kept abreast of the changing "committees" in Russia which had replaced the Czar.

But the Committee of Fifteen, following the promise of the *Union Record,* saw to it that milk was delivered to hospitals, to the ill and to families with babies. Light and power and gas continued, but not for the operation of private enterprise.

The second day of the strike passed much like the first. There was no picketing, no marching, no rousing radicals on soapboxes. A few owners of small shops made themselves available to customers, and were not molested, but no customers appeared.

Yet in the residential areas frightening rumors passed from house to house. From the rain shelters of porches, housewives, hands nervously clasped under aprons, shouted to one another what they had heard—or imagined. Some of the stories were ominous indeed. Mayor Hanson had been assassinated. The Committee of Fifteen was preparing a list of business leaders and civic administrators who would be lined up on the steps of the Post Office, blindfolded and shot. The water supply would be cut off, and certain water mains—particularly those leading to the homes of the rich on First Hill—were being poisoned. Representatives of the Committee of Fifteen would call upon every home for the purpose of interrogation and it would be wise to keep the flag out of sight.

Anything seemed possible in imaginations excited by memories of old anarchist news stories datelined Europe, and by flickering news reels of revolutionary violence smuggled from Russia and shown in Seattle movie houses now dark. Except for the *Union Record,* which had no home delivery, there were no newspapers and of course in 1919 no radios.

The switchboard at police headquarters was jammed with calls from hysterical women; the standard answer became, "Nothing to it, madame. Everything is quiet and in order." But it remained for those husbands who had ventured downtown to quell the rumors and calm frightened families.

It was true that nothing was happening, and by the third day of the strike it was apparent, to Mayor Hanson most of all, that the Seattle Revolution was petering out. Besides, every train from the East now was bringing national union leaders, who had come to smooth the tempers of laborites in what the Easterners felt was the Wild West. The war was over and a depression had set in; they were called "panics" then, and in peacetime they came with a certain regularity. The national union chiefs did not want to see hard-won contracts jeopardized by irresponsible laborites in what they considered Indian country.

Ole Hanson was aware of this, but in interviews with wire service reporters and writers from national magazines he continued to "smash" the general strike. He had prepared himself with two-hundred prints of a new portrait photograph which appeared eventually on the front pages of every major newspaper in the nation. The Committee of Fifteen might have closed down the Post Office and the telegraph offices in an attempt to silence the mayor. But they had no stomach for such drastic moves, and there was no way to muzzle the representatives of the national magazines and the big eastern papers which had sent reporters to the town on Elliott Bay. Mayor Hanson and his city already had become too widely known, and every national magazine was preparing articles on "The Seattle Revolution" and its courageous mayor.

On the fourth day the mayor's office was so filled with flowers from businessmen and Legionnaires that visitors could not find a chair unoccupied by floral tributes; they were scattered on the floor as well and lined the windowsills. The mayor was busy giving interviews to standee reporters and, between times, making a start on a book called *Americanism vs Bolshevism*.

As a politician he knew that the strike was failing and that now was the time to take credit. Some workers already had gone back to their jobs. In 1919 a large percentage of labor was made up of single men or "floaters," who saw that Seattle was headed for a depression and surmised, correctly, that employers would be more hard-nosed than ever. These realists began drifting out of town in search of better opportunities.

It was on the fourth day that the Committee of Fifteen voted thirteen to two to end the strike, with the proviso that it be extended one more day to include Lincoln's birthday. The shipyard workers had lost despite the brief support of other unions; they saw now that in a peaceful world there would be a decreased demand for ships and they would be lucky to hold their jobs when the yard gates opened. The national wage had begun to seem attractive.

Mayor Hanson was receiving invitations to lecture throughout the country and the fees offered were difficult to turn down. The money, together with political ambition, led him to resign as mayor and depart for the lecture platforms and chautauqua tents. The Republican convention was not far off, and Hanson—a Theodore Roosevelt "bull mooser" most of his life—decided that it was a good time to turn Republican. He was astute enough to realize that under normal conditions a nominee from the sparsely populated and relatively unknown Northwest would be a comic dream. But now he was a national figure and these were not normal conditions; he was a fighting superpatriot when superpatriotism was the popular thing, when young and active Legionnaires by the tens of thousands were backing the new slogan "America First."

Ole Hanson must not go into the record as a simple opportunist. There was iron in the second generation Danish blood. When the general strike began he had been in Seattle sixteen years and made remarkable progress.

He and his family arrived nearly destitute in a homemade covered wagon drawn by a team as emaciated as Hanson himself. Their journey was from Butte, Montana, where the pickings were poor, and Hanson had been hearing stories of a young town on Puget Sound that was filled with ambitious citizens, linked with Alaska's gold and commercial fisheries, and surrounded by great cedars and firs that formed the base of a rich lumber industry.

He was handicapped by an injury to his spine, but he did not let this detain him. He could not drive the team or bear to sit in the wagon seat. The driving fell to his wife and eldest son. The first day on the rugged road he tried lying on a battered mattress between him and the wagon bed. That first painful day made him realize that he could never reach Seattle as a reclining invalid. He fashioned a combination sling and belt of canvas, which he fastened to the tailgate of the wagon. For short distances he rode the sling, feet braced against the joggling rear axle. But for most of the unbelievable journey he walked, bracing his back against the belt to ease the pain. His wife and son had to pace the horses to this curious arrangement, literally dragging Hanson behind them. The journey was a slow one, with many rest periods and countless sleepless nights for the head of the family. The roads through Montana and Idaho were bad enough, but the passage up and over the Cascades was unmatched even by the travels of the pioneers before them. It was in that combination sling and belt that Ole Hanson covered seven hundred painful miles to the city of his adoption.

On their first night in Seattle the Hanson family camped atop Beacon Hill, from where they could look down at the lights flickering between the waving branches of tall trees. Naturally the covered wagon attracted wide attention, and word spread quickly of the odd latter-day pioneers. Despite a pouring night rain a sizable crowd gathered, and even then Hanson could not resist an audience. Actually his back had improved by means of the primitive therapy and Hanson was ready to speak.

In the light of two kerosene lanterns hanging from the wagon he explained the rig and told of the rugged journey from home. From there he launched into a political speech. As an admirer of Theodore Roosevelt he "bull moosed them for a while" as he put it years later, then audaciously avowed that some day he would run for the mayor's office and expected their votes when the time came.

Volubly he outlined a platform although at the time he had not the slightest idea as to what was right or wrong about the current city administration. As he reached the climax of his speech his thin voice ascended into a whining tone that was to be a characteristic of his political speeches in years to come. Some of his audience suspected that he was half out of his mind, but others pondered his excitable manner and all admired the stamina and courage his journey revealed.

Yet for a number of years not much was heard from Ole Hanson. The town was tight in the grip of second-generation men who had come from the loins of the founders and pioneers. For a time Hanson ran a tiny grocery store, but soon decided that "grocers were the greatest philanthropists in the world." Then he tried selling insurance, without much success. A friend pointed out that almost no insurance salesmen owned their own homes, but that almost all real estate men did. Then, as today, Seattle was noted for the large percentage of home owners. So Hanson went into real estate and found it to his liking. Until politics called him he was never a big operator, but he did make a modest success selling land and houses; and soon he did own his home.

Hanson's political bug really took hold about the time he became successful in real estate. A reformer, he went after the Seattle race track, something of a scandalous entity at that time, and was elected to the legislature. True to his promise, he introduced a bill outlawing horse racing in Washington—which became law and stood until pari-mutuel betting was legalized in 1933. By now he was big enough to attract attention. In 1918, he ran for mayor against Hi Gill as something of a superpatriot and the voters responded by turning Gill out. At the time of the general strike, Ole bought a residence of seventeen rooms and could be called a leading citizen even before he sat in the mayor's chair.

Following his lecture tour in the wake of the general strike, Hanson was on deck at the Republican convention. But he was lost in the corners of the smoke-filled rooms; he had no machinery or money behind him and only a few of his Seattle friends showed up to help. None was influential in Republican circles. The nomination prize went to Warren G. Harding, a small-town newspaper publisher not as well known as Hanson. But he looked like a President and the GOP wheels knew that he could be controlled in a period when a President had time for long poker sessions and was not criticized if he had a taste for bourbon and branch water.

(One of Harding's last public appearances was in Seattle, where he was cheered on his way to Alaska. On his return trip in a naval vessel he fell ill, and a few days later died in Portland. It was a heart attack, although for years afterward the rumor ran, strongly in Seattle, where Mrs. Harding's thin-lipped lack of enthusiasm was resented, that his wife had poisoned him in the knowledge of his infidelity. Still, Harding's reception in the city was happier than that of his predecessor, Woodrow Wilson. A parade was scheduled, and for several blocks on north Second Avenue the curbstones were occupied by early rising Wobblies and pacifist laborites. As the motorcade approached they stood shoulder to shoulder and several lines deep, arms folded, unseeing eyes straight ahead. In the downtown area he had received the kind of welcome a President might expect. Then suddenly, at Virginia Street on Second Avenue, he encountered the human canyon of silence. The misty air was heavy with hatred for the man who had said he would keep the country out of war. For a few moments Wilson tried to find response in the crowd, smiling and waving his top hat. Then, angered and visibly shaken, he slumped in his seat. Pacifists and International Workers of the

World had had their day and would afterward claim they had
started Wilson on his decline.)

Ole Hanson returned from the Republican convention a disappointed man with the feeling that the powerful men of his city
were ungrateful, had let him down and might even be contemptuous
at his improbable ambition. Insofar as labor was concerned, the
conservatives had matters well in hand. They realized now that Hanson had little to do with the failure of the general strike, that it had
fallen apart due to the confusion of the workers and the lack of aim
which Anna Louise Strong—perhaps subconsciously—had suggested
in her editorial. Soon Ole Hanson disappeared from the Seattle scene
and when last heard from was selling seashore property in California.
His death a few years later failed to make the Seattle papers until
long after his funeral.

Yet he popped up briefly in the news in 1925, when he announced he was "founding" a new town. Indeed, his real estate
dealings resulted in the town of San Clemente, California—where a
latter-day Republican of similar patriotic, anti-radical bent eventually
established the "western White House."

Anna Louise Strong was herself depressed and confused
when the strike had ended. She had long since lost her friends
among the Parent-Teachers Associations and the well-to-do women
of First Hill, the very people who had elected her to the school
board. Too, she found little warmth among her labor associates.
She had expected that the strike, despite its failure, would bring
the unions together. But now they were more divided than
ever, and some had lost members. Economically, Seattle was in
trouble again, as often it seems to be between wars and without the
luck of Alaska. The whole country, however, was in another of its
"panics" and a Seattle worker who had a job at any wage felt himself
fortunate. Work at the shipyards had slowed almost to a halt, and
the Navy Yard across the Sound at Bremerton was letting out civilian
employees by the hundreds.

Orders for lumber were down because of a building slump in
San Francisco and the rest of the country. The price of canned fish
had fallen so low that the product was featured as a "loss leader" in
grocery stores. The Fulton Fish Market in New York had canceled
orders for halibut and other unpacked species which once had regu-

larly sped across the nation in refrigerated railroad cars. And it was upon such a simple economy that Seattle had always rested: shipbuilding, the fisheries and lumber.

Soon after the general strike there came to Seattle the famous Socialist writer Lincoln Steffens and he and Miss Strong sought each other out. He was then the most famous of radical authors and he welcomed Miss Strong with well-meant advice. She told him how the unions, divided among themselves, seemed to have lost much of the strength they had prior to the strike. She described the demise of the *Union Record* and how the conservative papers, the *Post-Intelligencer* and the afternoon *Times*, had come back strong in favor of the Establishment, how even the *Star*, once in support of labor and studied in its refusal to publicize what then passed for high society in the town, was now merely a slim entertainment sheet specializing in humor and cleverness.

She expressed her disappointment in the Industrial Workers of the World, too, but Steffens already knew most of what she told him. He explained the Wobblies' hatred of Socialism and its lack of strong leadership; they were dreamers, he said, and really had little connection with a people's reform. Nonetheless, he heard her out and then, recognizing her confusion and that she had come to a turning point in her life, he offered advice.

"Anna," he said, "you can't stand in the middle and you can't expect a position of leadership in Seattle as things stand now. You have too much courage and determination to fall into oblivion, so you must decide once and for all which side you are on, and you must get away from here."

Steffens had recently returned from Russia; she gave him a long look, knowing that what was in his mind had been forming in her own. "You mean I should go to Moscow?" she asked.

Steffens assured her that this was exactly what he meant. "You will find confusions there, too. But there are also successes and they have a goal. They believe in the power of the people to run Russia and perhaps one day the world. They are actually doing what the IWWs of the Northwest are only singing and marching about. You must go there, perhaps for the rest of your life."

It was a hard decision for Anna Louise Strong. She loved the forests and mountains and the inland waterways of the Northwest, and there still lingered a love for Seattle. But she felt guilty as well as confused, believing that perhaps her uncertainty had doomed the general strike. Steffens scoffed at this, telling her that she should not go to Moscow as penance but to help a revolution that really meant something to the world.

It was not difficult to persuade her, and soon she was on her way with the best of recommendations from Steffens and at the invitation of Mother Russia herself.

She stayed for nearly thirty years and at last fell afoul of one of Moscow's own "Committees" and was expelled as a traitor and a spy. The elderly reformer, now in her sixties, returned to Seattle and found it much grown—and, to her surprise, a strong union town. For two or three days she was starred in the newspapers, hardly as a heroine and yet with a certain favoritism as a hometown girl who had become disillusioned with Russia. After this initial publicity she fades from the Seattle scene, yet stays in its history as a strong-minded woman who brought prominence, of a kind, to a town that often felt neglected.

What interested her most was the strength of the Central Labor Council, run by Jimmy Duncan, yet affiliated in a strange and unofficial way with business. And the man who interested her most, and who would have nothing to do with her, was a Seattleite on his way to stand shoulder to shoulder with Walter Reuther of the Automotive Workers and George Meany of the combined CIO-AFL. His name was Dave (not David) Beck.

Today Dave Beck is perhaps the calmest living eyewitness of the Seattle Revolution, and ready to take a little credit for its failure.

For years, except for the brief rise and decline of Ole Hanson, Beck was Seattle's only truly national figure. To look at him today, still vigorous in his seventies, one finds it difficult to believe all that has happened, good and bad, to the stocky, rosy-faced man who rose to the powerful post of president of the International Brotherhood of Teamsters.

He was raised in poverty in a ramshackle house in Seattle's old Belltown near the south end of Lake Union. Its occupants were a non-earning father about whom Beck has little to say, a hard-working mother who was her son's heroine all her long life, and a sister and brother.

"We were poor as hell," is the way Beck always describes his lonely boyhood. One way he helped out was to roam under the wharves of Lake Union with a borrowed .22 rifle, shooting rats. In those days Seattle was periodically disturbed by signs of the bubonic plague brought in by rats from ships out of the Orient.

"When I got a sack full of rats I would take them up to the Health Department, where they would nail them on wooden slabs and cut them open. For every rat which showed signs of the plague I got fifty cents. If my mother had ever found out I was carrying around sacks of dead rats she would have beat my head off, so I told her I made the money running errands or helping out an old fellow who ground horseradish and put it into jars to sell at the Public Market. Sometimes I really did help him and he'd give me a quarter if he was feeling good. He lived in a houseboat tied to an old pier on Lake Union, and I tell you that if the Health Department had ever thought to look into that houseboat they would have hung him!"

Beck's mother, the chief support of the family, brought up her son with no nonsense. "It wasn't her fault that I dodged the truant officer pretty good and never got past the sixth grade, although later I had a spell of night school at the old Broadway High. They weren't so tough then about absenteeism as they are now, not unless a kid was making trouble or getting into trouble. And what I could earn out of school was important to the family."

Beck has never forgotten how hard his mother worked to keep the home together. She had a job in a laundry near Belltown. There were no regular hours, except that she had to be at work at seven in the morning and she worked on the wet wash machine until the job was finished.

"My sister and I would go up to the laundry in the evening and wait outside until she was through. I remember nights when it was seven or eight o'clock before she was done—and there wasn't any overtime pay. I'd heard something about unions and, believe me, it was right there that I decided they were all to the good."

When his mother was through work she was too tired to prepare a meal. The three of them would go to the little cafe of a Chinese friend, where they got a big bowl of noodles with a little meat in them. "It cost thirty-five cents," Beck recalls, "and our Chinese friend would furnish us with three little empty bowls so we could divide up the dinner. Sometimes, even yet, in my dreams I can feel Chinese noodles coming out of my ears."

By the time Dave Beck was old enough to get a job driving a Model T laundry truck there was a union—the Teamsters he would one day lead. But he had been on the job only a few months when the United States entered World War I in 1917, and he joined the Navy. He never got overseas but the service pay was a great help to the family. "I found out I was lucky at craps," he remembers, "and almost all my Navy pay went home." Since then he's never been interested in gambling, and he's never taken a drink in his life. "I've seen too many guys go down the drain that way." Beck says he spent most of Navy time peeling potatoes and yearning to get back on the driver's seat of that laundry wagon; an unpublished biography is called *The Driver's Seat*.

When the Armistice was declared and Beck was mustered out at Pelham Bay Park he took the first train for home. Waiting for him was Jack Connors, an old family friend and strong union member. "Connors said there was plenty of trouble brewing in Seattle and he showed me some newspapers that warned of a general strike in sympathy with the shipyard workers who were walking out. There was a lot of stuff in the stories about Mayor Ole Hanson and he sounded like a political blowhard to me. But Connors insisted things were serious and urged that I make a speech at a meeting of our union that very night. I'd filled out considerably and the only clothing I could get into was the uniform on my back. Connors said maybe it was a good idea if I spoke in uniform, so my mother brushed up my blues and pressed them while Connors and I talked in the bedroom with the door shut. We didn't want to upset my mother and sister."

Connors seemed really worried, Beck recalls, and the idea of a general strike startled young Beck himself. Before the war he'd had a brief experience with a strike and hadn't liked it.

"I still don't like strikes," he says today. "Sure, the Teamsters had plenty of them under old Dan Tobin, and later when I was on the way to the presidency of the International. They'll probably have more, but I look at a strike as a last resort and I think I was the first union leader to take that view. Any wild-eyed guy can work up a strike vote, but it takes sensible effort—on both sides—to avoid one. Anyhow, the idea of a general strike struck cold chills down my back and I knew Connors was no alarmist. Some of the Teamster unions already had voted to hit the bricks and that worried me more. The idea of a general strike was only theory in this country; it was something that happened in Europe once in a while and always raised hell in the process. Connors told me the shipyard workers were demanding eight dollars a day for skilled labor, five and a half for unskilled, with a forty-four-hour week. I told Connors they must have gone nuts."

Nobody now remembers what Beck said that night; the meeting was not covered by the press, which, except for the *Union Record*, had worries of its own. But Beck seems to have convinced the membership that a general strike was a revolution—actually anarchy. "I don't know what I said, but I know damned well that I stood them on their feet, and how good that felt to a punk kid in a sailor suit."

What Beck remembers about that night must be fairly accurate. A hundred and ten unions already had voted for "anarchy" and the Laundry and Dye Works Drivers Local 566 was the single Teamster union which voted no.

If the general strike made a deep impression on the average citizen it made even a deeper one on Beck. "I was a union member," he says now, "and always will be. Unions are a part of the national economy, although there are still a few diehards trying to break them up. I believed in the war and, like a lot of others, figured it had been fought for democracy and a permanent peace. And I didn't see any way out of the Second World War."

Beck usually votes the Democratic ticket, but he became a firm supporter of Eisenhower when the general was elected President, and he is proud of the fact that as head of the International he was invited to one of the President's breakfasts.

Today he's not so sure about our adventures in the Far East. "I don't see how we can win a war over there, really win it, and it seems to me that some of those ruling gooks we support are as crooked as a dog's hind leg. A lot of money is going down the drain and a lot of our boys are being killed in a war they can't understand.

"Back there in 1919 I came home and before I could get back into a truck I ran into something—right in my own country and my own hometown—that was the direct opposite of democracy. That Anna Louise Strong they made so much fuss about was fuzzy in the head; she was an old-time suffragette in the wrong pew when it came to labor. It was then and there, during the general strike, that I had it proved to me that communism has nothing for labor. If ever they got the chance they would crucify labor right off the bat. Look what happened in Russia."

In retrospect Beck refers to the early day Socialists and radicals as communists. He has little use for doctrinaire hairsplitting as to the differences among socialism, communism, Marxism, anarchism or any other "ism" that isn't Americanism. To Beck anything that is "un-American" is harmful to both labor and employers and this feeling is just as strong in him today as it was before his decline and fall.

He likes to point out that his opposition to the general strike was not entirely due to his hatred of the Reds. "Our local had a contract, and so did the other Teamster unions. I was preaching the sanctity of contracts when a whole hell of a lot of union leaders were still preaching what amounted to class warfare."

Long after class warfare became a frayed and faded banner, Beck's regard for a contractual agreement made him stand out among labor leaders of earlier days. The word got around in Seattle and elsewhere that Beck's word, on or off paper, was as good as his bond.

As Beck rose in the Teamster ranks, journalists on assignment began to drift into Seattle to try to find out what made him tick. Their paths inevitably led to a pioneer businessman noted for objectivity and a mildly humorous cynicism. On the subject of Dave Beck he always told them this:

"I think the unions are getting too powerful and some of that power has gone to the leaders' heads. I'm not too sure it's good for Beck to have such power, but I will say that as long as such power is available we in Seattle are mighty glad that it is in the hands of Dave Beck."

The growing community acceptance of Beck moved onto a state level when in 1935 Governor Clarence D. Martin, Democrat, appointed him to the Washington State Parole Board. In view of subsequent events this was an ironic twist to the story of Dave Beck, but the governor was forced to delay the appointment following a wild protest from IWWs incarcerated in the state penitentiary. In effect, said their formal petition, they would have no chance whatsoever with Beck on the parole board. Beck was asked if this could be true. "How could I answer that?" he laughed. "I'd have to review each case and I'd do it objectively. But I can promise you that no Wobbly would get any edge from me."

The appointment finally went through and with it—besides the weakening of the Chamber of Commerce as a force in labor matters —labor came of age in the Pacific Northwest. Eventually Beck, by then president of the International Teamsters, would be appointed to the Board of Regents of the University of Washington. He says now,

1. A statue of Chief Sealth, after whom Seattle was named, stands with the Space Needle as background.

2, 3, and 4. Pioneers. Bertha K. Landes was Seattle's first and only woman mayor. (PHOTO BY GRADY) Arthur Denny led the city's early settlers and Henry Yesler (below) established its first major business, a sawmill.

5. An early picture of the Seattle waterfront showing Yesler's mill and the wharf. (WEBSTER & STEVENS)

6. The great fire of 1898 eats its way through the young town. (MINNEAPOLIS ART STUDIO)

7. First ship leaving for the Yukon as the Gold Rush begins.

8. Gold shipments like this one, worth $1,350,000 from the rich Yukon strikes, were not uncommon sights at the assay office around the turn of the century.

. For many years the L. C. Smith Tower reigned as Seattle's
allest building. (PHOTO BY W. H. [BILL] HOULTON)

0. San Francisco wasn't the only city with picturesque cable cars
nd turntables. A Seattle scene around 1900.

11. Future aviation tycoon William E. Boeing (right) and pilot
Eddie Hubbard deliver the mail on Lake Union in 1919.

12 and 13. In the city's earlier days, citizens had a choice of transportation vehicles ranging from an efficient trolley car system to the type of bicycle held by beloved pioneering figure Henry Broderick. (PHOTO BY BROWNELL)

14 and 15. Labor leaders. Anna Louise Strong became world renowned for her part in leading a strike that paralyzed the city. Later she was invited to visit heads of state in Red China and Russia. (PHOTO BY MILLER) Dave Beck, former president of the Teamsters Union, is shown below while under fire by the McClellan committee during its investigation of union racketeering.

16. Seattle's unusual underground city—remnant of some earlier bad planning—is explored by a tourist group as curator Bill Speidel lectures at far right. (PHOTO BY WEBBER)

17. In the seventies, Seattle displays the upward-soaring tendencies of a true metropolis, though efforts are being made to preserve the beauty of its natural surroundings.

"I told the Teamster board I wouldn't take their job unless I could continue to live in Seattle. I wasn't about to pick up my gear and move to Indianapolis or Detroit. In fact, I had in mind a big new Teamster headquarters in Washington, D.C., but I had no plans to move there and catch Potomac fever. What would be the point in this age of flying? Anyhow, the Pacific Northwest is my kind of country and Seattle is my kind of town."

By then Beck had as many friends among employers as he did among labor, probably more. One of his weaknesses was that he could not quite make up his mind whether he preferred being a labor leader or a Seattle business tycoon; he compromised by being both. He remembers his first meeting as a member of the University regents. "I didn't seem to detect any reserve or resentment. After all, I had been speaking before many business groups and they knew I wasn't out to wreck the University or business or anything else. I didn't feel out of harmony with my associates on the board in those first days—with one exception. I knew that sooner or later I'd have a run-in with him. I did, and the other regents backed me up. What bothered me most was that I was the only one on the board without a college or university education. I figured that maybe they, and the public too, would feel I couldn't have much of a grasp of the problems of education. But, hell, those were really business meetings, and I knew plenty about business, good and bad."

It was a period when an investigation was being conducted as to alleged communists on the faculty, what liberals called a witch hunt. Everybody expected the new regent to jump into the fray, but they were disappointed. It was an explosive situation at the time, but the leading Teamster didn't add to the confusion. "I could understand the faculty's concern about what they called academic freedom. We had to remember that out there on the campus were able, well-intentioned people who were really concerned about the investigation and really saw a danger to the freedom of their profession. I did think that some of them needed the advice of those who had been outside rubbing elbows—and knocking heads—with the commies. But at the same time I appreciated their concern." He disappointed newspapermen because he would make no stories at the expense of the accused or of the faculty as a whole.

He was riding high in the business community and possibly he didn't want to rock the regents' boat or embarrass the governor and the University president. But he served only four years of a five-year term and his final departure is interesting because it led back to his boyhood days when he was dodging truant officers. His resignation grew out of the advisability of raising tuition fees. "I found myself in a minority of one. Here was state institution, largely supported then by taxes and with unusual investments of its own. Hell, it had never let go of its original property in the middle of town, where some of the most prosperous office buildings and stores and banks now operate. At that time the idea of a state university was one that was practically free. I made a little speech about how John Rodgers of an early legislature had pushed through what was called 'The Barefoot Boy School Law,' the first of its kind in the nation. But mainly I knew that a lot of the University students were having a tough time as it was. I remembered when I couldn't afford high school and when the University was beyond my wildest dreams because I had to make a living. It seemed to me that there ought to be some ways to cut corners and not put the burden on the young people. I felt damned strong about it, and when I was outvoted by all the rest I figured it was time to get out."

Beck became Seattle's leading citizen, despite some enemies. There were businessmen who remembered that during the Great Depression he had made the rounds of all the local Teamster unions and persuaded the membership to take a cut in wages. "Nobody had ever heard of such a thing," he says, "and I barely got out of some of those union halls with my head on. But when the Depression tapered off I saw to it that the cuts were restored."

By now he lived in a not immodest home in the Sheridan Beach district a block from Lake Washington, and had the foresight to buy a vacant lot diagonally across the street, where he planned a private park which would give him access to the lake. Coming events were to prevent this, but Beck had created for himself at the side of his home a miniature of a wilderness spot in the Cascades with a twenty-foot waterfall that was illuminated at night for guests. Beck's home was sort of a manor house for an entire quarter block, in the center of which was a lawn featuring a gasoline-driven miniature train for the entertainment of children living in houses around the periphery of what was called "the compound." In one of the houses lived Beck's mother and sister; in half a dozen others were the families of his close friends who were relatively high in the hierarchy of the local Teamsters. The official engineers of the miniature railroad were Beck himself and Dick Klinge, former University of Washington football star and still today a top Teamster official.

Children living outside "the compound" were welcome as passengers of the train on weekends when Beck and Klinge were available to run it and see to their safety. On weekends they were also welcome to use the Beck swimming pool, which was hidden from the street by expensive landscaping. With no children of their own, Beck and his wife Dorothy seemed to enjoy playing Mr. and Mrs. Bountiful and often bought a bicycle for some youngster who lived on the other side of the tracks from the wealthier area. Some of Beck's neighbors were uncertain as to whether they welcomed the proximity of the Teamster compound and not every neighborhood child was allowed by parents to play there.

The layout was generally believed to be Beck's own, and it did not develop until later that it all had been built with Teamster funds from the International treasury. This was perfectly legal, for the constitution of the International gave the president complete authority as to the use of Teamster funds. By then it was one of wealthiest unions in the country, and Beck did not let it be forgotten that he was responsible. "Old Dan Tobin, who preceded me in the International chair, didn't know anything about business, and he cautiously let the money sit in the bank drawing three per cent. I built up a portfolio, buying blue-chip stocks, but chiefly I invested Teamster money in real estate or in distributive businesses that might be said to be allied to Teamster interests. That's how I made my own money, too."

Throughout his adult life Beck was secretive about his own worth, but it was believed that he was several times a millionaire. Inasmuch as he made investments, both for the Teamsters and himself, in the local area the Seattle banks were happy and so were a lot of other financiers. He became noted for coming to the rescue of local institutions; the most talked about was his saving of St. Mark's Cathedral, a high society church in which many prominent weddings took place. But St. Mark's fell into financial trouble on its mortgage. It was a Depression time and none of the rich members, singly or in groups, appeared willing to come forth with the needed cash that would prevent foreclosure. It was Beck, a non-member and not a religious man, who stepped forward to save the day.

Dorothy and Dave Beck did little entertaining, and when they did open their home to guests the pattern was always the same. In the basement was a complete movie theater with banked seats, and an area more than large enough for a buffet supper and dancing. In the corner was a well-supplied bar, but Beck, a teetotaler, never presided there or hired a bartender. Guests helped themselves and there is no report that indicates anybody ever got out of hand. Most of the guests were Teamster officials mixed with a few non-Teamster friends of long standing. He never invited prominent businessmen and their wives, and so far as anyone knows the Becks were not invited to the homes of the latter. Dorothy Beck was quite shy and not too well. She had been a department store clerk. Although a pleasant and ladylike person, she did not seem to enjoy even her husband's occasional parties built around a first-run film that Beck ordered from Hollywood, making certain that it had not been officially released. During the running of the film the host would usually wander off to some other part of the house; he found no enjoyment in films or the theater, and certainly not in the opera or the symphony. His study was lined with well-chosen classics but there was no evidence that he was familiar with any of them. Dave Beck's hobby was making money and unlike some of his wealthy acquaintances downtown he didn't coat the hobby with culture.

The peak of Beck's career came with the dedication of the multimillion-dollar International Teamster headquarters in Washington, D.C. In full view of many of the major buildings and landmarks of the capital, the union president's huge luxurious office enjoys a full sight of the Capitol building.

In advance of the dedication he made several speeches to Teamster officials in other cities. Militance was his theme; it was as if he feared that the new building, definitely his creation, might lead some of his underlings to get the idea that the union had gone soft and political. The very week in which the building was dedicated he reminded a visiting committee of organizers: "The Teamsters have always been a fighting union. We must never lose our alertness or go soft in the gut or we won't be worth a damn." To another group he said, "We're well off, and we belong to the national picture and this building proves it. We're proud of being well off, but remember that we're not going to get fat and lazy."

One of the nation's champion long-distance commuters, Dave Beck flew eastward—via New York, where he stayed in the Waldorf Towers "right next to General MacArthur," to take full charge of the dedication of the headquarters of the International Brotherhood of Teamsters. He was now telling members of the press that it had cost "somewhere between five and six million dollars" and as they wandered around its marble halls and waded through its plush carpets they could well believe it.

A moment after he entered the building the word spread fast from floor to floor: "Dave's on deck." The conferences he held each morning at the vast walnut table with leather inlay had an air which any high-placed advertising account executive would have found uncomfortably familiar. This was, in essence, a corporation's board listening to an agency's proposed campaign. The dedication had to go well, and this had to be it. The big boss was on hand.

Somewhere at the back of Dave Beck's mind troubles were looming, but nobody would have known it. And at his right sat James Hoffa, who always seemed to be in motion even when sitting down, like a prizefighter waiting on his stool for the bell of the first round. Hoffa felt Beck had been on the throne long enough, just as, years before, Beck had the same feeling about old Dan Tobin.

But the king was bland. Reports of the various committees were delivered informally but briefly. Occasionally Beck said, "That's good," and less often he would say, "That's damned good. Who thought that one up?" Sometimes, still listening, he read a memorandum brought in by his secretary. Around the walls of the great room were oil paintings of Teamster presidents; Beck's was already there, overhead behind his huge black leather chair.

So it went right up to the very day of the dedication. Parallel with the dedication planning was work on the variety show to be staged in Constitution Hall for the delegates and their families. (It is interesting to note that, despite Beck's background, no working Teamster and his family appeared to represent the rank-and-file membership.)

Beck arranged the variety show, too, and it was no little program thrown together for the entertainment of delegates in a strange and night-quiet town. It was a complete theatrical production featuring Scat Carruthers, the Tokayers' famous acrobatic act, and singers such as the Demarco Sisters, the Nota Belles, Earl Wrightson, Joan Holloway, Anne Crowley and Margaret Whiting. Nor was there just one master of ceremonies to keep the show moving. There were five, then all big movie names: Dan Dailey, Jack Haley, George Murphy, Pat O'Brien, and the urbane Walter Pidgeon.

Somebody had the courage to ask Beck if it wasn't a little too much. "What the hell," he answered with a flash of temper. "They're not here just as stars. They're all members of the AFL. They're here as unionized professional people in sympathy with the Teamsters. I'll make that plain."

He didn't make it plain that not a star or an agent or studio would have dared refuse. But the stars fell into the spirit of the evening. Pidgeon told how he had been called in years past by both Tobin and Beck and said he was always happy to respond. In a burst of Irish sentiment Pat O'Brien growled out a curtain call with: "You are a wonderful people. I love you and God bless you!"

In the closing minutes of the show the performers lured Beck onto the stage to cap the finale. He danced, clumsily but enthusiastically, with O'Brien and joined Margaret Whiting in a song. He acted like a man on top of the world. But rumors had been flying fast through headquarters that the big boss was in trouble with the Internal Revenue Service, that dozens of federal investigators were busy out in Seattle, and that already Beck had hired the best team of defense attorneys that money could find.

A big union is not a happy paradise, and that week of celebration there were those who greeted the rumors with satisfaction, and among them must have been James Hoffa, who was next in line. It began to look as if perhaps the place in the driver's seat might be available even sooner than he had hoped. Too, there were many in the International who resented Beck's insistence on running things from the farthest northwest corner of the United States.

When he returned to his hometown he was forced to plunge into a sea of trouble. His nemesis was a quiet federal investigator named Claude J. Watson; he had once been a neighbor and he and Beck had much in common as to their background. Watson quickly found that while Beck had reason to be proud of his businesslike operation of the International union, his accounting of personal financial affairs had been much more informal and certainly did not seem to match the figures on his income tax returns. But Watson knew that he had to have a watertight case; he and his helpers proceeded to construct one. They traveled thousands of miles and spent countless man-hours on the case.

On March 12, 1957, the blow fell, and it came in the form of a 445-page report turned in by Watson and some fifty agents assisting him. In a few weeks, after a grand jury hearing, Beck was indicted in Tacoma. The charge: income tax evasion. But long before that something called the U. S. Senate's Select Committee on Improper Activities in the Labor or Management Field—known then as the McClellan Committee—had dragged the teamster leader before the nation's television cameras. Beck's chief adversaries were Sen. John McClellan, of Arkansas, and the committee's counsel, a young man named Robert Kennedy.

Repeatedly, Beck refused to answer questions put to him by McClellan and Kennedy about his own or the union's financial affairs. He invoked the Fifth Amendent dozens of times, acting on the advice of attorneys who knew he would face trial in Tacoma. His later trial in Tacoma lasted several months, but at no time did Beck's attorneys permit him to take the stand. He was convicted in federal court, and the summary of Judge George Boldt was one of the bitterest denunciations of a defendant ever heard in the Northwest.

As Beck and his attorneys stood before the bench, Judge Boldt said, "No bootblack or newsboy of Horatio Alger's imagination ever rose from a more humble beginning to a greater height than Dave Beck. From the driver's place on a laundry wagon to the seats of the mighty, national and international, is a greater climb than even Alger conceived for his heroes.

"Did we not know what we now know of Mr. Beck, his success story would be as thrilling and inspirational as almost any in the history of opportunity, enterprise and ingenuity. The exposure of Mr. Beck's insatiable greed, resulting in his fall from a high place, is a sad and shocking story that cannot be contemplated by anyone with the slightest pleasure or satisfaction. A fair appraisal of the evidence shows beyond the glimmer of a doubt that, as an incident of his tax fraud, Mr. Beck plundered his union, his intimate associates, and in some instances personal friends, most of whom quite readily would have freely given him almost anything he asked. As more than one of his union executive witnesses put it, 'He could have written his own ticket.'"

Beck stood as stalwart and erect as a bluejacket before a superior officer at boot camp. But his round and usually rose-colored face was plum-colored. One of his attorneys touched his arm as if fearing an outburst from his client.

Beck attempted an appeal, which was futile, and finally he embarked on the launch to McNeil Island and a cell in the federal penitentiary there. His sentence was for five years. Privately he told friends he'd be out soon. "Even though I'm not guilty, I intend to be a model prisoner, expect no favors, and through friends outside I'll work on the parole board."

He was not quite a model prisoner, for he tried to slip a business letter past the warden. That lost him his first appeal to the parole board. But on December 11, 1964, after two and a half years he was released on parole.

There is an epilogue. When a freed Dave Beck stepped jauntily down the gangplank of the McNeil Island launch he repeated his contention that he was innocent, and would say no more on the subject except that he had no complaint about his treatment in prison, where he had worked at a menial job in the penitentiary cannery.

"I'm still in business," he told reporters, "and I've already arranged to open an office at 14 John Street."

Today he's a loner and rarely is seen downtown. It is still believed that he is a multimillionaire with most of his holdings in real estate, as always. As a sign that he has lost none of his astuteness he opened a block-square parking lot across from the state unemployment office. He had observed that most unemployed came for their checks in their own cars. "When I get bored," he says, "I go down and do the collecting myself. I'm not proud."

His first wife died of cancer soon after his release from prison, and six years after his release he married again, in 1970. His new wife is a white-haired motherly sort and for years has been a friend of the family. They live in one of the town's older tower apartments and regularly take long drives around the region and down the California coast. Apparently in his mind he is still an innocent man, but he will not discuss his conviction and imprisonment. It is as if he has drawn a curtain tightly over that troublesome period.

He is still a part of Seattle, and yet not a part of it in the way of former times. Once businessmen had crossed the street to greet him, and practically ran across the expanse of the old ornate dining room of the Olympic to pound him on the back and ask after his health.

Those days are gone. Now the leading businessmen pretend he

doesn't exist, and many a Seattleite believes him dead. But in his middle seventies he is still lively and ambitious.

"I've got a lot of deals on the fire," he says. "This is a place of opportunity and my wife and I wouldn't live anywhere else in the world even without those opportunities."

13

Young Boy, Young City

Ask a contemporary Seattleite if ours is an exciting city, and probably you will give him pause. After a moment's thought he may say, "Well, maybe not exciting, but I wouldn't want to live anywhere else."

Possibly he likes the setting, the awe-inspiring backdrop of rugged mountain ranges with peaks forever topped with snow—especially Mount Rainier, the giant which on most days withdraws into a veil of mist or nowadays, God help us all, a combination of mist and smog.

Or perhaps he likes Seattle because it offers the participant sports he prefers: skiing, boating, hiking and climbing, rock hounding, fishing and hunting, exploring. Maybe he—or she—likes gardening, which is extended by the year-around mild climate.

But exciting? Exciting as a city? Perhaps not, he will admit. Ours is not a city which takes you up and shakes you, like New York or San Francisco or New Orleans.

If he is a native it may occur to him that once it did seem

exciting, but he is remembering his youth, when all the world was a wonder, and when Seattle, youngest major city in the nation, was also in its breathless adolescence.

Henry Broderick, the pioneer realtor, recalls as most exciting the years before World War I, whereas I recall as most exciting the years between World War I and World War II. It all depends upon when you were very young. But boyhood in a town which is also in its growing-up stage—that is a heady combination.

My closest companion was a lad with the unlikely name of John Buckles, whose aunt and widowed mother ran a rooming house at the foot of Queen Anne Hill. In what seemed to John and me ancient times indeed they had been girls in a small town in the Deep South, and the aunt chewed snoose in an unobtrusive and ladylike way. Both women were ladies to the core, and their rooming house was respectable and impeccable. Their own living quarters were my second home. They felt sorry for me because at the time I lived in a hotel. Near the corner of Second Avenue and Virginia Street, the place is now known as the Commodore and has not changed much since the year of 1909, when my father and grandfather had it built. Those were the days when buildings were created to last, and when future progress singles it out for the wrecking ball, progress is going to have a hard time.

The reason that John Buckles' mother and aunt felt sorry for me was because I lived alone in the hotel in a room of my own. My parents and grandparents had their own suites, and I suppose the arrangement was unusual. But I saw nothing wrong with it. I enjoyed it.

It was a small hotel of a hundred rooms, on the American plan, meaning that it had no dining facilities. But at the rear of the lobby was one of the most elaborate bars in the town, for this was in a time before Prohibition when bootlegging added to the excitement of Seattle.

The bar was behind the Ladies' Parlor, where gentlemen were allowed to visit single female guests, and there was a large billiard room at one side of the lobby floor. It stretched the whole depth of the building, and once upon a time the famous Willie Hoppe practiced there in return for a free room. When he was practicing all other play ceased and there were plenty of spectators. I learned that before retiring to bed the world's champion rubbed his hands with cold cream and donned white silk gloves.

Sadly, the elaborate bar and the billiard room are gone now, and there are no uniformed bellhops; the elevator is self-operating and guests handle their own luggage. Some years ago, after ten exciting years in Manhattan, I registered at the old place, intending to stay there until we found permanent residence. There had been many renovations over the years, and the guests seemed as respectable as those in Mrs. Buckles' rooming house.

But I stayed only one night. Somehow the memories to which I had looked forward turned melancholy. I checked out the next day. As we all discover, as Thomas Wolfe knew, you can never go back. Besides, I had been away from Seattle for nearly a decade and I had a whole new city with which to become acquainted.

John Buckles and I had once discovered it, mostly on foot, and now and then on roller skates. Not then on bicycles, for when John and I were companions Seattle had even more hills than it has now. There was a period when we made scooters out of an old skate, nailing the two parts of the skate to a length of two-by-four, affixing a Carnation milk twenty-four-can box to the front, and attaching a wooden handlebar atop that. The motive power was still by one foot, or by gravity on the downgrade. The idea of acquiring an automobile never entered our heads. Indeed, it had not entered the heads of adults unless they were wealthy, or could adjust themselves, financially and psychologically to Henry Ford's Model T, which, as the joke went, you could have in any color you pleased so long as it was black.

Traffic was no problem. There were few automobiles, and perhaps a dozen elegant ladies operated their own electric carriages. Business houses made deliveries by horse and wagon. The Teamsters Union was rarely a subject of conversation.

Despite roller skates and homemade scooters, John and I rambled mostly afoot. If each of us had an extra nickel we took a trolley car, and soon learned that the transfer system could take us far afield and back. "Always ask the conductor for a transfer slip," was John's motto. Like his mother and aunt, he knew how to get the most from a nickel.

The fatherless little Buckles family considered me a spendthrift and were convinced that my family was wealthy. This was not the fact, for my father and grandfather had put themselves deeply in debt to build the hotel. They knew that the Alaska-Yukon-Pacific Exposition was on the way, and inasmuch as our hotel was only a block from the New Washington, the town's most luxurious inn, they planned to get an overflow of tourists from the larger establishments. While the exposition was on, the plan worked well. After the exposition closed, business was slower. Second Avenue and Virginia Street was then far, far north of what then was called "downtown."

Nonetheless, John was scandalized at my mode of life. On the way to school I stopped at the hotel desk, where the morning clerk was instructed to give me a quarter. It's difficult to believe now that this bought me a breakfast in a nearby Greek restaurant and a school lunch, and probably a nickel or so left over. Dinner time was even more lavish. At that hour my father was on duty at the desk (usually he had inspected the bar), where I received fifty cents. That was enough to buy dinner at the Greek's, from which I departed with enough to take me to a movie (silent) for a nickel or a dime, buy a candy bar and perhaps a second-hand book from a late-closing used book shop on First Avenue.

John Buckles envied me this life, but I could not share it with him at all, because his mother and aunt did not approve his being out at night until the scandalizing hour of nine or nine-thirty, and insisted that he do school "homework" or some housekeeping duty or other in the rooming house.

So it was on Saturdays or Sundays that we roamed the city together and there was scarcely a part of it we didn't know. We even knew (by reliable hearsay) the red light district below Skid Road, but it did not interest us much and as I remember we went there only two or three times, chiefly to brag about it to an overly wise schoolmate we detested because he was always enlightening younger kids about the facts of life.

Actually we were uncomfortable in the area of tolerated vice. We more or less tiptoed by the little ramshackle houses and the questionable run-down hotels. The "girls" were asleep or otherwise invisible during our hours of exploration. In any case, we were by no means prospective customers, hurrying along in knee pants and keeping eyes out for any policeman who might be on the beat. I can't recall that we ever glimpsed any woman who resembled our idea of a prostitute. I do remember that once John saw a crimson light burning near an upstairs window, and recall his half-frightened whisper and pointing finger. I think it likely that the room may have been occupied by some old lady who preferred a lively lampshade on an overcast day, for neither of us had been born when the "red light district" was a literal term. It was an expression we had over-heard from careless elders, and of course was not very far in the past, at that, for Seattle was then a town of not quite 300,000 people. It had grown amazingly in the last decade, spurred by the Gold Rush to the Yukon and Alaska near the turn of this century; and it was changing fast, although John and I did not realize this. To a boy his town is immutable.

To the south of the wicked area was a stretch of greasy brown tideflats not yet filled in to create new land. Curling around the tideflats was a trolley line built on piling, and if we possessed a couple of extra nickels we would embark—not forgetting to ask for the transfer slips which would get us back. The destination was West Seattle, and Alki Point, the very beginnings of the city where the founders had first landed.

In West Seattle there were a few houses half hidden among the tall trees on the high bluff, but we would head for the beach, a vast curving shingle with a long ebb tide that left pebbles and clam shells shining like jewels. When we were much younger there had been a little Coney Island there, with a roller coaster ride and a Ferris wheel and a huge natatorium with heated water. This had been in a time when we had been taken to West Seattle in the custody of parents, and it was all gone now. A natatorium in a city surrounded and divided by so much water seems curious now. But Seattleites then were not much addicted to surf bathing, and private swimming pools were years ahead in an era of which we did not even dream.

We would, however, take off our shoes and long black stockings and do some wading when the tide was in. And from there, on a clear day there was—as I have said—the best view of Seattle's skyline and waterfront.

There it stretched, just as our grammar school books said the founders envisioned it. I don't believe a word of those textbooks now. The founders had their hands full getting settled, then making a living and finally taking great profits.

But John and I, more or less serious students (both John's mother and my old man were hell on report cards) believed every word of those textbooks on local history. We never knew that Doctor Maynard, despite his many good qualities and his contributions to the infant village, was a dedicated boozer and a bigamist to boot.

So we would gaze at the skyline—our very own skyline—always in pride and wonder. The waterfront, the downtown buildings and the homes rising up the hillside to the gray sky. Or perhaps, if it was in summer, to the blue sky with Mount Rainier beyond. It was ours, all ours, and we were proudest of the town's only true skyscraper, the L. C. Smith Building (now Smith Tower and overshadowed by taller buildings) erected by the typewriter king and the tallest building west of Chicago, forty-two splendid stories high.

Finally we'd let our feet dry, brush the sand off, and resume our long black stockings and shoes, all in time to catch a trolley and get John home for dinner. There would not be time to wander around Pioneer Place—now stubbornly called Pioneer Square, although it's not a square but a triangle. That exploration would wait for another day.

Pioneer Square, as it must be called now by usage, was known as the "birthplace of Seattle" because it covered part of the original site of the platted city. It was surrounded by stolid Victorian-type office buildings and hotels, some of which still stand. At the peak of the V-shaped mall stood the giant restoration of an Indian totem pole, and at the base of the triangle was an ornate iron enclosure with a roof against the rain. Beneath were benches on which commuters waited for their transportation—a trolley car, or the long-gone cable cars, or the interurban train to Renton or Tacoma. Commuters shared the benches with loiterers or professional bums who had wandered dully up from Skid Road. The commuters ignored the smell of cheap wine, burying their noses in the evening papers, of which Seattle then had several besides the traditional Seattle *Times*. One was the pink-covered *Star*, said to be edited for a mythical "Mrs. Humblebridge" in West Seattle. It graduated some brilliant newspapermen and authors and was fun to read. In summer vacations I delivered it on a modest route around the foot of Queen Anne Hill because my grandfather believed earnestly that a boy should not be overly idle. I grossed twenty cents a week.

Then there was the *Union Record*, a labor paper which figured prominently in the Seattle Revolution. For a brief time there was the orange-covered *Sun*. Now, of course, there are only the morning *Post-Intelligencer* and the *Times*. Seattle today is one of few cities of its size with more than one newspaper. The *Post-Intelligencer* traces its lineage beyond a century and is the oldest business firm in town. The indestructible *Times* was founded by Alden J. Blethen, and it was inherited by his son, General Clarance (sic) Blethen, who was equally picturesque.

Around the Totem Pole were stolid buildings and a few hotels, whose tenants were somewhat mixed. Seattle's economy was then sparsely based on commercial fishing and lumber; the office spaces in the buildings were mainly taken up by firms involved in those fields, together with lawyers and a few doctors and dentists.

But there were some sports in the breed. One such who called himself a doctor—a "clap doctor," John and I termed him out of earshot of our parents—who featured, and widely advertised, what he called "an educational museum." You reached it by one flight of stairs from the street, and although John and I had never experienced sexual intercourse, we visited the museum whenever in need of horrors and chills. It was comprised of male and female wax figures, stark naked, very real although somewhat dusty.

These figures clearly demonstrated the possible progressive ravages of venereal diseases, which, apparently, could not only destroy sexual organs but destroy a leg or a nose or even half a face. I shudder now to think of their effect on the guilty sailor or landlubber. If they were sufficiently impressed, the doctor's office was conveniently at the back of the museum for a free examination and diagnosis. I do not know what his treatments cost, but the traffic was good and he was reputed to have amassed great wealth over many years—until the medical association and the public health people got around to putting him out of business.

This was on First Avenue, then a lively street, along with Second Avenue, which was just as lively but more reputable. The city was gradually moving north and east, and long after John and I were released from knickerbockers and black stockings and the annoying hidden harness which supported the latter, Fifth Avenue would replace Second as the fashionable avenue.

The Puget Sound Naval Shipyard was across the Sound at Bremerton and First Avenue catered greatly to bluejackets on leave or on a pass. It was crammed with nickelodeons and second-run movie houses, trick-and-puzzle stores and open-front shooting galleries side by side with entertainment establishments to which boys were not admitted. It was in the latter that a sailor or civilian could drop a nickel in the slot of a "moviescope," turn the crank, and enjoy an animated flirtation scene in which the female stripped right down to her bloomers and underwaist. Such entertainments still thrive on lower First Avenue, although I can't think why when you consider the modern "art" and avant-garde films uptown. I suppose the movie prices are too costly, and even now there are down-at-the-heel citizens who rarely venture north of Cherry Street. Indeed, there were visiting Alaskans or tourist farmers from east of the Cascades who never went north of the Frye Hotel, which wasn't far from the Totem Pole in Pioneer Place. That much of Seattle sufficed for them.

But John and I were less restrained. We would wander along First Avenue past the cross streets, and we knew the way to recall the order of them. They were James, Cherry, Columbia, Madison, Marion, Seneca, Union, Pike and Pine—and their initial capital letters stood for:

JESUS CHRIST MADE SEATTLE UNDER PROTEST.

Natives of Seattle still use this vestige of frontier days and pass it on to any newcomer who may be confused.

Along First Avenue, for a considerable distance north, we would now and then glimpse loitering in a doorway a flossily dressed young woman. Her dress and immobility, although she ignored us, whispered that she was a street walker at rest. This was one of a higher type than those found "below the line" and they were under the protection of a questionable police force, their madames or pimps having paid the required bribe.

While my companion and I learned our city well, we did not, of course, learn it all at once. We explored on Saturdays or holidays, and when we found something of particular interest we did not hurry. The waterfront was too fascinating to rush matters. There were always ships of foreign flags loading or unloading cargo. We never failed to drop into Ye Olde Curiosity Shop, which still flourishes.

It displayed and sold genuine Indian baskets, which now are scarce and expensive. But true to its name, there was little of the unusual that could not be found there. There were in Ye Olde Curiosity Shop alleged mummies, arrowheads, Indian artifacts, postcards and souvenirs of the city—the Lord only knew what all. It carried curiosities from all around the Pacific Rim, and despite a lively business was always so crammed with unrelated items that it was difficult to move about.

Some Saturday in April we would take a trolley to Fisherman's Wharf, where commercial fishermen of Scandinavian or Yugoslavian descent were readying for the coming salmon or halibut season in the North. They would be mending seine nets, or—grease to their elbows—tinkering with their diesel engines in the pit of a fishing vessel. Or with their gasoline engines, though Puget Sound fishermen and tugboat skippers had taken to Doctor Diesel's invention long before the Atlantic Coast workboat fleets.

All along the wharves beneath the south end of the old Ballard Bridge silent men were busy at the nets or on purse seiners, trawlers, miscellaneous double-enders, or in a few tall-mastered halibut schooners.

Scandinavians are not garrulous when sober, and we simply looked on, well out of the way, keeping our mouths shut. Today in April the scene has not changed much, except that the vessels are more modern in hull lines and equipment.

John and I did not venture beyond the wharves into Ballard because the Ballard district was—and still is—an entity of its own. Strangers were quickly spotted, and Ballard kids had the reputation of being fast and willing with their fists.

Ballard was self-sustained, self-respecting, a town of its own. Its citizens, largely Scandinavian, were good citizens and comfortably situated. They preferred the foods, the mores and the religions of the old countries. Their houses on Sunset Hill were neat and regularly painted, with gardens and lawns well cared for. Most downtown Seattleites did not realize that a man with a fishing vessel or a sizable share in a season's catch was his own man, with more than ample savings—a businessman, in fact, whose business was hard and dangerous when the fishing run was on.

In those days Ballard resented any inroads from downtowners, just as it had had doubts about annexation to Seattle. Today things have changed somewhat, for Ballard retains its identity and there is a Ballard Chamber of Commerce. But it has welcomed the giant "outside" moorage at Shilshole Bay, whose thousands of yachts belong to citizens from all over the Seattle area, pleasure boat skippers who want to avoid the trouble of negotiating the Chittenden Locks, which join Puget Sound with Lake Union and Lake Washington. They are proud of Walter Clark's big Windjammer restaurant, where the waitresses wear less than mini skirts and long black stockings sheer; a getup that would have scandalized Ballard housewives a generation ago.

The wharves of the fishermen were about as far as John Buckles and I ranged in our Saturday explorations. After all, we were rather small for our ages, and neither of us could boast a strain of Scandinavian blood.

Our grounds for adventure were in Seattle's downtown area, but were exclusive of First Hill, where the wealthy had their rather forbidding mansions, some with carriage houses over which servants lived. Our limited forays into the realms of the rich proved unrewarding. We were hardly interested in architecture, and a deathly stillness pervaded the area, particularly in summers, when the inhabitants covered the furniture and moved to summer places north of town, which in those days was "out in the country." John and I, no crystal-ball gazers, could not foresee the time when First Hill would be a place of tall hospitals, apartment houses and doctors' clinics, and some of the great mansions would fall in the path of progress or be transformed into rooming houses.

Now and then we took a cable car as far east as Madison Park.

This was a real adventure. You took a grip-cable car, with side seats open to the elements. (San Francisco had the foresight to keep their cable cars; Seattle's one surviving cable car is in the Museum of History and Industry.)

At the top of the route which led from the foot of Madison Street you changed to another cable car—with that transfer slip, of course—and this one operated from a second cable windlass, because from the top of the hill it was downward again, with gripman's greasy gloves tight and busy muscles bulging and the brake ready at hand. This was the breathless part of the journey, with the little car swaying on a high wooden trestle and a veritable forest on either side. (The forest is gone now, gone with the wind and the cable cars.) Then finally the sight of the big lake, and a level stretch to a wooden building with vertical shutters propped open for the sale of ice cream cones and soda pop. I don't remember that we took the lake launch or ferry to the thickly forested east side. That cost too much round trip and no transfer offered. If it was a Sunday afternoon we listened to the band that was sheltered on a platform with a peaked roof against the always possible rain. If it was a Saturday we walked the beach, skipping flat pebbles on the lake surface.

On the return trip, changing cars for the downhill slide back to the city, we peered fearfully into the wide doors of the brick powerhouse which held the cable windlasses, forever rolling. A chain stretched across the entrance and there was a huge red sign: DANGER! KEEP OUT! We obeyed.

On the way uptown we might climb to Third or Fourth or Fifth Avenue, where there were plenty of vacant lots. Many of these had been excavated for structures never built, dreams halted by some past recession or taxes that overcame the first owner unable to coax a bank into a loan. Some of these holes held a sizable pool of rainwater, trapped by the clay soil. Often in such tiny oceans there was a plank raft with a push pole, the property of older boys we made certain were not in view. We remembered our *Huckleberry Finn*, but did not pretend to be Huck and Jim. What we remembered more vividly was some silent movie of swashbuckling pirates and we sailed (by push pole) a treacherous ocean in search of treasure or ships to plunder. That Mississippi of Huck's and the runaway slave we remembered as too lazy.

If the excavation of our choice was miraculously dry it became a desert, or perhaps its far bank was a slope at Gettysburg. For we were often patrons of the old Alhambra Theatre, which in those days seemed to specialize in Civil War dramas spawned by the success of D. W. Griffith's *The Birth of a Nation*. Of course, being Northwesterners and wholly ignorant of the Deep South, we stormed the slope as young men in blue, firing our scantlings which had become Springfields and routing treasonous troops of the Confederacy. Sometimes, forgetting what our mothers would say when we got home, we fell dead on the spot, caught by enemy fire, rolling down the dusty bank to the bottom.

Of course there was John's weekly trip to the Pike Place Market to shop for staples for his mother's shelves. He carried a black knitted bag for his parcels while I, unencumbered, tagged along. In those days the fruit and vegetable stalls, presided over by truck gardeners of all nationalities, seemed to stretch for miles.

John Buckles, taught by his mother, was as canny a shopper as any poor old lady, choosing by his sharp eyes, probing fingers and sense of smell. Every week we pretty well covered the place, and it was always fascinating. It had more stores than a small town, and the smells of food were everywhere: freshly ground coffee, fish caught early that morning, meat that was aged just right. There were a lot of little restaurants, from "coffee and" to cafeterias. You could buy a pair of shoes or a second-hand pair of pants, and spices from all over the world. If a tooth began to ache, there was a dentist handy. If you wanted horseradish a man would grind it before your eyes and nose. If you had kitchen knives that needed sharpening, there was a fellow who honed them on a stone wheel powered by his feet and old bicycle pedals.

It was mainly a place for old people when I was a boy—or did they just look old to me? Later it has attracted young shopkeepers, "arty" youth selling bad paintings and batiks and beads and giant buttons espousing various causes, or ridiculing the Establishment or the military.

Inasmuch as John was finicky and pennywise, we'd cover pretty much all of it. But we were on the run, particularly in summer, because if the butter was melting through his mesh sack before he got home he was due for some ladylike but unadulterated hell when he got back to the rooming house.

So it was all our city, the Market and the rest: Magnolia Bluff, Queen Anne Hill, the University district, Lake Washington and Lake Union, the rain pools in the vacant lots. It was all ours, and we thought we knew it all, but there were things we didn't know.

We didn't know, for instance, that a full-rigged ship lay moldering under the foundations of the Colman Building, and we couldn't point out the spot where three men had been hanged by vigilantes, or where courageous Judge Thomas Burke had stopped an anti-Chinese mob by the sheer combined power of his presence and his oratory.

But as we moved toward the eighth grade at Warren School we, young as we were, began to see and sense change. Some of the clay hills had been partially leveled or graded by picks and shovels and wheelbarrows. Now we could witness an even greater engineering feat: the sluicing down of old Denny Hill by fire hoses, helped by some dynamite and steam shovels. The clay soil was moved six or seven blocks by endless canvas belts onto self-capsizing barges, so that now Denny Hill is spread along the vast deep of Elliott Bay. It was one of the great engineering feats of a time that was innocent technologically as otherwise—and what a show it was for young and old alike. More exciting than Ringling Brothers, and free.

Both the old Denny School and the cupola-crowned Sacred Heart School were perched atop the clay hill which the engineers had condemned to the bottom of Elliott Bay. There was a slippery path which led from the west bluff of the hill to the lower, newly made streets and the hotel that was home. The cross-cleated planks did not help much—and neither did the big Italian kids from Sacred Heart who now and then decided to speed my progress by giving chase, yelling threats in the language of their parents.

Actually they were harmless, even tender-hearted, although I never slowed down enough to make certain of this. It was then a tradition that Protestant-oriented Denny School and the pupils of Sacred Heart were enemies. That was why my parents transferred me to Warren Avenue School, near the trolley-car barns, on the graded flatland then called Belltown, and it was there I met John Buckles. A few years after that both Denny School and Sacred Heart came down, and the hill beneath them was demolished.

I doubt that most of the clay-greased shovelers and teamsters with their trap-door-bottomed wagons knew the reason for the destruction of the great hill in an area still known as the Denny Regrade District. But the civic leaders saw that the movement of the city would be northward, as indeed it is.

The movement was slower than anticipated. The final regrade is now mainly a sea of parking lots, outdated three- and four-story apartment houses; and, nearer downtown a few panel-constructed office buildings that somehow look temporary. The chief landmarks are the Seattle Center, cultural and scientific heritage of the 1962 World's Fair, and a tall apartment house beginning to show its age and tenanted mainly by well-to-do elderly widows. As they gradually pass away, the office space on lower floors moves upward. Soon the Grosvenor House will be entirely an office building, the pioneer of its kind in old Belltown. Across the street is the *Post-Intelligencer*, which is more than a pioneer of Belltown. It is the oldest business establishment in Seattle, and dug in its heels by spending seven million dollars for a third story, new presses and a colorful interior renovation.

The growing town was always changing under a boy's eyes. John and I took for granted cross streets of thick planking laid horizontally and scarred by the iron shoes of heavy draft horses. We paid little mind to a few cobblestoned streets that had been ballast in sailing ships making it empty into Puget Sound.

John and I may have been more or less oblivious to the changing hodgepodge that was Seattle in our boyhood. We didn't even notice that although the lady shoppers of Second Avenue were in the mode, the male citizens of the town were generally the worst-dressed in the nation. Of course hard derbies were in favor, but so was a broad-brimmed peaked hat that had a flavor of Alaska and the Gold Rush about it. Coats were rarely tailored, pants were baggy, and brightly shined shoes an affectation. The old photographs taken early in the century are hard to believe now. But the policemen were uniformed about as they were in any other city. There was the broad belt unsuccessfully trying to hold in a paunch, the long-skirted jacket, the helmet—older readers may recall the Keystone Kops of silent movie days, and ours resembled them.

If a boy could overlook many things, he could not miss the excitement in the air after an assassination in Sarajevo and a widening war broke out in Europe. It seemed as if the newspapers issued extras on the hour, with black headlines two inches high. There came the day that a German submarine docked on the waterfront and her ramrod crew and officers walked the streets unharmed, even welcomed, for President Wilson had proclaimed our neutrality and Seattle had a sizable, close-knit German population.

Three summers drifted by, and still the war seemed far away from the Pacific Northwest. Some of those summer days the precious sunlight was blotted out by the smoke of forest fires and the sky glowed red at night above the mountains. *Ecology* and *quality environment* were not yet in the Seattle vocabulary, and there was wood-smelling smog in the air that would shock the anti-air pollution groups today. Out in the still independent Ballard area, gray ashes fell from the sky, the product of sawmill burners which took care of chaff and slabwood. The lumbermen had not yet learned to make the most of the tree.

Then in the third summer of the European war even a boy could sense that our neutrality was shifting. Old and new shipyards south of town were coming to life. A new emigration sifted in from the East Coast, including many trained shipbuilders and their families. The rumor was that they received fabulous wages of seven to ten dollars a day.

When the town was 93 years old and the century seventeen, we were in the war. The shipyard workers became heroes, but not to the same degree as those who appeared in khaki. Fort Lewis, not far away near Tacoma, took young men from the cities and farms and tried to make them soldiers, something they would not really become until they got across the continent, into ships, and finally into the dark and bloody forests of Germany and France. From Seattle they had been preceded by a few adventurous young men who had joined the British Air Force, and some restless young women who departed to drive ambulances or become nurses of the Red Cross.

The tiny airplane shop owned by William Boeing built some navy training planes and shipped them to San Diego. In the woods the Army took over spruce mills, for that was the light sturdy wood from which to make frames for the first warcraft of the air. The Naval Shipyard at Bremerton came alive, and so did Bremerton. The German clubs disbanded, their Old Country songs silenced.

Boys like John and me learned the tunes and words to songs such as "Over There" and "Johnny, Get Your Gun," and tried to save up enough money to buy a War Bond. Failing that, we hoarded tinfoil and rolled it into balls big enough to be acceptable to Uncle Sam. We saved peach pits, too, and dropped them into barrels in front of department stores—where, so short a time ago, Indian women had spread their mats on the sidewalk to sell their hand-woven baskets. There was some mysterious property in a peach pit, we learned, that was necessary to the filters of gas masks.

John and I carried swagger sticks, about the size of a baton, aping the smarter United States officers, who were in turn aping British officers.

Seattle was booming and yeasting again, as it had during the Gold Rush. There were cynics who whispered privately that Kaiser Wilhelm was doing a lot for the town, just as, twenty-four years later, others would say, more openly and during the "Cold War" abroad, that Hitler was making us prosperous. In our hearts we knew that the second one would involve the Pacific, that it would be nearer. But by then we had no illusions about a World War, for we realized that in 1917–18 we had not at all made the world safe for democracy.

But John and I, as did our elders, believed it, when the city was young and so were we. It was a time when, in the unkept grass of what had come to be "parking strips" and among the weeds of vacant lots, little roses grew wild, descendants of those rose seeds that Louisa Boren Denny, first bride of Seattle, had carried across the plains in the pockets of her apron. You can see them still, in some unexpected places not covered by concrete, but soon will see them no more. Like so many other things in Seattle, their doom began on the day Pearl Harbor was attacked.

14

Politics and Circuses

Puzzling is the word to describe modern Seattle politics. Looking back, I am rather convinced that this has been true since the days of Populism and the period when Whigs became Republicans.

Although east of the Cascades the relatively sparse population can be depended upon to mark their ballots in the conservative squares, voters in Seattle and King County are unpredictable.

Shelby Scates, the sharp political observer for Seattle's morning paper, characterized the first general election of the present decade as like a pointillist painting by Georges Seurat. "I mean," he said, "that, statewide, it was perfectly focused in its general composition, but contradictory in its details." He might have added that most of our regional balloting is contradictory in details. Seattle and Washington State voters cross party lines with the greatest of ease. The general election in 1970 was a Democratic sweep on partisan matters, and a classic demonstration of Puget Sound voters' selectivity on ballot issues. It must be noted that Seattleites, and most of the state, frequently ignore newspaper and television editorials, campaign advertisements and the paid space of leading citizens endorsing this or that candidate or issue. Also, listen and look as they may, they pay little attention to campaign oratory or press conferences when they get behind the green curtain of the voting booth. This observer often wonders why the money is spent, so consistently has it been shown that much of the currency does not transform into support.

The initial general election of the seventies was in traditional puzzle form. It was to be expected that U. S. Senator Henry Jackson was the outstanding personal victor. But it could not be predicted that his victory would come about via the largest margin in state history. Jackson campaigned vigorously for the presidency in 1972. He and Senator Warren ("Maggie") Magnuson, who did not need to run in the 1970 race, have forged a strong political power out of a state which—until their rises in seniority—had been weak from the viewpoint of the national capital.

In the governor's mansion in Olympia, Republican Dan Evans must have sat some time before the fireplace in deep thought and future planning, for he is a stubborn fighter. He had campaigned strongly (also with charm, where appropriate) for tax reform. Evans' proposal to add a flat income tax to the state's taxing powers was defeated by the voters in 1970. Undaunted and more convinced than ever of the need for reform, Evans appointed a statewide citizens' committee in 1971 to overhaul the state's antiquated tax system. So far the committee has been unable to move its recommendations through the state legislature.

Liberalization of the abortion law carried the election day—yet for a month afterward a large percentage of Seattleites were boiling angry about the victory of "the killers" and not keeping quiet about the result. This, too, is a Seattle tradition. It would not surprise old-timers if the issue arose again, with an opposite result. In Seattle politics it is always reckless to assume that an issue has been decided and the story ended. Our voters are noted for second thoughts.

Yet one aspect of the abortion issue should not be overlooked. There was a vocal group of females, backed by a sizable number of churchmen, who threatened to bring murder charges against those who legally performed abortions. The smashing rejection by the voters of this sort of threat could improve the odor of future campaigns. But inasmuch as we are talking about politics on the shores of Elliott Bay I would not, as a native, bet on this. One of the fiercest and most disgraceful campaigns I ever witnessed in my hometown was staged by opponents of a dog-leash law. On both sides there was what is called on Skid Road "dirty pool"; and that dog-leash battle almost obscured other issues far more vital to the progress of the city.

When voting on public issues in 1970 our people again displayed their traditional selectivity. They turned down a proposed lid on state taxes, even as they rejected by an overwhelming majority the governor's tax reform bill. Proposals to lift the interest rate ceiling on bond issues for pollution control bills were adopted. Yet a proposal to lift it on bonds for state buildings was turned down. Seattleites and Washingtonians know exactly what they want—and when they want it. There's always time, a young city feels, to change the course.

Such varied decisions seem contradictory to some, and to others are sophisticated voting. It is clear now that we want quality environment—but it must be added that we may hedge a bit when the question of money arises. That we want quality environment at all is significant, because in the sixties the subject was rarely mentioned. Up until that decade our feeling was that, unquestionably, we lived in the best place in the world. Later came some doubts. There arrived also thousands of newcomers from cities which had waited too long to curb pollution, and these knew the tragedy procrastination can create. It appears almost certain that these newcomers have improved the conscience of the city and caused the natives to examine issues and candidates more cautiously, and perhaps with less emotion.

For example, at the time of the 1970 election the area—along with the nation—seemed headed for a recession that might be prolonged. It was particularly noted in the Puget Sound area due to the layoffs at Boeing and the spotty condition of the airline business.

One might have thought that this situation would work against incumbents, whether Democrats or Republicans. The voters moved to the contrary. Even in the most affected precinct areas the citizens stayed by the incumbents if they approved their past records in fair weather. They did not let their financial emotions affect their judgment. As a proud Seattleite I can say that it isn't in every city and county that you find many voters who realize that one man is not to blame for everything that is going wrong.

There have been extended periods when Seattle politics were simply dull. The citizenry seemed to prefer them that way. The town was usually prosperous, and it was growing, and Seattleites were in general pleased with themselves and their community.

Candidates were for the most part weak or rogues, and it looked as if their constituency preferred them to be one or the other. Excepting the pioneer days, the record shows that there was decade upon decade when it was almost impossible to persuade able and conscientious citizens to compete for office. These were the eras when our governors were meek and unimaginative, and when election to the Seattle City Council seemed a lifetime job. It appeared to be almost impossible to budge a councilman from his part-time chair. And in one such long period—probably a retrogression to the frontier spirit—a councilmanic post was indeed a part-time activity. Members often carried on extensive outside businesses, and absenteeism went almost unnoticed. There is no question that conflict of interest was, if not ignored, taken for granted.

At such times the mayor seemed either powerless or unwilling to change things, whatever his name. But among the councilmen, growing gray as they muddled along, there was a notable exception. He was David Levine, who spent many more than eight hours at his job and was for a time virtually the mayor insofar as power and action went. Like all dedicated men, he had his detractors, and there were ugly rumors that he was working for Dave Levine, not Seattle. But it was he who took the city through one of its most serious financial crises, even persuading merchants to accept "scrip" instead of the money which Seattle could not pay to its employees.

What was the reward for such a loyal public servant? Retired from the council after many years, he was given a small office at City Hall and unofficially he was called "adviser to the mayor." Certainly no mayor could have a better one, for Levine had seen Seattle through good times and bad. But soon grumblings were heard as to whether it was wise for a mayor to have Levine as an adviser, although in reality the post was mainly honorary. It was not long until Levine felt the doubt and enmity and departed from City Hall forever. Today he is almost forgotten, and almost half the population were unborn or babes in arms when he was fighting to keep Seattle moving.

Among the gray patches of Seattle politics there was a brief, bright interlude—really a foreshadowing of things to come. A group of young men banded themselves into an organization called Cincinnatus, christened for the Roman who now and then left his plow to defend Rome and returned to his weed-strewn fields in the piping times of peace.

"We were young then," says attorney Ralph Potts, one of the group's leading founders. "We wanted to get into politics but found it almost a closed corporation in Seattle. We explained what we were trying to do, which mainly was to get young men interested— and into office. The old wheelhorses at least pretended they thought we had a great idea, and offered to guide us. Some were sincere in this, but somehow we got the idea that others were trying to guide us the wrong way—I mean, out. But we went ahead, mainly on our own."

The life of the organization was relatively brief, due to depressions, rumors of wars and war itself. But Cincinnatus did show what could be done. The one-time members are now all well past middle age. "We were just a bit ahead of the times," Potts says now. "A lot of things we would do differently now, but then we were green as grass. But it is pleasant to see happening now what we had in mind more than thirty-five years ago."

Cincinnatus did show what might be done by young men weary of seeing old men of both main parties running the show. It must be remembered that these were the days prior to the discovery that the world belongs to young men and women of all races and creeds, and that they intend to take their claims to the hearts of people of all ages.

Cincinnatus threw some momentary fear into the wheelhorses, both Democrat and Republican. It did more. It succeeded in getting a young man, George Lockwood, on the council. "He looked like a high school kid among all those grandfathers," recalls one sympathetic former councilman. "But, believe me, he learned, and he worked, and he was an adept persuader. You might say he was sort of a pioneer, like the young founders of the city. He did a great deal for Seattle and hardly any of it made big stories in the papers. It would now, because the whole viewpoint has changed."

Cincinnatus did far more than put Lockwood at the council table. It elected young Arthur Langlie as mayor, and Langlie did such a good job that he proceeded to the governor's chair. In Olympia he showed ability, courage and a rocklike integrity. The late Miller Freeman, a leading citizen and one of the elders who had helped the Cincinnatus because he saw the need for younger men in office, told me: "Langlie was one of the state's outstanding governors and I hope that some day this will be recognized. I was in the House of Representatives down there for a while, so I think I speak from special knowledge. Langlie wasn't in Olympia as a politician, or the white-haired boy of the Republicans. He was a governor and he helped make the state greater than it had been. And no member of Cincinnatus, which had really got him there, received a favor he didn't deserve."

So actually, in its brief time, Cincinnatus accomplished considerable. Its accomplishments were in marked contrast to Seattle politics generally at that time. And, as Potts suggests now, the shadow they cast was longer than the Cincinnatans foresaw.

In 1968 an organization called CHECC, the acronym for Choose an Effective City Council, came into being. It was similar to, but smaller in scale than Cincinnatus, and consisted of young political activists of both parties. Their aim was to oust some of the old guard city councilmen and they campaigned on behalf of Phyllis Lamphere, a woman of intelligence, grace and charm, and Tim Hill, a straight-looking but strong-minded young man who might well have been one of their own. Both Mrs. Lamphere and Hill, who have turned out to be highly effective council members, were elected. Later in 1970, somewhat the same group of activists united behind John Miller, a young lawyer and conservationist, and Sam Smith, making a bid for re-election as Seattle's first black councilman. Mrs. Lamphere also received their support and all three were elected.

There have been times when Seattleites showed a preference for circuses mixed with their politics. In these years the rest of the country paid little attention to what was transpiring on Elliott Bay; the anti-Chinese riots and even the "Seattle Revolution" seemed far in the past. And some of the circuses were so purely local that they did not deserve national attention. Others happened when the nation as a whole was having troubles; there were political and social upheavals almost everywhere in the country—or so the Great Depression made it appear.

Sometimes Seattle cared more for an amusing show than it did for serious government. The examples are not all complimentary; perhaps none of them are, but they deserve their place in the record. They help to characterize the Seattleite as waging within himself a struggle between the frontier spirit and municipal sophistication.

At such times the police department inevitably becomes involved. But that pattern has meandered through the city's history for years. Commenting on a recent allegation of widespread bribery and conflict of interest, Maurice Kadish, veteran Seattle attorney, said, "When I look at the current picture I'm tempted to ask, 'What else is new?'" Gazing at his city out of a window high in our first skyscraper, the L. C. Smith Building, he was referring to reports of graft and protection money. "I remember the same kind of news. In 1929, for instance, Wendell Wasner, then special agent in charge of intelligence for what was called the Bureau of Internal Revenue, said that graft in police circles had become an institution in Seattle. He said the situation here was a lot worse than Seattle people realized."

Kadish went on: "I don't pretend to know the inside story today. But Wasner was certainly right in 1929, and only a world war halted an investigation which might have told the voters what Wasner said they'd find hard to believe. The fellow who said that history repeats itself was right. Just change the names today and you have the same old story."

In late July of 1971 Kadish's remarks were confirmed. A grand jury returned thirty-two indictments of conspiracy to defraud by city officials. Involved were a recently defeated prosecuting attorney, a former police chief and two councilmen. Named, but not indicted, was a councilman who was later elected mayor. All had not been as smooth and pure as most Seattleites believed.

There was once a Seattle mayor who tried it both ways. Hi (for Hiram) Gill was a gaunt, well-meaning Midwesterner with an Adam's apple as obvious as his thinking. He ran for mayor on a "wide-open town" campaign. He announced that if a man wanted to drink and gamble it was that man's business. He went even further. He confessed a belief that if a lonely man liked the ladies and had no close companionship among that sex he should have available to him a well-regulated district where he could find company suited to his taste. He spelled this out in campaign speeches, and to close friends added, "Hell, this is a seaport town, ain't it?"

Seattleites elected him.

But once the town was thrown wide open, a number of citizens began to experience pangs of conscience. Some of their guilt was set off by articles in national magazines and eastern newspapers which called Seattle "still a wide-open, wild Western town" where fun could be had where you found it, and where you could find it anywhere within the city limits. There were also citizens who believed that Gill was getting a huge rake-off on vice. "I don't believe it," a ninety-year-old resident told this writer. "I knew him well, and in his way he was honest. I visited him in a hospital one time and he told me that a madame had swept into his room one day and thrown a lot of high-denomination bills on the coverlet. It was a Catholic hospital and Gill said he called in one of the sisters and told her to gather up the money and see that it got to charity organizations. I believed him and I still do."

Yet Seattle's chronic split personality was badly disturbed. When Seattle is good it would like to be sinful, and when it is evil it will soon confess and don sackcloth and ashes. Once upon a time it decided that horse racing was a sin; today the Longacres track is one of the most popular in the West.

But dog racing? Absolutely not! It was once attractive to thousands of Seattleites, but now a lean dog running faster than a lope is as likely to find itself in jail as in the city pound.

Whatever the reason for Seattle's schizophrenia—and as yet no expert has analyzed it—Hiram Gill found himself in trouble and the populace impatient. Seattleites decided not to wait until the next election to atone for their sins. Recall petitions were circulated against Gill, and my father—who once had been a bookmaker at the old Meadows track, and operated a couple of small gambling houses—was in the forefront of the movement. He was so far in front that he and four others were cartooned in the Seattle *Times.* The cartoonist caricatured him as raising his hands to heaven, a gesture which revealed several hidden aces in his hip pockets. The cartoon was titled "Isn't Mr. Gill a Wicked Man!" Father never explained his change to me, but I suspect that he didn't want his son to grow up in immoral surroundings.

In any case, Mayor Gill was indeed recalled.

He bided his time, and in the very next election filed his candidacy for a second time. Now he had a different pitch. Over and over again he said to the voters, "You elected me because I promised you a wide-open town. I considered my election a mandate and gave you what you asked. Then you made a switch. I can do that, too. You know I keep my promises. If you elect me this time I promise you a city government that the most straitlaced clergyman will approve."

Hi Gill's refurbished campaign approach appealed to Seattle's sense of fair play. There is no other explanation for his victory. The moment he got into office he kept his campaign promise in ways that astonished the whole town. He banished games of chance, he sent fancy ladies packing, and transformed their "hotels" into respectable inns. He came near to closing movie houses on Sundays.

As for speakeasies, he didn't simply padlock them. He formed an official ax squad and these enthusiasts destroyed tens of thousands of dollars' worth of fixtures. If an operator opened elsewhere, he only furnished more work for the ax squad. This strange collection of lawmen poured hundreds of gallons of beer into the gutters. Many of them were former loggers and had never had so much fun in their lives or wielded an ax with more finesse.

There is a legend that denizens of the Skid Road rushed up-town when they heard of a raid, lined up prone in the gutters and lapped up the illicit liquor like cats. The story is apocryphal; the new Hi Gill would allow no such favoritism. But it is known that some of the ax squad sneaked a nip now and then to keep themselves at proper pitch.

Hi Gill strutted around City Hall in a gray suit (as always) which hung on his skinny frame like a sack. He wore a broad-brimmed Stetson cowboy hat and smoked a corncob pipe; they had become his trademarks. Now and then he left his desk and official halls to make a speech in which he dared the forces of evil to thwart him.

With some exceptions, Seattle loved it all. They found Hi Gill's new term twice as much fun and three times as exciting as the first truncated term. He tried a third time, but the voters wanted Ole Hanson for a change.

Only once, at this writing, has Seattle elected a woman mayor. She was Bertha K. Landes, wife of a political science professor at the University of Washington and chairman of the City Council. For several years she was openly hostile to Mayor Edwin J. Brown—and the issue in those Prohibition days was Wet *vs.* Dry. Mrs. Landes was all Dry. When Brown left town in 1924 to be present at the Democratic convention, Mrs. Landes became acting mayor. She straightaway fired the chief of police and set to work closing down the town as tightly as she could. Her actions caught the imagination of the voters—especially the women—and she was elected to succeed Brown in 1926.

Frequent liquor raids became increasingly unpopular as she goaded the police into a closed-town policy. Seattle quickly grew tired of Mrs. Landes and she was defeated by Frank Edwards after serving a two-year term. Seattle's next woman mayor? At this time there are a number of possibilities around, and some are experienced from service on the City Council, which has had several female members following the pioneers, Mrs. W. W. Powell and Mrs. Harland Edwards. Somehow these two trail-blazers also could think of little more than improving our parks, a point upon which they encountered no disagreement from their male associates. This was mild fare compared with that served up by councilwomen who followed them. The modern spirit of a Seattle councilwoman is to fight hard in the campaign and to keep on fighting if she wins. Today the male segment of our City Council may be in the majority, but when they hear a female voice at the table they have learned to stop, look and listen. The women who gain a place on the council today are also for improving parks—and for more of them—but they are for, or against, a lot of other matters. And when one of them gets the feeling that the male lawmakers, including the mayor, are getting off the track of progress and the humanities they take to the newspapers and television, and Seattleites pay attention.

Those who are unhappy with Seattle politics today should recall, or be told about, the Elliott Bay politics of a few decades ago. In times past we have been accused of attempting to rival California in supporting crackpots filled with panaceas. Industrialist Gene Tunney, former pugilist, once visited Seattle after a sojourn in Oregon's calm and conservative Portland. He took a jaundiced look around and said that Oregon was a bridge between two insane asylums.

The Franklin Delano Roosevelt landslide of 1932 brought

events which decrepit Seattle Republicans still regard as almost the beginning of the end. In that exciting November, when Herbert Hoover's only local memorial was "Hooverville"—a community of shacks and lean-tos on the tideflats—we elected an advertising dental parlor barker as a commissioner of King County. A county jail prisoner, charged with the rape of a twelve-year-old girl, was elevated to the eminence of state representative. And, most intriguing of all, a jazz bandleader turned up as lieutenant governor.

In that gray fall, which seemed like doomsday to hard-bitten Republicans, we witnessed candidates who suffered from a more or less common condition: lack of money with which to travel even to Olympia. These unfortunate victors usually were able to borrow a few dollars from their supporters, but about an equal number hitch-hiked.

It was certainly no disgrace to be without funds in 1932, but a number of our victorious candidates were lacking in other things as well. The main reason was that they had ridden to new heights on the coattails of President-elect Roosevelt.

Of them all, the most interesting was the bandleader, Victor Aloysius Meyers. His trail to statesmanship had not been direct; he had some political experience behind him. He had once run for mayor, under circumstances that were peculiar.

Meyers was a tall, bubbling, likable fellow who looked and acted exactly like a bandleader of his time. In this profession he was reasonably successful, although always broke. Nobody at the Plaza in New York ever heard his band, but he did record some Columbia discs, which sold fairly well. By design or circumstances, or lack of invitations from afar, Meyers and his boys stayed with the Pacific Northwest.

In the late twenties our locally famous bandleader converted a stuffy garage into what was the area's first night club. It was "the only place to go" insofar as young people were concerned. Of course it went broke, but for a while it carried Vic's name in illuminated letters two feet tall. When he had the money he hired a bus and played one-night stands around the Sound and in "the Big Palouse country" east of the Cascades. He became known throughout the state, and the day would come when this would help him on the way to the state capital.

Meyers' political career began in January, 1932, a year when the mayoralty campaign brought forth a vast disinterest. The candidates were so bad that the Seattle *Times* could not find it in its heart to support a single one. As for mayor, it decided to enter its own man and make sport of the whole campaign. The newspaper played safe by choosing the most obviously unqualified character they could find. Their man was Victor Aloysius Meyers. They paid his filing fee and promised him thirty days of front-page publicity. That couldn't hurt his band, and he and everybody else knew that he couldn't win.

The *Times* assigned to him a pair of its star reporters of humorous bent. They were to handle the candidate, write his speeches and furnish him with bright sayings which he could "ad lib" when caught in a corner. Catching the spirit of the extended exhibition he soon was spouting monologues of his own. An occasional comment that was his own invention startled the management of the *Times* and they warned his handlers to watch him more closely. Every day his reporters studied the campaign promises of the field and parodied them for Vic's use. Almost all editions of the paper carried a by-line piece by the jazz man, who was dubbed "The Harmony Candidate."

Meyers' suggestions for the improvement of Seattle delighted the citizens, whose minds were on the zooming stock market and who were paying small attention anyhow to the rhetoric of Vic's opponents. Soon Vic's campaign found space in eastern newspapers, which seemed to take it seriously. There were tens of thousands of out-of-towners who believed that a community on the shores of Elliott Bay had gone utterly mad. In the desert of Prohibition the bandleader was made to remark that he believed a sizable saloon could be made to pay. In addition to wet-minded Seattleites it would bring visitors and conventioneers by the trainload. Vic said he had been doing some figuring (everybody, particularly his bank, knew that his arithmetic was atrocious) and concluded that such an institution could defray all municipal expenses. He would see to it that the saloon was a monopoly by local law.

Vic contended that the midnight trolley runs should supply cracked ice for merry passengers, and that trolleys at all hours should be provided with pretty hostesses. These would distract regular patrons who were tired of the same old scenery day after day. Ahead of his time, without knowing it, he deplored the uglier parts of the city and advocated blossoming flower pots atop the fire hydrants.

He was ready for anything that would attract attention to his candidacy. He appeared at a business club luncheon draped as Mahatma Gandhi, complete with goat. Up and down the main avenues north and south he rode on a brewery truck drawn by handsome Percherons. He scattered leaflets and, more discriminatingly, flowers when he saw handsome working girls along the curb.

Addressing a crowd of workingmen he transported them with his candor. "I don't know for sure whether I have any qualifications to be a mayor," he confessed. "The truth is, I just would like to be one for a term. I would never run for a second term because I have noticed that this can be habit-forming. I think I would have a lot of fun at the job, and I certainly can use the wages."

At just what point Vic began to take his campaign seriously is not known. But toward the finish line his sponsors and his handlers began to have some trouble with him. The *Times* was paying him a small stipend, under the guise of a campaign contribution, and Vic bought a dark suit and began to walk and talk with dignity. Actually, the *Times* lost control of him in the final week of the campaign, and the top brass of the traditionally conservative newspaper began to fear that he might win.

Certainly before the show was over he had developed high hopes. His failure at the polls, a dismal defeat, did not discourage him. When the next opportunity showed itself he went down to Olympia and announced that he wanted to file for governor. To his great disappointment he found that his wallet did not carry enough to pay the filing fee. "Well," he drawled, "what else do you have that's important? How much for that—what do you call him? —lieutenant governor?" When they told him, he counted his bills and change again and found that he could make it, with enough left over for bus fare back to Seattle. "All right," he said jovially, "I'll try for that."

In the primaries he won by a comfortable plurality, as a plain western-type Democrat and no help from the *Times*. The following November he was swept into office on the Roosevelt flood of 1932. The *Times* was embarrassed, and took a great deal of criticism, for the Republicans blamed the paper for making Vic's name known beyond the saxophonic circles of jazz.

When a well-wisher warned him that he would have to preside over the state senate and therefore be familiar with parliamentary law, Vic retorted in heat: "To hell with Parliament. What's wrong with American law? It's good enough for me, and it'll do for the state of Washington."

His reply was sincere, for Meyers was green as a wheat field in spring when it came to his duties. But he was quick to learn, and determined that now people were going to take him seriously. He got hold of the rules of parliamentary law, studied them night after night and took a short course in public speaking. To the relief, and astonishment, of many citizens he presided over the senate with smooth dignity—and that was no small feat in that year when both houses were virtually untutored mobs. Both his enemies and supporters practically forgave him for packing the lieutenant governor's office with relatives and rounding them out with friends who needed jobs.

When the voters finally led Vic out of Olympia it was discovered that the political bug had bitten deep. In 1946 he made another try for mayor of Seattle, and he did not clown around about it. Defeated, he disappeared for a while, then made a political comeback in the 1950s, running successfully for the post of secretary of state. Which brings up another phenomenon of Washington's frequently offbeat political tastes—that is to say, we often elect our ex-football coaches and athletes to office.

John Cherberg, ousted as head football coach at Washington in 1955, rolled up an enormous vote in the '56 election and has served as Washington's lieutenant governor ever since. Howie Odell, fired as coach three years earlier, later was voted in as county commissioner; the same for Johnny O'Brien, Seattle University's first All-American basketball star. And when Jim Owens suffers an off season, the standard joke is, "Big Jim must be planning to run for governor."

Our final circus-style candidate failed to make it. This was a chap known only as Richard A. C. Greene, who filed to run as state land commissioner in 1968 as a Republican. Greene won the Republican primary handily before anybody discovered that he wasn't even in the state. He was teaching school in Hawaii.

Richard A. C. Greene's absentee campaign was run by a few local friends, somewhat in the Meyers vein, but on a more sophisticated level. Grave-faced press conferences were called by his supporters at the Warren G. Harding Memorial Bandstand in Woodland Park. Greene's ostensible campaign pledge as land commissioner was summed up by his supporters as "treat the land gently, but firmly." If elected, he promised, he would hire the Democratic incumbent, Bert Cole, as his assistant. Pictures showing Richard A. C. Greene campaigning from a beach in Hawaii were published in the papers. The whole thing fizzled out with a few giggles, but it was fun while it lasted.

One way to describe the mayoralty situation in Seattle in the years just prior to World War II is to compare John Dore with Arthur Langlie; the two were definitely political stars in the town's progress toward mature lawmaking.

As a young man, Dore had been a police reporter, a post in which he learned where the political bodies were buried, or how to find them if he didn't know already. It was in that early role that he learned to play poker with luck that some found suspicious, and developed a taste for bourbon that stayed with him as long as he lived. He was a round and raucous little man, with metal-rimmed spectacles and a very red face out of which could come language both charming and obscene.

He was ambitious and did not intend to spend his life as a police reporter. He studied law on his own time and passed the state bar examination. Considering his background on the police beat it was almost inevitable that he would become a criminal lawyer, and one of the sharpest in town at the time. As a lawyer his career was not exactly what the Seattle-King County Bar Association would call clinically clean. But John Dore was almost always about one step ahead of disbarment proceedings. At one point in his career he slipped out of court, ran to the rooms of the law library, and effectively hid a couple of volumes which he suddenly realized opposing counsel would need to convict Dore's client.

When he decided to run for mayor he won easily, for he knew almost everybody in town. Dore made sport of the mayor's office as he had made sport of the law. His political deals were legendary, and over the years he had built up secret files which helped him considerably when he needed support—or a favor—from some leading citizen whose outward mien hid matters which would do his reputation no good if revealed.

Seattle forgave Dore for many things because he never pretended to be more than he was: a hard-bitten former criminal lawyer who would cut a corner when he found it necessary to his welfare. He knew that people can be fooled, and that sometimes they even seem to enjoy it. The man most Seattleites called

"Johnny" Dore had the jovial effrontery to tell them so, and they appeared to enjoy that, too.

Arthur Langlie, the handsome young man Cincinnatus both put into the mayor's chair and later sent on to Olympia, was certainly the opposite of Johnny Dore. He had deep respect for his legal profession. His attitudes and conduct were impeccable, almost spiritual. That he was appreciated for such qualities was proved at the polls twice. Yet somehow he never captured the imagination of Seattleites and was never as popular as Dore. In the Pacific Northwest a majority of votes does not necessarily mean popularity of the kind that Johnny Dore brought forth. This is probably because, even in the seventies, the frontier spirit rises now and then.

When Langlie's political power waned—partly due to his Republicanism—he accepted the invitation of millionaire H. L. Hunt to become publisher of *McCall's* magazine. Seattle newspapermen, who had never understood Langlie and vice versa, were astonished. They could think of nobody anywhere who seemed less qualified for the rough-and-tumble world of national magazines. Nonetheless, Langlie moved to New York and was a success at his new job. When he and Hunt separated business relations by mutual but friendly agreement, Langlie and his attractive wife returned home to look toward the years of retirement. By then he had lost interest in politics and passed away a few years later.

In contrast, Johnny Dore might have continued in elective offices as long as he liked. But his battered physique was failing fast. In his last campaign there was a memorable evening when he had to be assisted to the rostrum. Once there he hung on tightly, now and then swaying, and some of the old fire showed through. But voters saw that he was near the finish, even if Dore did not. Defeated and ill, he was as popular as ever in a way that Langlie had never been, despite a superior character which even Dore's old friends recognized. Today, Johnny Dore, like Hi Gill, is remembered by a large segment of the older population whereas honest Arthur Langlie, the true knight in shining armor, is almost forgotten.

Our region has never produced a President of the United States, but in the middle of this century there was a feeling that we were getting warm. We have had several able men who came close to the vice-presidency, and we have more and more who have the ability and the youth popular these days. A certain fall of the cards and it could happen relatively soon.

Harry Truman very much wanted Supreme Court Justice William O. Douglas, raised in Wenatchee and graduated from Whitman College in Walla Walla, to be his running mate. Douglas is popular in the region for his interest in the natural environment, and for his regular summer sojourns in a cabin near the Rogue River. Truman's invitation was prior to Justice Douglas' run of marriages to young women, but at the time he gave the matter some long thoughts. "Finally I decided that I liked the law too much," Douglas told this writer. "And I felt that I was where I belonged. I think I am of some value to the Supreme Court, and I liked to be able to travel and write a book now and then."

Did Truman's apparently slim chance for victory have anything to do with the justice's decision? At the question the craggy outdoor lawmaker studied one of the eight-thousand-dollar chandeliers in the lobby of the new Washington Plaza, where we were talking. Suddenly his clear blue eyes fixed on me with something close to anger. "You and I have been acquainted since college days, and you know me better than that. I gave you the right answer the first time."

William O. Douglas is not the only one who might have been Vice-President, then President, from this state. Sen. Henry M. Jackson, widely popular in both parties here, very nearly was picked by John F. Kennedy as his running mate in 1960. As noted before, Jackson campaigned for the presidential nomination in 1972, although the early going was tough, since he bucked the difficult problem of names familiar on a nationwide scale.

President or not, Jackson is a powerful force for his state in the U. S. Senate. So is his senior colleague, fellow Democrat Warren G. Magnuson. Another bright young lawmaker from Seattle is Brock Adams (often mentioned here as a gubernatorial prospect), but I tend to think of Jackson, Magnuson and the veteran Republican Congressman Tom Pelly as forming a most powerful trio for Seattle and the state. At any rate, their efforts have brought the state literally billions of dollars in federally funded projects, providing thousands of jobs and turning the limelight on the Evergreen Land.

That much of what they have done for their constituencies has been connected with war or preparations for war has disturbed some people.

It was in that period of the "Cold War" across the Atlantic that many senators and representatives were very unhappy with the billions of dollars pouring into Washington State, sparsely populated and out on the edge of nowhere. Some blamed "maneuverings and deals" on the part of Magnuson and Jackson. In a way, their feelings were valid—for our two senators are lawmakers who work hard and pay attention to the people who put them where they are. But it must be noted that geography, geology, the Navy Yard and shipyards, and the chance that made Boeing synonymous with the Northwest, were of assistance to our senators and representatives. Yet in the big Union of states there are places with similar advantages, so plenty of credit must be chalked up to Magnuson, Jackson and Pelly—the trio who helped create such great changes in the area and in the process more than made up for the antiquated "silly seasons" when the region's politics were chautauquas featuring clowns and opportunist demagogues.

Doubtless Magnuson and Jackson were fortunate in that they began their political careers when the Scandinavian population of the area was somewhat higher in percentage than now. Jackson was born in Everett; his parents were Norwegian immigrants. Magnuson was born of Swedish parents in Moorhead, Minnesota, but the family moved early to Seattle, where the tremendously popular "Maggie" graduated from the University of Washington Law School.

Jackson moved from the House to the Senate in 1952. Magnuson is senior to him by several years, having been elected senator in 1941. Ignoring possible exemption, "Maggie" joined the Naval Reserve and made several tours on active duty.

Before he reached the capital he carried considerable experience under his belt as special prosecutor for King County, member of the state legislature and assistant U.S. district attorney. He seemed to carry all this background lightly. For years he was a merry bachelor, and sometimes it was difficult for voters to feel that he was serious enough. But they could never find a man who seemed to equal him. His friends are both Democrats and Republicans, and many of the latter have contributed to his campaigns.

Small and somewhat heavy, "Maggie" is a good storyteller and has a sense of humor that tops the occasional gaiety of Jackson and Pelly. His modesty projects sincerely. This writer remembers a talk he gave to members of the Seattle baking industry during his first term in the House. "Every once in a while," he told them, "one of the page boys asks me a question. Usually I have to tell them that I'm just a little Swede from out West in a place called Seattle and trying to find out what this is all about myself." At that time such innocent frankness was popular in Seattle. But now Seattle knows that Magnuson has found out plenty, and puts the knowledge to good use. As a lately married man he carries himself with more dignity. As always the shrewd mind is working behind the pleasant but now more serious façade. In the late sixties and early seventies he began to show a practical interest in more protection for the consumer, and some now call him "the Ralph Nader of the Senate." His close and old-time friends have told him that they suspect that his wife turned him toward this path. "She's a help," he admits, "because she is a consumer with a mind of her own, and she doesn't believe all that guff you read in some advertising and on some packaging. But I think maybe it all started when I quit smoking."

It is reported that "Maggie" was predominant in the creation of the law which demands that the Surgeon General's warning be printed on every cigarette package. His friends of younger days often ask him when he intends to see that a similar warning is printed on every bottle of liquor. He's been asked that so often that now he just winks and replies, "It's easy to quit drinking, but it's damned hard to kick the cigarette habit. That's why I don't like to see young people fooled into the habit."

As for Magnuson's many services in bringing jobs and projects to the state, he refuses to take all the credit. He shares it with Jackson, and with Representative Pelly and other members of the House. And he admits that somehow Washington State and the Puget Sound area are naturals for the projects that the country has needed in time or threat of war.

"I got a lot of credit for the Grand Coulee Dam, and Bonneville, and the other dams," he told me one day in the Senate dining room. "But don't forget the President was pitching, and the Army Engineers knew the score. Anyhow, I didn't create the Columbia River. God fixed that up. And as for the Hanford Atomic Works project—well, the Army wanted a place with a hell of a lot of room and a big cold river running through it. The Hanford location was it."

In the dining room we were interrupted for a moment by one of those old-fashioned politicians with a gray mane curling up the

back of his neck. He had weaved around a dozen tables just to clap
"Maggie" on the shoulder and give him a word or two of greeting.
In terms of both congressional service and actual years "Maggie"
was very much his junior. But the incident reflected Magnuson's
popularity, as well as the recognition that he can be valuable to his
colleagues.

Elected to the House in 1952, Congressman Thomas M.
Pelly bears no resemblance to our pair of senators. Tall, bald-
headed and somewhat heavy in facial features, he has attained a
most distinguished air as the years rolled by. A Republican, at times
he seems to carry a rabbit's foot that really works. He is representative of the First District, which is a rough one to ride. It includes a
part of Kitsap County, the Navy Yard, Bainbridge Island (home of
many millionaires) and a part of King County. No district in the
state contains such a mixture of voters, yet despite occasional strong
opposition and the times of peace, when Kitsap County sags economically, Tom Pelly has held it all together and returned to the
Potomac practically unscathed.

He puzzles the press, seeming at times to freeze when faced
with reporters. He does not have the flair of either Jackson or
Magnuson. But people trust him, and the voters have recognized
a job well done. A native Seattleite whose father was connected with
the British embassy, he worked in banking, and paralleling his banking phase went a strong appreciation of literature. He was once one
of the best booksellers in Seattle.

A more unlikely background for a successful career in politics
can scarcely be imagined. Yet Pelly started with top marks because
he had become a leading businessman who wanted to be of service
to his country politically. There are not nearly enough of them in
the Pacific Northwest—or anywhere else, for that matter—and Pelly
has deserved his successful campaigns, which at this writing stretch
over more than ten years.

So, as King County and Seattle moved haltingly into the
seventies—stumbling a bit—they clearly matured in the field of politics. It is unlikely that we'll ever see again the like of Vic Meyers and
Hi Gill in high offices, much less minor posts.

In fact, Seattleites were a bit startled in 1968 when a conservative Seattle lawyer, John Ehrlichman, who had long admired Richard

Nixon and helped manage his national campaign in 1968, was picked
to be one of the new President's inner circle of advisers. When
Ehrlichman's appointment made headlines, many a Seattleite asked,
"Who in the world is that?"

As governor in the sixties we twice elected Daniel J. Evans, an
engineer turned politician who was a state representative. Backed by
a forceful group of young Republicans, Evans won the confidence
of the older crowd, and was elected in 1964. At first, he seemed a bit
stiff and distant, but developed a warmer image among the elector-
ate. "He brings a slide rule to every problem," said one Seattleite.
Indeed, it's true that in some of his informal interviews in his office
he lightly taps the palm of one hand with a small plastic slide rule.
And when explaining a tax measure, he does bring a slide rule into
play and so covers a blackboard with the neat figures and symbols of
engineering that has reporters and legislative committees with
mouths agape. But it's all quite clear to Dan Evans and proof of
what he is saying.

But his is not only a slide rule mentality by any means. He
is strong for the humanities, civil rights and a fair deal for the
minorities. Of course he would like to see the budget balanced, as
what governor would not? But these matters are not political with
Dan Evans. They reflect the kind of young man he is.

Perhaps it is television that seems to be leading the state and
Seattle toward attractive candidates. Evans is tall, dark and good-
looking. He has a warm smile, but is not given to laughter and
certainly his initiation into politics was hardly a time for laughter. He
is not always a smooth or convincing speaker, probably because you
simply cannot bring a slide rule and a blackboard to the voters. But
obviously he speaks from honestly held beliefs and convictions.
When he is successfully opposed by a legislature or the voters on one
of his favorite bills he refuses to drop the subject. He readies himself
for another attempt, and tries hard to make his position more clear.

In the second year of his first term he was still battling hard for a
tax program which was proving unpopular, and there was no suggestion that he would welcome modifications. He was making this
attempt at the same time he was putting the finishing touches on a
bill which would give the governor stronger powers. And atop all this
he submitted a proposal for a department of transportation. When
this attempt failed, he girded for another try.

If he continues in office Governor Evans is determined that a state department of transportation should become a part of our machinery. "He's like a fighter who gets knocked flat, but springs up and charges forward again," said one reporter covering Olympia for a wire service. "I've never seen anything like him down here, and I've seen several state chiefs come and go."

Town wits and columnists call Dan Evans "Straight Arrow" but as a cynicism which is a vestige of the area's Indian days the label falls flat. Like him or not, Dan Evans is truly "Straight Arrow" and the state has not had very many in its political quiver.

In the seventies, at last, Seattleites began to recognize the importance of a solid City Council. Early in the new decade it had one, including an able black and two women, who proved themselves the equal of their male colleagues. We had in Mayor Wesley Uhlman a city leader who was "mod" in appearance, and—within the boundaries with which the charter surrounds the mayor—a fighter for Seattle. Young and inexperienced in his honeymoon months in office, he was not showing remarkable progress, but neither had Arthur Langlie, another young mayor who turned out to be a governor with similarities to Dan Evans.

Too, we now have a Metro Council, which in its infancy was not at all popular. But when it set to work under the determined direction of James Ellis to clean up Lake Washington—and, what's more, accomplished it—Metro gained what seems to be a permanent place in our area's scene.

The lake—a mile and a half wide and more than four miles long —for years had been a sparkling playground for boat owners, fishermen, water skiers and swimmers. It was also, without anybody noticing it much, a reservoir for sewage. The communities around the lake were growing fast, and parallel with the sewage problem came marine biological changes understood only by the appropriate scientists. To the majority of Seattleites the dangerous transformation seemed sudden, but for a long time Jim Ellis and his Metro group had realized that it was becoming a giant cesspool. "No Swimming" signs had to be posted along what once had been popular lake beaches, in the interest of public health. It was a very big job that Metro took on, and there were a lot of pessimists who said they had waited too long. But Metro did indeed clean up Lake Washington, and the giant feat—coming at a time when the whole nation was awakening to pollution and quality environment—brought wide prominence to Seattle, and to Metro. Actually it was the area's first almost insurmountable and vital step toward quality environment.

In 1957 the state legislature responded to an imaginative solution calling for a federated government. It enacted the Metropolitan Municipal Corporation Act, now known as Metro. Led by the stocky, energetic and persuasive Jim Ellis, literally hundreds of people worked through hundreds of meetings to make Metro effective. The job was to pull together the co-operative efforts of mayors, councils and other officials of towns and cities surrounding polluted Lake Washington. It was, in retrospect, a minor miracle of politics that Ellis and his group performed—a task of persuasion that cut through long-standing rivalries, jealousies and the self-interests of these municipalities.

The people were asked to respond to the crisis and voted to create Metro and to authorize $145 million worth of revenue bonds. Metro established extensive treatment plants at Renton and West Point at the entrance to Elliott Bay. Other treatment plants were spotted in key locations. Slightly more than one hundred miles of sewage trunk lines were completed. Gradually, over the next decade, Lake Washington became cleaner and at the end of the sixties came the complete elimination of sewage from Lake Washington. It is interesting to note that when Metro completed its construction in 1970, the cost was within one half of 1 per cent of the original estimate made by Ellis more than ten years before.

Even before Metro was completed, in fact in November of 1965, Ellis appeared before the Seattle Rotary Club to make a speech that would also improve the quality of the Seattle-King County environment for decades to come.

In that speech, attorney Ellis challenged the politicians and the people of the county and of all the cities within the county to come together to analyze the goals and needs of the area. He called his plan a forward thrust, and the name caught on. Soon Mayor Dorm Braman and King County Commission President Ed Munro picked up Ellis' challenge and set up a steering committee. Letters were sent out over the signatures of the two elected officials to hundreds of county and city people, including bankers, labor leaders, housewives, businessmen and architects among others, inviting them to become part of a Forward Thrust Committee which would set up the priorities of local government spending in the coming twelve years. Each person was asked to sign a pledge agreeing to spend "six hours a week of work." Incredibly, 300 of these busy community leaders did sign and then met, under Ellis' chairmanship, for the next two years. Their recommendations were presented for approval to the voters at an election held in February 1968.

While four of the issues failed—a rapid transit plan being the most controversial—seven passed, including capital bonds for parks and recreation, a youth service center, community fire stations, neighborhood improvements, sewers and a domed stadium. The park and recreation issue alone authorized $118 million in bonding, which is to this day the largest ever voted and approved in any local jurisdiction in the United States.

It was a fantastic effort, almost all of it by volunteers, and can not be downgraded by the fact that voters turned down all four proposals in a second Forward Thrust election in 1970. For by then Seattle was reeling under the Boeing layoff and people were not willing to approve any issue that might increase taxes.

In 1968 we came at last to face the reality that King County was becoming too complex and populous for all its problems to be solved by three county commissioners. The county whose official seal features the crown of a king added more than 220,000 residents between 1960 and 1970. The Bureau of the Census reports this upward surge for a decade which had a number of gray spots economically. It amounts to a 23.7 per cent population increase in ten years, so what is likely to happen in a following decade which already promises projects the like of which the Pacific Northwest has never known? From the viewpoint of administration problems it is pertinent to note that in 1970 the population of the county was 92.5 per cent urban and 7.5 per cent rural. It was indeed high time to modernize the 114-year-old government. When the three-man commission refused, it was, again, a citizens' group, headed by the crusading and indomitable Madeline LeMere, who had also helped spearhead Metro, that took matters to the people. A small army of volunteers from the Municipal League and the League of Women Voters marched across King County carrying petitions and explaining the need for a new kind of government. Apparently the people listened, for they approved a new charter and elected freeholders to write it in November of 1968.

John Spellman, a Seattle attorney, became the first county executive and the old commission was changed to a nine-man council. The King County Council seems to have shown that it is worthwhile. Some still feel that the council membership ought to be lessened by two or three, but that is a detail which time will prove valid or invalid.

Unquestionably the King County Council has tightened the government within its province, and there seems no doubt that county operations are moving more efficiently. It can show, for example, that it has reduced the county debt, and it offers the voters a more visible accounting of the control of county finances.

In 1971 it was working hard on the economic problems of the region, and apparently making some progress in articulating its aims to the federal government. The new county council established a public defender system to provide additional legal aid to the indigent. And it opened a seven-million-dollar administration building, whose design naturally drew frowns from the more esoteric of our architects and environmental protectors. "Well, it's a place to work," retorts John Spellman bluntly.

What's going to happen regarding the King County Council vis-à-vis the various city councils? As some ask—in fear or approval—will it gradually encircle and overshadow the more local lawmaking bodies? That could happen in time, but to what degree, and what changes may need to be made in the liaison between the King County Council and the city councils, nobody can predict now.

Much of our more mature view of politics is due, of course, to the tens of thousands of newcomers. They arrive with no preconceived views as to regional politics. They heartily approve the things they cannot (and would not) change. They are enchanted with Mount Rainier, and Puget Sound, and the Cascade and Olympic ranges, the vast and meandering inland seas and the environment in general. To them our climate is mild and attractive, for most have come from areas where the weather can be violent. As time goes on, and they become more attached to their new home, they often grow unhappy with our politics and set out to help in some changes. Certainly they are not smug—as were the old-time Seattleites. So much of the new political sophistication approaches from their quarter. And they in turn are producing their own native Seattleites, whose ideas and ambitions for their home place can hardly be predicted, except that we may be certain they will be more complex and definitive than those of the days when you and I were in knee pants.

New things are happening now in the area's politics in the legislature. There are "youngsters" who do not worry too much or too steadily as to who is a Democrat and who a Republican. "Don't quote me," said one, "because I don't want to get read out of my party. But we get together—donkeys and elephants both—and have our little meetings. Some of us, and I am one, consider these gatherings more vital to the state than our party caucuses. I'm not going to worry whether I'll be re-elected—not until campaign time anyhow. Maybe I'll be a one-termer. But like the rest of us 'freshmen' I'm not going to spend any time in Olympia trying to survive politically. I'm here to translate into legislation, if I can, the ideas which I believe are good for the cities and the state."

Those are strange new words from a new breed of lawmakers. They do have a few recent ancestors who served in Olympia, but they are indeed few. Never in our political history have we had so many as now. Like attracts like, and there'll be more.

The political circuses have folded their tents and disappeared into the fog of Puget Sound, probably forever. Politics in Seattle and its neighboring communities is a serious business today. We find our fun and games in other fields.

15

The Sporting Life

Is Seattle a good sports town?

Ask that question of a well-informed fan of any major sports and you'll get the quick, honest answer. It's a great sports town for its size and age, and a better sports town than many a city older and larger.

In professional basketball the Seattle Sonics easily average 9,000 people per game, and nobody is surprised if, given the right weather and other unpredictables, more than 13,000 come to see the fast fun.

Hockey has taken a nose dive in recent years but there is growing talk about bringing a major league franchise into Seattle. As for varsity football, the University of Washington Huskies always usher 58–60,000 into their big stadium. They come by charter bus and city bus, private cars, on foot and—because the east goal posts are near the Lake Washington shoreline—by dory, outboard motorboat, cruiser or yacht. A football Saturday very nearly rivals Opening Day of the boating season on the vast lake. When the Huskies play out of town more than two thousand spectators follow them through the sky or wheel below them on the highways.

There are no dependable figures on boxing fans. But they are numerous as well as hopeful, and of late years this has been mainly due to a promoter, not the fighters. The promoter is Jack Hurley, called the "Deacon" because of his long face and funereal garb. He arrived in Seattle in 1950 for a two weeks' stay. He has been here ever since, and in the same cluttered room at the Olympic Hotel. He's an admitted hypochondriac ready to die in the next minute, but he doesn't sound like it and is easily the liveliest fight promoter Seattle has ever seen. Says one of his reluctant admirers, "The Deacon will take a young fighter—almost any boxer who won't jump out of the ring—and it's just a question of how big he estimates that the boxer can be blown up for the drooling fans."

He's had some near misses at the big time, and a lot of flops, but he remains one of the town's best-known sports characters. In private he may tell the truth about his man and it's always a picturesque truth. Of one he said, "I had to take the fear out of him. He'd run like the Forty Thieves, and when he got close to his opponent he couldn't have knocked his hat off if the rules allowed the guy to wear a hat. But when I took him on he didn't have a dime, and I made $300,000 for him and he went into business for himself."

A clue to the crowds that Jack Hurley can produce from nowhere was shown when the Seattle Restaurant Owners Association gave an appreciation dinner for him. They wanted to thank him for the business he had created for them over a couple of decades. The charge was twenty-five dollars a plate, and the cafe leaders presented him with a beautiful vicuna coat. In his response the Deacon said: "I've been accused of some swindles in my time, but twenty-five bucks a plate for a dinner to honor *me*—boy, that is a *swindle*. But I appreciate the vicuna coat. I doubt if I'll ever wear it. In the first place, you don't need a coat this heavy in Seattle and in the second place, if I hung it on a hook in one of your joints I'd be afraid somebody would steal it." He meant what he said; the vicuna coat has never been out of Hurley's closet to this day.

Various boxing commissions now and then have tried to clip his wings. They claim to want to give new and younger promoters a chance at the game. Hurley has his own views of boxing commissions: "They don't know a damn thing about the fight game. They've never been in it, and they try to tell *me* what to do. They don't get paid, you know, and they're worth every cent of it."

The Deacon was born in Moorhead, Minnesota, and was a neighbor of the Magnusons. Senator Warren Magnuson was one of his first fighters. "I put Maggie in the ring at sixteen in a bout across the river in Fargo. He was a stocky kid with courage, and a slugger, but he took a licking. When he got home and his mother saw the marks on him he got a second licking. I was fond of the old lady and touched when Maggie brought her to Seattle for burial when she died. I think Maggie could have developed into a good middleweight, but he's doing all right as a heavyweight in the Senate."

Horse racing is a prime sport in Seattle and this is traditional, going back to the days of the old Meadows Race Track when bookmakers took the bets and the state finally quashed the sport. When the pari-mutuel system was legalized a couple of young fellows named Joe Gottstein and William Edris got busy and built the Longacres track. The pair had made plenty of money in Seattle real estate, and had not a little to do with the legalizing of the pari-mutuel system.

Gottstein, who passed away in 1971, spearheaded the Longacres track. In 1933 he chose a spot between the Duwamish River and Renton and said to the architect, "Build it here—and fast." When Gottstein spoke, things happened and the track was finished in twenty-seven days. There have been many enlargements and improvements since, and today it is one of the most beautiful tracks in the nation. And, as the advertisements correctly state, "just minutes away from Seattle by freeway." In good racing weather ten thousand will crowd the stands and grounds to put down a bet or just watch the horses run.

The Seattle area has produced its share of national and world champions. Al Hostak and Freddie Steele were middleweight title holders before Deacon Hurley arrived on the scene, which possibly was fortunate for them.

In golf it has been an extended Ladies' Day. Both Anne Quast and Jo Ann Gunderson clubbed their way to the U. S. Women's Amateur national title. The distaff side, too, furnished our all-time swimming champion. She was Helene Madison, protégé of Ray Daughters when he was swimming instructor at the Washington Athletic Club. She took about all the national aquatic titles available, and swamped the world's opposition at the Olympic Games held in Los Angeles in 1932, splashing through 400 meters in 1:06:8, which then was an all-time mark.

Seattle adopted—that is, Seattle University recruited—two of the most colorful basketball players in the history of the sport. The first was Johnny O'Brien, a five-nine court wizard who came here from New Jersey with his identical twin, Eddie. Johnny O'Brien —playing at center, of all places—became an All-American and the first big-time collegiate player ever to score 1,000 points in a single season. This was in the early fifties, and today Johnny O'Brien is a rotund, cigar-smoking Irish politician, serving on the County Council. Eddie is now athletic director at Seattle U.

The second great player was Elgin Baylor, who came to Seattle from Washington, D.C., with a one-year stopover at Idaho State. Baylor, an incredible performer, was an All-American selection who almost single-handedly vaulted Seattle U.'s Chieftains into the finals of the NCAA national playoff. He later played for the Los Angeles Lakers, then retired in mid-season of 1972. Experts tag him everywhere as one of the greatest all-around players in the game's history.

The Husky football team produced a flock of All-Americans, two of the most illustrious being George Wilson and Charles O. Carroll, both now included in collegiate football's Hall of Fame. Wilson drifted away from Seattle, while Carroll became county prosecuting attorney and held the post for two decades. But the kingpin of Husky gridders was Hugh McElhenny, a powerful, elusive runner, an All-American, who went on to the San Francisco 49ers and was later inducted into pro football's Hall of Fame. McElhenny returned to Seattle in 1972 to head up a drive to get a pro football franchise for the city.

Fred Hutchinson was another giant of Seattle sports lore. As a kid pitcher he hurled his first curves on the sandlots of a Rainier Beach and was signed out of Franklin High School by the old Pacific Coast League Rainiers. Incredibly, this eighteen-year-old youngster won twenty-five games in his first season, then was sold in 1938 to Detroit for the then-illustrious price of $100,000. He later managed Detroit, the St. Louis Cardinals and Cincinnati, the latter into a World Series. In two intervals, 1955 and 1958, he returned to manage the Rainiers. The entire city mourned—indeed, so did the entire sporting world—when Hutch died of cancer at the age of forty-five. Today, Seattle citizens donate generously to the Fred Hutchinson Cancer Foundation, headed by his brother, Dr. William B. Hutchinson, one of Seattle's best-known surgeons.

In many ways, Seattle's most imposing sports figure is big Jim Whittaker, the first American to reach the top of Mt. Everest. The fact that Whittaker was first almost obscures the fact that three other Seattleites, Richard Emerson, who teaches sociology at the UW, Willy Unseld, a philosophy professor at Evergreen College, and a Seattle anesthesiologist, Dr. Tom Hornbein, were along on the historic climb. Two years after conquering Everest, Whittaker led the late Robert Kennedy to the crest of a 13,905-foot peak in the mountain range of St. Elias in the Yukon. They christened the mountain in memory of the late President John F. Kennedy.

As late as 1972, Seattle was without professional football or baseball, and that hurts. Pro football, it is predicted, will surely come, once the lawsuit-plagued, but already funded domed stadium is built near King Street Station.

Seattle's entry into major league baseball was short and not at all sweet. In 1970, a group headed up by Dewey Soriano, another prominent baseball player of the Hutchinson era, acquired an American League franchise. Nicknamed the Pilots, the team out-drew several other major league teams, asking the highest ticket prices in baseball history. But in the end, the ownership turned out to be financially unstable and went into bankruptcy. Despite a herculean effort by local people, headed by Edward Carlson, president of Western Hotels, to save the team for Seattle, the franchise was, instead, moved to Milwaukee. As one sports writer put it, "Seattle didn't realize it was merely getting a team passing through town."

Seattle likes to think of itself as home base for the biggest and best athletes to be had. With exceptions, some of whom have been mentioned in foregoing pages, this is of course mythology. But inasmuch as mythology in the Puget country has a way of transforming into reality, the base of the belief is worth examining.

Few Seattle fans realize that no less an author than Jonathan Swift began the mythology of "giants" in the Northwest. Paul Bunyan was a Johnny-come-lately and was born in the Midwest anyhow. Around 1703 Swift drew, or caused to be drawn, a map of the coast of North America which included a coastal outline roughly in the location of our own Olympic Peninsula and almost identical in shape. It was on this outthrust of land that Swift's hero, Lemuel Gulliver, encountered giants. The place was known as Brobdingnag.

Our gargantuan image of ourselves has periods of resurgence and one came in the twenties and thirties when Washington crews seemed unbeatable and the sport was at the height of its popularity. One Husky crew won the Olympics in 1936 and they would often sweep to victory at Poughkeepsie, winning even more handily at home on Lake Washington.

About this time the Husky football teams were doing well, too, and so in the twenties and thirties the mythology of giants was perpetuated by alumni in the Washington Athletic Club, which even now is the monument to the myth.

Aside from the oarsmen, two of the reasons for the consistently winning crews were a series of great coaches and an invention of George Pocock, a local builder of racing shells. The Pocock shell was a light fast job, hardly more than a sliver of native cedar with lines beautifully designed to resist water friction. Naturally for a time it was used exclusively by the University of Washington. It was aided by a form of propulsion known as the "Conibear stroke," named after one of our shrewd early coaches and carried on with refinements by Coach Al Ulbrickson, another local immortal in the sports world.

In those days the athletes came mainly from the region. And so began the belief that the young men of Puget Sound country were just a bit bigger, and stronger, and more courageous, and better co-ordinated, than the young men of any other area in the United States.

Things were to change a bit. Other crews at other universities, even eastern prep schools, became owners of Conibear's once exclusive stroke and of Pocock shells. As for football, recruiters later began to go beyond the borders of the Northwest, a practice they once had thought wholly unnecessary.

For some years crew racing fell afoul of Seattle's periodic apathy, and part of this was probably due to the rise of excitement in hydroplane racing, where speed and daring are involved. In comparison with the bouncing hydros and the almost frightening rhythmic whine of their engines the sweating crewmen and their cox-swain seemed pretty tame.

In Seattle today it is easy to find an argument as to whether hydroplane racing is a sport. But it has to be admitted that it is, even if you consider only the skill and sheer guts of the drivers of those ever faster boats.

At one time, anyhow, the Gold Cup Race was indisputably a great marine event, though pretty well confined to the Detroit River. Then Seattle, boating capital of the world, as we shall see, decided to make a try for it. This was through the efforts of a Bellevue millionaire, Stanley Sayres, and a designer named Ted Jones, as-sisted, report has it, by advice from Boeing engineers. They created a craft called *Slo-Mo-Shun*. It was anything but slow; the first of a series of the same name, it practically flew. Sayres took the first one to Detroit, grabbed the wheel, stomped on the accelerator, and returned a hero with the Gold Cup in his hefty arms.

Some feel that it has been unfortunate that thereafter Seattle made the Gold Cup Race the climax of its annual summer festival called Seafair. Somehow, reviving the myth of the bigger the better, the Gold Cup Race was transformed into a maritime Roman circus. Every summer it brings no less than 150,000 people to the west shore of Lake Washington, and hundreds more on cruisers and yachts moored to a log boom on the east side of the course. The rules of the race are complicated and actually few really know who is in the lead while the contest is on. The majority of spectators, some of whom camp out during the night to assure themselves of standing room, simply like the thrill of the "rooster-tail" water spray thrown up from the stern. And there is always the possibility, sometimes fulfilled, that a boat will disintegrate, maiming or even killing the driver. Shoreline residents go through a trying time on "Hydroplane Sunday." The city provides portable sanitary facilities, but these are inadequate. So a shoreline homeowner is resigned to a steady queue of men, women and bawling children seeking the nearest bathroom in the house.

The race became so expensive for participants that mere mil-lionaires, excepting the Texas variety, had to drop out. Entries now are largely craft owned by corporations or commercial groups.

Of course Seattle eventually lost the Gold Cup. The reaction

was immediate and predictable. We decided that the Gold Cup
was a bit tarnished anyhow, and created the Seafair Trophy. So the
huge water show still goes on annually, and the morning after the
race the shoreline of beautiful Lake Washington is a shambles of
litter, scarred trees, trampled plants, and God knows what. Next
day the city cleans up at a cost of around ten thousand dollars
—and shoreline residents restore their yards and repair interior
damage.

As we have seen, Seattle and the Puget Sound country love
"firsts" and having the "biggest." It may be moot whether some
of our firsts and biggests are relevant in a chapter on sports. As a
Seattleite, I contend that they are. They are both participant and
spectator sports in this remarkable region. So stand back, please,
and brace yourself:

Already you know that Jim Whittaker was the first American to
climb Mount Everest, the world's tallest mountain: that Grand
Coulee Dam is the largest man-made monument in the world; that
Boeing has built the largest manufacturing plant, with a capacity
of two hundred million cubic feet and a floor area of thirty-six
acres. And that therein it built the first Jumbo Jet, the 747—
and now we know that Boeing plans to add another deck to the
747s so that each can carry 350-plus passengers.

But there are some other matters we must consider in talking
about Seattle and the region. Over in Tonasket they bred the
world's champion rodeo steer, a Brahman-Hereford crossbreed who
has unseated 476 of 482 reckless cowboys.

The world's largest cake was a six-sider, baked for the World's
Fair of 1962, and weighing 25,000 pounds. It was twenty-three feet
high with a circumference of sixty feet. It took 18,000 eggs, over
10,000 pounds of flour, 4,000 pounds of Hawaiian sugar, 7,000
raisins, over 2,000 pounds of pecans and a hundred pounds of
salt. What's more, fair-goers ate every crumb, which in itself must
be a first of some kind.

Steve McPeak of Seattle Pacific College mastered the world's
largest unicycle, which put him thirty-two feet in the air. Then
he set a duration record by traveling on a thirteen-foot unicycle from
Chicago to Las Vegas, a distance of two thousand miles.

Then in 1970–71 we had the world's greatest twelve-month
snowfall. No, not in Seattle, but quite close, at the Paradise Ranger

Station on Mount Rainier. The statistics: 1,027 inches, or more than eighty-five feet.

We are proud of the longest undefended international boundary because we are part of it. That is the invisible line between Canada and the United States and it is commemorated by the Peace Arch at Blaine, near Seattle. Irrelevantly, we made the world's largest bottle, measuring eighteen feet by five feet in diameter. The non-alcoholic content was a ship's model, and this expertise by a Navy Yard worker won a prize in a Seafair parade.

Lake Washington is spanned by the world's longest floating bridge, 12,596 feet in length. Already we had the first floating bridge west of Chicago. A third and fourth are planned, and surely we will figure out a way to make them "firsts" or biggest. They'll be the tallest or widest or something, and you may bet on it.

We have the world's most powerful fire boat, the *Duwamish,* which pumps over 22,000 gallons of water per minute; and combined with the *Alki* makes the most powerful fire boat fleet on the globe. About 60,000 people annually visit the waterfront boathouse which shelters them, so we believe we have the most visited fire station in the world, too.

In Whidbey we have the world's longest island, over sixty miles. Which for no reason at all reminds me that Clinton Locy (sic) of West Richland delivered a sermon which lasted forty-eight hours and fifteen minutes. The record does not say how many, if any, stayed to the finish.

And in Ernest Yogg we have the fastest ice cream eater. He took fifty-five scoops of ice cream, with topping, in fifteen minutes.

In a more serious vein, we built Northgate, the nation's first full-dress shopping center, in 1950. And over east a few miles away the towns of McCleary and Shelton stormed up the biggest bear stew ever seen—and eaten. Naturally that brings to mind a dessert, so be it known that Marysville built the world's largest strawberry shortcake and none of it was wasted.

And we built the world's first service station, at East Marginal Way and Holgate Street, in 1907. It did not supply air for tires or clean your windshield. Just gas and oil, and water for the radiator.

That these kinds of records amuse or delight or fill us with pride probably tells something about the character of Seattleites. And those out-of-town readers who feel that this indicates a lingering immaturity or a vestige of the frontier spirit (or anxiety) may be perfectly right. That angle no longer disturbs us. We still like "firsts" and "biggests."

But I haven't yet touched on the complex phenomenon that really makes Seattle and the Puget Sound country a great sports center of the nation and the whole wide world. With a flourish of trumpets the many-faceted "participant sports" must be ushered in.

Participant sports are those in which you and your family can engage, not as mere onlookers but as part of the game. Even hard-bitten, enthusiastic sports writers, experts in their various specialties, admit that when it comes to numbers of people and crass economics, participant sports are the greatest.

In the Puget Sound region there is no business quite like snow business, and skiing is one of our really big participant sports. Just how big is skiing hereabouts? You can get all kinds of astounding answers to that question. In King County alone, informed estimates are that 69,000 hit the many nearby slopes regularly. On any given Saturday or Sunday, when the weather is good, an estimated 25,000 ski the Cascades, and all 12 Puget Sound counties contribute to this mass migration. More and more ski schools proliferate, and the best guess now is that there are some fifty ski schools in operation.

The snowy Cascades entice ever growing numbers of learners. No less than 1,600 certified ski instructors work on the various slopes, and given an average of ten pupils per class, that adds up to 16,000 people learning to ski every year! There are many midweek classes for harried housewifes, who can now make the slopes, make the snow fly, have lunch, slalom some more, and be home in time to fix dinner. Several areas are lighted and open for skiing six nights a week.

Skiing had no dramatic impetus here. It simply grew from a small group of hardy outdoorsmen who hiked up and skied down. The first lift, a rope tow, was installed by Webb and Virginia Moffett, at Snoqualmie Pass, and they are generally credited with being the pioneers of this massive phenomena. One of the early climber-skiers was Don Fraser, whose wife, Gretchen, became the first American woman ever to win a gold medal in the Winter Olympics. Gretchen hit the headlines in 1948, and since then the Northwest has produced two other Olympics competitors, Kathy and Judy Nagel, whose father Jack also competed many years before.

Until she moved to Idaho, Susan Corrack, the girl who won a bronze medal at Sapporo, Japan, in 1972, got much of her early training at Crystal Mountain.

Bellingham skiers are neighbors to Mount Baker Lodge facilities as well as to other skiing areas. Tacomans can easily choose Paradise Inn at the foot of Mount Rainier; or Crystal Mountain, one of the newer and more posh ski resorts with heated swimming pools, condominiums and a lodge—much like the fancier ski resorts on the European continent. Seattleites also are enthusiastic about Crystal Mountain. From its ski lift there is a hitherto impossible view of Mount Rainier that is amazingly beautiful and inspiring. Seattle also favors Yodelin, Alpental, Snoqualmie Summit, Ski Acres and Hyak. Everett skiers are most familiar with the slopes of Mount Pilchuck. Leavenworth, a popular skiing community, a few years ago refurbished itself completely to resemble a Bavarian village.

Other ski areas in the world receive more public acclaim, but for sheer force of numbers we get the flag. There are few big metropolitan areas so close to first-class skiing.

Golf has always been popular here, as well as elsewhere. But now it's a mass participant sport, with literally hundreds of private and public courses. Tennis is in resurgence throughout western Washington, partly due to the building of covered courts to meet the uncertainty of our climate.

We are a hilly country and the big surprise has been the tremendous revival of bicycling. Two things brought the bike back with a rush: the popularity of outdoor exercise for all ages, and the new multi-geared cycles. Whole families take to the road on our too few bicycle paths (there's a roar for more of these) and bike manufacturers have drastically revised their quotas for the Pacific Northwest. Many dealers were running out of bicycles before Christmas, making thousands of youngsters unhappy.

Everybody knows that hunting and fishing are big in the Pacific Northwest. They too are part of the life style that helps bring so many new people. In saltwater fishing salmon (cohoe and chinook) is the big thing, and salmon derbies abound in every Puget Sound port. In stream fishing rainbow trout are still the wily prize, although many other species are down there for the man who knows his business. Fishing areas are almost everywhere you look, but some of the more adventurous Puget Sounders have taken to stretching it by means of float planes that can reach the higher mountain lakes and some of the otherwise difficult fishing grounds in western Canada and the Panhandle of Alaska.

Deer and elk are the star targets in hunting, and so close to civilization that "Watch Out for Deer" signs are common on many highways. If you are really athletic, and patient about game department red tape, you can make a brave try for mountain goat or the often irascible black bear. For bird hunters it is duck, pheasant, geese and doves in about that order. They all feed not too far from the homes of Seattleites.

Truly the year-around sportsman knows no season. If you don't believe it, write for the sportsman's calendar, addressing the Tourism Department, Olympia, Washington. Beginning in January the all-year outdoor man may start with some duck hunting in the cornfields across the Cascades, find some kind of fishing, somewhere, all through the year, and barely get home for Christmas after goose hunting in the McNary Wildlife Recreation Area, trying for sturgeon in the Chehalis River or floating the Skagit for steelhead.

Mountain climbing is by no means confined to champions like Jim Whittaker, but neophytes are warned to take along an experienced climber. And newcomers—this is important—should not consider experience in the East as sufficient to tackle even our smaller peaks. There are marked differences in the cols and crevasses and rock, and it would be wise to join The Mountaineers, whose address is Post Office Box 122, Seattle, Washington 98111.

Hiking is another participant sport in the region. The Mountaineers have issued three small but instructive books: *101 Hikes*, *102 Hikes* and *50 Hikes*, yet all three scarcely scratch the surfaces of the North Cascades, the South Cascades, the Olympics, the Alpine Lakes area and Mount Rainier National Park. They'll keep you walking for many a season, though, and if you like to hit the trails and by-paths, the Puget country is for you.

We have some unusual participant sports, and probably the most popular of these is rock hounding. At last estimate there were at least 25,000 dedicated rock searchers in the King County area alone. Most have complete field gear, many have trailers and also equipment at home for polishing their finds and making them into various kinds of jewelry and doodads.

Boating is the most popular participant sport in the region. There is no question but that Seattle is the boating capital of the nation and perhaps the world. And here it is an all-year-around sport. April is the traditional outfitting month, of course, but in Seattle and other Puget Sound ports few pleasure boat owners "put their boats up" for any part of the winter. Some of the most popular class racing is in the fall and winter. Mainly, however, boating hereabouts is a family affair or a part of the fisherman's equipment.

The most recent official survey was taken in 1966 by the U. S. Army Corps of Engineers and the Washington State Bureau of Outdoor Recreation. They counted 186,000 craft and estimated a growth figure of 4.1 per cent a year. The Northwest Marine Industries Association estimates the growth at 5 per cent. Lieutenant Commander James Hadley of the Coast Guard Safety Division is certain that the growth rate is 8 per cent. Whichever rate you prefer you come out with a lot of boating. It is now generally accepted that one out of every five families in the Puget Sound area owns a boat of some type.

Another clue is the Seattle National Boat Show, one of the ten largest boating exhibitions in the country. In 1971 it drew 65,000 people, which represented an increase of 15 per cent over the previous year. This was in the face of the highest unemployment rate of any metropolitan area (due to the Boeing downturn) and there was snow on the ground four of the nine show days.

It is reasonable to assume that in the twelve counties of the Puget Sound region we are dealing with at least 200,000 craft. The official forecast: 299,000 pleasure craft by 1980; 593,000 by the year 2000; and not less than 1,239,000 by the year 2020. Right now there is an average of ninety-four privately owned boats for every thousand persons in the region. That compares with 41 per cent on the national average. That's mainly because there are over 2,246 miles of shoreline in the Puget region, partly because they are very accessible, and partly because Puget Sounders and Seattleites are "seafaring" by nature. Paradoxically, that goes double for emigrants from regions where folks have never seen an oar. Or perhaps this is not paradoxical, for most of the great navy admirals of World War II came from towns far inland.

Naturally enough, due to the mobility and power of the overhang motor these days, 50.7 per cent of our craft are outboards; 9.8

per cent are inboard powered; 4.2 per cent are sailing craft with or without auxiliary power; and about 35 per cent are miscellaneous. And I do mean miscellaneous; they include balsa rafts, catamarans, folboats and kayaks, prams, canoes, dories and even tiny steamers.

The big problem now is how to jar public officials as to the need for additional mooring facilities. In the early 1970s twenty more miles of shoreline were already sorely needed for this purpose. It might help to force lackadaisical authorities into taking a good close look at the Shilshole Bay marina. That is the lively, colorful marina in the Ballard district of Seattle. It handles 1,600 craft of all types and sizes. And what Puget Sound boat owners are going to need *are the equivalent of 168 Shilshole Bay marinas or ramps!*

The economic impact of this participant sport is already impressive. In the early 1970s Puget Sounders were spending $55 million a year on recreational boating. And—whoops and avast—some $850,000 to repair damaged craft. Naturally enough, many of our skippers are in the learning stage, as the Coast Guard unhappily can testify.

Where to cruise? Well, there is plenty of water everywhere, most of it protected from ocean storms. If you rent mooring space it will be only a few minutes or an hour or so from home. If you own a trailer boat you can start your voyage from one of literally thousands of inlets and ports. The late Stewart Edward White, a popular author in the old *Saturday Evening Post,* owned a yacht called the *Simba.* Like several well-to-do Californians he kept her at Lake Union in Seattle and spent summers cruising Puget Sound, British Columbia and Alaska. I remember him telling me: "I've been doing this for twenty-five years, and I tell you that in this country a man could spend a lifetime dropping anchor in the bays and inlets—and he'd have made landfall on about an eighth of them. It's the greatest cruising area in the world, and I've seen them all."

So Seattle claims just about every participant sport there is, and the important thing is that they are so available, so near to home. But there is something more. A transplanted couple told me that they engage in no particular participant sport and attend few spectator sports. Then why, I asked, were they so enthusiastic about the Puget Sound country as compared with their old home in the Midwest? They looked at each other, seemed silently to agree on the answer, **and** the husband stated it:

"Well, we just walk and ride around and somehow seem to be involved with nature and the whole outdoors. It's that kind of place here. And I suppose you'd call riding in a car and walking—you'd call them participant sports, wouldn't you?"

Yes, indeed.

16

Our Culture Kick

Some time after the Indian wars, on the lush flats of the Nisqually River, an early settler built a lean-to cabin. A visiting neighbor from several miles away was impressed to note that the Nisqually man had constructed also an outbuilding, which was furnished with *two* copies of a mail-order catalogue.

When queried, the settler testily replied, "Got the Injuns chased out, got my trees down to stumps, the spuds in the ground, and a lean-to that I expect to make into a real cabin. Now I got a little leisure for some culture. The other catalogue is for readin' purposes."

The grizzled pioneer seems to have understood what modern folks are beginning to realize: that a mail-order catalogue is a fair picture of what is going on in the world at any given time. The anecdote does illustrate that marked impatience, that determination not unmixed with commercialism, with which Seattleites approach culture even now.

We have come a long way—not in time, but in distance, from

the days when questionable practitioners from the East Coast and Europe fared well here. There is a lengthy history of fancy fakirs who made themselves at home at the best tables and in the most exclusive salons of the town. There have been spurious dukes, foreign officers, shady diplomats, Continental philosophers, translators from Hindustani, collectors of paintings and sculpture (unseen) and heaven knows what else. When and if exposed they went scot free, or already were on their way, for none of the first families liked to admit they had been duped; and most of the imposters borrowed only a little money, usually enough to move across the state to Spokane or across the Columbia to Portland, Oregon. There is no record that the police or anybody else sent warnings to these fresh targets.

Seattle was, after all, only following the pattern of the gullible rich on the East Coast less than fifty years before. Of course we are still young—the last region of all to develop cities and sizable towns. Our relative innocence makes us a haven for literally hundreds of irresponsible bohemian painters and sculptors. This writer has witnessed scores of Seattleites buying, at unbelievable prices, various kinds of arts and crafts on the theory that because they are "original" they are of value.

So what? We want to learn, we want to appreciate, and we want to become "cultured" almost as quickly as we want to build and grow. Many of us are conscious of the reality that Seattle has a reputation as a greedy community where the fast buck is more to be desired than a long-term investment. Perhaps we feel that something must be done to offset this dubious reputation.

Nonetheless our new adoration of the arts and the humanities is something more than an outgrowth of pioneer days when the traveling "professor" and his lecture offered the only cultural entertainment aside from the music of church or dance hall.

And we aren't as gullible as we were, not all of us. The newspapers, the newsreels, and finally radio and television and the airplane, have brought the nation so cozily together that it is relatively unsafe for a character to blow into Puget Sound and let it be known that he is a famous international artist, a nephew of the Duchess of Kent or a brother of James Branch Cabell. But our innocent era did not quite come to an end until the beginning of World War II. At the beginning of that Armageddon it was plain that money was to be made, and as a vital part of Franklin Roosevelt's "arsenal of democracy" Seattle temporarily forgot about the arts.

Our welcome newcomers are not at first aware of how dogged we have been in our search for culture, despite the interruptions of two great wars and a full-size Depression. Not infrequently in our dogged pursuit of culture, we have stood fast for insults—or developed a thin skin. A classic example involved the late Sir Thomas Beecham, who, for a time, led the Seattle Symphony. Shortly before his departure Sir Thomas spoke of the need for support of the symphony to a group of ladies, adding that it was needed unless Seattle wanted to be looked upon as "a cultural dustbin." Poor Sir Thomas! He was irascible and outspoken (he once stopped his orchestra in mid-passage and ordered a photographer out of the hall), but even he must have been surprised by the reaction to his remarks. People seized upon his words as though he, himself, had called our city "a cultural dustbin," which, in fact, he did not. But for years after, he remained a thorny memory in Seattle's cultural hide.

In any case, here we are in the midst (several well-appointed critics say it is only the beginning) of the greatest cultural boom the region has ever known. Only in Seattle does one hear the word *boom* applied to the arts, which is fair enough because our own artistic explosion is not merely a part of the national urge. What sets our region apart is that the present resurgence of interest in the arts regionally has few historical roots. It was only in the sixties and the beginning of the seventies that we took note of the Indian arts and crafts in a serious way.

With our boundless energy we embrace, along with the arts and the humanities, many more things: the conservation of natural resources and the beautification of cities and highways—even some aspects of civil rights and opportunities for racial minorities.

It is important to note that those two world wars and that great panic of the thirties were more damaging to the cultural thread of a young region than they were to older areas of the nation, where the arts were deeply rooted. Yet now we have discovered that our historical roots in the arts, although few, are strong and important indeed. The early Indians, on the narrow strip of seacoast stretching from Puget Sound to British Columbia and Alaska had a definite and curious culture all their own.

By the time of the first white seafaring explorers the apogee of this culture was on Vancouver Island. It was not apparent to the early settlers of Seattle, but it was a strong culture that persisted because it had escaped—perhaps avoided—the kind of traffic which had come to the lower Sound. Today we can understand that rediscovered culture because it is strongly familiar, particularly to Seattleites. Beneath its arts was an economy based on a seemingly endless supply of cedar and salmon and it was a way of living that stressed wealth and prerogatives. The art was bold and exotic, and as competent as any achieved by primitive tribes anywhere on this continent.

It was an art of mask and totem pole, rich in the symbols of raven, bear and whale and of the mythical creatures lurking in the dense forest behind the carver's village. Collections of Kwakiatl and other Northwest Coast art can be found in the great museums of the world, in London, and Paris and New York. But for a long time here in Seattle only a few anthropologists, such as Dr. Erna Gunther, working in the old musty University of Washington museum, knew or cared about the exotic art of the Northwest Coast Indian. Now of course, Indian art is a feature of many private collections in the city, and the handsome new Thomas A. Burke Memorial Museum, built on the edge of the University campus, is a popular spot for those wanting to know more about the art and heritage of our Indians' past.

What the overpowering scenery has done to our arts and crafts is a question not yet fully answered. The pioneer amateurs, the "Grandma Moseses" of late in the last century and early in the present one were inevitably impelled to paint Mount Rainier or Mount Baker with the inland seas, or their own growing hamlets, in the foreground. The forests they often ignored, probably because the painting of a forest requires a technique beyond that of the amateur, whose brush and concept is likely to be literal. Our modern artists —with some subtle exceptions unrecognized by an innocent viewer —seem inclined to ignore their awesome surroundings. That they find it inspirational, however, is revealed by the fact that many of our artists accepted by competent critics seek hermit abodes in mountains and forests far enough from Seattle to avoid its ugliness—which we seek now to repair—yet close enough to keep in touch with the galleries and those few taverns and art centers where the conversation is compatible with their talents and soul-searching.

Certainly the will to create in Seattle and environs would have suffered far more from wars and depressions had it not been for the

federal Work Projects Administration. The WPA was much maligned in our city, which at that time was not yet in full cry after the
arts. Not incidentally, it is curious to note that the old WPA is not
mentioned in news stories about the government's revival of interest in cultural pursuits. Yet, at least insofar as the Northwest is
concerned, the WPA helped many a Northwest artist and writer to
survive, and it left worthy and permanent works behind it as well.
The book *Washington,* one of the first products of the Writers
Project of the WPA, is a classic, and in revised editions has become
the most comprehensive reference volume available.

Seattle's modern cultural era began during the Great Depression
when in 1933 Dr. Richard E. Fuller and his mother, Mrs. Eugene
Fuller, built and donated to the city the Seattle Art Museum in
Volunteer Park.

After the First World War the Fuller family of Boston made a
year's trip to the Orient, which awakened Richard's interest in
oriental art objects. In 1918 Mrs. Fuller began a collection of snuff
bottles and small Chinese antiques as a hobby. Richard was first
lured by jade and this was the beginning of the famous jade collection always on display in the Seattle Art Museum.

Later the Fullers moved to Seattle permanently and established
the family home there. In 1930 Richard Fuller was elected president
of the Art Institute of Seattle, which until then had been housed
in the old Henry home but was losing that location. In the same year,
Richard's father died, leaving a considerable estate acquired from
astute investments. His widow and son decided to co-donate an art
museum to the city with a part of this inheritance. Thus in 1931 they
offered the Art Institute, a corporation, the sum of $250,000 (a most
sizable sum in that worst of the Depression years) for the purpose of
constructing a museum on the location of the pergola in Volunteer
Park.

Doctor Fuller has served without salary as president and director of the museum since its founding. This makes him unique
among museum directors, even among those with large independent
means. He has quietly encouraged young artists by purchases for the
museum. Among them was the internationally known Mark Tobey.
The tall, white-haired and distinguished-looking artist, now living in
Switzerland, has never lost his love for the region, although he expresses his disappointment at what commerical development has done
to it.

Doctor Fuller began his adult career in business. It was a brief encounter. He says, "I was a clerk in 1921 in the Ladd and Bush Bank down in Salem, Oregon. I hadn't quite completed a year when I fell ill." His comment is accompanied with his quiet, hesitant smile. Despite his athletic build, which persists in his seventies, everything about the museum's director is quiet and shy. But this is deceptive, and he still knows his way around the world of commerce—only now it is as board member of many Seattle institutions. He finds time for public service beyond the museum; his awards for civic accomplishments make a long list.

His wife Betty is the daughter of latter-day pioneers of prominence and as a former member of the museum staff, she is a well-informed partner for the man who unquestionably is the dean and indirect ruler of Seattle arts.

Like the city it adorns, the Seattle Art Museum is young. Yet during its relatively brief history it has attained literally world renown for its oriental collection, and each year augments its exhibits to present a visual knowledge of the history of the world by reflecting, as Doctor Fuller says, "the creative artistic progress of mankind. Our programs and 'historical' exhibits each year are focused on a specific part of the world or concentrated on one general period or culture."

Despite the fragmentation of the interests of Seattleites—and their devotion to the outdoors and various sports—the Seattle Art Museum has recorded some remarkable attendance records. It broke the record for the Official Exhibition of Japanese Painting and Sculpture, even though that same show visited such centers as Boston, Chicago and New York City. A part of this success may have been due to Seattle's traditional interest in the Orient and its sizable Japanese population. Yet that record was exceeded by the attendance at the Walter Chrysler Collection, when at least eighty thousand passed through the gates of the museum.

The museum building itself is a most attractive addition to the city scene. Its setting is perfect, for Volunteer Park is one of the town's most beautifully landscaped parks. The museum overlooks a well-designed reservoir which has the appearance of a natural lake; beyond is the bay, and, on a clear day, the jagged peaks of the Olympic Range, perpetually spotted with snow, are visible. Recently the museum's director approved the installation of a fifteen-ton granite sculpture adjacent to the building. It is Isamu Noguchi's "Black Sun" and its appearance was an important artistic milestone in Seattle's cultural history.

Soon after the close of the Century 21 World's Fair the Seattle Art Museum established at the fair site an Arts Pavilion which essentially is an arm of the museum. It is designed to capture an audience which, on its own, might not find its way to the Volunteer Park exhibitions.

The Seattle Art Museum is by no means the only one in Seattle and environs. Visitors and old-timers alike are somewhat surprised to find three solid columns listed in the telephone directory under "Art Galleries and Dealers," and they are scattered all over the city and found in what seems to be unlikely neighborhoods. Many are small and struggling—a few are co-ops, owned by artists—but many feature important works by well-known artists, some of whose works command stiff prices. Among them is an astonishing variety—galleries which feature oriental art, primitive art, Eskimo soap carvings, antique oriental rugs, as well as paintings ranging from conventional to *avant-garde*.

The Richard White Gallery often features important shows, along with the Manolides Gallery (*avant-garde*), both located in the rapidly reviving Pioneer Square area. Some, like the Woodside Gallery in the upper part of the Broadway district, are located in restored old homes. Even many of the churches regularly exhibit works of prominent Northwest artists. Indeed, in the five years between 1965 and 1970, the number of galleries in Seattle almost tripled and the field is still growing.

The Century 21 site is now called the Seattle Center and one observer of the Seattle arts has called it "a visual jewel within the concrete maze of the city." The main features of the center are the Pacific Science Center with its quiet pools and lacelike towers, which give a much needed lift to the city skyline; the Opera House, one of the most beautiful in the country; the Repertory Theater; and the Space Needle. Doubts have been cast upon the architectural perfection of the latter, but it became a symbol of the Century 21 Exposition and is now firmly placed in the prideful hearts of Seattleites, who rarely fail to show it off to visitors.

There are dozens of arts groups in Seattle, far too many for focusing on the part of the average citizen and, indeed, unknown to all but the most studious reader of the newspapers. They vary in purpose, but all have a common denominator: lack of sufficient funds to achieve their ambitions.

A tremendous help to all the arts, as well as to selected charities, is the organization known officially as Patrons of Northwest Civic, Cultural and Charitable Organizations and unofficially, thanks be, as PONCHO. This is a non-profit corporation dedicated to the support of cultural activities which raises funds through an annual auction of donated goods and services. The proceeds of the auction go to previously designated organizations selected among applicants to the PONCHO Beneficiary Committee, whose difficult job nobody can envy.

The annual auction is a high point in the city's social calendar and provides considerable fun for the cognoscenti. Some of the gifts for auction are lavish; in some years a completely furnished mansion will lead the list. Other gifts are exotic, possibly a baby kangaroo (promptly given to the zoo by the high bidder) or—remember this is still the frontier—a chamber pot decorated with peace symbols. But beneath the amusement of the yearly auction party is a truly serious bent and one that does not overlook the urge of minorities toward the arts. For example, a usual beneficiary is the performing arts department of the Central Area Motivation Program, which chiefly is concerned with the cultural works of blacks.

Paul Friedlander is one of the citizens responsible for the founding of PONCHO, and he is one of all too few city leaders who work with boundless energy for the arts. Some struggling Seattle artists owe their presence in the city to the interests of the John Haubergs, Ann Gerber and the Bagley Wrights. The Wrights are the owners of one of the most valuable collections of modern art in the country, and Mrs. Wright has a gallery of her own.

Mr. Wright has been president of the Seattle Repertory Theater since its inception and has led it through some rocky periods with both time and money. There are others who really get down to work and provide cash for the arts around Puget Sound, but they are comparatively few as yet.

Committees, of course, are without number—and some are effective. The Municipal Arts Commission deserves an accolade if only because it keeps a sharp eye on the status of culture in Seattle. It issues an annual report by means of which those interested can see where we stand. For many years architect Ibsen Nelson, one of our leading environmentalists, was its chairman.

It says a great deal for Seattle that it has been able to hold the Seattle Symphony Orchestra as directed and inspired by Milton Katims, and the Seattle Opera (once an orphan child in what was still a fish and lumbering town), directed by the irrepressible Glynn Ross. He's been called "a Nebraskan by birth, impresario by profession, and salesman by nature." Popular newspaper columnist Emmett Watson closed himself in a room with Ross for a couple of hours, and came out muttering admiringly, "He's 220 volts coming in on a 110-volt line." Another has said, "Talking with Ross is like being plugged into an open switchboard with all lines busy."

I once spent a three-hour lunch with Ross and can vouch for his dynamic flow. It's always about the opera and it's always valid. It could hardly be otherwise when one notes that, with very little help, he put Seattle fourth in opera behind New York, San Francisco and Chicago. As Glynn Ross sees it, "To sell opera you have a four-way problem. First you have to get their attention with a little razzle-dazzle. You've got to be sympatico. You have to be able to communicate, and you have to deliver your message with the best possible product you can manage."

The one-time Golden Gloves fighter with the broken nose delivers the product and doesn't mind talking like a huckster or hustling a few tickets if need be. Unaided, he made opera popular with a sizable percentage of Seattle young people.

He won the reluctant admiration of critic H. C. Schonberg of the New York *Times*, who, after noting that the Met was "down a bit" in 1970, added, "In Seattle they order things differently. Out there Glynn Ross sells opera. Out there you see campaign buttons with the legend *Opera Lives*. It is in Seattle where you can look at the sky and find an airplane skywriting the virtues of Seattle Opera. There are even auto bumper stickers about the opera."

Mr. Schonberg rates Seattle Opera highly professional, but it is clear that it is Ross who fascinates him. "Provincialism is gone," he says. "The commissars of Seattle opera are just as bright, just as knowledgeable, as those anywhere else. Brighter, indeed, because they are younger and around the Seattle Opera there is an air of freshness and experimentation that contrasts vividly with the dull, tried and true, tired professionalism in other opera houses one could mention."

Regularly Seattle's few professional critics bemoan the drain of Seattle talent to other cities where opportunities are more numerous than they are on the shores of Puget Sound. But this is a situation familiar to most cities outside New York City; and now and then we win a few.

In 1967 the Philadelphia String Quartet became unhappy in the Quaker City and cast eyes toward Seattle. It took a while to straighten out a contractual agreement. While this was going on, Seattle was cheering loudly and the great day came when, at the Seattle International Airport, the state governor and his lady met Veda Reynolds, Irwin Eisenberg, Alan Iglitzin and Charles Brennand. They have proved greatly popular, and residence in Seattle has not tied them down. Among other wanderings the quartet has made a European tour, and at Carnegie Hall performed the music of University of Washington composers.

Recently added to the faculty of the University is the Soni Ventorum Wind Quintet previously in residence at the Conservatory of Music of Hato Rey, Puerto Rico, where the group had been in association with Pablo Casals.

The local culture scene seemed to have reached a high-water mark in the late sixties, when a group from industry, headed by Pacific Northwest Bell, made arrangements to bring the entire Robert Joffrey Ballet Company to the Seattle-Tacoma area for summer workshops. But the industrialists were unable to raise enough money to remodel theater facilities and Joffrey switched his workshop to San Francisco.

Ballet was not unknown locally before the Joffrey arrival, chiefly due to the activities of teacher-choreographer Martha Nishitani and her company. And the town has always been friendly to visiting ballet companies.

The late Nellie Cornish of the still existing Cornish School deserves a prominent place in the history of Seattle arts, as does the pioneer theater work of the late Glenn Hughes, whose Glenn Hughes Playhouse and the Showboat Theater are still landmarks and useful ones on the campus. Hughes was the West Coast innovator of theater-in-the-round, and several of his students made Broadway in the twenties when the New York theater was in one of its most vigorous periods. Today Dr. Gregory Falls, executive director of the University's School of Drama, and Duncan Ross, director of the Experimental Program for Professional Training in Acting, have brought a national recognition to the campus.

Seattle University, a Catholic institution which is vastly expanding in the center of the city, has demanded a place in undergraduate and postgraduate theater. Its success thus far is promising.

The Seattle Repertory cannot, of course, absorb all the budding theatrical talent on the shores of Elliott Bay, and this has given rise to "Off Center" theaters (corresponding to Manhattan's "off-Broadway" theater) and these, while operating with uneven success and more or less sporadically, have given opportunities to numberless young people interested in various aspects of the stage. Most important, they have been able to do more experimenting than, thus far, the Seattle Repertory seems willing to attempt.

Parker Cooke, music director at Garfield High School, organized a citizens' group to raise funds for the Garfield Magnet program and was able to convince the Seattle School Board of its importance to the Central Area (where a large segment of blacks reside) and the idea has been important in arousing cultural interest in many of the city's schools.

An important recent development has been the organization of the United Arts Council of Puget Sound. Its purpose is to solicit support from the local business community for sustaining funds for Seattle's major cultural institutions. This has been a far more difficult undertaking than it should be in a city which at least pretends a broad interest in the arts. It is a bitter truth that too often "business is business" and the arts are considered none of the city's business.

One of the most remarkable cultural phenomena in the Puget Sound area is the Pacific Northwest Arts and Crafts Fair held every summer in Bellevue. It was founded almost by happenstance in 1947, when the Crabapple Restaurant offered to display paintings on its walls and around its courtyard, a feature of the Bellevue Shopping Square, which had been completed the year before from a brilliant design by young architect Bliss Moore.

The idea of a changing "gallery" of paintings proved so popular with artists, owners of original art and the general public, that arrangements were made for an annual fair. The program, modest at first, was led by Kemper Freeman, aided by interested Bellevue groups and individuals.

Now the Pacific Northwest Arts and Crafts Fair covers the entire forty acres embraced by the square and is the largest affair of its kind in the nation. Indeed, with its many innovations, it is the only one of its kind. In two and a half days near the end of every July more than 110,000 visit the fair, and around $100,000 in paintings and crafts are bought by the public. The show is arranged so that the artists, their works, and the viewers are "integrated," and spectators practically become participants. A feature added in recent years is a program of *avant-garde* films entered from all over the nation. It has been widely acclaimed by the country's leading film critics.

The success of the Pacific Northwest Arts and Crafts Fair has matured the summer festivals of many towns around the Puget Sound area, although none have been able to match the Bellevue institution. Edmonds, Port Townsend, Mercer Island, La Conner and other neighboring communities now include arts in their more traditional annual festivities.

There has been a steady, although not wholly satisfactory restoration of the area in and around Pioneer Square in Seattle. This part of the city, now at the very edge of what was called Skid Road, was once a lively center of what was becoming a metropolis after the Great Fire. Around the central attraction, a totem pole, stood many fine old office buildings and a few hotels which had seen their prime in the Gold Rush. Tragically, some of these were destroyed for parking lots before a group of citizens got around to seeing what might be done to preserve them. The early leaders in restoring Main Street and the Occidental Avenue area were architect Ralph Anderson, publicist and writer Bill Speidel and the interior decorator Allen Vance Salsbury, who were among the first to locate there permanently. Later came more architects, and now the area proliferates with writers, publicists, law offices, restaurants, antique shops, galleries; even the King County Democratic headquarters has its office there.

Also in the refurbished Pioneer Square area is a series of offices that house another remarkable Seattle success story. This is a large booking agency known as Northwest Releasing, whose impact fans out across the nation and into large parts of Canada and Hawaii. But before detailing this unique operation, run from a far corner of the U.S., a flashback is necessary.

For a long time in the thirties and forties, Seattle's leading impresario was a shrewd, often tough, but at times lovable woman named Cecelia Schultz. Working mainly out of the Moore Theater on Second Avenue and Virginia Street, Cecelia was the den mother of Seattle culture. This redoubtable woman wheeled, dealed, bargained and browbeat to bring good attractions, both serious and light, to her city. She was sharp and penny-wise. At times, she would even shut off the drinking fountain in the Moore's lobby to stimulate the sale of soft drinks. For many years she was a success, and Seattle owes much to her, because her labors kept us from becoming a culturally deprived area. Cecelia stayed active into the fifties, but by then bigger things were in the works.

In 1952, a pair of close friends in the theater business, Zollie Volchok and Jack Engerman, formed Northwest Releasing. At first they merely distributed motion pictures and worked as a promotion team for visiting artists. But gradually they branched out and formed a big-time entertainment circuit with Seattle as its hub, but including Portland, Spokane and virtually all of western Canada. Exuberant and energetic, Volchok and Engerman booked such top-ranked artists as Victor Borge, Harry Belafonte, Frank Sinatra, Elvis Presley and the Beatles. Using this network of cities, they were able to offer top sums to attractions and personalities that would never have come to play Seattle alone. They retired in 1968. Engerman was killed in a private plane crash and Volchok is now a vice-president of the Seattle Supersonics basketball team.

Northwest Releasing was taken over by a pair of relatively young men named Bill Owens and Burke Garrett. Owens, with a background as talent booker and deejay, and Garrett, a musician and booking agent for small clubs, moved the uptown offices of Northwest Releasing down to 119 South Main in Pioneer Square. Their expansion and success has been nothing less than staggering. When Volchok and Engerman retired, the firm had grossed $1.3 million on its entire circuit. By 1962, Owens and Garrett had booked fifty shows which grossed $1.5 million in Seattle alone! They switched the emphasis to rock and the newer forms of entertainment, but frequently bring in such things as Eugene Ormandy's Philadelphia Symphony, "just to sort of balance things out." They use the Opera House, the Arena, and downtown theaters like the Coliseum, Paramount and Moore. "We take anything we can get," says Owens.

Almost unnoticed, by 1972 this pair had expanded the original Northwest Releasing circuit all over the U.S.—booking shows in Miami, New York, Philadelphia, much of Canada and Hawaii. They brought in the New York company of *Hair*, which—filled out with local talent—played for seventeen weeks and grossed $750,000. A big attraction, like The Who, easily packs 14,000 into the Coliseum.

Together, operating out of the old Skid Road area, they have formed one of the largest such operations in the country.

Those who feel that Seattle is near the peak in cultural achievements are by no means in the majority. The spokesman for the pessimists and the impatient is Rolf Stromberg, formerly of the New York *Times* and now head of the culture department on the *Post-Intelligencer*. Says he: "In Seattle the arts continually lose out to the intangibles, and right now we are sitting fat and flat on our plateau insofar as culture is concerned. A number of things will have to change before there is an appreciable move upward in the arts."

Business he excoriates in particular. "In general business has no interest in culture in Seattle, seeming not to recognize how important the arts can be to the commercial welfare of a city. Look at some of our biggest industries and institutions; in order to attract a high type employee they advertise our cultural pursuits—in addition to participant and spectator sports, which is fine—but at home what do they do for the arts, and what genuine interest do they have in our ecology, in the quality of our environment? Damn little, when you compare Seattle with other major cities. And look at that freeway!"

Let's look at it, since freeways are, beyond doubt, a blight on the aesthetic beauty of a city like Seattle. Freeway fights have been going on for years, with many of our cultural leaders and more enlightened architects fighting against them. What we got, eventually, were great ribbons of concrete that bisect the very heart of the city north and south, and the desecration goes on with access roads and egress roads and cloverleafs over cloverleafs. As one disgruntled citizen put it, "Seattle has been taken over by the cement lobby." When somebody proposed a fourth Lake Washington Bridge (a third is in process) the same fellow growled, "Why don't they drain Lake Washington, fill it with cement, and let those commuters from the East Side whip back and forth like open-field runners?"

But there are signs that Seattle is weary of freeways—that they have awakened to the fact that the lovely city is being marred by gigantic blocks, pillars and embankments. In 1972, for example, the citizens were asked to approve two more big projects. One was the Bay Freeway, connecting the central freeway with the waterfront viaduct traffic—a scheme that would virtually wall off Lake Union from the city. The other was the R. H. Thomson Expressway, which would abut Seattle's lovely Arboretum, near Lake Washington. In both cases, the citizens voted a resounding "no" at the polls, leaving embarrassed city planners with $12,000 worth of blueprints made up in expectation of voter approval.

As in most cities, literature in Seattle seems forced to stand on the sidelines of its arts and culture. As a writer, I have never been able to understand why this is so—unless it is because books cannot be hung upon a wall or granite-based in a park. Books are not always likely to increase in money value. Moreover, the seeker after culture must bring something of himself to a book and therein, I fear, lies the rub.

The region is still too young, perhaps, to have developed what honestly could be called literature. True, the Northwest has developed writers of originality and vigor. One thinks of Stewart Holbrook, an historian of Portland, who gained a measure of national fame. There is, of course, James Stevens, who created the magnificent Paul Bunyan legends for us, and H. L. Davis, who captured wide acceptance with *Honey in the Horn*. *Skid Road*, a history of Seattle's seamier past, published in 1951, is a minor classic written by Murray Morgan, and his many other books have gained him wide attention. Yet in their own field writers have not reached the level of the painters: Mark Tobey, Morris Graves, Kenneth Callahan, Guy Anderson, Ambrose Patterson, and the more traditional Eustace Zeigler and Ernest Norling.

Plenty of books are now published by Northwest writers, in both fiction and non-fiction, but the quality suffers in comparison with older regions and only half a dozen titles can be said to transcend the region. Something mysterious and undefined silences young promising writers in the Northwest. Again, it may be that the awe-inspiring scenery depresses rather than lifts them. H. L. Davis, probably the finest novelist that the region has produced, did his best work after moving to California, from where he was able to view his homeland in perspective. Thus his characters are as strong as his backgrounds, which can be said of almost no other novelist of the Seattle area. In the non-fiction field only Morgan, dividing his time between Tacoma and Seattle, can be said to fit the shoes of the late Stewart Holbrook, a transplanted New Englander whose *Age of the Moguls* and stories of the early lumber camps are excellent.

For several decades after the twenties the literature of the area suffered a decline, but there are some signs that new writers are developing who have the vigor and originality of the earlier professionals. These are in the *avant-garde* category and most of them choose to ignore the rugged forests and peaks and rivers, concentrating on narrative and characterization and sometimes venturing into the satirical. Among these are David Wagoner (although his poetry is better than his novels), and a newcomer named Tom Robbins, whose novel *Another Roadside Attraction* shows amazing originality, adept writing and tremendous promise for the future. It appears likely that the time has come when Northwest writers are about to ignore the canvas backdrop for the play itself.

It is in poetry that the region really shines on a national level. For an untold number of years the newspapers inflicted upon their readers what the cynics called "housewife poetry" or a dubious kind of rhyming that celebrated nature (Puget Sound nature, of course) and a Pollyanna attitude toward life and Man. When most of the newspapers had had enough, countless self-published volumes appeared, and there were formed poetry clubs whose members read their verse to each other.

Surely the appearance of Theodore Roethke at the University of Washington did much to break up this unhappy state of affairs. Curiously, it was only a year or two before his untimely death that Seattle realized it had this genius in residence, and this apathy or ignorance was a source of sadness to a poet who certainly needed no additional burden to his depressed state. Nonetheless there built around Roethke—although perhaps not entirely due to him—a valid Northwest school of poetry. The well may be deep, for many Seattle public schools issue publications in which the verse is surprising in its techniques, conscience and maturity.

Unlike other major cities Seattle was without a slick-paper magazine of its own, and in 1964 Stimson Bullitt, the liberal and wealthy chief of King Broadcasting Company, decided to give it one of quality. For editor he lured able Peter Bunzel away from the Time-Life organization. Bunzel chose his staff carefully and trained them with a strong hand. The first few issues, thoroughly professional, startled the Establishment and some other sensitive categories in the town. *Seattle* magazine dug deeply into such issues as abortion, proliferation of freeways, the homosexual community and other almost unexplored areas. It did a bit of muckraking, but was never a liberal magazine except in the minds of arch-conservatives. It drew fire as well as bouquets.

"We were carpetbaggers," Bunzel says now from the editor's chair of the Los Angeles *Times'* lavish Sunday roto magazine *West*. "We were charged with writing down our noses from an eastern point of view. It took us a while to catch onto the temper of Seattle and become fond of it. There always was a love-hate relationship between the magazine and the city, but I think people realized finally that our love for the city was predominate."

Many of the articles reflected this, but the magazine "dug into some pretty dirty corners," as Bunzel puts it. Some advertisers were aroused and tried to retaliate by pulling advertising from both the magazine and the radio-TV station. However, Bullitt and Bunzel continued to exercise "exploratory skepticism" wherever they felt it was required. Bunzel's editorials were thoughtful and constructive.

It reached a peak circulation of 28,000 and every copy was read by three or four persons, which provoked plenty of needed discussion. But over a six-year period it could not attract a fair slice of national or local advertising as do such magazines in San Francisco, Los Angeles, Philadelphia and other cities. Publisher and editor refused to transform it into a booster-tourism type of publication, and in September of 1970 Bullitt decided to give it up. Seattle was simply not ready for the kind of magazine *Seattle* insisted upon being.

Puget Soundings keeps rolling along under the high-flown banner of the Junior League. It has featured admirable articles by top-flight experts on fairly touchy subjects, offering prestige instead of money, although it carries paid advertising. But it has never, as did *Seattle*, mustered the courage to downgrade Washington wines or poke into dark corners such as automobile repair rackets and other subjects likely to drive advertisers wild. The Junior Leaguers, however, deserve high praise for uncovering some new writers, poets and photographers of merit.

Meanwhile, in the late 1960s and early 1970s, the Sunday magazines of the newspapers became more daring and sophisticated, and the feature articles took on magazine quality.

Largely due to the two great wars and following depressions, there were many moons of non-cultural sleep. But now the region is being enlivened by tens of thousands of newcomers with their own cultural needs and memories and contributions. Also there is a new generation of native-born who have caught the enthusiasm of the newcomers.

I can agree with Mr. Stromberg that too often we sit on our fatuous plateau before the next "thrust." But this is characteristic of the whole area, which progresses by means of what my grandmother called "fits and starts." I haven't a doubt that the cultural movement will continue and grow stronger, and that more of Seattle's unquestioned wealth will drain toward the arts.

This simply has to be, for the schooling of the average Northwesterner extends over twelve years and three months—meaning that, statistically, every person in the region has had a touch of college. Atop this is an easily visible determination that the minorities and underprivileged shall prevail.

The remarkable educational level is still on the rise. This is relevant to the influx of highly literate people brought in by firms such as Boeing, Battelle-Northwest, Heath-tecna, Rocket Research and the amazingly diversified, and research-oriented timber-using business.

There have been times when our culture seemed to be one vast borrowing, and when I was younger—therefore much wiser than now!—I was certain that regionalism would disappear entirely in the Northwest. Now I know better; our distinctive pattern was never more apparent. We do seek the traditional and we do want to know more about the history of the arts. But also we demonstrate the will to create, to go our own way, to become superior if possible.

There was the time when the mountains and the forests and our rivers and inland seas overshadowed the artist and writer, even made musicians and singers timid. One has to see our surroundings to understand this wholly. But now even our natural setting seems to recede, to assume a reasonable perspective in relation to the humanity collected on our shores, as more and more Seattleites and neighbors express themselves and seek to respond to the creativity of others.

17

Our Racial Climate

IN ITS compressed history of a bit more than a hundred and twenty years Seattle has had considerable experience with racial problems. It might therefore be expected that its handling of the inevitable integration of the minorities with the majority would be more satisfactory than is the fact.

The first experience of Seattleites with the race problem of course involved the Indians. In the context of American history the tiny settlement did not regard the Indians as a problem in the exact sense of the word. On Puget Sound there were no violent encounters between white and red men, except for one abortive confrontation, the Battle of Seattle.

The attitude of the first settlers was that of all frontier people. It was not considered openly that the whites were the interlopers, actually stealing the land of the original population and later attempting to make the robbery legal by means of treaties which the natives did not fully understand. They were treaties which would move tribes to areas designated by the whites in return for money which was sometimes paid in full and sometimes not. It is an old story which until recent years weighed lightly on the conscience of the whites. But modern Indians have created a sophisticated rebellion which seeks to bring to light the venality and cruelty of the old treaties.

Seattle was no different than other settlements in its attitude, and fortunate in the fact that the tribes it encountered were in a low state and willing to make liaisons with the whites both for protection against their enemies, and sometimes out of curiosity about the white man's God, who seemed to favor his children with great powers. The town had its favorite Indians, the most notable of whom were Chief Sealth and later his daughter, Princess Angeline. But beneath the surface of the village's calm was a contempt for the original owners of the land. Seattleites approved natives when they were useful, but they did not like them too close and in sizable numbers. In his memoirs, Arthur Denny expressed concern when Indians "up to a thousand" crowded onto land which had been "claimed" by the whites or land they intended to stake out. Although these red men were friendly, they were overcome by curiosity and became what these pioneers regarded as a nuisance. A few Seattleites—few indeed, but Arthur Denny was among them—recognized the Indian's rights before the laws. Those laws did not, significantly, include Indian rights to their home grounds.

The solution, as the settlers and government officials saw it, was to move them. But they did not come to this conclusion until it was felt that the red men were a threat to white lives and property. Even as late as the first quarter of this century an Indian was a "Siwash," a term of denigration. Half-breeds were usually considered dangerous. In the land that would become Washington State there was a curious difference, still existing, between the whites on the west side of the Cascades and those east of that range. In eastern Washington mixed bloods are considered as whites, and many families in the region of the big ranches are proud of having strong strains of Indian blood. This is probably due to the contrast between the eastern tribes and those on the coast.

The coastal natives, as Chief Sealth recognized, appeared to be unalterably in a state of deterioration—an opinion which would be proved wrong. But the Indians east of the Cascades, notably the Nez Percé, possessed characteristics admired by the white man. They were highly intelligent, brave and warlike against tribes farther east. They were expert horsemen and had a flair for costuming and for decorating their horses. In every way they appeared superior to the coast natives, who were quick to accept the white man's cast-off clothing; and—half naked and half covered with a threadbare coat or merely a crushed top hat—they became ludicrous to the whites and this lent further strength to the term "Siwash." The Indians of the eastern range were forced to hunt for game, whereas the coastal tribes depended on fish and clams and easily found edible roots. Theirs was a soft life, conducive to laziness. Naturally they were not satisfactory as workers for the white man.

Some of their descendants, victims of the white man's scorn and neglect, can still be seen in doorways and around Seattle's taverns near Pioneer Square, or lolling on the area's few park benches. But the Indian of today—the modern, proud militant, whose new awareness has spread over the United States—is a strong element in Seattle's contemporary scene. Many of the new generation of Indians seen in Seattle descended, no doubt, from the warlike tribes of eastern Washington and throughout the Midwest. But the sons and daughters of the once scorned "Siwashes" are very much a part of this new and long-overdue striving for rights, dignity and power.

It was in the middle of this century when the first signs appeared that "trouble" with the Indians was not buried permanently in the biased annals of the pioneers.

There have been modern "uprisings," which the majority of Seattleites do not take seriously enough, or ignore entirely. At the outset the troubles centered around fishing rights, an ancient point that goes back to the first treaties. The modern Indians disturbed commercial and sports fishermen, some of whom claim that the Indians are going beyond the treaties, endangering the fish run and violating regulations of the state game department. The white men are not now up against ignorant natives, futile arrows and crooked-bore muskets. They face intelligent young Indians, both men and women, with sophisticated leaders. And employed by the Indians are attorneys of the first class.

Many tribes and several reservations are involved. The Puyallups, for example, stated their claims through attorney John Sennhauser. Speaking for the Puyallup Indian Tribal Council he stated that Indians have been taunted, threatened and harassed by "sportsmen" on fishing grounds, that Indian nets have been cut or destroyed by shotguns. The Puyallups claim that hundreds of sports fishermen have entered Indian land in an attempt to frighten these descendants of the original settlers, and warned them to keep away from fishing grounds. The Puyallups also contend that whites have staged "fish-ins" on streams and other bodies of water which belong to the Indians by treaty. The Puyallups continue to make claims to the U. S. Civil Rights Commission, and they have warned that unless their rightful demands are met there will be "more violence and disharmony."

The new "Indian warfare" moves on several fronts. Some Puyallups have demanded exemption from the draft because "a state of hostility" between the Army and Nisqually Indians has existed. The Puyallups insist that state officers have entered Fort Lewis by permission of the Army, where attempt is made to enforce fishing regulations, and that this violates an Army-state agreement covering a property known as Frank's Landing on the Nisqually, an Indian fishing area.

Now and then Indians enter into conflict with the state game department and win. This happened when the Indians foiled—in court and not from ambush—an attempt to enjoin them from fishing for steelhead on the Puyallup River. The Quinaults won a major skirmish when attempts were made to limit their fishing. They blocked roads to reservation beaches. That, and other drastic actions brought national publicity and now and then a film or television star, perhaps sincere, perhaps seeking newspaper space. These prominent outsiders were not welcomed by the Indians, who felt that this kind of gaudy support confused the legal issues and did more harm than good.

At one point in the new Indian warfare the Indians blocked roads in an action which left the state highway department with a $3.5 million plan for a road that would lead nowhere, and the program had to be shelved.

Indians also objected to prices offered for their fish. So the Puyallup, Nisqually and Muckleshoots began shipment of salmon to New York. They had been offered as low as ten cents per pound locally, while dressed salmon in Manhattan brought as much as eighty cents a pound. Ramona Adams, a handsome and prominent young Indian "warrior" told the press that a co-operative was being created to serve the East Coast market. She was joined in her plan by Hank Adams, project director of the Survival of the American Indian Association, who told this writer that "the market in the East for

'genuine Indian-caught salmon' seems unlimited. It looks permanent, too," he said, "because the big hotels feature this fish and it's
very popular with the customers."

So the regional Indians have resolved to avoid the role of
patsies, and a processing plant went into the general planning. Oddly
enough, the plant idea was the result of a clash of sixty-two Indians
with armed Tacoma police at an encampment on the Puyallup River.
No shot was fired, but at gunpoint the police arrested—with the aid
of the now hated Game Commission—the sixty-two Indians and
took them to jail. A bail fund of more than $9,000 was raised, but
not nearly that much was needed. The remaining amount was used
to get the processing plant under way.

The resurgence of Indian activity is not wholly connected with
fishing rights. The Indians object to the directive which would juggle
around Indian agency superintendents every two years. The Indians
charged that this was an attempt to create schisms among the tribes,
and at this writing they seem to be upheld by Indian Superintendent
George Felshaw.

The old conception of Indian reservations, core of the yellow-
ing treaties, seems to be waning in the Indian's mind. When Fort
Lawton in Seattle was marked obsolete by the Army, the Indians—
among others—were quick to show an interest in at least a part of it.
The spirit of Geronimo, who surrendered far east of the Rockies
to General Lawton, was invoked at a mass meeting of Indians in an
attempt to solidify their claim to a piece of the beautifully forested
"fort" just north of Seattle. The approximately 10,000 Indians of
Seattle were implored to unite behind a plan which would include
the Indian claim in the city's hopeful program for a refurbished
Fort Lawton, which will become one of the largest parks in the city
system.

The U. S. Indian commissioner had withdrawn an Indian bid
for part of the surplus land. But not Bernie Whitebear, head of
United Indians of All Tribes, who thumped the war drum for a
multiservice complex to serve the social, educational and cultural
needs of urban Indians. "I don't like the word compromise," he
told the meeting. "But I don't want to look at myself in the mirror
and know that I was willing to accept nothing at all for the Indian
people." The Indians were disappointed not to have won the whole
property, but Blair Paul, Indian attorney, indicated an enthusiastic
interest in the idea of a cultural center in the old fort. "We don't

want to make the mistake of thinking that our mayor is an Indian at heart," the lawyer told the audience. "But he's a man—a political man, and I think he's shapable." Blair Paul's comment reflected the sophistication of the modern Indian in his revived confrontation with the white man.

There was help, too, from the nation's capital. Said U. S. Senator Henry M. Jackson, representing Washington State: "I've encouraged the Indians to work with Seattle and put together the best possible proposal."

Buoyed by the idea of a cultural center, I asked a young Indian if he thought reservations were a thing of the past.

"They'll be 'way in the past," he answered. "We were the first North Americans and it's about time we became really a part of the whole. My hunch is that long before the end of this century you'll see Indian lands, as always, but nothing in the way of reservations as people think of them, and smugly accept them, right now."

I asked him if the demands of the blacks had set off the renewal of Indian concern with their rights and culture. "In no way," he said. "What is happening is our idea, although we see the viewpoint of the blacks and sympathize with it. We'll welcome their cooperation, but I don't see us butting into their affairs. We're all Indian now, man. You're not talking about the days of Chief Seattle now. He and some of the others couldn't make up their minds whether they were Indians or white men—and you know what happened. Somehow the Apaches and the Hopis get more attention, and God knows they need it, than the Northwest tribes. But I think we're on the right trail now. Too many people in Seattle have forgotten the Indians and we're going to take care of that."

It looks that way. The Northwest Allied Tribes have become a politically powerful alliance of Washington, Oregon, Idaho and Montana tribes. If regional white fishermen are shaken by it, so are the top men with the U. S. Indian Commission.

As Chief Seattle said, "Perhaps we are brothers, after all. We shall see."

Seattle's next racial problem—and perhaps its most shameful—was with the Chinese. It did not erupt until the late 1880s. The Chinese had helped build the railroads across the nation. They were willing workers, at wages which consisted of pennies and three bowls of rice a day. They were useful in the expanding fish canneries both on the Sound and in Alaska. They washed the clothing of the whites, and were quick and anxious to learn any kind of manual labor. Due to immigration restrictions, few had families, and so were unable to demonstrate to the Seattleites that they could create a community of their own that would be an asset to the town. That would come much later in the city's history.

In the minds of whites there were too many Chinese once the railroads were built. The lid blew off. Seattle's handling of the situation was hardly commendable.

Here was a race which, like the Indians, had shown a certain usefulness and now seemed dangerous—dangerous to the economy of the white man. The answer to the whites seemed to be to forget them, or move them on. There were too many Indians and later too many Chinese to simply ignore.

In 1886 the attitude of most Seattleites against the Chinese amounted to a craze. Yet the anti-Chinese attitude was by no means new, or entirely local. The immigration of the Chinese began in the early 1850s. Almost at once the anti-Chinese movement took ragged shape. It continued—in fluctuating waves, always depending to an extent upon the state of the economy—for nearly forty years. A chief argument was that the Chinese did not intend to become assimilated; they wanted to earn here what would be more than sufficient in China, then return home. A more specious argument could not be imagined, for the anti-Chinese of the West Coast did not really want the Chinese to assimilate. Yet they were compared unfavorably with immigrants from Europe, who also sought to escape oppression and substandard living and live in a land of freedom. People in the eastern states were puzzled by the anti-Chinese violence out west. There were few Chinese on the eastern seaboard; they offered little or no competition to white labor, and their roles in the communities were limited.

On the West Coast the situation was different. White workers in almost every branch of industry felt the influence of the Chinese. Among the whites' most closely organized groups was the Knights of Labor, a pioneer attempt at unionism in the Seattle area. Its members were strong and active in the coal mining areas of Issaquah, Renton, Newcastle and other neighboring towns. But their power was increasingly felt in Seattle; they formed one root of a condition which has made Seattle the strongest "union town" on the western coast.

Economic conditions sharpened the danger to the Chinese. The collapse of the so-called "Villard boom" in 1883 was followed by five years of precarious times in Seattle. The first outbreak against the Chinese, however, occurred in Rock Springs, Wyoming. At that community there was an uprising of white men who murdered eleven Chinese and drove out five hundred more.

The Rock Springs massacre was important because it set off anti-Chinese action at several points on the Coast, particularly in Seattle and surrounding towns. In the Issaquah Valley a night attack was made on hop pickers as they slept in tents. Three were shot dead and many beaten badly. Most escaped by plunging into a stream and hiding in the brush. The leaders of the Issaquah attack were known, but no effort was made to apprehend and punish them. The outrages at Rock Springs and Issaquah, although widely separated as to geography, were the start of a series of mob meetings around Puget Sound. The speeches were wildly incendiary and urged every town to rid itself of the Chinese. As yet there was no opposition to this kind of oratory. Soon after the meetings, miners at Black Diamond, near Seattle, drove the Chinese out of town, injuring nine seriously.

Finally, on September 19, 1886, Mayor Henry Yesler, builder of the town's first sawmill and thus its first industry, called a public gathering of a far more conservative nature than those which had preceded it. Yesler pleaded for law and order, but was supported openly by hardly more than a dozen leading citizens. He might not have received even this meager support if he had not promised to aid in the removal of the Chinese by lawful means.

Later in the month an "anti-Chinese congress" met. The labor groups were represented strongly, and many fraternal orders saw to it that a sizable percentage of their membership was present. No objection was made to the entrance of known troublemakers and anarchists, some from Seattle, others reaching town "on the rods" of freight trains. The resolutions they adopted were afire with hatred. The so-called "congress" produced a proclamation ordering that all Chinese must leave western Washington not later than the following November 15. A day or two later a mass meeting in Tacoma endorsed the action.

John H. McGraw, then sheriff of King County, showed commendable effort to halt the vigilante spirit. He increased the number of deputies and issued additional arms and ammunition. The local police were unready and undermanned for a major crisis. Every freight train brought more vicious outsiders who were out of work and blamed it on the Chinese. Seattle expected pillage, arson and even open murder of both Chinese and those believed to be in sympathy with them.

A scattering of leading citizens—some out of fear and others in the cause of humanity—decided to hold an emergency meeting in Frye's Opera House. To keep out the agitators, tickets of admission were prepared and cautiously distributed. About six hundred tickets were taken up. The purpose was to make plans for mutual protection, and thus was born the "Opera House Party," which soon was opposed by the "Anti-Chinese Party." The schism was widening, and open warfare—with the poor frightened Chinese in the middle—seemed probable.

Few if any of the Chinese could speak or read English, but if they had translated to them the essence of the meeting of the Opera House Party, they could find small comfort in it. This was the resolution adopted by acclamation:

> Resolved, that we regard the existence of the Chinese among us as a disturbing element, and are strongly in favor of the Restriction Act, and of any amendments thereto that may be necessary to accomplish its beneficent purpose, and we fully recognize and advocate the paramount claims of all laborers, who are or may become citizens of the United States, and we recommend their employment by individuals and corporations; but we are also, as a matter of honor, right and safety, both as individuals and as a community, in favor of law and order. We hereby pledge ourselves to the constituted authorities within this jurisdiction, whether the same be Federal, territorial, county or municipal, to aid them to the fullest extent in the suppression of all attempts to destroy life or property or to endanger the public peace and tranquility.

In brief, the Chinese had to go, and peace was requested until that could be accomplished. Meanwhile they were afforded no assistance in shelter or food, and got along as best they could in shacks and tents beyond the south end of town.

A few days after the Opera House proclamation, the territorial court convened and a grand jury was called. At this time Judge Roger S. Greene, Chief Justice of the territorial Supreme Court, after reading parts of the criminal code, made a comment which must strike the modern reader as amazing inasmuch as he represented the law and was regarded as a most conservative citizen. Among other things he said:

"If any breach of these provisions has passed it has probably had something to do with the Chinese . . . You probably share, as do I, the conviction of the people of the Pacific States and territories that under present conditions, and viewed from an economic stand-point, the Chinese are out of place in America and their presence in this city and on this coast is an obstacle to the highest business prosperity . . ."

This from a high court judge representing a large melting pot of the world! After making a stand for law and order in the manner of the removal of the Chinese, but making no concrete suggestions as to method, the judge said also:

"As it seems to me, the presence of the Chinese on this coast is a real grievance which may be summed up under five heads: Undercompetitive cheapness of Chinese labor. . . . Alienage of Chinese labor. . . . Export of the earnings of that labor. . . . Padding the population with the Chinese element. . . . and race and class irritations which are a perpetual menace to the social order."

He was referring to a group which had helped build the railroads, mine the coal for ships and locomotives, and had contributed generally to the upbuilding of the nation, particularly the western coast and the Pacific Northwest. However, in fairness to a judge pressured by economic conditions and an influx of agitators for whom nobody was prepared, he added: "The presence of the Chinese is an evil, but the project of driving them out by lawless violence is suicidal."

This was indeed a pretty dish to set before those kings of the area who held humanity in their hearts, and how they would make away with that dish was still a puzzle. Nowhere in the judge's remarks did he refer to the venality of businessmen who had caused the "padding of the population with Chinese."

All the while, of course, there was considerable official correspondence and discussion. The governor was in touch with the Chinese consul at San Francisco, as well as with authorities at the national capital, most of whom could not understand the problem at all and wished they could close their eyes to it. The governor was also corresponding with the sheriffs of King and Pierce counties and the mayors of Seattle and Tacoma. Every response from the regional officials of the law tried to calm the governor; they pointed out that a state of quiet prevailed and was likely to continue because of the abilities of their various departments to maintain law and order.

Suddenly the anti-Chinese in Tacoma undertook direct action. In wagons, several hundred agitators moved into the Chinese quarter. The day was cold and a driving rain was pouring down. The mob forced the Chinese to move their meager goods and themselves into the wagons, and drove them in the near-freezing rain to the Lake View rail station several miles away. At least one Chinese died from exposure and the sick were given no comfort. From the Lake View Station they were sent to Portland, Oregon.

The action was called peaceable expulsion. Not a citizen objected, and one wrote the governor a letter which probably reflected the general air in Tacoma: "It affords me genuine delight to recall my assurances to you at Olympia and here that the Chinese could be got out of Tacoma without any trouble, and point to the denouement in confirmation. Those who predicted differently were partly swayed by their wishes and greatly underrated the intelligence, character and resolution of the men who worked up the movement and were flippantly called 'a rabble' by their moral and intellectual inferiors."

While Portland was receiving the Tacoma Chinese with less than welcome, and attempting to send them on to California or out over the Columbia bar by ship, the Tacoma mob had returned to the Chinese quarters to burn the shacks, then went on to destroy the few shops which had been operated by the hated foreigners.

Nobody was punished for these acts, or even sought out for questioning.

The governor, now near panic and not soothed by the Tacoman's letter, realized that what had happened on Commencement Bay would only increase the tension in Seattle and small nearby settlements where Chinese had been employed. He issued a proclamation, urging Washingtonians to "array yourselves on the side of the law." There was no visible effect. Even members of the

Opera House Party advised the Chinese to be ready for deportation at any moment.

Yet there were many who felt the danger was past. To attempt to insure this, a mass meeting was held and speeches were made by both the lawful and the agitators. The most notable speech was by Judge Thomas Burke, son of Irish immigrants and a hero of the struggle for the railroads. He admitted that the time had come for a new treaty covering Chinese immigration, but this was a problem for which Seattle and the territory could not muster much force. What Judge Burke stressed was that Seattle was "face-to-face with the question as to whether we shall act as becomes free, law-abiding and justice-loving Americans, or as turbulent and lawless foreigners."

Not expecting any practical results from all this speechmaking the governor telegraphed the Secretaries of War and of the Interior that the presence of United States troops was an absolute necessity. This time the national capital took sharper notice, and three hundred and fifty troops were ordered to Seattle from Fort Vancouver on the north side of the Columbia River. They were not to stay long, but there would be a second emergency call for the regulars.

When the troops came they had only vague orders and were practically ignored by the anti-Chinese, who merely conducted their plans and actions less openly. They were so quiet that the U.S. troops were sent back to Fort Vancouver, and just at a time when the *Queen of Victoria* came into dock, offering the rabble the opportunity they wanted. A Committee of Fifteen marched to the Chinese quarters led by the chief of police himself. At their rear a quickly growing mob gathered. Using the city's sanitary regulations as a blind, the committee and their volunteer helpers began moving the Chinese to the waterfront. There was of course no resistance from the frightened "coolies," who were now ready for almost anything that would get them out of Seattle and headed for home.

During these maneuvers the position of the mayor is lost to the records. But Sheriff McGraw appeared as soon as he got the word. His command to disperse was greeted with jeers, whereupon he assembled a posse as large as could be gathered in such a short time. The posse was hopelessly outnumbered by the mob. They could do nothing unless they wanted to resort to gunfire, and that they did not want to do. So the sheriff tried another move. He caused the fire bell to ring its signal for assembly of the Home

Guards, who appeared almost at once under Captain George Kinnear; the Seattle Rifles commanded by Captain Joseph Green, and Company D with Captain J. C. Haines at its head. Governor Squier was in town at the time, protected by the walls of the courthouse. He issued another proclamation and caused it to be posted throughout the downtown area.

The hometown soldiers were not taken seriously by the anti-Chinese, who went on with their plans. They soon had about three hundred and fifty Chinese herded on the wharf, but were denied the gangplank of the *Queen* until her master could see the color of passage money.

The downtown area was jammed with men and a few raucous women who liked trouble. Between the mob and the bay the shivering Chinese were trapped. An early observer said that the town had never been so thronged with strangers—"hard and idle characters," he called them. They were alleged to have come from Victoria in British Columbia and as far south as San Diego. Seattleites claimed that the crisis would not have developed without the strangers. Judge Roger Greene now sent a dispatch to President Grover Cleveland, urging suspension of the writ of habeas corpus and the return of the troops. And he stressed the need for martial law.

Events were developing rapidly. Some of the Chinese, whose fare had been paid, were taken from the *Queen* and brought to Judge Greene's court under protection of the Home Guards and the two militia companies. The mob followed to the courthouse, threatening and brandishing clubs and stones.

They were not allowed inside the courthouse. Gently, through an interpreter, Judge Greene frankly told the Chinese present that almost all in the city favored their departure, but he would not allow force. He promised that all Chinese who wanted to stay would be protected. But an informal vote of raised hands showed that only sixteen out of eighty-nine present wanted to stay. Exactly why the sixteen wanted to stay remains a mystery in Seattle's history. One suspects that they misunderstood the question.

Those who voted to leave were escorted back to the ship, but when a certain number had climbed the gangplank the ship's captain announced that under maritime regulations he could take no more. About a hundred were left on the wharf with fares in hand—fares raised by passing the hat among anti-Chinese forces.

But the steamer *George S. Elder* was due. Until her arrival nothing could be done except to escort the waiting Chinese back to the "yellow ghetto." This dangerous duty was assigned to the Home Guards. The Chinese were formed in single file and moved back to the southern end of town. At Main and First Avenue South a howling mob was waiting. Those at the head rushed the guards and attempted to wrest away their arms, apparently confident that the guards would not fire. The local troops tried to beat off their assailants with rifle butts, but inevitably a few shots were let go, wounding five men and killing Charles Stewart, a loud-voiced leader of the anti-Chinese mob, who turned out to be a Canadian.

No order on the spot had been given to fire, but in retrospect it developed that Captain Kinnear had told his men to be cautious, but if they and the Chinese seemed to be in danger the troops were at liberty to fire.

At the single volley the mob fell back, leaving their slain leader and their wounded in the clay mud of the street. Some citizens felt that they would have reformed and attacked again except for the arrival of the Seattle Rifles from the wharf and Company D from the courthouse. Now the three local outfits formed a hollow square within which the Chinese dropped to the ground in terror. Finally they were lifted or persuaded to move with their protectors.

Now the agitators sought the aid of the law they had flouted. Their anger was focused on Judge Burke, the Reverend L. A. Banks, E. M. Carr, Frank Hanford and David Webster. A complaint was sworn before Justice of the Peace George Hill, and a warrant for their arrest went to a constable. All the defendants were at the courthouse at the time and it was considered certain that if Judge Burke left the building he would be lynched. The mob was particularly angered at Burke both for his speech at the mass meeting and his position as counsel to railroads which had employed the Chinese.

The group was temporarily saved by Judge Greene, at the time holding territorial District Court in Seattle. He told the constable that the five were officers of his court and that he would not allow them to be arrested there. Accepting this until further orders, the constable withdrew with his warrant for arrest.

Governor Squier was still taking refuge in the courthouse and Judge Greene told him that the constable would be back. "Governor," he said, "it's my judgment that the situation can be controlled if you declare martial law in Seattle."

"Martial law?" exclaimed the nervous governor. "You mean right now?"

"I mean right now. You've already advised the President of the need."

"Will you write the declaration for me?" asked Squier.

The judge dropped to a chair by the table and drew a sheet of paper toward him. He began to write: "Whereas, heretofore, on the 7th day of February, 1886, in consequence of the inflamed condition of the public in the City of Seattle and a grave disturbance of the peace therein, I, Watson C. Squier, Governor of the Territory of Washington, issued my proclamation warning all citizens to cease and desist from breaches of the peace . . . Whereas, said proclamation has proved ineffectual to quiet the public mind and preserve the peace. . . . Numerous breaches of the peace have occurred and more are threatened . . . Therefore be it known that as Governor of said Territory and commander-in-chief of the military command of said City of Seattle, I do hereby order that no person exercise any office or authority in said city which may be inconsistent with the laws of said Territory, and do hereby suspend the writ of habeas corpus and declare martial law within said city . . ."

The governor read the declaration and signed it. This was about noon. By three o'clock copies had been printed and posted about the town. Then, when the governor and the judge were certain that the news was abroad, they walked down the slippery wooden sidewalk (crisscrossed with cleats for safety against the steep grade) to test the temper of the town.

They found streets and sidewalks crowded, and were the targets of pointing fingers and loud taunts that were not only uncomplimentary but obscene. But nothing more dangerous seemed probable, and the high officials made their way with what calm and dignity they could manage. Nobody was more relieved than the constable, who, without the existence of martial law, would have been forced to take five men to jail through at least a thousand angry mobsters. Now his duty was suspended. Later a charge of murder was lodged against the five, but the justice of the peace accepted bail and they were allowed abroad. The case never came to trial.

At the time of the shooting some unknown citizen had discharged a load of buckshot which lodged in the siding of the court-house. During the night somebody had circled the pellet marks with a chalked circle under which was lettered "Burke's Mark." The once wholly popular little Irishman withstood threats on the street and whenever he appeared in public meetings. For a time he and Mrs. Burke received hundreds of abusive letters. His landlord was advised that his office building would be dynamited if he allowed Burke to continue as a tenant. Landlord and tenant ignored the threat, and nothing happened. Gradually the letters and taunts wore out, but it was a sad—and doubtless dangerous—period for the Burkes, who had been so admired by the city.

The President quickly approved the governor's martial law, and ordered the return of United States troops. They stayed on for a couple of months after martial law ceased on February 22 of the following year. Martial law was in existence for only two weeks, but that was sufficient. Itinerant idlers and agitators soon departed. Hardly more than a dozen Chinese were in town now, and they were not molested. Symbolically at least, these courageous few can be called the founders of Seattle's later, admirable Chinese community.

Yet the issue was kept alive by demagogues and a few Puget Sound newspapers seeking sensational news. The municipal election of that year demonstrated how strongly bigoted feelings were continuing. A "People's Party" organized by the anti-Chinese was strong. Even a candidate as eminent as Arthur Denny, a founder of the city, was defeated by William Shoudy for the office of mayor. The vote was close, but considering the reputation of Denny the latter's defeat was significant. To the council were elected four of the "People's Party" and four members of the "Loyal League," formed by those who had shown respect for law and order.

The edge was taken from this fifty-fifty split by the general election which followed a few months later. In that balloting the "People's Party" made a clean sweep of all county offices. This caused a switch by opportunist politicians who until then had been openly supporting the judges and the governor.

However, the power of the "People Party" was not to last long, and the apparent reason was the disappearance of the recession and a marked improvement in Seattle's business climate. As money began to loosen, so did tension. The town entered another era of population growth, which saw the addition of many businessmen from the East. This was attributed in part to national publicity given to Seattle's period of martial law.

In any case, the racial troubles of the city seemed to have evaporated and all concerned smugly felt that the Chinese problem had been "solved."

It is interesting to note that today there are oriental student unions at some of the many new community colleges in the region. At the University of Washington there is an Asian-American Student Coalition, and a community group called the Asian Coalition for Equality. Their activities have been quiet. Sometimes they have been joined in their aims by the black student unions, and also the Brown Berets, an organization of Mexican-Americans usually called "Chicanos." Filipino-Americans, particularly the younger ones, are a quietly strong factor in the Coalition. What these groups usually seek is representation in administrative posts on the campuses, and their record of accomplishment is good.

The "new" Chinese, when their time came, participated in civic enterprises but remained proud of their race and culture. They raised distinguished families which were a pride of the city. They created a "Chinatown" that was not as ornate and well defined as San Francisco's, but definitely it reflected the enormous changes wrought since the gray days of the late eighties in the last century. They rarely entered politics and it was not until 1962 that Wing Luke, son of a pioneer Chinese family, was elected to become the first of his race on the Seattle City Council.

Wing Luke had been active in attempting to lead Chinese into the center of municipal programs. One effort—illustrating the variety of his interests—was his attempt to save and restore the *Wawona*, an ancient schooner which had been prominent on the waterfront decades before. Unfortunately Luke's influence was all too brief, for as a comparatively young man he was killed in the crash of a private plane three years after his election to the council. Today the Wing Luke Memorial Center is a fitting reminder of his work and his ambitions for his people in a city he loved. It features exhibits of Chinese art, culture and history, and is one of the most popular attractions in the city.

Four lears later, in May 1969, another distinguished citizen of Chinese ancestry, Liem Eng Tuai, an attorney, was appointed by the City Council to fill the unexpired term of Councilman Paul

Alexander, who died in office. That fall Tuai ran for the council in the city's general election and received more votes than any other council candidate.

There was, eventually, a Japanese crisis, but its origins were far different from that of the anti-Chinese troubles.

The troubles with the Japanese came directly from the effects of the attack on Pearl Harbor in Hawaii, and transformed into a kind of panic when it was obvious that the whole West Coast, particularly Seattle and Alaska, were woefully unprotected from an enemy.

The Japanese crisis might be called a phenomenon of fear, and was much more marked in Seattle than elsewhere. Actually, San Francisco was almost as vulnerable as Seattle—yet thousands of Seattleites, gripped by panic, sent securities and other valuables to friends and banks in San Francisco, and were ready to follow their financial gains at an instant's notice.

The best one can say of the handling of the Japanese crisis is that it was unfair and cruel, but under the evil circumstances of war it also was inevitable. Aside from the inhumanity involved, and the admirable local record of the Japanese, it is of interest as a demonstration of the population's susceptibility to fear in Seattle. There were indeed hawkish citizens who for years had talked of the certainty of war with Japan. That feeling had been an underlying concern of Seattle and other West Coast cities for many years, long before most people worried about Hitler in the Pacific Northwest. Actually there was no real hatred of the Japanese in Seattle; even in a time when nobody quite trusted them there was considerable sympathy for a people so easily recognized as having antecedents in an enemy nation. There were no outside agitators involved, nor were unions and economics involved. This was a matter of the military against the Japanese.

Interwoven with displacement of the Japanese in Seattle was the influx of workers heading for the shipyards and Boeing plants. Among the newcomers were several thousand blacks, and Seattle —which had harbored less than 4,000—viewed them with something like awe. The truth of the matter was that Seattle did not welcome the great immigration of war workers. Underneath there was the traditional suspicion of Seattleites toward strangers in numbers.

But in the Second World War many changes took place—and quickly—in towns throughout the state, but particularly in those in the Puget Sound area. Bremerton, equated always with the Puget Sound Navy Yard, came alive instantly when the United States entered the war, just as it had at the outbreak of World War I.

The swift expansion of Bremerton was to be expected, but there were other areas where changes came as a surprise. Rural Whidbey Island, north of Seattle, whose only warlike atmosphere emanated from the rotting logs of a blockhouse, became one of our Navy's "anchored" aircraft carriers. Disgruntled and grizzled pioneers moved before the bulldozers, and cringed at the roar of planes overhead. A man who lived on Whidbey as a youth told me, "The Japanese weren't the only ones who were displaced. You should have heard my father when the Navy moved in—and moved us. We had to vacate a house we'd lived in for seventeen years, and where I'd been born. 'Talk about the Japanese,' he said. 'What about us? It's enough to make a man want to join the other side.'"

Of all the towns and cities in the state only Seattle and Tacoma and Bremerton were old hands at building war materials. There were still many veteran shipbuilders from World War I. When war came again, the three towns of Seattle, Tacoma and Bremerton hitched up their breeches with a knowing air and went to work. Once again, Seattleites thought, their city would become a most vital part of what President Franklin D. Roosevelt had called "an arsenal of democracy." Most citizens had the uncomfortable feeling that once more we would be engaged in the war, but we tried to put it out of our minds. Perhaps this time it wouldn't happen.

Of course events did not turn out that way. In Seattle on that dread Sunday of December 7, 1941, a momentary shock and paralysis took over the city by Puget Sound. We would need to be more than part of the arsenal of democracy. Hawaii suddenly seemed very close to home.

Lieutenant General John DeWitt, commanding general of the Pacific Coast, and Vice Admiral Charles S. Freeman, commandant of the Thirteenth Naval District (and soon of the Northwest Sea Frontier, meaning Alaska and her Aleutian chain) appeared to be the only ones not puzzled or shocked. Both were quoted in the newspapers as having expected an attack in the Pacific although they did not pretend to know where the enemy would strike.

Because it was the Army which had to look after land defense in the air raid which almost all on the Coast now expected, it was General DeWitt upon whom most of the responsibility fell. Within a few hours, the general had set the pattern under which Seattle and the Coast would live for a long time. Seattleites, like people on the East Coast, were living in blackness at night. For a short time DeWitt silenced all radio stations on the theory that their broadcasts might unwittingly breach security, and also create a point of electronic reference for enemy submarines lurking off the coast. Night office workers toiled behind blackout windows and crept along halls with blue-shaded flashlights. There was almost no traffic on the streets, but all cars were required to mask their lights with dark blue cellophane.

It was a strange new world, a strange way of living. People on the West Coast sensed that they were unprotected—Seattleites most of all because of their nearness to Alaska. It was easy to imagine the Japanese landing on the Aleutians and moving south, invading with infantry and island-jumping with air strikes. It was a time of uneasiness and fear, and suddenly Seattleites became aware—sharply aware—of the Japanese among them. Though the city contained only 6,975 Japanese at the time, now it seemed like more, and stories multiplied. Then it was noticed that some Japanese (how many nobody knew for sure) had returned to Japan. Talk of these departures was rampant and rumor-filled.

What information had the returning Japanese taken home? What photographs did they have? Of Boeing? Of our harbor? Of the Bremerton Navy Yard? Nobody knew, of course, but Seattle and its environs fretted over those departed Japanese.

Yet in all the months between the December attack on Pearl Harbor and the chilling strike on Dutch Harbor the following June there is not a single record of violence between remaining Japanese and other Seattleites. Mob hysteria was not a problem, except for one instance, when a merchant forgot to turn off his window display lights before locking up for the night. Before the police could inform him, a mob formed to smash the windows and destroy the lights with bricks and clubs. The forgetful merchant, who was then thoroughly investigated, was not a Japanese.

Nontheless the fear of the local Japanese was mounting, and General DeWitt established a curfew for them on the excuse that it was for their own protection. The telephones of the daily newspapers rang more or less continuously with curious reports from excited citizens.

An old lady who lived in West Seattle reported that the body of a Japanese flier had washed ashore. It turned out to be a bundle of sodden gunnysacks. An imaginative citizen insisted that a large open field near the Sand Point Naval Station had a pattern of mustard weed in the form of a double arrow, one pointing toward Bremerton, the other toward the air station. He insisted the bright yellow weed was to aid enemy fliers. Investigation proved that the whole field was scattered with mustard weed, and in no particular pattern. A man in the north end was certain that he had seen three enemy planes aloft, heading for the Navy Yard. He insisted that he was familiar with the appearance of all Allied planes and these were none of ours. Such wild reports were rampant in the early days after the Pearl Harbor disaster.

Because of the fear of espionage, the military was making plans to evacuate the Japanese. The Italians and Germans, of whom Seattle had several thousand, were unmolested. Of their own volition some of the many German organizations abandoned or reduced the number of their regular meetings. The Italian Club remained popular, but every night and part of the day a Naval Intelligence officer, out of uniform and friendly with many of the members, moved from bar to tables, from group to group.

The Japanese were given ample warning that they would be moved to comfortable areas being prepared for them, and given a probable date. Curiously and coincidentally, the movement of the Japanese and Nippon's attack on the Aleutian chain occurred within a few days of one another in June. Men, women and children were moved by train to Idaho on June first, leaving not a single Japanese in the city. Moving single file onto obsolescent railroad passenger trains, they were a sad sight in the pelting rain. Many younger couples had babes in arms or tagging along at skirts or trousers; it seemed that every young Nisei couple in Seattle had children. Some of the elders carried keepsakes that they had not wanted to trust to the baggage cars. Something had gone wrong with the heating system of the train. The windows, smeared and dirty, were dripping with rain and on the inside fogged with the cold. The military in charge had not planned this kind of travel. Those were days when it was difficult to put a passenger train together, any kind of a passenger train. Some of the occupants, young and old, rubbed at the fogged panes seeking what might be a last look at the bay or the hills of the city which they had come to love—and which now had forsaken them.

By chance I was night duty officer for intelligence in what Seattleites had come to call the U.S.S. *Exchange Building*. And by even more curious coincidence I was in the communications room, looking over the shoulder of a yeoman who sat at a teletype machine. Suddenly I did not hear the din of tapping keys all over the room. All I could hear—or see—was the teletype in front of me and the unbelievable message it was spelling out:

JAPANESE ATTACKING DUTCH WITH ZEROS. THIS FROM DUTCH HARBOR. THIS IS NO DRILL.

The machine stuttered a string of meaningless letters, then repeated THIS IS NO DRILL. LOOKS LIKE. . . . Then the machine stopped. Seconds went by that seemed like hours. I remember thinking that the operator up north on Kodiak Island must have been killed. Then in what seemed like slow motion the yeoman whirled the knobs, tore off the narrow strip of green paper and headed for the office of the night chief of staff.

It was five minutes after six on Kodiak when the fifteen Zeros and four large bombers slid down out of the murk to have a closer look at Dutch Harbor, where our Navy was constructing a base. Ed Hume, a construction worker, told me later that they seemed so close that he thought he could see goggled yellow faces peering down at him. The planes rose into the fog, then came down again in a wide circle and Hume could see black specks dropping lazily out of the bellies of the bombers. For a moment the black specks seemed to disappear in the fog, then tore in a red frenzy of explosions at the earth and the hangars and the oil tanks huddled in revetments near the shoreline. The Zeroes followed, very low, spitting shells—it seemed to Ed Hume—at random.

The Navy did not announce the attack until almost twenty-four hours later, but it was still near enough to the moving of Japanese to seem like a retaliation. Of course it was nothing of the kind, although few non-military Seattleites could be made to believe this. The attack on Kodiak Island and the later occupation of Aleutian islands far to the west had been set in motion as early as May 5 with an order from the Imperial Japanese Headquarters that read in part: "COMMANDER IN CHIEF OF COMBINED FLEET WILL,

IN COOPERATION WITH THE ARMY, INVADE AND OCCUPY STRATEGIC
POINTS IN THE WESTERN ALEUTIANS AND MIDWAY ISLAND."

The United States forces had by then broken most of the
Japanese code and Admiral Nimitz guessed that the attack on the
Aleutians was mainly a diversionary tactic to draw some or all of
our fleet near Midway into the far northern fog. Nimitz knew that
the enemy was partial to diversionary moves. He decided to let
the Aleutians wait a while and it was a fortunate hunch. But it
won no votes for the Navy from Seattleites. As a part of the great
two-ocean war the Aleutian campaign was minor, but certainly not to
Alaska and Seattle. Everybody now agreed that General DeWitt had
moved the West Coast Japanese just in time to avoid confrontations
that could have resembled the anti-Chinese riots eighty-five years
before.

Seattle was even more uptight when later the Japanese occupied
the island of Attu in the Aleutian chain. The bitterest of battles
drove them out, and the community by Elliott Bay was angered
when that engagement remained half cloaked in secrecy. Nimitz
was not able to get a sizable fleet into the North until the enemy
had taken over Kiska. On the streets of Seattle it was rumored
that Kiska was held by no less than 10,000 well-equipped Japanese
marines. But they had disappeared as if by legerdemain by the time
our forces arrived.

Even after the disappearance of the enemy from the Aleutians,
citizens of Seattle were both nervous and angry. The anger was
directed at the administration, which seemed (to Seattleites) to play
down the danger to the Northwest and Alaska. Our hawks were
convinced that the President, his advisers and the military wanted
to keep the public's main attention on Hitler and the Axis. Seattle
had felt—and now more strongly—that eastern citizens had always
had "one foot in Europe." Until late in the world holocaust, the
community felt that more attention should be given to the Pacific
war. This emotion, as natural as the rain, reached a peak of bitterness. But it began to cool when great numbers of marines, most
of them looking startlingly young, were brought to the naval hospital at the Sand Point Naval Station. When that happened Seattleites felt a little ashamed, and were willing to concede that these
youngsters, some terribly wounded, had accepted a duty to protect not
just one city, but the whole United States of America.

Over a period of time, at war's end, the Japanese began to return to Seattle and the Northwest. For a time they were greeted with hostility. Signs saying "We don't want any Japs back here— ever," appeared in storefronts and in agricultural areas near the city where Japanese had once farmed the land. And there was a "Remember Pearl Harbor League." For their part, many of the Japanese were bitter—in many cases they were virtually dispossessed of their property by sharp dealings. Recent studies have shown that West Coast Japanese lost (or were forced to sell) property valued in the millions. The majority had lost almost four years out of their lives, and many were forced to bury parents far away from their old homes in Seattle.

But come back they did. And so did news of the courage of the fighting Nisei in U.S. uniforms—many from Seattle—who had suffered casualties in battles all over the world.

Gradually, the Japanese began to move back into the fabric of Seattle life. In time, the bitterness on both sides diminished and the term "Jap" was no longer heard. The Japanese, resilient in spirit, began to enter—and even excel—in the professions, the arts, business, teaching and music, making notable contributions to the postwar vitality of Seattle life.

The situation of the blacks in Seattle did not become noticeable to the great majority of citizens until late in the 1960s. And the majority by no means have begun to understand it fully. Like the city itself, it is a situation in broad transition.

A part of the reason for the blindness of white Seattleites to the problems of the blacks is that the city is so young that it has not yet developed conditions which have set off violence to such a tragic degree as in other cities. About 9 per cent of Seattleites are black, which places the number around 48,000. But it is noticed by too few people that this number has grown from somewhere between 15,000 and 20,000 in the years following the last world war.

In spite of the knowledge that a city like Chicago is about 50 per cent Negro and that Los Angeles has developed areas that are ghettos in every sense of the word, too many Seattleites see nothing to worry about. There have indeed been confrontations between blacks and the police and other officials. There have been marches which threatened violence but did not reach that pitch. There have been bombings which brought the blacks into suspicion, but it has not been proved beyond doubt that they were involved. There have been demonstrations on the campuses of the University of Washington, of Seattle University and of some of the new community colleges. But as late as 1972 there were no face-to-face encounters of mobs of blacks and whites. The holocaust at Watts, California, did more to awaken Seattleites to the possibility of crisis than has any event on the shores of Elliott Bay.

"When there is an outbreak," says Arthur Wheeler, a black with the state Parole Board, "people in Seattle are surprised for the most part. The whites, I'm afraid, have been virtually asleep to the problem, or simply apathetic about it. Surprised, they ask, 'What in the world do they want?' as if the blacks haven't made it pretty plain. It's true, of course, that Seattle is too young to have fully faced what is happening, but there is no time to waste now." The opinion is valuable, for both Wheeler and his wife have been careful observers of racial trends and both have many friends among whites who, it must be said, have been educated by them.

Abruptly, in the late sixties, racial tension exploded at the University of Washington—centering on its football team, an entity worshiped by large parts of Seattle, which annually packs the UW's 60,000-seat stadium to capacity for virtually every game. The architect of this pigskin worship is a tall, handsome and highly successful coach named Jim Owens—and Owens was the target of black wrath. Emphasizing discipline, self-restraint and an almost fanatical devotion to hard blocking and tackling, Owens had given Washington three Rose Bowl teams; this success, along with his ease and charm among the public and the more fervid alumni, gave him a unique stature in the community. As one student cracked when Owens built a home across Union Bay in Laurelhurst, in full view of the stadium, "Big Jim can now walk to work on water."

Moreover, he had created teams which, out of uniform, gave the appearance of being advance agents for Billy Graham. "I'm not a religious man," a Washington Athletic Club member told me, "but I'm damned if he hasn't put something together that seems almost spiritual."

He was, by then, both athletic director and coach. His position was lofty and unchallenged. Then the black revolt struck. Former black stars of his Rose Bowl teams indicted him for "blatant racism." They detailed their grievances in the press—charges of "stacking" black players in one position to avoid having too many blacks on the field at one time; ignoring blacks' problems within the university and brushing aside their job and housing needs. They demanded that the team trainer be fired. Their demands—and by now, the current black players on the varsity had joined the black alums—included the hiring of a black coach.

Such charges, aired in national magazines and the local press, shook the city visibly. Did the godlike Owens have feet of clay? The more fervent WASP supporters of Husky football remained firm behind Owens; so did the University administration. But many thoughtful people, who may have liked their football but could also sympathize with blacks, began to wonder. One faculty committee criticized Owens' handling of black players. Big Jim eventually resigned as athletic director and was replaced by his assistant, Joe Kearney. No admission was made that the black revolt had caused this reshuffling—but the implications were plain.

The lowest point came prior to the UCLA game in 1969, when every black player refused to board the bus on the way to the airport and the trip to Los Angeles. The bus was surrounded by angry young black militants. One black player was heard to say fearfully, "I'd like to go along and play down there, but there's no WAY I'd get aboard that bus." The Huskies finished with a dismal 1–9 record. Rumors abounded that Owens would be fired in the interests of campus unity with the troubled black students and, in fact, the entire black Seattle community. Owens rallied his forces for a successful season the following year—a team keyed to an Indian quarterback, by the way—yet five black players quit the team at the end of the season. One was a star defensive back who declared he would never play for Owens again. Yet he and other blacks returned to Washington and the Huskies played out a successful 1971 season without incident. But by now the blacks had won their points—Washington not only has a black assistant coach, but a black assistant to Kearney.

Whether Owens is, as the blacks charged, a racist, is a moot point. Certainly, he seems to have adjusted to the changing times. But for a while, it seemed to me, there was no subtlety among some of the assistants. I once overheard one of them explaining the loss of a game. "We had just one trouble," he grumbled, "not enough nigger power in the backfield."

Gary Gayton, black attorney and former University of Washington athlete, blames the whole community for Washington's football troubles. "What has happened is an indictment against Seattle," he has said. "It is an indictment also against Joe Kearney, the athletic director, and Jim Owens. But if we are to be honest we must admit that we want Jim Owens and as a community we'll try to keep him here. Referring to the boycott on the part of black athletes prior to the UCLA game in 1969, it isn't true that it was caused by the black community. There wasn't any pressure, but we tried to make it look that way to keep the kids out of trouble. My advice to the black players was to stay on the team and play. I told them that if they boycotted it would look as if the blacks were causing the trouble, and that would not reflect the facts. The troubles this year [1971] probably did not hinge on any specific incidents. I agree that most of the things the black players complained about were coach's decisions, such as who should play what position, who got starting assignments and how much game time each player got. But there have been problems out there between the blacks and the whites ever since Owens got into town."

In a talk before the Seattle-King County Bar Association, Gayton declared: "The track record on race relations at the University of Washington is one all of us should be ashamed of." But it has to be noted that as recently as the winter of 1972, a faculty committee, with blacks well represented, gave the coach good marks for improving race relations and commended the athletic department as a whole.

At the start of the seventies it could not be said honestly that a sizable percentage of the ministry, black or white, had taken much interest in the blacks' problems. Most gave the appearance of being as unaware as their parishioners, or perhaps of succumbing to warnings from the latter not to rock the boat.

There were, of course, notable exceptions. It was a great loss to the solution of the problem when the Reverend John Adams of Seattle's First African Methodist Church, chairman in the late sixties of the Central Area Civil Rights Committee, departed for a pulpit in California. He was a courageous activist, and took part in an early Alabama Freedom March. At the time of the march his decision was considered by a majority of Seattle whites as a radical move. "That's going a hell of a distance to borrow trouble that will rub off him here," one white citizen complained to this writer. The Reverend Adams brought back no trouble that was not already in Seattle, and his supporters were proud to have had such a distinguished representative in the Alabama demonstration. Moreover, in 1969 the B'nai B'rith recognized his firm but quiet work and named him their "Man of the Year."

The so-called Central Area is "the black district." It is roughly bounded by Madison Street, South Jackson Street, Broadway Avenue and parts of Lake Washington's shoreline. And the ghetto is expanding. A fairly recent example is Beacon Hill, just above the southern downtown area, where obsolescent dwellings have naturally attracted blacks of modest income. Efforts are being made to refurbish the areas which could become larger ghettos in fact. But from the viewpoint of the blacks this effort is slow and lacks both enthusiasm and leadership.

Throughout the early sixties, it cannot be said that either of the city's two newspapers, the morning *Post-Intelligencer* and the evening Seattle *Times*, zeroed in on Seattle's race problems with vigor. But it should be noted that the *Post-Intelligencer* did some hard and valuable work beginning in the latter part of the decade. The paper's managing editor, Louis R. Guzzo, was hired away from the *Times*, where he covered the symphony, opera, visual arts and the theater. Coming to the P-I (as the *Post-Intelligencer* is commonly called in Seattle) he strongly felt that Seattle had civil rights problems (among many other problems, including environment) and that neither paper was alerting the public to the whole story. Moreover, there had been many slights to minority citizens. For example, not in years had a photograph of a black bride appeared in the women's departments of either paper.

Heading up the P-I at this time—he had, in fact, hired Guzzo away from the *Times*—was an active young man named Daniel L. Starr. His experience included advertising work on the Washington *Post*, some years in radio and advertising sales. William Randolph Hearst, Jr., well aware that Seattleites preferred local newspaper chiefs, elevated Starr to publisher from his position as the P-I's retail advertising manager.

The pairing of Starr and Guzzo paralleled the growing militancy on the part of Seattle's blacks. To report on that situation, Guzzo chose Hilda Bryant, whose background included newspaper experience, schoolteaching and specialized studies at the University of Washington, where she once edited the UW *Daily*. Moreover, her family of three adopted children included two Orientals.

Out of an editorial conference headed by the new publisher,

it was decided to form a team, headed by Mrs. Bryant and including the locally respected political reporter Shelby Scates. Scates, in fact, broke the first story in Seattle of racial trouble in the UW athletic department. The vigorous, attractive Mrs. Bryant developed many meaningful and valuable stories on Seattle's race problems—some to the shock and dismay of many Seattle conservatives. The real objection was the raising of the subject, and the *Post-Intelligencer* knew it—they had, in fact, fully discussed the probability of a temporary loss of circulation, and objections by advertisers.

Mrs. Bryant's stories had a steady influence on the city's thinking. By now, and to its credit, the *Times* began attending to the problems of the blacks, and among local TV stations, KOMO and KING were the leaders. The latter now features a number of black news announcers and commentators. *Seattle* magazine, a quality publication owned by KING Broadcasting, also developed a number of stories focusing on the black community before the magazine folded.

It was determined by the circulation manager of the *Post-Intelligencer* that the number of "stops"—subscription cancellations —was surprisingly few, and most of them were back on the paid list within a few weeks after the cancellations.

This was in a period which most Seattleites considered violent, but compared with cities of similar size it was hardly that. In general the violence was not half as marked as would be the later anti-war demonstrations.

Meanwhile, known only to half a dozen people, a quiet, meaningful story was unfolding in Seattle. No comment on the racial climate of the city would be complete without reference to Lori Newquist. Young, handsome, a top-grade student at the University of Washington, she had been interested in the plight of the blacks for some time. She had talked with her parents about it, and they had tried to discourage her interest, not from bigotry but because they felt there was nothing she could do alone and that her preoccupation with the black minority could only divert her from a career.

"I had a steadily growing urge to try to see the situation as the blacks themselves saw it," she said. "And there seemed no way to do this other than to become a black and live as most of them were forced to."

She was aware that her idea was not new, but she realized that in Seattle it would be daring and original, and that many would regard it with lewd suspicions. Nonetheless, after long thought, she determined to "pass for black." She consulted her physician, who told her that there was medication which would darken the color of her skin and need not be permanent. But he attempted to discourage her, although she had gone to a black physician because she felt one of his race would be more understanding. At last, after several visits, he decided that she was a young woman of determined integrity and not a seeker of sensationalism. After a complete physical examination he began to administer medication which gradually turned her dark complexion wholly black. Her dark eyes and hair, and certain facial structures often observed in the black race, contributed to what she would come to believe was an unfair deception. Vivacious and a bit of an actress, she entered wholeheartedly into her new role. Her parents were dismayed, but at last became convinced of her sincere need to go through with the experience. During her transformation she moved from her parents' home and neighborhood and stayed, more or less in hiding, with a white schoolmate from the University. She knew four or five blacks, whom she needed to make her transformation complete. "I learned to walk with the fluidity of most black girls. I studied their gestures, their expressions, the tones of their speech. A couple of them were a bit standoffish at first, and seemed to think that I was being condescending. But the more we talked together, the better they understood. Soon the whole little group was with me, and in a serious way."

She added thoughtfully when it was all over, "A curious thing happened. I found myself more adept as my skin grew darker. That convinced me early of something I always had believed—that much of the racial thing is, literally, only skin-deep. As time went on I was delighted—and later ashamed—when I found that blacks were accepting me as one of their own. I mean those who were not in on my secret."

She found housing in a ramshackle dwelling in the Central Area, rooming with a black middle-aged woman who had little regard for housekeeping. "My father had offered to put me on an allowance, but I felt this would be unfair. I got a job in a rundown estate office. It paid very little, but at least I could help my roommate with the rent, and contribute to the food bill. At first I was shocked by her. She seemed years beyond her actual age. Her husband had left her some years before and she had no children, and no relations nearer than Mississippi, and seemed to just go through the motions of living. Sometimes the natural humor of her race would come through, but not often, and the place was a mess. She worked in a laundry, and it was a hard job. By the time she got home at night she was completely bushed, and just didn't give a damn. For a while I tried to improve the housekeeping, but it was such a run-down place to start with that I just about gave up."

Lori Newquist remembers the exact moment when she felt that she was really a black person. "It was a silly, small thing," she said, "and I don't know whether you'll understand it. Anyhow, a group of us were sitting on the sagging front steps. It was Sunday, and there wasn't much traffic. It was too chilly to go to the beach, so we were just lolling on the steps, drinking Cokes and kidding one another. My landlady was inside taking a nap."

She paused a moment, and I knew she was seeing it again and wondering if I'd see it, too. "Suddenly around the corner there came a couple of white men in a brand new green Tornado. There was a funny noise and the car stopped dead almost in front of us. You could see that they were nervous, because all of a sudden they had no wheels going around and there they were right in the middle of the Central Area. I think maybe the owner was taking a visitor on a slumming trip. The driver kept pressing buttons, and pulling little levers on the instrument board. Then they got out and lifted the hood. One of them measured the gas with a wooden stick picked off the street. Somehow they were all uptight and nervous, and kept glancing at us. We were two boys and three girls, just drinking Cokes, and now we were watching the two whites trying to get that green car going.

"Somehow—it's hard now to explain why—we got to laughing at them. We weren't taunting or cruel. We didn't have much sympathy, either, I suppose. But the thing struck us as funny. We began to laugh, and I was laughing so hard that I couldn't stop. I don't know—the whole little incident seemed so futile. I think my two black boy friends could have probably found the trouble. But the white men would glare at us and it was plain they didn't want any help from us, and were half afraid. Finally one of them got up enough courage to look at us—he didn't really look at us, but sort of through us—and said, 'I don't suppose you got a telephone in there we could use?'

"That could have made us angry," Lori Newquist says now. "But some way it set us off laughing all the more. Of course that ramshackle place didn't have a telephone. The elderly lady and I couldn't afford one, and wouldn't have had much use for one if we could have."

Then a two-man patrol car rolled up. "The police—I thought of them as fuzz, I remember—looked first at us, as if we'd done something. Then they began fooling around with the Tornado. That didn't help stop our crazy laughing, but the police ignored it. The upshot was that one of them got onto his radiophone, and in a few minutes a tow truck showed up and took the white men and their car out of there. Believe it or not, we were still laughing, practically rolling on the steps. Somehow the happening made our whole Sunday afternoon."

Lori stopped and looked at me, silent a while. "That's all there was to it. I don't know how to explain it now, but it was then that I felt all black. Two white men who were helpless and didn't like us, and two policemen whose first thought on the scene was a notion that maybe *we* had been up to something."

She was white again as she told me this, but somehow a Negro tone and manner came back for an instant. "I do remember that the realization that I felt really black didn't bother me a bit. I think I sort of gloried in it. If I didn't feel superior to those white men, at least I felt equal—whether right then I had equal rights or not. The police didn't bother me. They had a job to do, and I think I got the impression they didn't much like patrolling that area. But the police have learned a lot in Seattle in the last two or three years. That much I know."

Lori was right on the head of the nail regarding the Seattle police. There was a period in Seattle, lasting several decades, when the very few blacks hadn't a chance to get legal rights. The police—then all were white—were particularly rough on any black seen in the company of a white girl. For these and other "crimes" a black would be given ten hours to get out of town, and the order was followed up in deadly fashion by the men on the beat. Neither the orders nor the subsequent "riding 'em out on a rail" came from headquarters, but it is to be suspected that the various chiefs in that period knew what was going on.

As for administrative attitudes, a retread marine and former policeman told me with obvious pride: "Whenever we got a nigger or a homo or anything like that down there we didn't lead them to the desk or a cell. We kicked their asses all the way, and I never heard any of them yell for a lawyer. Believe me, we had the situation in hand in those days."

It was a simple situation and no wonder they had it in hand. But times have changed.

By 1971—despite a succession of chiefs and discoveries of bribery in the force—the Seattle Police Department requested the City Council to create a division of community service officers recruited from the ghetto districts. The request suggested training by the police and funding from the Model Cities grant. Because the recruits would be undereducated by selection and poor by any standard, almost automatically they would come from minority groups, chiefly blacks. They would carry no arms and would wear a uniform distinguishable from that of the police. Their chief purpose would be the prevention of crime, a relating to youth and an attempt at liaison with the police. They would have no power of arrest but would be encouraged to lead the police to criminals. Moreover, very important, they would in effect be trainees for the regular force.

The moment that Lori Newquist felt that she was "really black" did not disturb her, then or later.

"The traumatic experience came when I had to decide whether to keep on being black. I still cannot explain or describe it clearly, even in my own mind. But it was really an awful time when I realized I did not want to be white again, yet felt I must because I couldn't go on living a lie. I suppose lots of people would not accept this as truth. They'd say I'd had my fun—fun, they'd call it! —and my experience, and now I could get back to comfort and the power and protection of the whites.

"It surely helped when I had the decision made for me. My doctor told me that the medication I had been taking was showing side effects for which he did not want to be responsible. It was then that the terrible part came. I had to step back across the line, didn't really want to, and had to explain to a lot of black friends what I had done. You know, there wasn't a single one who didn't understand what I'd been trying to do and who didn't appreciate it. Most of them said that more whites ought to try it and learn a few things. Believe me, I treasure those friends now."

So now Lori Newquist is white again. She still has her black friends, and she did learn a great deal. Although she expresses herself clearly and honestly, she made no attempt to write a book about her experience, and the thought had not entered her head until white schoolmates suggested it. She made no attempt to cash in on her "life as a black" even in a short series of syndicated articles. To try to help the local blacks she did write two or three brief articles for a Seattle newspaper, but she is doubtful that they had an appreciably helpful effect. "It was hard to write because I felt I sounded as if I was making a heroine of myself, and that wasn't the idea at all."

As one who had been through the black mill, if only for a little while, does she think that other white Seattleites are improving in their attitudes toward the minorities, particularly the blacks? "Yes," she answers, "but not nearly enough of them—and certainly not quickly enough." Does she feel there will be more troubles, even violence? "I'm afraid so," she said quickly, "and if I'm right, and I hope I'm not, it will be doubly tragic for all the citizens of Seattle, because if Seattle and the surrounding communities hit the civil rights thing now, wholly and with integrity, we could offer an example to the whole nation. If that could be done it would save people in this region a lot of heartaches, and probably some lives. Sometimes I feel encouraged. Most times I'm fearful, because we don't seem to be going at this with the determination we've shown in other things that are not nearly as important. Not nearly."

As Lori Newquist said this she wasn't writing off a happy ending. "The city is young and we could learn. But we won't have our chance long," she added, sorrow in her dark eyes. "When I think of that, then is when I become doubtful."

That really sums up the feeling of many blacks and a lot of whites who are doing what they can to guide Seattle toward a humanitarian path instead of toward the ugly freeways which get us home in time for an extra highball before dinner. What Lori Newquist feels is important, because she is our only white person who has tried literally to see the town by Elliott Bay as the blacks see it.

As in the days of the anti-Chinese troubles, the unions, even as late as the closing of the sixties, were absent from the forefront of civil rights efforts. Some of the important ones were dragging their feet in hiring blacks and seemed to be attempting to stand aside from controversies involving minorities. But the legal rights of non-whites were being tightened. The state Board against Discrimination forcefully announced that it had no intention of tolerance toward bigoted practices in the building trades unions. And the blacks involved were learning to take their grievances to court. The first result of this came in 1971, when two blacks charged discrimination on the part of a welders' union and were awarded $10,000 each.

In that same year there was a more significant development. This was the so-called "Seattle Plan," which was signed February 19, 1971, with the U. S. Labor Department acting as a firm mediator. It is a simple voluntary agreement among labor, management and minorities. Some say it won't work satisfactorily because it is voluntary, but possibly these overlook that it provides for an arbitrator when an agreement becomes difficult. The appearance of management in the triple-pronged plan is one of its encouraging aspects. It took over the activities of a labor program called "Outreach," which frankly wasn't reaching far. The new plan was not easy to come by. It took three years to hammer it out. "Whether it works or not," said one observer, "depends upon the convictions of those involved. If it turns out to be just another piece of paper with signatures on it, we'll try another course."

Unions were not the only laggards in the civil rights problem in Seattle. Private clubs have generally shown little enthusiasm in encouraging applications for membership on the part of blacks. In the first year of this decade, small progress had been made among the clubs. Some fraternal organizations were almost openly firming up an all-white stand. The state can bring hard pressure to bear by denying liquor licenses to recalcitrant organizations. And the Seattle City Council voted six to two in favor of a resolution disapproving fraternal and social clubs which were restricting memberships on the basis of race. The resolution included a paragraph which discouraged councilmen themselves from using the facilities of biased clubs or continuing membership in them. Said Councilwoman Jeanette Williams, "I think at the very least we who represent the people should represent *all* the people."

Recently a group of whites has been encouraging successfully the formation of businesses owned and operated by blacks. Among them is Mike Stanley, a Caucasian who built The Plaza shopping center for the purpose of leasing it to two blacks, R. J. Brown and

Tom Preston. Other examples of new black-owned firms were under way as the seventies began.

    The last major address of Whitney Young, executive director of the Urban League, who died a few days later, was in Seattle. On the platform with him should have been Edward T. Pratt, local leader of the league, who was gunned down fatally in the doorway of his home in 1969 by an unknown enemy. It was apparent from Young's speech to a capacity audience that Pratt had followed closely the pattern set by his chief. The clear association of the two demonstrated to many Seattleites why the martyred Pratt is near the top of the list in the history of active blacks in Seattle. The progress of the local league in the sixties was in contrast with the weakness of the National Association for the Advancement of Colored People, whose Seattle chapter appeared to reflect the difficulties of the national group.

Pratt was gone, but the Reverend Leon Sullivan, the league's founder, was present. The two nationally known blacks were attending the annual conference of Opportunities Industrialization Centers. Inasmuch as Young's final public words were in the city's new Washington Plaza Hotel it is appropriate to note the comment he made.

Whitney Young stressed a situation which has become apparent in Seattle, although development has been slow.

"We need a co-operation among black groups, from Panthers to Baptists," he told Seattleites. "We need to forge political power —black political and economical power. Once we learn to harmonize we can move toward coalitions with other minorities such as the Mexican-Americans. Then we can negotiate from a position of strength."

Young noted that now black people occupy key spots on the boards of major corporations and banks. "These are signs of progress, but it shows only what more can be done. We must go farther, much farther. Even these gains are not secure so long as masses of black people are trapped at the lowest economic levels."

Pragmatic and candid, Young said, "Figuratively speaking, fire power is quickest, but one must be certain who has the fire power, and I mean among ourselves. It is by no means easy to be responsible and militant at the same time. And certainly the name of the game is not lung power, although it may be useful for a while."

He could have been speaking specifically of Seattle, where, a relatively short time before, the first appearance of the militant Black Panthers almost jarred the city out of its apathy and certainly frightened many of the whites. Officials of the Panthers say they are still at work, but have simply quieted their approach. Those Seattleites who fear them believe they have "gone underground" and are planning violent "spots of rebellion" throughout the town.

Most blacks admit that they have changed their tactics and want it clearly understood that they have not become discouraged, and have not been slowed down by any white backlash, real or imagined. Part of their new sophisticated stance is due to education; black students, like those of another color, grow up fast and create a more intelligent opposition to the Establishment. Also, funds were raised to allow many black leaders to travel to other parts of the country, from which they returned with new attitudes, new confidence and a more sophisticated manner in dealing with whites who have the power to help them.

They fully recognize now that much can be done at the ballot box, and the seventies ushered in tangible results from this recognition. Blacks discovered that a victory at the polls awakens the formerly apathetic Seattle leaders to the reality of black influence. This in turn has led more and more businessmen to seek able blacks for corporate positions.

One influential black is Arthur Fletcher, who became Assistant Secretary of Labor in the Nixon administration. He had been active in the "Tri-Cities" east of the Cascades: Pasco, Kennewick and Richland, towns that had become sizable and complex cities, chiefly due to irrigation projects and the Hanford Atomic Works. Despite strong anti-black sentiment, Fletcher won a place on the Pasco City Council, where he further proved his ability and won new white friends. A Republican, he ran for lieutenant governor in 1968 and made a good race of it; his colorful personality, vigor and eloquence made a strong impact on the entire state. This led to his federal appointment. He has since resigned and, as of this writing, he is believed to have plans to return to Seattle and run for Congress.

Disquieting is the opposition of many citizens and the 1971 legislature to the proposed bussing of students from one area to another to create schools which are sufficiently representative of all colors, races and creeds. Particularly adamant has been an organization called Citizens against Mandatory Bussing, which brought court actions and threatened a recall of the school board. The latter idea got nowhere. Backed by the school board, Seattle School Superintendent Forbes Bottomley has stood firm in favor of mandatory bussing, as he has in similar critical situations for more than a decade. He has remained unmoved by the claim of his opponents that the issue is not desegregation at all, but a change in the structure of the school system. Although naturally open in his belief in equal rights for all students, Bottomley has retained an amazing claim in dealing with his seemingly insurmountable problems. He has spoken as strongly to unreasonable blacks as he has to bigoted whites. But he strongly favors one of the demands of defiant blacks, namely the need for more black teacher aides, who often make up the critical link between minority students and white teachers. He is backed in this position by state Superintendent of Education Louis Bruno.

Bottomley has said that it may take four or five years before Seattle schools are completely desegregated. His black opponents say that this is far too long a time, but Bottomley realizes what a complex problem it is and that it involves far more than emotionalism. There are a great many schools and neighborhoods in states of obsolescence, and the transitions in all fields in the city are difficult. Bottomley knows what a job he has on his hands, but since his arrival in Seattle he has never shown a sign of evading an issue.

That the future holds more problems for Bottomley and all of us is clear in recent statistics from the state's public schools. Although the schools enrolled 3,000 less students in 1971, due to the economic decline, there were almost 2,000 more blacks, Oriental, Indian and Mexican-American students—with the blacks markedly predominant in the increase. "Yet, totally, there are now about half as many Orientals in the schools as there are blacks," says state Superintendent of Education Bruno.

"And," he says, "there are more American Indians than Orientals. It should be, but apparently is not, clear to the majority of Seattleites that the Seattle and Tacoma areas show 21,000 black students, 15,000 Mexican-American students and more than 10,000 Orientals. The Indians and the Chicanos (Mexican-Americans) are scattered throughout the state, but the black increase is concentrated in the Seattle-Tacoma area, which accounts for about 75 per cent of the total black enrollment. The Seattle School District has the highest percentage of black students with almost 11,000 registered."

It is pertinent in the King County statistics that in the last decade Seattle declined in population by 26,256 as King County suburbia gained over eight times this much, or 247,875. Unfortunately, there is no way to ascertain what percentage of Seattle's expatriates is due to the Boeing difficulties at the start of the seventies, and what percentage is due to those attempting an "escape" from minority difficulties. In any case, such escape can be only temporary.

Curiously, a large drop in the Seattle population is in the five years and younger age group, insofar as the schools are concerned. The decrease, from 51,946 in 1960 to 16,952 in 1970, is reflected in the approximate one-third enrollment drop in the Seattle kindergartens.

Only one age group, twenty to twenty-four years, increased in Seattle in the decade of 1960–70 and it is believed that many of the 13,000 who moved to the city may have come to attend the University of Washington, whose enrollment increased from 18,000 in 1960 to 33,000 in 1970.

Governor Dan Evans has taken a firm stand on equal rights for minorities, and regularly has sessions with their representatives in his office, chiefly those of the blacks.

Prominent among black trailblazers attempting understanding without violence were Walter Hundley, director of Model Cities; Alfred Cowles, of the Seattle School Board; David Mills, assistant to the public defender; Les McIntosh, with the local office of the federal Department of Health, Education and Welfare; Republican Mike Ross and Democrat George Fleming, both Seattle blacks, won election to the state legislature.

Two pioneering blacks were Sam Smith, first black to be elected to the Seattle City Council, and Alfred Petty, a former Boeing engineer, appointed by Mayor Wes Uhlman to head the city's building department. Among the blacks in earlier periods of strong action have been such triggers of change as Carl Miller, Larry Gossett and Aaron Dixon, the latter in his role as head of the Black Panthers.

Thus for the first time in the city's history, blacks were appearing in positions of power or were holding positions influential in Seattle's progress. It was only a beginning in the early seventies. It was an encouragement to the blacks and to white exponents of equal opportunities for all.

What of the future of Seattle's racial climate? Hilda Bryant, the woman reporter who helped crack open the subject for all to see, is hopeful but dubious. "At the present rate of progress," she says, "there is in my opinion a real danger of further trouble. Any Seattleite who will use his eyes and judgment can hardly overlook that possibility."

But Roberta Byrd Barr, acting principal of Seattle's Franklin High School, poses in her characteristically wry manner a broader allied question. "What about the whites?" she asks. "I tell my young people at Franklin High: take a good look and tell me exactly what we have to envy."

Mrs. Barr, a handsome black woman born and raised in Tacoma, attended public school there, "then traveled across the country picking up a higher education and a lot of experience." When she returned to Seattle she became active as a private citizen in the problems of the local blacks and the attitudes of the Seattle majority. In 1964 she became the persuasive moderator of a weekly color television program which has one of the top ratings in town. This brought her to the attention of School Superintendent Forbes Bottomley and she occupied various administrative posts dealing with minorities in the schools, leading eventually to the vice-principalship of Franklin High School, which enrolls a large number of blacks. With a soft speech, a smile that lights the world around her, and a brilliant mind, she has been tremendously influential.

"I'm neither pessimistic nor optimistic," she says. "I think I am simply realistic. It seems to me that we are witnessing the end of the Industrial Revolution and obviously have handed ourselves over to the scientists. Many doubt whether they have put us on the right track. I tell my black students, 'Don't get too uptight at this point. Look closely at the majority. Exactly what should be our course when all around us we see the whites coming unglued?'"

Nevertheless, it could be, she seems to suggest, a period when we will, by force of events, come together to attempt a better world.

18

Two Expositions

I<small>N ITS</small> brief time Seattle has staged two great expositions, the first a sprawling affair of gingerbread-trimmed buildings, the later one compact but naturally far outranking its predecessor in theme and imagination. Both left important permanent legacies to the city.

They began in almost the same way—with three or four men, guzzling from glasses of spirits, talking about the future of Seattle and wondering how its progress could be brought to the attention of the nation and the world.

The first was the Alaska-Yukon-Pacific Exposition of 1909.

The second was an exposition certified from a hole-in-the-wall office in Paris as a genuine "world's fair." The office was the headquarters of the Bureau of International Expositions, which was not in existence when the first Seattle fair was built. This second exposition was sometimes called "Century 21" or, more formally, the Century 21 Exposition. Later, and with pride, it was the Seattle World's Fair 1962.

The two fairs took their definite shapes in the quiet bar of a club. The Alaska-Yukon-Pacific Exposition of 1909 assumed probability in the bar of the Alaska Club.

The idea of the Seattle World's Fair 1962 spread from a few hundred casual words of conversation by four men in the bar of the Washington Athletic Club.

There is no question as to the identity of the man who fathered the Alaska-Yukon-Pacific Exposition—still known as the "AYP" by those who remember it fondly. He bore the ornate name of Godfrey Chealander. He had spent several years in Alaska and was Grand Secretary of the Arctic Brotherhood, at that time a strong organization both in Puget Sound cities and in the North. It was a brotherhood in the genuine sense of the word, for early in the century a sizable percentage of Seattle's population had tried their fortunes in Alaska or were in businesses largely based on trade with the vast territory to the north. Successful or not, these men—and women as well—were forged together by extraordinarily strong ties. Literally, they all knew one another, and deep friendships were born out of commerce or sentiment or both.

In 1905 the Lewis and Clark Exposition had taken place in Portland, Oregon. Godfrey Chealander was the obvious choice as manager of the small Alaska exhibit there, and the official representative of the Golden North. The Alaska Territory did not have much money for exhibitions, yet the exhibit drew tremendous interest. The Alaska Gold Rush was still fresh in the minds of Portlanders and many of the visitors to the fair. Chealander soon arrived at the idea that in Seattle there should be a permanent and more comprehensive exhibit.

When the Portland fair closed Chealander came to Seattle and looked up his old friend William Sheffield, secretary of the Alaska Club, whose office was appropriately on the top floor of the Alaska Building. Quickly he outlined his plan, and together he and Sheffield called on James A. Wood, then city editor of the Seattle *Times*. Wood had never met Chealander until then, and was impressed by his enthusiasm. In brief, Chealander urged a modest permanent building whose exhibits would keep alive the ties between Seattle and the Northland. It would be a constant reminder of a then distant land that could be somewhat forgotten as the old-timers passed on.

Wood was open to the idea, as he had been kicking around in

his mind something related, but on a far larger scale. As a devoted Seattleite he was irked that Portland had brought off an exposition ahead of the town on Elliott Bay. Those were the years when rivalry —even enmity—was the usual thing between neighboring communities of the Pacific Northwest.

"I've been thinking about something that would tie in with your idea," he told Chealander. "If Portland can have a successful exposition, why can't we? Here we are, over fifty years old now, and we've had nothing such as Portland came up with. I saw it, and liked it—but I'm sure we can do better. Let me test it out with the public through the paper. I think we'll get a good reaction, and that will help."

At first Chealander was a little crestfallen to see his idea swallowed by a possible exposition. He feared his Alaska show might turn out to be small potatoes at the bottom of the bin. But he saw the value of the *Times*'s support and held his peace.

He was delighted when the *Times* began its series of conjectural stories, for almost every one referred to an exposition related to the North. The paper carried interviews with prominent citizens, and they were all favorable. With so many former Alaskans in town, hundreds of letters came into the *Times* and Wood printed all that his space would allow.

When Chealander, Wood and Sheffield next met it was in a corner of the bar of the Alaska Club. It was there that the idea became a probability. Wood said that he had the full backing of his publisher, the powerful Alden Blethen, and that meant a great deal. Neither had Chealander and Sheffield been idle. While they appreciated the support of the *Times* they did not want to see the plan become a newspaper promotion and wanted the blessing of the morning newspaper, too. The *Post-Intelligencer* management confessed that they didn't want to seem to be following in the shadow of their competition. But it certainly was not a program they would oppose, and gradually the entire press of the Puget Sound region, weeklies and dailies, began to "back into" the story and publish editorials favorable to "an Alaskan exposition."

The point of crystallization was a luncheon attended by a few Seattle leaders early in 1906. By now the proponents were up against the money question, and it was decided to form an association of businessmen for the purpose of financing a full-fledged exposition. All of the men at the luncheon were members of the Chamber of

Commerce, so naturally the committee grew from that membership. The trustees were all chamber members.

Appointed to head the exposition was J. E. Chilberg, prominent banker who had come to Seattle with his parents as a child and grown up there. It was inevitable that James Wood would be "director of exploitation" or what today would be called public relations director.

Compared with the fair which would come along fifty-three years later the exposition of 1909 had fairly smooth sailing. There was little time for debate and quibbling. The opening was scheduled for 1907—the tenth anniversary of the discovery of gold in the Klondike, which was in Canada, not Alaska, but was the forerunner of the other strikes in the Far North.

Professor Edmond S. Meany, probably the most popular faculty member in the whole history of the University of Washington and an early historian of regional note, proposed the campus of the University of Washington as a site. This was the university founded by Asa Mercer that for several years had operated in a single building, just east of where the modern IBM Building now stands downtown, and in 1893 had moved to a large forested area on the shores of Lake Washington and Union Bay. Wisely, the regents saw to it that the University retained title to its downtown acreage. This is now known as the Metropolitan District and is a vital source of income to the University. At the time of Meany's proposal the new site was considered "far out in the boondocks" and was reached mainly by trolley car service. It comprised only three modest buildings. They were so well hidden by the tall firs and cedars that an innocent freshman had to do some searching through the wilds after he had stepped from a streetcar on his first day. In 1905 almost no attempt had been made at landscaping. The campus was simply a wild natural park with romantic meandering paths and a clearing for an athletic field of sorts.

Meany's suggestion did not receive anything like unanimous approval. Many believed that the site was too far away for out-of-town visitors and that attendance would be affected seriously by the distance. Meany did not agree. He insisted that the forest park itself was an attraction, and people were accustomed to the trolley cars. Besides, he said, the trip would be a sightseeing tour for non-Seattleites. Meany had the foresight also to appreciate that the exposition could do a lot for the campus. A large part of the wilderness would need to be landscaped, and surely some of the buildings would be permanent and of practical use to the University in years to come.

The state legislature agreed after only a token debate. It had experienced a more or less constant pressure for money to add buildings that would begin the kind of school of higher learning that the state deserved. This led the solons not only to go along with Meany's choice, but the legislature—now feeling pressure from the Chamber of Commerce and the influential brotherhood of former Alaskans—added the proviso that most of the state money should go into four permanent buildings. The final result topped the proviso. When the exposition was over there was a vastly expanded and improved campus—the most beautiful in the nation, proud Seattleites claimed—with no fewer than twenty buildings for the use of the University. After the state had shown its faith, the federal government was not slow in getting into the act. Congress promised $600,000, quite an appropriation for the time, if Seattle proved it could raise a million dollars. The town was quick to respond with the amount suggested.

Then King County came forward, agreeing to build a $300,000 forestry exhibit with an additional $78,000 for exhibits. Actually, the Forestry Building was the largest "log cabin" ever built, and the size of its components awed visitors from beyond the Pacific Northwest. Its portals were literally whole trees of tremendous size with branches cut off and the bark left intact. For many years afterward the University's Forestry Building attracted visitors from all over the world.

The name of the fair began to grow. Beginning simply and informally as the "Alaska Exposition" it soon became, at the suggestion of the brotherhood of the North Country, the Alaska-Yukon Exposition. After all, the first big strikes that created the Gold Rush were in the Yukon Territory. Canada naturally would be pleased at this acknowledgment.

By now, as one old-timer put it, Seattle was becoming as excited as a pregnant fox in a forest fire. Citizens followed the progress through the newspapers, and on Sundays thousands visited the site to see how things were coming along. About this time Professor Meany reminded fellow citizens that the whole Pacific Rim was involved in Seattle's commerce and culture, and that Washington's own coastline on the far side of the Olympic Peninsula was a part of that Pacific Rim.

Seattleites responded to Meany's imaginative concept. In effect they said, "As long as we're doing it, let's do it big." No sooner said than attempted; probably the town had never shown so much enthusiasm and acceleration. Out on the high Pacific seas went E. F. Blaine, Harry Whitney Treat and Judge Thomas Burke, who had taken a leading role in the battle for rail connections. The emissaries to far Pacific lands were not as successful as they had hoped, but there were other delegates "on the trail." Scott Calhoun was sent to California, and exposition chief Chilberg went to Ottawa. Henry Reed, who had been publicity director of the Lewis and Clark Exposition, arrived in Seattle with the indorsement of Portland and the promise of a reasonable contribution from the people of Oregon. Now the whole Pacific Coast was engaged, and in Ottawa the answer to Chilberg was that Canada would participate.

So now the name of the fair just had to be the Alaska-Yukon-Pacific Exposition—the famous "AYP" probably more loved by Seattleites than any other project in all its history up to the present time. Professor Meany enlisted Reginald de Koven to create music for Meany's lyrics, resulting in a song honoring the fair. It was called "Washington Beloved" and may not have been the most successful of either composer, but at least its beginning was often on the lips of many during the exposition.

> Thy name, of Washington renowned,
> We hail, we hail from far and near;
> Thy glories joyfully resound
> In song of praise and mighty cheer.

The Alaska-Yukon-Pacific Exposition was widely exploited as "the fair that will be ready on time," a gentle jibe at other cities whose expositions rarely had been completed on opening day.

Then out of the blue came a disappointment that may have been a blessing in disguise because it insured Seattle's promise of an opening with its exposition in full swing. Early in 1906 the governors of the Jamestown Exposition in Virginia pointed out that they had 1907 in mind inasmuch as it was the tercentenary of the landing at Jamestown. Therefore would it be possible for Seattle to postpone the Alaska-Yukon-Pacific Exposition?

Saddened, but resigned, the leaders of the Seattle fair convened and decided that there was no alternative to postponement. They could open in 1908, but that would be too close to the Jamestown celebration. They chose 1909 and consoled themselves with the thought that more time might allow for the creation of an exposition even more dramatic than already planned. They sent a gracious message to Norfolk and wished the Jamestown Exposition all success.

Despite the delay, the members of the Chamber of Commerce maintained their enthusiasm. They were feeling tip-top or, as the Chinook jargon would have it, *copacete*. Their plans were coming along famously and in 1907, the year originally chosen, they felt even better. For that year turned out to be a producer of one of the nation's periodic "panics." Seattle was far away from heavily populated areas and the recession would certainly have affected the fair.

Ignoring the "panic," Seattleites, persuaded chiefly by Will H. Parry, bought up all the capital stock of the exposition in a single day. Seattle's response, in a period when the nation's business was uncertain, made inspiring news everywhere.

Ground was broken in June of 1907 and the famous Olmsted Brothers, who designed much of the Lake Washington Boulevard, were persuaded to produce the overall plan of the fair. They assigned the job to James Frederick Dawson. He took full advantage of the spaciousness of the grounds and of the natural forests. A central feature (underlighted at night) was a long pool which descended gently by means of a series of short waterfalls. This was fascinating to visitors, who watched it for hours at a time and returned again and again to succumb to its magic. Dawson's whole plan resulted in what many visiting reporters called the most beautiful exposition ever held anywhere in the world. Near the end of the first decade of the century traveling critics were not inclined to denigrate the heavily trimmed buildings or the simplicity of some of the exhibitions. It was an innocent age, and most of the big city newspaper writers sent to cover the fair were so astonished at the accomplishment of an infant frontier community that there were few adverse reports—and of course Seattleites saw no reason why there should be any. Certainly, as Meany had foreseen, the exposition left in its wake one of the most unusual university campuses in the country.

As the New Year of 1909 dawned it was plain that the AYP would indeed be fully completed by the opening date of June first. By the end of March most of the main attractions were up and some of them were ready for the crowds.

Indicative of the simplicity of the nation's technology and the ease with which people could be entertained was an exhibit at the King County Building. It was a perfect scale model of the Newcastle coal mine, which was only a few miles away from Seattle. And although the exposition was a mere trolley ride from downtown, many Seattle scenes were also reproduced in the form of dioramas and models of prominent buildings. Even hometowners found these fascinating. Also nearly ready by April was the Alaska Building, and Chealander and the brotherhood of the North had made certain that it was a star of the show. Japan and Canada were the only foreign nations to come up with buildings of their own, but they were enough to validate the name Alaska-Yukon-Pacific Exposition. Other foreign nations sent representatives and articles typical of their industry and culture.

This was long before the Women's Liberation movement, but the ladies of the region were represented by the Washington State Woman's Building. The interior booths and exhibits made certain that males would not forget the courageous roles women had played as pioneers, or the leadership many of them were taking in civic charities and other enterprises.

Inevitably the question arose as to whether the fair should have a section devoted to popular entertainment. Half a century later, Seattleites would have difficulty making up their minds about that. But in 1909 the answer was easy. The St. Louis Fair had had its "Pike" and Chicago its "Midway," whose belly dancer, Little Egypt, even today shows signs of immortality whenever the subject of expositions arises. Seattle decided not to go as far as Chicago's Little Egypt—possibly because there was an area downtown that shocked the timid and had been the subject of sermons for years. But the name of the amusement section was easily chosen. It was called the "Pay Streak," although most of the games of chance did not pay off to the satisfaction of all visitors. But then, as many pointed out, not every cheechako had struck it rich in the Gold Rush, either.

A curious feature of amusement row was a reproduction of the battle of the *Monitor* and the *Merrimac* of Civil War fame. Of course it was popular with veterans of the War between the States,

and was just as exciting for youngsters. Today one can find Seattleites who recalled the simulated battle above everything else at the
fair.

Well ahead of time, Mayor John T. Miller declared the opening
day a legal holiday, and by that day—he strongly urged—the city
should shine for the visitors. Downtown streets, he promised, would
be sluiced three times daily during the exposition. In the days of
the horse-drawn vehicle this was sensible, but he pressed further.
Every citizen should make certain that lawn and garden were
trimmed, and, if necessary, homes should be freshly painted. The
results he obtained were most satisfactory. On June 1, 1909, Seattle
assumed the reputation of being the cleanest and neatest city in the
nation. This was a title it held—rightly or not—for several decades.

Late in May the streets downtown were arched with banners,
and recently cleaned buildings showed the national colors in a pro-
fusion of flags and bunting. Seattle was in a great state of excitement, and on opening day 80,000 people crowded through the gates.
Inasmuch as expositions are unpredictable, and considering that
most out-of-town visitors had not yet arrived, this maiden attendance
was considered promising.

The great day dawned clear with only a slight overcast. Most of
the crowd had already been excited by a downtown parade, chiefly
military, which had been honored by the presence of the Duke of
Connaught's Own Rifles. At ten o'clock Pacific Standard Time, bells
began to ring and whistles screamed along the waterfront. In Washington, D.C., President Taft had pressed an Alaska gold nugget
which by telegraph set the Alaska-Yukon-Pacific Exposition in motion. For the time being the easy-going William Howard Taft had
done his duty to the fair. But he would be along later to see it all
and, just as important to him, beat capitalist A. S. Kerry at golf. It
was reported later that the President's white knickers were the most
capacious ever seen on Seattle links and in fact resembled the tent
of an oil-rich sheik in size and conspicuousness.

Opening day speakers were J. E. Chilberg, president of the
exposition; Director General I. A. Nadeau; and Seattle's adopted
son James J. Hill, chief of the Great Northern. He was the one who
held the crowd quiet. As always, he spoke with hardly a gesture and
short arms akimbo. Alongside a black patch his one good eye was
fiery with pride and the certainty that Seattle and the Puget Sound

region had only begun to fight for national recognition. A more acceptable opening day speaker could not have been found. Seattleites believed every word he growled from the depths of his gray-streaked beard.

You'll glimpse the names of many activists in the Alaska-Yukon-Pacific Exposition on street signs and a few Victorian buildings not yet victims of the wrecking ball. You'll find the descendants of some scattered through the vital commerce of the town. Today it seems odd that among these movers and shakers were no blacks, Indians, Eskimos, Japanese or Chinese. These omissions were not calculated; it simply did not occur to the whites that there should be representatives of these races.

Designer Dawson properly included a "permanent" statue on the fairgrounds. It was of Secretary William H. Seward, the cabinet member of Lincoln's administration who engineered the purchase of Alaska from Russia. The statue was unveiled with ceremony. Engraved on its base were the words "Let us sign the treaty tonight." The statue is now half hidden in an obscure corner of Volunteer Park.

The fair's best attendance was, naturally enough, on Seattle Day, when a record 117,013 people shoved into the magic forest. These Seattleites made a particular effort to achieve that record, thus proving to the nation its belief in the Alaska-Yukon-Pacific Exposition. The town was ready with a special Seattle Day song by George Beck, and for some years after the big show it was sung or hummed by many proud citizens. It began:

> Two hundred thousand people, including me, will stay,
>   Until the day is over, for it is Seattle Day.
> So wake and call me early, for we're going to the fair;
>   For it's Seattle Day, mother, and believe me, I'll be there!

That the song overestimated the actual attendance troubled nobody. The composition was sung as written, then and later.

Every day was a special day, and those concerned did their best to see that theirs was notable as to attendance. Accurate records are not now available, but the town's ethnic proportions in 1909 made certain that some of the most successful days were those celebrated by Scandinavians, Japanese and Germans. There were also days marked for the Chinese, the Elks, Tacoma, Portland, Snohomish, and those from Minnesota, Oregon, California and British Columbia.

Distinguished visitors helped swell attendance. William Jennings Bryan appeared on Bryan Day, October 10, and it is said that the golden-voiced orator drew more people than President Taft. True or not, only 25,000 gathered at the amphitheater to hear the President urge a national committee to establish more laws for Alaska, thereby proving that the jovial Commander-in-Chief did not understand the high-spirited Alaskans too well. At this period the territory was not anxious for additional laws, and only halfheartedly looked toward statehood, because that would mean more regulation for a certainty.

When the Alaska-Yukon exposition closed—and that was a letdown for Seattle—it had accomplished two distinctions which fairs in the United States had not achieved. It had opened with every building and exhibit ready, and when the gates were closed on the final day it was in the black. Within the hundred and thirty-eight days there was a total of 3,740,551 paid admissions on the books; translated into money that meant $1,096,475 in the big hard, round dollars of 1909.

Did the exposition succeed in other goals? Seattleites were sure that it had. They believed that the AYP forcefully had reminded the nation and the world that Alaska was of enormous value, and that Seattle was its entrance and there was no other gateway worth mentioning.

Too, the exposition had been created with tremendous bursts of energy and enthusiasm, and it gave Seattle a confidence which at the time it needed. Yet in retrospect it seems probable that the most lasting result was the new campus it created for the University of Washington.

That legacy is marked by a simple bronze tablet inscribed:

> On these grounds, was held, between June 1st and October 16th, 1909, the Alaska-Yukon Exposition, and this tablet is erected by the Seattle Chamber of Commerce as a testimonial to those citizens of Seattle who, from a sense of civic loyalty, and at great personal sacrifice, created and carried to success an exposition of lasting benefit not only to this city but to the entire Northwest.

Untold until now was an effect of the Alaska-Yukon exposition on the town's social and cultural segment. In the early part of the century Seattle was markedly imitative, and sometimes, in its comparative youth, it still is. In the days of the exposition the city did not, of course, have four hundred persons who moved in what was then called high society. But the wealthiest had congregated on First Hill, just above the downtown area. From there, in ornate mansions, they looked down on the bay and the "outsiders" of Seattle's world, and were referred to as the "Four Hundred."

When the exposition began to take shape a social crisis developed, wholly unnoticed by the majority. J. E. Chilberg, the banker, had been named chief of the fair simply because businessmen recognized a self-made man who had grown with the town and got things done.

Probably it occurred to none on the committees that the Chilbergs, for reasons lost in time's passage, were not members of Seattle's "Four Hundred." They lived in a sizable house at the edge of First Hill, but were not, as the term then in fashion had it, "accepted." They had friends, none of whom belonged to the elite, and visits and dinners were exchanged. But the Chilbergs were never invited to the homes of the upper crust and their names were never on the invitation lists when a distinguished visitor was entertained. What the Chilbergs thought of this is not known, and probably they did not care.

True, Chilberg was not broadly educated, his conversation was dull and his grammar could be astonishingly bad. Nonetheless he accepted the leadership of the exposition from those who ignored him except in matters involving his bank. Certainly he had no thought of revenge in assuming his role as chief of the fair. Those who remember him say that he was by no means vindictive, and in any case the inevitable social aspects of the exposition were not considered in the beginning. Had they been, it is probable that someone else would have been chosen in Chilberg's place. As matters stood, Chilberg and his lady would of necessity take on the unaccustomed roles of exposition royalty.

It was a First Hill matron who more or less immediately saw the situation—too late. "Why, this simply turns everything upside down!" she is reported to have exclaimed.

It did indeed turn everything upside down in the little world the lady valued so highly. But there was nothing to be done about it as the fair got under way. When the Chilbergs held a reception near the beginning of the exposition, it could not be ignored by Chilberg's associates in the project. They appeared, with their wives, and among the latter was the lady whose world had been inverted. When the Kerrys entertained President Taft, the Chilbergs were, of course, on the list to receive an invitation. When the Treats opened their doors to a close relative of the Emperor of Japan, the Chilbergs were there. And obviously they were learning, for it was the Chilbergs who gave a dinner for the Ambassador from France.

But it remained for Henry Struve to fix the actual number of the "Four Hundred" in Seattle. His method was dramatic, and doubtless unwitting, but it crystallized the town's high society for some years. Struve was a friend of Chauncey Olcott, then perhaps the most popular entertainer in North America. Struve invited Olcott to be a house guest, and in honor of the occasion hurriedly built a fashionable wing to his First Hill mansion. The addition was somewhat in the form of a theater with a slightly sloping floor (which could be raised level to create a ballroom) and there was a sizable dais at one end. It was from this platform that Olcott enchanged the chosen few of Seattle.

That addition to the Struve home held just one hundred chairs. No more and no less. As the Struve plans developed, excitement ran like a hurricane around First Hill. Nobody will ever know the full extent of the machinations that took place to insure an invitation. It was such a notable affair, and Struve's preparations were so remarkable, that First Hill was forced to accept the reality that Seattle's "Four Hundred" was more precisely the "One Hundred" privileged to hear Olcott on that brilliant evening. I suspect that social historians would consider this about right for a city of 237,000 people.

If the Struves set the number of the elite for some years, they also destroyed the idea that in Seattle there are those who belong and those who do not. Today Seattle has no "One Hundred" who rise above all in beauty, wealth, brilliance and general acceptability. The majority would ignore such pretensions if they did, and there is no certification that any cohesive group entertains the ambition of the woman whose world was turned upside down by the Chilbergs and the Alaska-Yukon-Pacific Exposition. It is true that the town's well-to-do and upper middle class run in cliques, and equally a fact that highly selective subdivisions—such as The Highlands, Broadmoor and Medina, the latter east of Lake Washington—create de facto social groups. Yet Seattle is markedly democratic. Wealth alone is not a sure key to the majority of groups and clubs. And the many newcomers from the East and Midwest have much diluted the importance of descendance from pioneer families.

The beginning of Seattle's next exposition was so similar that one would almost suspect that the four participants who first put the idea into words had looked into the sparse records of the old AYP. Only one of the four had seen the first fair; he was in knee pants at the time and was highly imaginative about the exposition in later years.

The second fair burst forth in all its miniature glory—sometimes it was called "the exposition in a jewel box"—in 1962. Yet only ten years later there was a difference of opinion as to whether three or four were present at its conception.

There were four. Casually and without planning a meeting, they came together in the bar of the Washington Athletic Club on a wintry day in January of 1955. Although all were relatively young, there are only three survivors. Nobody recalls the momentous day of the month. There was no reason to; they engaged in small talk, half in earnest, half in jest, and there were highballs. The four were Ross Cunningham, a top senior brain and political writer at the Seattle *Times* who knew that a former city editor of his paper had been an inventor of the old AYP; Don Follett, manager of the Chamber of Commerce; Al Rochester, a member of the City Council and descendant of a prominent pioneer family; and Denny Givens of the Seattle Area Industrial Council, an arm of the Chamber of Commerce.

At the time of the talk in the Washington Athletic Club, the city had become addicted to steady prosperity. But business was sagging and, as Follett said, Seattle needed a shot in the arm. Inasmuch as tourism was beginning to be recognized as a vital industry, with plenty of potential, city leaders were hoping for a city center of varied interests.

The city owned considerable property committed to a center. But the progress on the site lying between Mercer Street on the north and Denny Way on the south had been rather halfhearted, and part of the center already was obsolescent. The main buildings were a high school memorial stadium, an ice-skating arena, an all-purpose auditorium and a state armory, none of them things of beauty. Landscaping, inasmuch as Seattle is a garden-oriented city, was virtually nonexistent.

There is little doubt that the first desultory conversations leading to a fair were focused merely on dreaming up a lively series of events that would attract tourists the year around, with something that would create a climax in the summer. Seattle held an annual celebration called Seafair, highlighted by an extremely popular hydroplane race on Lake Washington. But many citizens were growing a bit weary of Seafair, just as, many years before, they had tired of an annual week-long event called The Potlatch.

The chief criticism of Seafair was that it had been borrowed and, except for the appropriate name, had little to do with the city's traditions. It was, said the cynics, just an adaptation of carnivals of other cities. The "story line" of Seafair involved King Neptune, uninhibited pirates and of course a beautiful Seafair Queen with a retinue of princesses and escorts. The costuming was something out of Graustark. Nobody spotted the basic weakness until recognition came that we were living in the Space Age, and that because of Boeing the community was a Space Age city. The main parades were attractive, and several neighborhoods simultaneously staged their own versions of Seafair. The hydroplane contest, brought to Lake Washington following the winning of the Gold Cup in Detroit by Seattle merchant-sportsman Stan Sayers and his *Slo-Mo-Shun*, was what kept Seafair going.

So, during the seedling conversations, there was talk of refurbishing Seafair, bringing it up to date and integrating it with a vague something or other called, perhaps, "Festival of the West." It would be staged at the city center and bring some life and beauty to that area.

As yet, none of the talk about exposition sites was taken seriously. But Al Rochester and a few other stubborn Seattleites kept on talking about another fair. It should be, they said, in 1959, which would be just a half-century after the first exposition. It was not long, however, until even the ubiquitous and excitable councilman recognized that this target date would be too soon. It was clear that the Seattle Chamber, sizable as the membership had become, could not perform the miracle alone.

Yet, without a site, without money, and with no organization, the fair was given a name—and this was no small help. Its author was advertising executive Gerald Hoeck, who at a small informal luncheon at the popular 410 restaurant, suggested "The Twenty-First Century Exposition." One of his associates, Marlowe Hartung, said, "Let's try turning it around and maybe it will sound better. Make it 'Century 21 Exposition.'"

So that is what it became, at least until an unforeseen development relegated it to a subtitle. "We didn't make our decision too quickly," recalls Murray Morgan, official historian of the fair. "Our little group had been asked to come up with a suitable name, and Hoeck and Hartung had produced one. But we kicked around a lot of names that day. We didn't want to dry up the refreshments too soon."

Certainly Hoeck was in orbit, for the Russians had let go with Sputnik I on October 4, 1957, a feat which electrified the world and did much for Seattle's second fair. "Our exposition," Hoeck said, "should take a giant leap into the next century."

Actually, this seemed quite a leap to the group there in the 410 cafe. But Al Rochester didn't see it that way. So to move the idea out of dreamland he persuaded the City Council to memorialize the state legislature. The plea from Seattle stimulated most of them to grab their wallets, convinced that Seattle was merely hatching a plot to create a great civic center with as little cost to itself as possible. But at last the state lawmakers, pushed by lobbyists and less visible pressures, voted for a world's fair study commission. Governor Arthur Langlie, who saw plenty of troubles ahead and did not intend to stand for re-election (he would run for the U. S. Senate, unsuccessfully), signed the bill without enthusiasm. This created the World's Fair Commission. Then he had an inspiration: he would ask Edward Carlson, now head of United Air Lines, to accept the position as chairman.

Carlson received the news under interesting circumstances. He was then president of Western International Hotels, a Seattle-born and based institution. S. W. Thurston, board chairman, was a close friend despite their difference in age. Their beginnings and progress in the hotel business were markedly similar. Tacoma-born Carlson had started as a garage attendant at that city's leading hotel. Sedric Thurston had begun as a bellhop.

Carlson had been called into Thurston's office and after a bit of general conversation about the business, the older man began a gentle lecture regarding Carlson's many civic activities. In his seventies, Thurston foresaw the younger man sitting as board chairman; the older man's monologue was much like that of father to son.

He mentioned Carlson's steadily increasing outside activities. "Mind you," he said, "I'm not saying that an outfit like ours should shirk its corporate citizenship, and certainly I'm not suggesting that you haven't been doing your job and doing it damned well. But some of these extracurricular activities have a way of growing. You do any difficult job well and people know it. Also they know you are willing to work hard at anything you undertake. Personally, I have avoided these things—and I realize now that times are changing and that maybe I've stayed too much under cover. But I've been wondering if a little moderation . . ."

Thurston was interrupted by the ringing of his telephone. He listened briefly and said, "Yes, he's right here." The board chairman handed the instrument across his desk with the comment, "It's the governor." Fearing the worst, Carlson took the telephone and heard the words that would get the exposition off the ground. "How are you, Ed?" said Langlie. "As you know, I've authorized a World's Fair Commission and it has to have a leader. I want you as chairman."

Carlson admits that his face felt as if it was growing beet red. "Just a second, Governor. I'd better check with the boss." He looked at Thurston sheepishly. "Langlie wants me to take the chairmanship of the World's Fair Commission."

Thurston almost never laughed, but his smile now was broad. "You can't turn down the governor. Besides, if there really is a fair it will be good for the hotel business."

Carlson returned to Langlie. "Mr. Thurston says to go ahead and do my best."

Quickly now there formed the three main groups which would shape up the exposition. There were the World's Fair Commission, and later a larger group called in deference to the newly minted title for the fair, Century 21 Exposition, Incorporated, and, eventually, a group of architects whose collective genius would inspire the admiration of tens of thousands of people from all over the world. Literally they did create "a fair in a jewel box."

Inevitably the majority more or less agreed that the civic center would be the ideal site. One of the strongest arguments was that an exposition would leave a legacy of permanent buildings, as had the Alaska-Yukon-Pacific Exposition.

Of course property prices adjacent to the center began to soar. The Seattle Diocese of the Roman Catholic Church, which had just completed a place of worship at the western edge of the center, refused to sell at any price. The nearby Masonic Building took the same attitude. At this point, when the organizers were struggling to enlarge the site, Ed Carlson sighed, "Well, nobody can say we haven't made any progress at all. We've got the Catholics and the Masons together at last!" Eventually, however, the Masons entered into an agreement with the city whereby the Masonic Order leased its building with the proviso that it would be restored for its original pupose at the end of the fair.

On the commission, headed by Carlson as chairman, were Victor Rosellini, Alfred Rochester, Lieutenant Governor John Cherberg, Councilman J. D. Braman, Clarence C. Dill, Paul S. Friedlander, H. Dewayne Kreager, state senators Howard Bargreen, Herbert H. Friese, Reuben A. Knobloch; and state representatives Audley F. Mahaffey, Ray Olson, Leonard Sawyer, and Jeanette Testu.

William S. Street, retired president of the Frederick and Nelson department store and big game hunter, was chairman of the larger group Century 21 Exposition, Incorporated. He was later assisted by Joseph P. Gandy, who forsook a profitable law practice to become a partner in one of Ford Motor Company's most important dealerships in the Northwest.

Other members of this group included Ewen C. Dingwall who would become director-manager of the fair; Otto Brandt, Lee Moran, Iver H. Cederwall, Robert B. Colwell, L. E. Karrer, D. E. Skinner, Michael Dederer, Norman Davis, Edward P. Tremper, Lowell Hunt, A. W. Morton, Harry L. Carr, James B. Douglas, D. Roy Johnson, J. McElroy McCaw, Fred Paulsell, Harry Henke III, Willis Camp, Arthur Copperstein, Jay Rockey, Donald I. Foster, George K. Whitney, Clayton Young, Frederick Schumacher, Donald Fry, Louis Larson and Harold Shaw.

Paul Thiry, prominent architect and planner of national reputation, was primary designer of the fair and creator of the Washington State Coliseum. The United States Science Pavilion was designed by Minoru Yamasaki with the co-operation of Naramore, Bain,

Brady and Johanson. Designer of the Space Needle was John Graham and his associates.

There also came into being a board of trustees numbering well over a hundred. Certainly the memberships of the various groups formed the most representative cross section of Seattleites ever brought together in all its history.

Yet of the many hazards thrown into the way of the fair the most long-lived and discouraging was the disinterest of the general public. The city had slid into one of its periods of apathy. There were no bursts of enthusiasm and energy such as those that had so greatly helped preparations for the Alaska-Yukon-Pacific Exposition. This indifference was more damaging than were the relatively few active opponents, most of whom argued that there were more sensible ways to spend the money.

These also claimed that materials and labor were far too high for an exposition on a scale that would attract widespread attention. Many said that fairs were going out of style, as dated now as a chautauqua. The civic center seemed to be inevitable as a site, and the cynics believed that it was far too small.

The first meeting of the World's Fair Commission must have given momentary pause even to a man as enthusiastic as Ed Carlson. It was held at the Olympic Hotel, August 19, 1955. There were only seven members present, and seven guests. One of the guests asked, "What kind of a fair can be built on only seventy-five acres?"

"A really great one," answered Carlson quickly. He had been talking to the architects and looking at drawings.

As the commission appeared to be treading water, a typical Seattle paradox occurred. The City Council put a $7,500,000 civic center bond issue on the ballot. It passed with a vote of 187,053 to 63,752. Then, having taken advantage of the system of democracy, the people relapsed into the old apathy. Most voters had no idea of the hopeful plans of the commissioners and the fair planners. Their attitude seemed to be, "If they can put on even a little fair for $7,500,000, let them go ahead and try."

Of course more money would be needed and it would have to show up regionally before other steps could be taken beyond the mountains and the seas. Two emergency pleas were sent to Olympia. Neither received a reply. Finally Carlson wrote his personal report to the governor. The report began calmly, but its summary was characteristically Carlson and in capital letters: "WE CANNOT OVER-EMPHASIZE THE GREAT OPPORTUNITY THAT IS AVAILABLE TO US TO CREATE AN AREA THAT COULD BE AS DRAMATIC AS THE AGE WE LIVE IN."

Langlie probably did not doubt Carlson, but as a lame-duck governor with hopes for the U. S. Senate he was in no mood to react to his own appointee's enthusiasm. Things began to look brighter with the election of Albert D. Rosellini as governor. The optimistic Carlson and the extrovert Rosellini got along famously.

The new governor asked, "How much do you think we down here in Olympia ought to come in for?"

"I think Washington State and the city of Seattle ought to be fifty-fifty partners," Carlson said.

"On that basis I believe I can get what you want," the governor replied.

The governor's promise, while unduly optimistic, was finally realized when the 1957 legislature—after weeks of some of the most adroit broken field running that body had witnessed, finally authorized a $7,500,000 bond issue "for a world's fair to be held in the city of Seattle."

One of the major results of that appropriation was the Washington State Coliseum, a major attraction both as to architecture and theme. Designed by Paul Thiry, the Coliseum was financed and built by the state at a cost of $4.5 million. It turned out to be worth much more, both during the fair and later. Its initial purpose was to give the public a view into the world of the future. And the ingenious Thiry design allowed for its conversion, following the exposition, into a sports arena and convention facility seating 18,500.

Despite the high caliber of the fair leaders, the two committees and the trustees, the road to Seattle's second fair was a rocky one. There were two postponements totaling three years and, as one commissioner put it, "a public disbelief that at times seemed total."

The doubt was hardly total, for more and more Seattleites began to recognize that something had started that would have to be finished and must be a success. Three moments require notice as vitally important before the going got rough. One was when Langlie appointed Carlson as chairman of the World's Fair Commission. Another was the choice of Joe Gandy as president of Century 21 Exposition, Incorporated, backed up by William Street.

Another most important moment was when the telephone rang in the office of Ewen Dingwall, a tall fellow of sober mien who looked as if he were on a diet and not pleased about it. He had been manager of the Seattle Municipal League, and assistant to the mayor. When he answered the telephone call that was to change his life style he heard Harold Shefelman. This prominent attorney avoided committees, although he was a regent of the University of Washington, but was modestly invisible in many an important step in the city's progress. He asked Dingwall to come to his office "right away" and in the town on Elliott Bay when Shefelman says to come at once you do that. Dingwall put on hat and raincoat and jogged to the lawyer's office, then in the Northern Life Tower. When he arrived he found Ed Carlson there. Dingwall, who once or twice a month let go with a flash of humor, recalled that "Ed was smiling and I could swear there was a trace of canary feathers on his lips."

The lawyer broke the news. "Ding," he said, without preamble, "we want you to be project director of the fair. We're at the point where somebody has to take up all four corners and make one package. We think you're the man."

Dingwall protested. "Harold, I don't know a damned thing about a fair."

Carlson laughed. "Look, Ding, don't let that disturb you. All of us are amateurs in this, and Harold and I think you're the man for the job."

What they really wanted was an intelligent workhorse—and they got him. Dingwall hit the new duty head-on. One could find him on the fairgrounds almost any time, day or late at night. Near the finish he looked like a ghost, but the amateur had become a professional, promoted to vice-president and general manager. San Antonio, planning a fair, wanted him, if there was anything left, when the Seattle show closed. Eventually Ding became a nationally known consultant on expositions and exhibitions large enough to make the work worth his time.

Naturally the fair leaders had engaged some expert opinions on what the show could expect in the way of attendance. The estimates ranged from 7,500,000 to 12,500,000.

The main concern was still money. There was fifteen million coming, but the fair was still lacking in funds to sell its wares to potential exhibitors. At one ticklish point in the financial progress a few Seattle leaders came through handsomely by taking up notes of debenture, really glorified IOUs. Among those who came to the rescue for interim expenses were Lawrence Arnold, Henry Broderick, Maxwell Carlson, Frank Dupar, Ben Ehrlichman, Emil Sick, William Blethen, Charles Lindeman (the last two being publishers respectively of the *Times* and the *Post-Intelligencer*), William Street, Ben Bowling, D. Roy Johnson, O. D. Fisher, Norton Clapp, Horace McCurdy, Nat Rogers, S. W. Thurston, Frank McLaughlin, William Reed, the Clearing House Association and the Weyerhaeuser Company. These adventurers were representative of almost every section of commerce in the city. The names themselves were of value when the fair's "salesmen" took to the air. It was clearer than ever that Seattle's big wheels believed in the exposition.

But there was still a big name missing and everybody in eastern industry and those representing foreign nations spotted the omission. "It seemed to me," reported one traveling salesman, "that every single man I talked with asked, 'What is Boeing going to do?'"

It was a tough question to answer and about all that could be said was that Boeing's participation was still under discussion. So it was, but not by anybody from Boeing, whose top men had said NO in capital letters. The giant aircraft company had an unbreakable policy regarding involvement in promotional ventures—regardless of who sponsored them. At this time Boeing insisted that its customers were the airlines, not the general public.

Boeing did not break its policy by contributing money or a building of its own. It did something far more dramatic and appropriate. The big aircraft firm created and installed in the United States Science Pavilion a space age Spacearium, a permanent addition to the center and one of the most attractive features of the fair. Four times an hour a sixty-thousand-billion-billion-mile round-trip voyage began and ended in this amazing exhibit. This writer made the trip may times, "traveling" at ten trillion times the speed of light. Of course the first trip was the most exciting. Out of nowhere the narrator's voice warned, "We're leaving the Milky Way Galaxy and setting a course for Andromeda. Grasp the handrails, please." Already I was holding fast to a handrail; looking down I saw that my knuckles were white in the eerie half-light.

In a civilization that has almost lost the art of walking, people were still asking how out-of-town visitors were going to get to the fair. Actually, the civic center grounds were within walking distance from central downtown hotels and the scores of motels near the site. "It's too damned easy to walk to the fair," a disgruntled taxi driver told me. "That's what burns me about this town. They worry about business, but I never see 'em worrying about us hack drivers."

More exciting news was on the way, and doubtless added to the cab driver's unhappiness. All over the country a number of companies were promoting their versions of a monorail. Out of the blue came a proposition from Alweg of Sweden. This firm was ready to build a monorail installation of two high-speed trains, to be financed by taking twenty-five cents off the top of each admission ticket. When the fair was over and the cost amortized, the monorail would revert to the city. The route was to and from the fair and the Westlake Mall downtown. The distance was only 1.2 miles and could be traversed in ninety-five seconds. At the Westlake Mall moving sidewalks added interest to loading and unloading of passengers. Said the guide on each of the two trains, "You are making use of the rapid transit system of the future." Both visitors and hometown folks let their jaws drop, enjoyed the ride and made the trip many times. It was not really the first monorail in the region; early in the century a Tacoma inventor had built and operated a brief monorail run to demonstrate to the city fathers that he had the answer to the town's future transportation. Tacomans did not agree, and the pioneer monorail disappeared into dreamland. In Seattle the Alweg monorail is an almost unnoticed fixture now, doing a brisk business in summers, skirting the fountain statue of Chief Seattle as it makes the long curve in and out of the center.

On the legislature's bill it was felt appropriate to retain the designation "World's Fair" even though thousands of Seattleites, although warming up now, considered it amusing to apply such an all-embracing title to an exposition confined to a bit less than seventy-five acres. Then a discovery was made that revealed the innocence of the public and the leaders as well.

There was a somewhat mysterious international organization in Paris, and in 1928 it had taken unto itself the power to confer the title "World's Fair." If the Bureau of International Expositions, apparently directed by a Madame Michel Isaac, declared an exposition "a world's fair," then so it was. If the bureau withheld approval, the show was not a "world's fair" and should not make a claim as such.

About the time Seattle heard of the bureau in Paris it was learned that New York, planning another fair, already had made formal application to the organization.

A hurried trip to Paris by Governor Rosellini, state house speaker John O'Brien and James Faber, a savvy former newspaperman, was unsuccessful. Faber found the mysterious but all-powerful Madame Isaac in her BIE office, which he could only describe later as "a loft in an obscure building on a back street of Paris." Madame Isaac ushered him out. She would, she said, talk only to a representative of the United States government.

After still another rebuff, Gandy and other fair officials began to pull wires in Washington, D.C. A salesman by instinct, Gandy went to Paris and won over Michel Isaac by emphasizing that Seattle would, indeed, abide by every rule and regulation of the BIE. He had learned that New York had offended the lady by spelling out all sorts of changes they wanted in the regulations. Gandy took the soft-sell line as opposed to New York's hard one. An objection arose as to the possibility of labor troubles hurting the fair. Gandy hurried home and got a no-strike pledge from the King County Labor Council. He returned to Paris again with his no-strike pledge, then continued his salesmanship on Michel Isaac and other BIE officials. Some weeks later, Gandy, the seller of Fords, had won approval. Sanction came from Leon Barety, president of the Bureau des Expositions, Ancien Mistre. It showed up in Ewen Dingwall's hands, written in French. Dingwall hastened off to have the message translated. The part that brought cheers said:

> The BIE has been very appreciative of the desires of the Seattle Exposition to organize this important display in conformity with the rules contained in the Convention of 22 November, 1928, and it has followed with the greatest satisfaction the efforts displayed to that effect. . . . It is therefore with pleasure that the Board of Directors of BIE, in the course of its 47th session of 8 November, 1960, has authorized its members to take part in this exposition of particular interest as it is intended to exhibit in particular and in advance the scientific aspects of the world of tomorrow . . .

Now the representatives of Seattle's fair could go forth armed with the certification of the bureau. Immediately the name Seattle World's Fair 1962 took precedence over "Century 21 Exposition." The latter description was retained, but in a minor way.

It is regrettable that most Seattleites were pleased when New York was refused BIE approval. Seattle sometimes harbors the hallucination that it is competing directly with the great eastern city of eight million people. This occasional mirage doubtless is rooted in the abortive decision of the founders to name the town New York. However, Manhattan was not unnerved by the slight from BIE and called its show a "World's Fair" anyhow. But of course the approval from that dingy hole-in-the-wall in Paris meant a great deal to Seattle's "jewel box exposition" and was of marked help toward the finish line.

Soon it could announce definitely participation by African nations, Berlin, Brazil, Canada, Denmark, the European Economic Community, France, India, Japan, Korea, Mexico, the Philippines, Republic of China, San Marino, Sweden, Thailand, the United Arab Republic, the United Kingdom, the United Nations and the United States of America. That was quite a package for a tiny exposition in the upper left-hand corner of the country.

The United States Science Pavilion (still very much in business) changed local apathy to a mood of enthusiasm. It was not exactly the wild excitement that accompanied the building of the old AYP, but of course in the sixties the community, like the nation, was more sophisticated than it had been in the first decade of the century. There were still those who were dubious about the smallness of the site, but these did not yet realize that although the fair would not sprawl, it would soar into the skies of the future.

Jim Faber, an ex-newspaper reporter who joined the fair staff as public relations director in 1957, deserves considerable credit for the presence of the United States Pavilion. He had visited the Brussels exposition and on his return stopped off in the nation's capital for sessions with the state's powerful Senator Warren Magnuson. Curiously, "Maggie" had not been very enthusiastic about the fair. In a sense he was in a transitional period, becoming a protector of the consumer. But somehow Faber—and doubtless others—directed "Maggie's" attention to the fair. Whatever magic began to work after Faber's visit, the end result was $12,500,000 from the federal government—and that made up for a lot of troubles, such as lawsuits involving property rights.

The catalyst for the federal exhibit turned out to be a "character," and that was good. Seattle needed one just then. He was the able Dr. Athelstan Spilhaus, dean of the Institute of Technology at the University of Minnesota. He was loaned to the fair to become commisssioner of the science exhibit. During his regime he fell in love with Seattle and its surroundings and soon was skipper of a miniature steamboat. He had joined the great Seattle boating community in a typically Spilhaus manner.

The United States Science Pavilion was—and is—a beautiful poem in architecture. It was designed by Minoru Yamasaki of Detroit with Seattle associate architects Naramore, Bain, Brady and Johanson. The exhibit designers were Walter Dorwin Teague Associates, Charles Eames, Raymond Loewy, George Snaith and George Nelson. They used just about every technique in or out of the book—but most of all, they created. This house of science more than brought to actuality a proclamation by President Dwight Eisenhower long before the passage of the Science Pavilion bill:

> . . . Now, therefore I, Dwight D. Eisenhower, President of the United States of America, and pursuant to the aforesaid Act of Congress and at the request of the Governor of the State of Washington do hereby invite appropriate foreign countries to participate in the World Science Pan-Pacific Exposition to be held at Seattle, Washington, from May 1961 to October 1961. In witness whereof I hereunto set my hand and cause the Seal of the United States of America to be affixed . . .

No more than the Seattle leaders could Ike foresee the postponement to April 1962—and where he got the name he gave the exposition is still a minor mystery.

The Science Pavilion brought more people back for a second look than the next five top exhibits combined. It was always crowded, and at one point tired visitors sat on the floor, waiting until there was room for a closer engagement with the exhibits. A startled aide reported this to Doctor Spilhaus, whose unruffled comment was, "Why not? It's their house."

Alistair Cooke of the Manchester *Guardian,* one of many

reporters from all over the world, was generally critical of the fair. But he could not resist the showcase of science:

> It lies happily along the southwestern edge of the fair, away from the main architectural babel . . . five slender aluminum arches rising above graceful plots of buildings enclosing a court of pools punctuated by jetting fountains. The six flanking buildings are slabs of pre-stressed concrete of such crystalline purity that even on dull days their reflection was as difficult to bear as Alpine snows . . . The delicate interplay of light and water, arches and scintillating stone, makes one think that it is as if the Gothic style had passed without a break through the Renaissance and the 18th Century in and out of Spain and had achieved a final sensuous purity in the 20th Century. It is as if Venice had just been built.

Carlson had been inspired by the revolving television tower in Stuttgart. Immediately there leaped into his mind a tower restaurant and observation platform for the fair. It should revolve once every hour, giving diners a leisurely 360-degree view of what Carlson felt was the most beautiful sight in the world. The name came to him at the same moment. It would be called the Space Needle, but he did not dream that it would somehow become the symbol of the fair.

Carlson took the first available plane back to Seattle and went into huddles with architects and engineers. They came up with a flame-crowned tower more than six hundred feet high. It was the tallest structure in Seattle until almost a decade later, when Seattle-First National Bank—descended from Dexter Horton's frontier institution—built its headquarters skyscraper.

The Needle is topped by a popular glass-enclosed restaurant in the shape of a flying saucer and seating two hundred and sixty diners. The observation platform is just above. Both are supported by three gracefully curved steel legs and are reached by two high-speed elevators ascending in the outside of the central support.

Although a private enterprise, the Space Needle's gradual rise made the fair real to tens of thousands of Seattleites who had until then been dubious. The anchor which holds the structure is bolted together in concrete thirty feet below ground.

The rising of the Space Needle could be seen—on a clear day, of course—from Cape Flattery out on the tip of the Olympic Peninsula, and from the foothills of the Cascades. Its rather swift construction became a barometer indicating the nearness of the fair's opening.

Except for the delicate towers of the United States Pavilion, the Needle was all that the great majority of Seattleites could see of what was going on behind the walls and fences that Ewen Dingwall's workers had erected. Now and then a distinguished visitor was given a preview. President John Kennedy, in town for the centennial celebration of the University of Washington, was shown the progress that had been made. Of course a date for his formal appearance was on the calendar, but this had to be canceled due to the confrontation with Russia in the Cuban crisis. The President did not get to see the finished fair in its active glory, and it was left for Vice-President Lyndon B. Johnson to represent the White House.

Unfortunately for Johnson, that day his companion was John Glenn, the pioneer of space travel, and Glenn's presence put Johnson in the shade to such a marked degree that fair officials were embarrassed. The Century 21 setting was perfect for the astronaut. Moreover, he turned out to be a hero in the classic mold. Children and adults both crowded around him, trying to get his autograph or just to touch his hand. The only other visitor who approached him in popularity during a fair visit was handsome Prince Philip of Great Britain.

To Joe Gandy and Bill Street went major credit for the impressive commercial exhibits, which numbered nearly a hundred. Few of the big companies were easy to persuade unless they had sizable investments in the region. The big New York fair was coming, and Seattle was a far piece of land from the men of Manhattan who made top decisions. Joe Gandy had some difficulty with Ford Motor Company, which he represented in Seattle. That scalp he simply had to bring home and he confessed as much to Henry Ford II. On the final attempt the two had a pleasant luncheon during which Gandy was craftily silent on the subject of the fair. But he asked if Henry could spare a few minutes after lunch in the motor mogul's office.

When they got there Gandy said, "Henry, I simply must bring up our fair again. What am I going to look like as a Ford salesman if I can't persuade your company to participate? But that's not the main point. The Seattle fair will mean a lot to Ford business out there. I'm sure of it."

At that point Ford raised his custom-made moccasins to the top of his desk and leaned back in his chair with a broad smile. Smith-Gandy was one of the most satisfactory dealerships the company had under contract. Henry knew it, and so did Gandy.

"Well," said the descendant of the first Henry Ford, "now we're talking business. I'm not going to let you down. We'll be there—and in a way that will make you proud of us." Ford and his associates kept that promise with a circular building whose show was "An Adventure in Outer Space." During the fair the word spread fast that it was worth seeing, and people stood in line for hours to get into the huge aluminum-trimmed geodesic dome at the south entrance of the fair.

Originally it was decided that fun and games would be omitted, that Seattle's fair would be dedicated in the main to science, technology and culture, the latter to include theater and opera. Then the cry went up that no city—absolutely no city— could hold a fair that ignored kiddies and those who liked a bit of the risqué. So there came into being Show Street and the Gayway.

Appropriately, Gracie Hanson's Paradise International, a plush 700-seat theater restaurant, was at the head of Show Street. It was a quality girl show, mainly, and the really beautiful young women were "topless" as to costuming. How many local laws this venture broke nobody knew, or cared to find out. Somehow the law never got around to Show Street in its official role. Gracie Hanson became a big hit, fully clothed as mistress of ceremonies. As to measurements, there was a lot of Gracie (she was a logger's daughter from the village of Morton) but she proved a thorough professional and later continued in show business in Portland. So far as fair visitors were concerned, the Seattle production was Gracie's show, but it was financed by a group of well-to-do from the Chinese community.

Yet to everybody's surprise, the fine arts drew more people than all the girlie shows combined. Dingwall had his troubles keeping many of the ring-toss variety of games on their feet as paying lessees. The rise of science and the arts over fun and sex caused Seattleites to take a new look at themselves. Fine arts became "the thing" and after the fair the Seattle Repertory, the Opera, and the Seattle

Symphony Orchestra climbed in popularity, and in settings the like of which the town had never seen.

So, at 3 P.M. Eastern Standard Time, April 21, 1962, President John F. Kennedy pressed the same gold nugget key that had set the Alaska-Yukon-Pacific Exposition in motion back in 1909. But now the Commander-in-Chief's finger set off a chain of impulses far more sophisticated than the telegraphic spark created by President Taft's pudgy forefinger. President Kennedy's touch activated a computer in Andover, Maine, which focused a radio-telescope on the star Cassiopeia A. The star was 60,000,000,000,000,000 miles away. The telescope picked up a vibration from that star which had started across space ten thousand years before and relayed it to Seattle, where bells rang and whistles shrieked along the waterfront. The fair had begun.

By almost any measure the small, compact Seattle World's Fair, which ran for six months, was a smashing success. Largely due to taxpayer financing and federal participation, the exposition finished in the black. But more important, the concept of the fair was another Seattle dream come true. The city, as planned, was left with the magnificent legacy now known as the Seattle Center. Intact and flourishing are such things as the Opera House, the ever-busier Coliseum, a huge fountain, a refurbished Arena, pools, playhouses and lovely tree-lined boulevards. The Seattle Center now plays host to an incredible variety of attractions, everything from fly casting to rock and roll. A miniature carnival operates all through the summer months.

The entire complex now draws more than 7.5 million people a year—ranging from gawkers and strollers to fans clamoring to attend basketball games, opera, symphony, craft shows and all the rest. Center officials estimate that 3.5 million people come onto the grounds with no other purpose but to stroll, relax and listen to occasional free band concerts. The Science Center, under the dynamic Dr. Dixy Lee Ray, draws 250,000 paying customers a year.

Truly, the center is a jewel in the city.

19

The Big Kite Factory

D ESPITE serious difficulties at the opening of the seventies, the name Boeing will forever be a magic word in Seattle's history and the town will be proud of it. The plant that commemorates the great William E. Boeing has its own magic, too, around the world— and in outer space as well.

Most modern Seattleites do not realize that the early seventies did not mark the lowest point in Boeing annals. Founded in July 15, 1916, the company all but perished in the aviation slump after World War I. To keep in business and hold its work force together it did what it is doing now: found diversified non-flying products to build. Those early products bring smiles today. Most of Boeing's skilled workers were carpenters, inasmuch as air frames were made of wood. So Boeing built umbrella stands, telephone booths, hat racks and at least fifty library tables. Finally it branched out into bedroom suites, but this line proved unprofitable and was discontinued. The dire word went out that at the end of 1919 the company would finish $90,000 in the red, and practical Bill Boeing said, "If we can't get some business with an assured income we'll have to close."

But the air age was just beginning, and Boeing didn't close. Today the little company which became an industrial giant is again looking toward diversification—of course much more sophisticated in kind than in 1916—and Boeing officials still have faith in the air and outer space.

However, let's take the Boeing story from the beginning, and that means going back to William Boeing's arrival in Seattle and his meeting with Conrad Westerveldt.

Bill Boeing was born to fly and to build planes. He realized this the first time he saw a plane in the air, and he never missed one of the big international "air meets" that were coming into fashion. It seemed inevitable that he would encounter another man born to seek the clouds, and their meeting place was the city on the shore of Elliott Bay. The other man was Conrad Westerveldt, who by chance was assistant naval constructor at the Navy Yard in Bremerton, and later was assigned to the big Moran shipyards in Seattle.

He and Boeing met at Seattle's very exclusive University Club. Until then the young millionaire from Minnesota had been more or less a loner. But he and Westerveldt hit it off at once. The youthful Boeing was having difficulties with a yacht he had under construction and elicited Westerveldt's help. Thus began a long friendship that eventually forged the greatest aircraft plant in the world.

Young Boeing's money came from family holdings of ore and timber in Minnesota's famed Mesabi Range. He was the son of a German-born father who died when Bill was eight. His Viennese mother raised him strictly, but he had plenty of spending money and went to school in both Switzerland and America. He easily could have developed into a non-productive offspring of wealthy parents, but that did not happen. Instead he grew into a tall, handsome, studious young fellow wearing sensible narrow-rimmed spectacles to help him watch for opportunities that would satisfy his restless, industrious nature.

His mother remarried, and Bill and his stepfather couldn't get along together. So in 1903 he decided to pass up his final year at Yale and move west. To the twenty-two-year-old that meant Seattle. The town had never seen a young man quite like him. He began acquiring timber. He outfitted expeditions to Alaska. He bought a shipyard on the Duwamish River to finish the yacht that was not coming along to his satisfaction.

And he was keenly interested when a flier named Terah Maroney brought a Curtiss-type hydroplane to Seattle. Several times, at the aviation meets, Boeing had tried to hitch a ride in the air, but somehow his yearning never was satisfied. He decided to corner Maroney and invited Westerveldt along.

It was a perfect day. The Cascades and Olympics were holding a bowl of beauty that Boeing never forgot. Boeing was not as certain of Maroney's plane as he was of the weather and that beauty. But he was game, and so was Westerveldt. The skinny wings were covered with muslin, and the whole machine was supported by rods anchored to a sled-shaped float. The little engine hung between the two wings. Only one passenger could be managed, and Boeing volunteered to be first. He climbed onto the lower wing, braced his feet on a metal footrest, and hung on with both hands. Maroney's speed is not recorded, but he took Boeing to an altitude of a thousand feet. Later the young Seattleite admitted anxious moments, but when he got his feet on the landing ramp again he told Westerveldt that he was convinced that man was meant to fly. "The question is," he added practically, "is there a future in aviation?"

Neither he nor Westerveldt was certain about that, but now they were ready to find out. "You know," Westerveldt said, "we could build a plane a hell of a lot better than that one."

"All right," said Boeing, "let's do it!"

Thus the Big Kite Factory began. Bill Boeing guided its destiny through peace times and two world wars, retired for a period, then returned to the company in an advisory capacity before his death in 1956.

There naturally are paradoxes attending the presence of this remarkable company which had its ups and downs but prospers in a highly competitive business. When things are going well for it, Boeing is not always popular, although we don't forget to take pride in its products and their records. If you linger in Seattle long enough you will hear a cynic declare that we would all be better off if Boeing packed up and went away, and that we are a "company town," just as we were when Henry Yesler's sawmill was the only industry. You'll hear the wry comment, "Everytime Boeing sneezes, Seattle comes down with a cold." But the tune changes quickly when Boeing suffers. In the early seventies, when 747 sales came in drastically below expectations and the SST program was scuttled by Congress, the company dropped to about 30,000 employees from a peak of 100,000. Then the cynics yearn and pray for Bill Boeing's heritage to the city. The effect of Boeing's cutbacks was traumatic. It was a shaking experience to the entire area, both psychologically and economically; we didn't like being called "a major disaster area." It hurt our pride.

Although Boeing operates in what is known as "greater Seattle," it does not actually function entirely within the boundaries of the city itself. True, there is a sizable Boeing complex between the downtown area and the International Airport, but the southern boundary of the town was gerrymandered years ago so that the semi-sacred institution would be spared the pain of certain city assessments and taxes. There are, of course, other Boeing operations in Renton, south of Seattle, and near Everett in Snohomish County on the north.

Thus in Seattle, itself, which gets almost all publicity connected with Boeing, there is really no design or production done. The retail merchants and the banks of the city and suburbs are keenly aware of the huge company, however, and so are the people of neighboring communities. Indeed, in prosperous times in some of those communities as many as seven out of ten families are "Boeing families."

An indestructible joke around Seattle is that every employee of Boeing is an engineer. The employee may, of course, be a gatekeeper or a janitor, but to the great outside he is a Boeing engineer. His spouse will back him up. In normal times the phrase "My husband is a Boeing engineer" is heard throughout the Puget Sound country. Of course there's always the chance that the lady speaks the truth, for since World War II the ratio of engineers to members of the skilled and miscellaneous trades has markedly changed.

Of course Boeing's customers are not the average citizen, but the big airlines and the military. Although it has an excellent public relations department whose personnel know their business, there are times when the Big B seems to care little for its public image. Its relations with news media have not always been smooth. As individuals, its top men are pleasant, with a genuine liking for their city and region, but there are periods when the company seems unable to avoid an impression of arrogance earned by its long-term performance.

Critics of the company do not always allow for the stresses and strains of the business. Millions of dollars ride on the success of a new model, which always carries innovations. As the time nears for a maiden flight the employees of a vital department have been known to break out in psychosomatic rashes or other ills for which there is no medical answer.

Naturally when Boeing is on the upswing the unemployment figures locally are minimal, and the company will send out recruiters adept at picturing the joys of working for Boeing and living in the Pacific Northwest. Seasoned engineers know that they gamble with the fates that guide the aerospace business, and live from day to day. But given the high salaries and the attractive setting of the region most cannot resist the temptation to sign for a mortgage loan that will mean a split-level home and a garage big enough for a couple of cars and a boat or mobile camper. If a recession comes, they can be in a tough spot, faced with the necessity of moving on, and the real estate market is temporarily shot down. The aircraft business is not child's play, and even twenty-year tenure is no safeguard when the Lazy B Ranch has to reduce its payroll to not more than 30,000 people.

Men in the high echelons of Boeing are wary of being quoted, and the one I quote now asked that his name be omitted. "Really, it isn't a happy situation, knowing that Boeing means so much to the region's economy," he said. "We take a sort of pleasure in the fact, and certainly we're proud of our half-century of success. But the truth is that Boeing management will be happy when we don't stand so much alone in supporting the local economy. It's gotten so that, when the aircraft business sags, and so do we, Seattle and all the towns around start pointing their fingers at us and asking for a magic answer."

July 15, 1916, is the date that marks the founding of the Boeing company. After their ride with Maroney, and the subsequent decision to build a plane of their own, Boeing and Westerveldt decided to talk with Herb Munter, a Seattle stunt flier who was building a plane.

The trio are given credit for the first Seattle-built planes, but actually they weren't quite the first. It isn't in the record, until this minute, but the first Seattle-built planes were the secretive work of Robert Vinton Jones from Ohio. His interest in flying, like that of thousands of others, began with the flight of the Wright brothers at Kitty Hawk. It is possible that my grandfather Jones was further influenced by the curious fact that the maiden name of his wife, my paternal grandmother, was Catherine Hawk. And to him she was always "Kitty."

I remember well the rented shack down near the old Meadows Race Track where he and a helper built a monoplane and biplane. These were the days when a lot of farm-reared Americans were inventors of a sort, and my grandfather was of the breed. He had designed and built a stabilizer which he hoped would keep a flying machine automatically on an even keel. His first—and last—model was a copper cylinder with valves around its rim. That's all I recall about it, except that it must have weighed about as much as the planes which were intended to test it.

Robert had given his promise to Kitty Hawk that he would not try to fly the planes himself. So he imported a French aviator; American fliers were few in North America about 1914, and there were none in the Northwest until Herb Munter came along. I remember the Frenchman well. Goggles always hung around his neck and he continually twirled the ends of a smart mustache. In retrospect I think his flying credentials lost nothing in the telling; otherwise he could hardly have been attracted to Elliott Bay by an unknown named Jones. He had acquired a motorcycle, and I can see it all now: taking off for the hangar with my grandfather hanging on tandem. I remember the planes because I was allowed to sit in them while they were grounded, and a child does not forget such an experience.

I'm not certain whether it was the biplane or the monoplane which was tried first. All I know is that it did not gain altitude enough to clear a fence and crashed nose-down. A shaken Frenchman announced in broken English that my grandfather was no aircraft engineer, a veritable truth, and refused to try the other plane. He departed for France in the first available ship, and my grandfather forgot the whole business to go gallivanting off to Brazil and attempt a farm colony. That didn't work out, either, and the best I can say for Robert Vinton Jones is that it's too bad he didn't meet Herb Munter and that he was overimaginative and undercapitalized. The story seems to me to be a relevant curiosity because it indicates how firmly dreams of the air were percolating in an area as isolated as Seattle.

Young Bill Boeing had a number of things my grandfather was short on. Two were money and a general astuteness. The latter caused Boeing to associate with men who knew their business. With Westerveldt he began an inquiry into aircraft technology. When they talked with Herb Munter, he asked the question that would not leave his mind: "Do you think the public is really interested in flying?"

Munter had the early-day stunt flier's view of the public. "They come to see me crash, Mr. Boeing. So I give them a dive close to the ground—I'm going only forty-five or so—then pull on the stick. In a plane as slow as mine it's really not much of a trick."

Boeing could not rid himself of the feeling that there was much more to flying than thrilling a crowd. Too, he was mindful that in World War I there was conflict in the air. Soon Boeing had talked Munter into joining the partnership of Boeing and Westerveldt, and they began building two planes that would be called B&Ws. A couple of shipyards were put to work on the wings, and Bill Boeing took the train to Los Angeles to learn to fly under pioneer aviator Glenn Martin.

The day came when the first B&W, shining with dark varnish, sat on a Lake Union ramp with a 125-horsepower engine ready to sputter and turn. The wing span was fifty-two feet. Test pilot was Boeing himself, but he was cautious. He barely got the plane off the water. When Munter's turn came he followed Boeing's advice for a few days, then, as a stunt flier would, got bored, pulled back the stick and flew into the wild blue yonder. When he descended and taxied to the ramp he faced an enraged Bill Boeing. "Don't ever do that again unless I give you the word," warned the boss. But he couldn't hide his pride in the first B&W, and he wouldn't be the last Boeing chief to chide an overenthusiastic test pilot.

Two young fellows named Claire Egtvedt and Phil Johnson were taken into the design department not long after the United States got into World War I. They were individualists, perhaps the first and last of their kind at Boeing. Egtvedt was a soft-spoken engineer whose second love was sailing. Phil Johnson was an outgoing roly-poly who, when the long day was over, liked to head for the old College Club at Sixth and Spring and belt down a few in the bar. When he figured he'd had enough he would call a cab, tumble into the rear seat and unbuckle his belt for a nap. Every cabbie in

Seattle knew where he lived; what they didn't know was that home for Johnson would one day be a million-dollar castle north of town.

The nation's relatively brief time in the big war kept the infant company healthy but uncertain as to the future. The Navy was dubious about a special design Boeing turned out for them.

Legend grew that Seattle progress had to be based on wars or rumors of wars, or something like an Alaska Gold Rush. Years later the legend would grow with mysterious doings at Richland, across the Cascades—doings that needed the Grand Coulee Dam and had to do with nuclear fission. It is a legend not without basis in fact; Seattle's luck is sometimes based on tragic matters elsewhere in the world, or benign influences from outside its boundaries.

With peace in Europe, Bill Boeing was faced with a problem the company would confront more than once: what next? Boeing tried the simple diversification already mentioned, but clung to the idea that people—lots of people—would want to fly as passengers. Also, being a worldly man, widely traveled, and with German and Viennese blood in his veins, he was convinced that some day another world war, or a war with powers in the East, was probable.

He had other dreams, among them fast mail by air. Early in 1919, the year it was predicted the company would wind up $90,000 in the red making furniture, he and test pilot Eddie Hubbard fought a snowstorm and head winds to fly to Vancouver, British Columbia, and back. They were in the Model C that our Navy had doubts about, and they brought back sixty letters—thus creating the first Air Mail service.

Boeing never let up on the efforts to seek government contracts, for Uncle Sam was the big potential customer and the great airlines were far in the future. With Johnson and Egtvedt and a newcomer named Ed Gott, whom he had named general manager, Boeing nagged the military with ideas for pursuit planes and training planes, and kept after the Post Office Department with his design for a mail-carrying plane. Also he turned out the Model 40 that could handle a few passengers as well as mail. Stubbornly he operated the Model 40 through a subsidiary company that one day would become United Air Lines now headed by a Puget Sounder named Ed Carlson.

Then the Army Air Corps showed signs of being interested in a long-range bomber. Bill Boeing was ready, when the time came, with the B-17, the plane that was to be known worldwide as the Flying Fortress. One week after the attack on Pearl Harbor the plane's name was forged.

After the Pearl Harbor disaster Seattle had a world war in which it could become interested to a far greater degree than it had been in World War I, even though it had built more ships for that war than any other port in the nation. World War II embraced the imagination and excitement of the city as the first world conflict never had, not just because Boeing was so vital to victory, but also because it was the war that was close to home.

The name Flying Fortress was coined in battle, December 14, 1941, when a B-17 became separated from its formation in the fog and suddenly encountered eighteen Japanese Zeros. The Zero, with the innards of a katydid, was swift and deadly.

It looked like another downed plane for the United States, which already was outnumbered in the Pacific in ships, planes and men. But Captain Hewett Wheeless decided it was best to attack, not attempt escape to home base under fog cover. He stayed on his bomb run and the turrets of the B-17 blasted at the tricky Zeros. Committed to the bombing run, and alone, the Boeing plane was at a great disadvantage and suffered fatalities almost at once. But so did the enemy; in a few moments there were fourteen Zeros instead of eighteen. But those fourteen were circling and diving for the kill.

The number one engine of the Fortress went dead under Japanese fire, and the waist gun jammed out of action. Then half the cable controls frayed out from Zero bullets. The oxygen system failed. Radio, front tires, and fuel tank were riddled. Screaming air rushed through the plane's body.

It looked like the end when an odd thing happened. All except one Zero turned back into the fog. The lagging Zero drew alongside the B-17 cabin, so close that Wheeless could see his adversary's jaw agape. Then Wheeless realized the situation; the Zeros had exhausted their ammunition!

As dusk compounded the fog, Wheeless nursed the crippled plane toward the Philippines, never dreaming that he'd make it. He did, however, and the great crippled bird tore through the barricades on the runway, tipped on its nose, seemed about to flop over on its back, then sighed into the dust at the edge of the runway and lay in silence. Miraculously it did not burst into flame. The seven survivors tumbled out of the plane and gazed in disbelief at the wreckage which had brought them to a landing.

The sight was beyond belief, but Boeing and the Flying Fortress had earned their glorious names in the Two-Ocean War. Not until April 28, 1942, in a fireside chat, did President Franklin Roosevelt tell the public the story of the intrepid Wheeless, his crew and the mangled Flying Fortress. Nine days later, at Boeing plant Number 2, eighteen thousand employees gathered on the concrete and listened to the story from Wheeless himself.

The captain drawled, "We were just getting onto the knack of shooting them down, when they had to go home. But we survivors and my departed buddies, God rest them, don't get all the credit. For us and a lot of other B-17 outfits I want to thank you for the design and the workmanship in that great plane. Keep it up and we can't lose this war."

A cheer went up from eighteen thousand throats and Seattleites in general swelled with pride.

Wellwood Beall, who had become chief engineer at Boeing, sold the B-29 to the Army after that. In doing so he laid his word and Boeing's reputation on the line. Things weren't going too well around the world. The Allies had been practically driven from Europe and Montgomery was having plenty of trouble with Rommel in Africa. In the Pacific some said the United States was finished for years to come. Only a few knew that an awesome new weapon was being developed at Alamogordo. But, oddly, almost no Seattleite recognized the affiliated alchemy transpiring just across the Cascades at Richland, Washington. That was perhaps the best-kept secret of the war, a masterpiece of security, but Wellwood Beall knew that Boeing had been spending thousands upon thousands of man-hours on the B-29, a plane that hadn't left the ground as yet. He was convinced that the Army needed such a plane—a Superfortress, faster and more dangerous than the Flying Fortress.

The validity of Beall's hunch was proved in a visit to Seattle of General Oliver Echols, the Army Air Corps' engineering chief. "We're ready to spend more money on one project than any other in the war so far," the general told Beall. "We want to know if you've really got something in the B-29. You're the chief engineer of Boeing and you ought to know. I'll take your word rather than a mock-up and a lot of damned drawings. Could be the outcome of the war will depend on what you tell me and how accurate you are."

Beall, last of the Boeing "characters" among the firm's top brass, replied: "General, it's going to be a hell of a plane. It'll do what I think you want it to do. But give us top priority in testing. Give us a chance to speed up and do all the testing we have to do—and we'll come through."

Echols took the word to General Hap Arnold, who took it to the other war chiefs and to the Commander-in-Chief, the President himself. And Echols returned to Seattle to advise Beall personally that three billion dollars had been earmarked for the Superfortress.

The historic mission of the Superfortress called *Enola Gay* is still on the conscience of the nation; she was the plane that dropped death on 100,000 people in Hiroshima. Yet the Japanese refused to surrender, and another B-29 let go the nuclear bomb on Nagasaki. That one did it, and the surrender of the enemy took place on the U.S.S. *Missouri*, now a tourist attraction at the Navy Yard in Bremerton across the Sound from Seattle.

Now came the B-47, the medium bomber that put the Army into the jet age, where Boeing was to shine so brightly in the 1950s and 1960s. The Big Kite Factory would produce ten commercial jets if you want to count in the SST, which I do. They would range in length from forty-five feet to 231 feet four inches for the 747, which would precede the controversial SST (which is 318 feet on the drawing boards).

The B-47, popularly known as the Stratojet, first flew on April 15, 1952, although its prototype, the XB-47 flew as early as 1947. The war days were seemingly over, and everybody knew that once again Boeing was faced with cutbacks for a time. Later, after some disagreements among the company's top brass, Wellwood Beall would cut loose from Boeing and fly south to Douglas Aircraft. But on that day in April of 1952, he, General Morb Bradley and company counselor William E. Allen were out to see the B-47's maiden takeoff.

Flying the plane was Tex Johnston, a test pilot who had worn cowboy boots on every trial flight since he'd won the Thompson Trophy race in 1946. Perhaps the last of the reckless stunt fliers, he resisted temptation on this occasion and behaved himself nicely. So did the B-47, and the test was a success.

It was a different story when the first air-ready plane of the 707 transport line came along. Tex wasn't able to hold himself in. He was bored that day as he flew the 707 over a crowd of thousands watching a hydroplane race from the shores of Lake Washington. Distracting from the water sport, he dropped close to the crowd, zoomed up into the sky and did a slow roll. The crowd could hardly believe what it was seeing, but to make certain they'd understand, Tex did it again.

Next day he was on the carpet before recently elected president Bill Allen's desk—just as Herb Munter had stood before Bill Boeing. "What the hell did you have in mind," Allen asked, "pulling a stunt like that with fifteen million dollars' worth of airplane and endangering all those people?"

Legend says that Tex replied that he was up there with the greatest plane ever built, and down there was a big audience. "Any airplane that you can't roll," he added, "just ain't safe to fly."

Allan, the stony-faced attorney had been counsel for the company for many years, but when the board chose him as president in 1945 he protested that he knew nothing about planes and was just a country lawyer. Actually he'd had considerable experience, flying tens of thousands of miles in all kinds of planes in the interests of the company. He would lead Boeing through a long tenure into the jet and aerospace age. Not all the years would be good, and some of those who called him Uncle Bill behind his back did not do so with love. It seemed that the only time he showed emotion was when a new Boeing design took to the air. Then he would seem to help lift it with clenched fists, opening his mouth in a wild cheer.

But the directors had not conducted a personal popularity contest when they chose Bill Allen. They wanted a firm hand and a good mind and they got both. Allen has a right to be proud of his record and of Boeing under his leadership. It is significant of a new era in aircraft, however, that when Allen moved up to board chairman the directors picked an engineer, T. A. Wilson, as the chief, in April 1968.

War was something different now (for example, there are hundreds of Boeing helicopters in Vietnam) and Boeing was heading into a new world of aerospace and travel. Some 51 per cent of North Americans have never flown in a plane at all. That means optimism; the potential for growth of air travel is sizable, and already enough people are enthusiastic about high, fast travel to make Boeing feel vitally necessary to the jet set which wants to see the world in a hurry.

Of course the big Boeing 747 is not directed entirely at the luxury-minded jet set. It was built for mass travel, and the big plane has to be seen to be believed. Its 231-foot length is considerably more than the length of the flight of Orville Wright at Kitty Hawk. The wingspan is 195 feet, eight inches. A bulge atop the forward section shields quarters for the operating crew, and to the rear of that is space for a lounge connected to the main deck by a spiral staircase. A readily recognizable characteristic of the plane is its lofty tail, standing higher than a five-story building.

The 747's first flight was one of Seattle's great days. Crowds gathered from miles around as the word spread, and those too late for the takeoff were astonished at the landing. The plane was so gigantic that they expected the test pilot to step out in something like an astronaut's suit. But test skipper Ted Allard calmly emerged in an Establishment jacket and slacks, his conservative necktie only slightly awry. Quietly he commented: "The easiest plane to fly in my experience."

Imagine, if you can, the scene at an airport or in a city when two or three such planes land within the space of a few minutes. The 747 already has changed the future plans of airports, and caused hotel chains to review their methods for receiving such a gaggle of flying guests all at the same time.

Small wonder that the 747, and its cargo counterpart, will be an important vertebra in the backbone of Seattle's economy for years to come. However, there's a minus factor most Seattleites haven't considered in their characteristic optimism. This is that 65 per cent of the airframe weight is being built by firms other than Boeing, and in the future some of these subcontractors could be some distance from Puget Sound. Seattle may have to adjust to this reality, among other grim ones, or make plans to see that such subcontractors are close to home.

Such realities did not lessen the excitement of the town following the test flight and subsequent news of sales to airlines. Of course air-oriented Seattle knew that airlines were running into trouble at the opening of the seventies, but there certainly was no reason to believe that this situation would persist. Always impressed by sheer size, Seattle loved the plane and worshiped the fact that the plant near Everett, on a 780-acre site, is the world's largest building, encompassing 200 million cubic feet. That's where the 747 comes together and it is from there that each of the beautiful ladies takes off on her maiden flight.

What's next for Boeing?

Boeing officials are not garrulous, partly because so much depends upon factors outside the company's control. But even after some setbacks to begin the seventies, Seattle was unbowed insofar as its biggest industry is concerned. It knows that Boeing engineers are busy at the drawing boards, and that there are Boeing geniuses who in essence are paid to anticipate the future and dream a little. Not only about products for the skies and interplanetary space, but about mundane yet vital items that have nothing to do with flying and orbiting. Get near any Boeing plant and you'll hear the sound of hundreds of computers clicking away. Who knows what they will spew forth?

It will be most unusual if Boeing is not in the anti-pollution picture. It seems most probable that Boeing would be allied with the automotive industry in the anti-pollution field, a paradoxical probability when one considers that one of the chief concerns of the environmentalists about the SST had to do with air pollution. It's no secret that Boeing has been examining possibilities in recreation, in extensive real estate developments and in industrial parks. Nor is it a secret that Boeing has secrets as tight in security as any wartime project.

However, there's plenty ahead that's bright in the aerospace business. Admitting that the climb from the depths of 1970 will be slow and turbulent, the most conservative experts see the ingredients of an upturn. A favorable sign is the award of a contract amounting to $169 million for the development of an airborne warning and control system to detect enemy bombers. Almost inevitably, there will be increased air traffic and a parallel increase in orders for the jumbo jets, which is where Boeing shines. And few realists can imagine that the United States is going to see billions lost to overseas competition in the world projected by the SST. Even at the end of 1971, when Boeing employment was down to 30,000, there were company officials who would opine in a whisper that they could not believe that Congress would continue to stand in the way of the SST. At this time, too, there were top secret talks with the military about new designs.

To have confidence in Boeing's future one need only look at its past, with perhaps a sly glance at Seattle's historic luck. Boeing has built nearly 30,000 aircraft. As one observer put it, were that Boeing fleet to fly over the city it would blot out the sun and deafen the beholders. Of course no such mass flight would be possible now, for most of those planes no longer exist. But Boeing's history is written in superlatives. Since that first brightly varnished plane of cloth and wood it has built at least 188 models and submodels, and they've all been successes. With justifiable pride the company calls them the "Parade of Champions."

Seattleites, above all others, will back the company's right to use the phrase. Occasionally we become a bit miffed with Boeing. There even have been dark moments when downtown wizards have doubted the sagacity of the management and suspected flaws in the crystal ball at the Lazy B Ranch. In truth, there has sometimes developed a kind of mutual love-hate between Seattle and Boeing.

But actually the town and the region, deep in the hearts of their people, have great faith in the gigantic kite factory. For Boeing is part of the Seattle style. And in this instance we are talking of high style—high, fast, big and booming. That is how Seattle likes it, and—you may depend upon it—that is how it will be.

20

Pugetopolis: Eden No More?

As we move along in the 1970s, a fairly bright picture is seen for the Seattle area by H. Dewayne Kreager, an economist who has been a consultant for the federal government, the state and on behalf of private companies. He is now president of Pacific First Federal Savings and Loan Association.

"Diversification," he says, "may be the most important thing that has been happening to us. Long an economy based on raw materials—shipping agricultural and forest products East and bringing finished materials back West—we are now rapidly becoming diversified into a consumer product manufacturing area, with all the values which that implies. And we don't want to lose sight of the fact that the Pacific Northwest, from Vancouver to Eugene, has become the second largest and fastest-growing consumer market in the West."

Kreager admits that we need a strong national housing market because of its impact on our lumber and plywood industries. More people make their living directly or indirectly from forest products than from any other source of income in the Pacific Northwest.

The rising national housing market in 1971, apparently assured for 1972 and beyond, has helped greatly in recovery from the 1969–70 depths of recession in the Seattle area.

On the basis of advance bookings for hotel space, he also looks to an improved tourist and convention business in the early seventies.

Summarizing, Kreager cited other basic and continuing strengths, namely the very substantial level of savings accounts and bank deposits, which represent a solid base of consumer purchasing power once the consumer gains more confidence. He also emphasized the booming port business of Seattle and Puget Sound, and this, he said, "is permanent." Although the port has been discussed elsewhere in this book, Kreager's analysis is an important consideration. He remarked to this writer, "Now the second port on the coast, Seattle will be first in a few years. Nowhere else on the West Coast is there so much available deep water with adequate land service facilities and sufficient areas for growth on adjacent land. Only on Puget Sound can the 200,000- to 400,000-ton bulk or container carriers of the future find forty-five to eighty-five feet of minimum water and wharfage necessary to fast, efficient operations. Reopening of the China trade must eventually help Puget Sound more than any other West Coast port area."

What about the Alaska oil development? "It is of importance to us," Kreager says, "because it is, like the greater ocean traffic, part of the industrial and employment wave of the future. This Alaska oil will not be a two- or three-year boom, like the Boeing boom of 1965–68. Development on the North Slope will go on for fifty years or more. Its importance to Seattle is not really the oil coming in vessels to Puget Sound, but the vast supply market every year for heavy equipment and provisioning that has been built into Seattle since the early years of the forest products industry."

Seattleites often use the name of their city loosely, for it means more than is confined within municipal boundaries.

Seattle is King County, or vice versa. And one cannot view Chief Sealth's town without taking into consideration such communities as Tacoma, Bremerton, Bellevue, Everett, Olympia, even Bellingham, which is close to the Canadian border. There are hundreds of neighboring communities, linked to us—and we to them—by freeways or waterways. We need these places with names like

Puyallup, Auburn, Kent, Issaquah, Renton, Redmond, Marysville, Mount Vernon, Port Townsend, Port Angeles and Anacortes. Even smaller communities have meaning for us: social, economic and cultural meaning. Buckley, Enumclaw, Snohomish, Mukilteo, Edmonds, Port Orchard, Dungeness and scores of others, not forgetting the beautiful San Juan Islands, are part of our thinking and our way of living.

Take a map of western Washington and draw a rectangle with, say, Bellingham on the north, Port Angeles and Victoria, British Columbia, on the west, Duvall or Roslyn on the east, and Centralia and Chehalis on the south. Observe how all are linked together with ferries and bridges and freeways and four-lane highways.

Within that rectangle, one of these days—some say by the year 2000, less than thirty years away—is something that will become Pugetopolis. I have been unable to discover who invented the name, but it began to be heard a few years ago when national publications published articles about "strip cities." These were heavily populated areas, each embracing several cities of considerable size. As for the Northwest, the "strip city" of the future was projected as beginning at Bellingham or Everett on the north, stretching as far south as Olympia on the south. The western edge would certainly extend as far as Bremerton and the eastern boundary would be the foothills of the Cascades.

Should Pugetopolis come to pass, it would be almost entirely urban. Man-made parks and stretches of farmland and near-wilderness would be up to the planners, and I am sure it is not too early for our younger population—say the group between eighteen and thirty-five—to make their own suggestions, insist upon them, and keep sharp eyes on those planning committees, onto which some commercial land developers will certainly have infiltrated.

If this is not done we will have a Pugetopolis, right enough, but our lovely region will no longer be the Garden of Eden which, comparatively, it still is. If we do have a Pugetopolis or a strip city, Seattle is certain to be its center, not only geographically but sociologically, culturally and commercially. I venture that by then Seattle, Bellevue and Renton will have joined, creating without question the largest metropolis in the Northwest. If there are Seattleites who think this is nonsensical crystal-gazing, they simply have not been paying attention to the growth patterns in the various areas of that rectangle we have drawn.

There is not much the land developers with their earth-shaking machines can do about the mountains and the inland seas. Mount Rainier, Baker, Shuksan and the crags of the Cascades and Olympics will still look down upon the doings of man if Pugetopolis arrives. Those inland seas will do much to prevent the extinction of our Eden.

The warnings are in the air. When King County commissioners decided to float a bond issue to buy an expensive "show farm" for a county park, the president of the Citizens Planning Council addressed the people in an enthusiastic open letter: "The population projections show that within less than thirty years the Puget Sound area will be completely urbanized from the water's edge to the mountains. Future generations will regard this purchase . . . as we now regard the vision of those who, in 1856, five years after the founding of Seattle, purchased 840 acres of farm land which later became Manhattan's Central Park."

The planning director told the citizens that by 1985 King County would show a population increase equivalent to "another Seattle, which means an additional 600,000 people. And that means, too, that there will be 240,000 more homes, 267,000 more cars, 1,700 more miles of roads, 7,200 more stores, 158 more schools, and 277,000 more workers." Perhaps he should have added that it all will be either planned or haphazard growth.

So truly the young people had better watch out for the extravagantly beautiful 2,136 square miles that stretch from sea level to ski level in the Puget country. They had better guard the tall timber, the state and national parks, the rushing rivers, the pounding surf of the virgin seashore, the quieter streams and the hundreds of lakes. Already we have seen enough to know what can happen to these if man does not put up a fight—and, believe me, it will be a tremendous fight—to preserve the quality of our environment.

Not long ago I read a letter from a boy in Vietnam. Among other things it said, "They tell us a lot, and I read a lot, about what we are fighting for over here. I guess most of it is over my head, but I know what I'm fighting for. I'm fighting to get it over with so I can see those green hills of home . . ."

Yes, the green hills of home. The cedar and hemlock and fir, in all the darker shades of green, seeming to climb the slopes to the timberline, looking a little different every day because of sun or fog or mist or rain.

Mention "home" to a Seattleite and there is no certainty as to what may spring to his mind. It could well be those green hills the young soldier in Vietnam dreamed about. Or, if he is about the same age, he may be thinking of a canoe ride among the tule rushes of Lake Washington, with the moon shining down on the girl of the moment.

Or he could be thinking—past, present or future, you understand—of riding along a lofty ridge of the Cascades in the warm sun, listening to the wind scuttling through the scrub trees.

He might be remembering himself at the wheel of a fishing boat in waters off Point Roberts, that shred of Washington State that can be reached by land only through Canada because it juts south over the international boundary line. Or it could be down by Dungeness, watching the stern rise and fall in the swell that is rolling up the Strait of Juan de Fuca from the greatest of oceans.

Mention home to a Seattleite and he may think of a Chinese pheasant whirring out of the bracken in the dawn, or of a doe leaping a fallen cedar in a forest floor so sheltered that the sun never reaches it. He might be thinking of the mountains only, the blue ice in the yawning crevasses and the trees all twisted from the kind of wind that doesn't come into the meadows with their wild flowers swaying so gently.

He might be thinking of king salmon leaping the waterfalls of the river or flashing the surface of Elliott Bay. He could be remembering a little fishing shack on the bank of the Hoh. Or a big old-fashioned summer place where he played as a child, on the lee side of Port Blakely; the place where folks came of a Sunday, bringing their cars on the ferry or heaving a line from the bow of a cruiser—and never a telephone call beforehand as is the custom on the Atlantic shore. Perhaps he thinks of the calm digging or the tennis, or remembers his elders talking politics in the cool of the long porch.

What a Seattleite thinks of when you mention home will depend on his age and interests, naturally. In the off season he may miss the Monday Morning Quarterbacks breakfast at the Washington Athletic Club when football is in the air and last Saturday's game is dissected play by play. Or he may think of the big table at the Rainier Club, reserved at luncheon for men who have seen all of the modern city go by and a lot of old Seattle as well.

It is seldom that you can find half a dozen Seattleites together at one time to whom the town means quite the same thing. It's a big area, the region we embrace with the word Seattle, and we dream statewide, even beyond fabled Pugetopolis, and each of the region's parts is different from the rest.

What used to call itself the "Queen City" (a term almost abandoned now because of a homosexual twist of semantics) is, as we have seen, mildly schizophrenic. Many a visitor has observed that we sometimes seem unable to make up our minds whether we want to be a truly great city or a sprawling small town. But these visitors are a bit behind the times and somewhat myopic. It is true enough that many of us regret the inevitable, a bigger city. However, a vast majority are agreeing that it should be a better city, and that Seattleites must become more responsible as citizens to make it so.

You might put it this way: we welcome the newcomers, but there are some of us who wish they would choose another target. My old friend Stewart Holbrook was one such, and on his annual trips to the East would spread fantastic stories about the Northwest in the hope they would catch on as rumors to be considered. One of the popular author's yarns was that the Rocky Mountain tick had spread throughout Oregon and Washington. He did not fail to explain that the boring of this insect into the human epidermis could be fatal.

Seattleites are a paradoxical people, as a rule. We waver between a desire to be a quiet town after sunset, and a city with a much livelier night life. Our paradoxes are small as well as large. We love our ferry fleet (largest in the world, of course!) and proudly advertise it to the world. At the same time we build ever more bridges, which threaten to make ferries a part of the past.

We write ecstatically of the romance of our halibut fleet, and of the bravery of the men who sail three thousand miles through the North Pacific for this fish. But the best markets for the product are the stalls of fish houses on the eastern seaboard. Our highest gastronomic praise is reserved for salmon baked fresh, but our children prefer California tuna, a regrettable state of affairs.

We defend our climate passionately. But within my circle of friends who can afford the time and money are many who spend as many weeks or months as possible in Palm Springs, Tucson or

Phoenix, Hawaii or some even more exotic islands. These prodigal sons and daughters all return from far-off places with the deep suntan that is a status symbol hereabouts, affirming that all year around Seattle has the best climate in the world. I always want to reply, "That's true, but how do *you* know?"

We are indeed a family people, much given to doing things together, and dining at home—barbecue style when the weather permits. Yet we are proud of our increasing number of nationally acclaimed restaurants and choose to ignore the fact that only about 7 per cent of us furnish 90 per cent of their business.

It is a paradox that even those of us who were born in Seattle and have lived here most of our lives cannot say with precision what it is that we like about it. Nowadays we tend to listen to those who were attracted here for a variety of their own reasons, and who have brought with them certain habits and ways of thought they did not care to leave behind.

That is good.

We needed new blood, new ways of viewing things, and we are losing the old smug detachment. There are many reasons for this, as I hope has been demonstrated in the foregoing pages of this book.

In the year of the World's Fair of 1962 we said that we were going to really soar into the next century, and when you make a boast like that you had better be alert and guard against the complacency of other times.

So we try to do that now. As a native Seattleite I am convinced that we will bring it off.

BIBLIOGRAPHY

BOOKS

BAGLEY, CLARENCE B. *History of Seattle from the Earliest Settlement to the Present Time*. 3 vols. Chicago: J. Clarke, 1916.

BINNS, ARCHIE. *The Sea in the Forest*. Garden City, N.Y.: Doubleday, 1953.

DENNY, ARTHUR A. *Pioneer Days on Puget Sound*. Seattle: Alice Harriman, 1908.

DENNY, EMILY INEZ. *Blazing the Way*. Seattle: Rainier Printing Co., 1909.

HOLBROOK, STEWART. *James J. Hill*. New York: Knopf, 1955.

HOLBROOK, STEWART; JONES, NARD; HAIG-BROWN, ROGER. *The Pacific Northwest*. Garden City, N.Y.: Doubleday, 1963.

JONES, NARD. *Evergreen Land*. New York: Dodd, 1947.

MANSFIELD, HAROLD. *Vision, a Saga of the Skies*. New York: Duell, 1966.

MORGAN, MURRAY. *Century 21, a History of the 1962 World's Fair*. Seattle: Acme Press, 1963.

MORGAN, MURRAY. *Skid Road: An Informal Portrait of Seattle*. Rev. ed. New York: Viking, 1960.

NESBIT, ROBERT. *He Built Seattle.* Seattle: Washington Press, 1961.
OLSON, GENE and JOAN. *Washington Times and Trails.* Grant's Pass, Oregon: Windyridge Press, 1970.
RICH, JOHN M. *Chief Seattle's Unanswered Challenge.* Reprint. Fairfield, Wash.: Ye Galleon Press, 1970.
SPEIDEL, WILLIAM C. *Sons of the Profits.* Seattle: Nettle Creek Publishing Co., 1967.

PAMPHLET

SNYDER, WARREN. *Old Man House.* Pullman, Wash.: Washington State College, 1951.

UNPUBLISHED SOURCE

The Bagley Papers. University of Washington Library.

NEWSPAPERS AND PERIODICALS

Argus
Pacific Northwest Quarterly
Puget Soundings
Seattle *Guide*
Seattle *Post-Intelligencer*
Seattle *Times*
Washington Historical Quarterly

INDEX